PRAISE FOR
I'M SORRY FOR MY LOSS

"Powerful, eye-opening, and vital, *I'm Sorry for My Loss* shines a light on one of the biggest taboos in women's lives. It's a must-read for policymakers, healthcare professionals, and everybody who wants a better understanding of the gray areas between a perfect pregnancy and abortion."

—Marina Gerner, journalist and author of *The Vagina Business*

"A riveting, compassionate, and comprehensive exploration of the roots of America's current nightmarish landscape of reproductive care. *I'm Sorry for My Loss* is compelling, heartbreaking, and whip-smart, and should be read by every American, no matter their politics, gender, or where they are in their reproductive journey. Long and Little paint a vivid portrait of how many Americans are rendered powerless in pregnancy and childbirth through lack of information and demonstrate just how empowering knowledge can be."

—Katherine Leyton, author of *Motherlike* and *All the Gold Hurts My Mouth*

"This richly reported and deeply personal book is not just for people who have experienced pregnancy loss but for anyone who cares about women living in America today."

—Jessica Zucker, PhD, psychologist and author of *I Had a Miscarriage: A Memoir, a Movement*

T0190954

"Required reading to grasp the fascinating history behind our nation's befuddled and often hypocritical culture around pregnancy loss—with enough wry humor to cushion the inevitable outrage. (If we don't laugh, we'll cry!) As a stillbirth mother, I found it incredibly validating. As a maternal health activist, invaluably enlightening."

—Samantha Banerjee, executive director
of PUSH for Empowered Pregnancy

"Written with compassion and rigorous research, this is a book America needs right now."

—Leah Hazard, midwife and author of *Womb: The Inside Story of Where We All Began*

"Rejecting the stigma that surrounds discussing the mixed emotions and painful realities of our reproductive lives, this book powerfully and meaningfully connects the personal with the political in its description of intimate experiences of shame, racism, and misogyny. Nothing could be more important in this critical moment of reproductive health politics."

—Sarah Handley-Cousins,
Nursing Clio and *Dig: A History Podcast*

I'm Sorry for My

~~Miscarriage~~

~~Stillbirth~~

~~Abortion~~

~~Rights~~

~~Grief~~

LOSS

I'm Sorry for My Loss

An Urgent Examination of Reproductive Care in America

REBECCA LITTLE

COLLEEN LONG

For our babies—all of them

Copyright © 2024 by Rebecca Little and Colleen Long
Cover and internal design © 2024 by Sourcebooks
Cover design by Erin Fitzsimmons/Sourcebooks
Internal design by Tara Jaggers/Sourcebooks
Internal images © Pakin Songmor

Sourcebooks and the colophon are registered trademarks of Sourcebooks.

This publication is designed to provide accurate and authoritative information in regard to the subject
matter covered. It is sold with the understanding that the publisher is not engaged in rendering legal,
accounting, or other professional service. If legal advice or other expert assistance is required, the services
of a competent professional person should be sought.—*From a Declaration of Principles Jointly Adopted
by a Committee of the American Bar Association and a Committee of Publishers and Associations*

This book is not intended as a substitute for medical advice from a qualified physician. The intent of this
book is to provide accurate general information in regard to the subject matter covered. If medical advice
or other expert help is needed, the services of an appropriate medical professional should be sought.

Published by Sourcebooks
P.O. Box 4410, Naperville, Illinois 60567-4410
(630) 961-3900
sourcebooks.com

Cataloging-in-Publication Data is on file with the Library of Congress.

Printed and bound in the United States of America.
MA 10 9 8 7 6 5 4 3 2 1

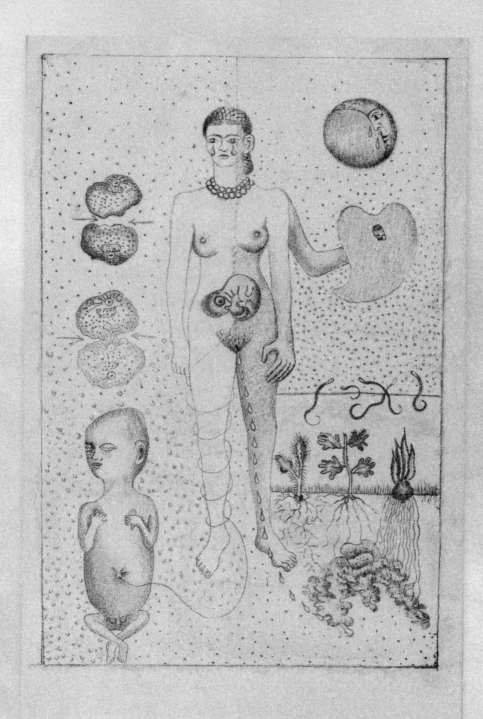

13ª prueba

CONTENTS

Part IV: The Making of Meaning

AUTHORS' NOTE
ON WORD CHOICE

Language matters. When it comes to pregnancy loss, the euphemisms, metaphors, medical jargon, politically loaded terms, and taboos blend into a confusing, emotional knot. What we do in these pages is attempt to untangle that knot, but first we want to explain our word choices.

We lay out the medical definitions of pregnancy loss in language as plain as possible, but we also reflect the words each person uses for their own loss.

We are not making political assertions when we use *baby*, *fetus*, or *embryo*. We used the terms that line up with the definitions outlined by the American College of Obstetricians and Gynecologists when discussing medicine, but those we interviewed use a variety of language to describe themselves and their pregnancies, and we have not altered their quotes. If they said "woman," we left it as woman. If they said "baby," we followed their lead. Part of our discovery through our research is that pregnancy—and pregnancy loss is circumstantial and hits every person differently. Reflecting language is not only a therapy tool but relevant to the mission of our book.

We use *women, birthing parent,* and *pregnant people* throughout, and all are necessary. *Women* excludes the experiences of girls, trans men, or gender nonbinary people who can become pregnant, lose pregnancies, and be affected by stigma, inequities, and barriers to care. (It is also in some ways too broad, because not every woman becomes pregnant.) Trans and nonbinary people are fighting for more just access to healthcare and equal rights, especially as a spate of laws winnow away protections. Still, abortion, miscarriage, and pregnancy loss have all been marked by gendered policy decisions. We use *women* when we are talking about historical contexts and inequities relating to gender in healthcare and as it pertains to female emotions being discounted. We use *pregnant people* or *birthing parent* when we're discussing pregnancy and loss more generally over the last twenty years. Sometimes we use *mother* and sometimes *parent*. We respect the fluidity of gender and identity, and we try to allow for fluidity in our language as well. While a lot of these problems are as old as time, the language around gender and binaries is changing quickly. We want to draw attention to the inadequacies of the language while also doing our best to use what is most appropriate in each context. Our intentions are journalistic accuracy, and respect for bodily autonomy for everyone who can become pregnant.

We interviewed dozens of people who have experienced some kind of pregnancy loss. In some cases, we use their full names. In other instances, we refer to them by a first name and last initial to protect their privacy. A handful chose to use a pseudonym. We let our sources decide how they would like to be identified so they could consider their personal and professional circumstances while still frankly sharing their stories.

We also use irreverent humor, which we realize may seem unexpected in a book about pregnancy loss. That's how we've always talked to each other, and we both grew up steeped in the Irish American tradition, where laughter and tears are separated by a hair's breadth. We take shots at systemic failures, historical absurdities, and sometimes ourselves but never those who opened their hearts to talk to us, nor the devastation our current political climate has unleashed on people experiencing pregnancy loss. The Venn diagram of laughter, rage, and sorrow is our wheelhouse. We hope to meet you there.

INTRODUCTION

In 2020, Colleen Long texted childhood friend Rebecca Little while both were juggling pandemic parenthood, writing, and enduring the full force of America's indifference to caretakers, mothers, and working parents. You know, just generally having it all.

"I have an idea. I think we should write a book about all this," Colleen texted.

"About what? Our shitty, cursed wombs?" Rebecca wrote back.

"Yes. Pregnancy loss in America. And why our culture sucks at it."

"I'm in. We ride at dawn. Or more likely midnight when these mofos are finally asleep."

We first met when we were ten, fourth grade desk mates in Catholic school. We had similar senses of humor, lived within biking distance of each other in the south suburbs of Chicago, and had last names that beautifully paired together for our amateur detective agency: Little and Long, Super Sleuths. Being young girls in the early 1990s, our choices were to become great friends or to wage mean girl warfare on our way to social dominance, and thirty years later, we think we made the right choice.

As we grew up, our lives ran on parallel tracks. We both became journalists (sleuths of a different sort) and were the kind of friends who would occasionally lose touch and then instantly pick up where we left off, in that way you can when you spent your childhood running in and out of each other's houses. And if movie marathon sleepovers are the glue stick to tween friendship, pregnancy loss is the industrial epoxy to an adult one. We frequently checked in with each other, knowing there would be a judgment-free, sympathetic ear. Because unfortunately, both of us are premier members of what Rebecca calls the Dead Baby Club.

And now, our bummer bona fides:

Pregnant with her third son, Rebecca was headed to a routine twenty-week anatomy scan. She put on her favorite maternity shirt—an orange varsity-style T-shirt with three-quarter sleeves and the number 9 printed across the belly. But just before she made her way downstairs, she turned around and changed clothes, because a part of her already knew she wasn't going to be pregnant for nine months. She hadn't felt the baby move in days—maybe four?—despite drinking juice and doing jumping jacks to prompt some activity. She never would have said it out loud, but deep down, she knew she wouldn't be leaving that scan with a sonogram printout of the baby.

The gel went on her stomach, the wand moved around, and instead of the spinning little spirograph she'd seen with her older two sons, there was an unmoving fetus with no heart flicker. She stared at her husband, who was leaning forward with a furrowed brow. "Is something wrong?" she asked the ultrasound tech, who said nothing. (It is a fundamental truism of ultrasounds that if the tech goes silent, you're screwed.)

Within minutes, the obstetrician confirmed that their son was dead at twenty weeks gestation. They were whisked up to the maternity floor, through the back stairs to avoid the waiting room full of pregnant people, and taken to "the sad room," as Rebecca and her husband referred to it, because it was tucked away from the cries of healthy babies. In less time than it would have taken for a normal ultrasound appointment to unfold, Rebecca was in a gown, on an IV drip, and gently told she needed to make a lot of decisions fairly quickly: Did they want to see the baby? Did they want to hold the baby? Did they want his remains? Would they want the complimentary hospital service to take photographs of him? Did she consent to have a D&C (a procedure that removes excess tissue from the uterus) if necessary after delivery? (They saw him, they held him, they buried him, they have photographs, and she had both a delivery and a D&C when the placenta didn't detach.)

Rebecca has been pregnant six times. She is raising three boys and has buried three others. She had a chemical pregnancy, a missed miscarriage at eight weeks, and following this stillbirth experience in 2014, she would go on to have a medical termination at twenty-three weeks with identical twin boys who had fatal heart conditions in 2015. That delivery would go catastrophically wrong and end with a uterine rupture, a near-fatal hemorrhage, and an emergency hysterectomy that would leave her with just one ovary, which she now pictures swinging around down there like a bare basement light bulb.

Three states away in 2012, Colleen had been busy pretending she wasn't pregnant at all. She had just gotten married and had complicated feelings of shame about being six months pregnant on her wedding day. Her new husband, though, was thrilled about their soon-to-be baby boy.

The sonogram was five days after the wedding, and she had the curious deep-down feeling that something was off. The cold goop on her stomach and the technician hunting for the heartbeat and the quiet "something must be wrong with the machine" angel-of-death speech. But Colleen and her husband were not whisked upstairs. A doctor she didn't know came in and told them the baby was dead, and she should go see her own doctor. They were quickly shuttled into a taxi and up Manhattan's West Side Highway, the gel still smeared on her abdomen. Their doctor was waiting for them in the lobby and brought them directly into her office, past a room full of other pregnant people, and laid out the options. Colleen could wait to go into labor and deliver the stillborn baby or, because she was still within the legal limit in New York State, head to an abortion clinic. Her doctor, though, didn't do "that kind of thing," so whatever they decided, they were on their own.

They chose the clinic, mainly because Colleen felt like if she had to deliver a dead baby, she'd never be able to handle being pregnant again. She didn't calculate how she might feel after the two-day procedure, after she'd walked past anti-abortion protesters yelling at her that she was killing their (already dead) baby, after she sat there in the clinic, sobbing, while other people wondered what was wrong with her. She didn't realize at the time—and no one suggested it to her—that it wasn't something you could just erase with a procedure, and that she might need something more formal to help with grief.

With this first experience lodged in the back of her mind, Colleen's two other pregnancies would be defined by anxious months of sadness and dread, expecting both babies to die while watching other pregnant people be happy, ethereal, and glowing. She felt guilty that they did not know where the remains of their first baby ended up and conflicted they'd never named him. Different circumstances, different cities, and different women, but very similar emotional and traumatic side effects, as we would discover.

The research for this book began with text messages. Quick check-ins, sharing an article with a "did you see this shit" caption, gallows humor about our unfortunate wombs. ("Lady at Target wouldn't stop asking me when I'm going to try for a girl. I said, 'I'm barren now. Bye.'") We came to rely on each other as the sounding board who wouldn't back away with wide eyes when the other said something gruesome. It was an attempt to process what happened, sure, but it was also something else: we wanted to know why. Not just why it happened but why we felt so uncomfortable and ashamed. And we had evidence that we weren't as alone as we felt. Both of us were inundated with messages after people found out, saying they too had experienced a stillbirth, a medical termination, a miscarriage. Some from people we had known for years! It seemed like one rule for being a member of this shitty club was not to talk about this shitty club. What if the culture around pregnancy loss could take fewer (or, ideally, zero) cues from Chuck Palahniuk? What if we could put it all out in the open for everyone?

In the immediate aftermath of our respective experiences, we each read books about grief. Colleen received three copies of the memoir *An Exact Replica of a Figment of My Imagination* by Elizabeth McCracken from well-meaning friends. She was offered nothing more formal to help with the anxiety and sadness though, not by her doctors or by the clinic. Rebecca was given hospital pamphlets about how to process stillbirths and lost pregnancies. Generalized grief manuals don't quite hit all the unique circumstances for pregnancy; they don't capture the uncertain state of ambiguous loss or what it's like to feel the weight of a political movement against a palliative choice. The handful of grief books tailored to pregnancy loss were an essential resource for Rebecca in the first ten weeks of the fog. But many of them used religious language—heaven, angels, souls—that just didn't quite land for her and often focused on how she could simply have another baby. Suggesting she could look forward to another pregnancy felt like a betrayal, swapping one baby for the next, and there was no guarantee it was even possible.

Colleen was shocked by how infrequently people would talk about what happened; some of her family never even mentioned it once. She felt like she couldn't talk about it either. After her stillborn son, a priest told Rebecca that he didn't need to pray for the baby because he was already in heaven, so she shouldn't feel sad. This was far from a comfort; it was enraging and invalidating. Conversely, the deacon who performed the funeral told her that holding a service would be hard, but she wouldn't regret it. He told her when he visited elderly women for end-of-life counseling, many of them were fixated on babies they had lost and never got to hold or see or talk about, sometimes more than seventy years prior. (Which is to say: society has been handling this wrong for a very long time.)

Today, we have a different cultural silencing method—the trendy lexicon of "the journey," which short-circuits any rage or sadness by insisting it was all essential to get you where you are today. That every loss has a silver lining, every misfortune is worth it, even if the ensuing road is a hellscape. America's idea of comfort is deeply discomfiting. Particularly for assholes like us, who want to feel angry and sad and will never be grateful it happened no matter how many essential oils we sniff. (If you want to lose an hour or two of your life, say, "Everything happens for a reason" to either one of us. You will beg for death.)

And then, in the middle of our research, the constitutional right to abortion was overturned by the Supreme Court through its decision in the case *Dobbs v. Jackson Women's Health Organization.* Suddenly, the system of reproductive healthcare that had been in place since before we were born was gone. It wasn't only access to abortion that vanished; complications from pregnancies were also swiftly caught up in the legal and political confusion surrounding the ruling.

It became clear that while pregnancy, miscarriage, and abortion are all part of the same spectrum of reproductive life, they've never been more separate culturally. We have isolated abortion into a political and legislative box, while we've pumped up the idea of a perfect pregnancy so dramatically that we are striving for ever more ridiculous standards. As a society, we almost exclusively fixate on abortion and healthy, nine-month pregnancies and ignore how routinely and regularly things go south. That ignorance not only leaves out a huge swath of people, but it also helped lay the groundwork to overturn *Roe v. Wade,* and it is making life for pregnant people today more deadly and dangerous.

So what are we actually talking about here? What falls under the category of pregnancy loss? Among the possibilities:

- An ectopic pregnancy, when the fertilized egg lands in a spot outside the uterus, won't result in a healthy pregnancy, and must be terminated to save the pregnant person.
- A miscarriage, which is the loss of an embryo or fetus before the twentieth week.

- A stillbirth, when a baby dies past the twenty-week mark up until the due date.
- Termination for medical reasons (TFMR), a newish term to describe abortions that a pregnant person chooses because of fetal diagnoses or because their own health would be affected by continuing the pregnancy.
- Selective reduction, the removal of an embryo or fetus in the case of multiple gestation to give the other or others a better chance to grow.
- Abortion, which is the purposeful termination of a pregnancy, nearly 90 percent of which take place before twelve weeks.

Ten to 20 percent of known pregnancies end in miscarriage annually, affecting about 750,000 to one million women every year. Stillbirths are a smaller subset of that number, closer to 1 to 5 percent, yet not as rare as people assume. One pseudo statistic that often gets repeated and was mentioned by most of the stillbirth parents we interviewed is "you're more likely to get struck by lightning than have a stillbirth." According to the Centers for Disease Control and Prevention, stillbirth affects one in 175 births. The odds of being struck by lightning, also per the CDC, are less than one in a million in any given year. (So go ahead and swing a golf club around in a thunderstorm, we guess. That's a lot less likely to get you than a pregnancy loss after twenty weeks.) Statistics are harder to come by for those who end pregnancies for medical reasons because abortion statistics are not really broken out that way. Abortion rights supporters purposely avoid the possibility of ranking reasons for abortion, and state policies on data gathering are greatly affected by politics. What we do know is that these terminations generally come after an early genetic screening test or in the wake of the twenty-week anatomy scan, and those for the pregnant person's health, even rarer, come throughout the forty weeks.

Why do we consider all these to be different things entirely? Why do we act like none of this ever happens when those of us who don't effortlessly glide from pregnancy test to delivery have a lot of company? These losses are all part of the same medical universe. The body doesn't distinguish between them. It's American culture that puts a premium on the intention behind it.

The state we find ourselves in has actually been the culmination of many different pressures sliding over each other like tectonic plates. The experience of modern pregnancy would be unrecognizable to women from earlier eras; even our mothers' experiences vary dramatically from ours. For most of human history, it didn't change much. A woman knew for sure that she was pregnant when she felt kicks, known as quickening, somewhere after sixteen weeks on the early side. Before that time, if she miscarried, she may not have even noticed. The idea of mourning a miscarriage would have made no sense at all to most women prior to the twentieth century, and abortion was largely a nonissue until the mid-nineteenth century.

Our views on reproduction have changed dramatically over the fifty years or so since *Roe* was first codified, shaped by the increasing ability of many people to *choose* pregnancy rather than have their lives dictated by the inevitability of it. This is also tied into the American notion that hard work leads to reward. "I did everything right, and I'm choosing this pregnancy, so everything will turn out OK."

The way we quite literally see pregnancies changed again after 1980. Sonograms became more widely available, so parents were able to get a peek of their fetus on-screen, and images of a growing fetus (usually made to look more babylike than is developmentally accurate) proliferated alongside antiabortion messages on billboards, bumper stickers, and in religious literature. The gestational parent, though, was hardly present at all. That has led to the increasing notion that a fetus is a person with the same rights as the mother or birthing parent.

Today, we can find out we're pregnant almost instantly. We're encouraged to bond the moment the pee strip turns pink. We see ultrasound images of our growing fetus at eight weeks. We get weekly emails telling us how big our "babies" are at each stage. All this affects how we handle it when it doesn't work out. It has led to the moment we're living through, where we separate pregnancy loss into categories of "good" and "bad," "wanted" and "unwanted."

The very words we use (and the words we don't have) to discuss pregnancy loss contribute to this problem. Medical jargon like *incompetent cervix* and *lazy ovary* add to stigma and blame, and political rhetoric has become so heated that it leaves those trying to share their experiences at the mercy of inadequate vocabulary.

If America is bad at talking about pregnancy loss, it's even worse at legislating it. This was true even before the Supreme Court upended the constitutional right to abortion but is even more so now that there's a free-for-all in states, some restricting abortion and others trying to make it more accessible. These regulations and restrictions go beyond access to abortion, and laws meant to curb abortion have consequences that deeply impact pregnant people who never intended to end a pregnancy. There's already increased criminalization of those who miscarry and who seek abortions in states where it is restricted. Some providers must check every day to determine what's legal in their state. U.S. laws around women's bodies, pregnancy, miscarriage, or abortions are rooted in a lack of understanding of how it all works, so it's no surprise laws don't align with what women and doctors need in a specific situation.

We're now at a particularly fraught moment for pregnancy in the United States. Nobody would be nostalgic for earlier eras when people could expect to be pregnant from the start of their marriage until menopause with a high risk of death in childbirth and when it was unlikely that all their children would survive until adulthood. But today, those in about half the country have no or very limited access to abortion care in their home state, which can also affect miscarriages. To give medical care, doctors in states like Texas, Louisiana, and Tennessee now must decide whether the pregnant person is sick enough with a potentially life-threatening complication to intervene on their behalf. Depending on the state where they reside, pregnant people and their doctors can be prosecuted for abortions or investigated for miscarriages, and their neighbors can earn a bounty for informing on their behavior. At nearly no other point in history was the growing baby prioritized over the mother. But now the laws are so murky and in some states so punitive, doctors tell us they don't know what to do. Many legislators still don't understand that the same procedures (and medicine) are used for a miscarriage and an elective abortion, and these laws are increasingly at the cost of the health and well-being of the pregnant person.

The argument against abortion in the 1970s was that it wasn't good for the woman—it harmed her mental and physical health. (That's been repeatedly disproven, most notably by the groundbreaking book, *The Turnaway Study*. Restricting access and abortion stigma has been shown to cause mental health issues including depression and anxiety.) Now the argument has shifted to criminalizing the woman and prioritizing the fetus, an unprecedented switch.

Meanwhile, America is also the only developed nation where maternal mortality rates are actually *increasing*. The United States has 32.9 deaths per 100,000 live births, the highest in the developed world. Maternal deaths across the United States more than doubled over the course of two decades. Black mothers are more than three times as likely to die from pregnancy-related issues than white mothers, a mind-boggling statistic that demonstrates the urgent public health imperative behind our current attitudes toward pregnancy. People of color generally are more likely to suffer miscarriage and stillbirth. Black, Hispanic, and Indigenous communities also receive worse care, are more vilified, and are less believed when they articulate suffering, physical pain, and grief. Black patients we interviewed told us of insidious systemic racism—not being consulted or given choices about whether to deliver their doomed babies or have a late-term abortion, being dismissed by their medical team, and, in the case of Black male partners, having to check their emotions in high-stress deliveries so they weren't deemed a threat. The racial disparities of medical care and reproductive justice are inextricably linked with complications in pregnancy loss. Scientific advances have made safer outcomes more possible than ever before, which is why it's so heartbreaking to know that access to such care is being restricted.

The helplessness and loneliness so many of us feel after pregnancy loss are not a coincidence. They are the result of a culture that is deeply uncomfortable with grief, particularly female grief. Add in the realities of the current moment—if the fetus has increasing primacy over the pregnant person's health, it's no wonder grief barely ranks. Politics, history, racism, misogyny, and medicine are working—separately and together—to choke off grief related to pregnancy loss, because it's too complicated, almost un-American, to allow all these contradictory feelings into the atmosphere. We found that so many of our restrictive views on pregnancy and by extension loss come from how we view women and mothers. This is all even worse for people of color and nonbinary and transgender pregnant people who face a different subset of obstacles to medical care, safe pregnancies and birth, and parenthood.

We are both aware of how much privilege we have as middle-class, cis white women and how our experiences were not overlaid by the additional obstacles that Black, Hispanic, Indigenous, and gender-nonconforming people experience, and we recognize how much more dangerous the future is for them if federal, state, and hospital policies do not change. We sought to be inclusive in our research, and we are grateful to everyone who spoke with us. We interviewed a diverse group of more than one hundred people who experienced pregnancy loss in addition to dozens of scholars, therapists, experts, and doctors. Some wanted to share because they are actively rejecting the silence and taboo, particularly those under forty, who are speaking openly about their losses on social media and elsewhere. Others have become activists, fighting for improved care or more compassionate laws. Some wanted to feel less alone. People of color and queer people wanted their voices to be heard above the din of the white cis narrative that permeates what discussion there is. (Right now, there is little scientific or scholarly research about how gender-nonconforming people in particular experience pregnancy loss. We hope that changes.) Many felt compelled to share after the sea change in laws governing abortion and miscarriage care.

These conversations were almost sacred. Person after person shared their trauma, their grief, their hurt, their recommendations for how it can be better. Sometimes our friends and family would ask, "Isn't it so sad to hear these stories day in and day out?" But it wasn't. Yes, the stories are gut-wrenching, but there's so much power in sharing them. You cannot feel empathy for people whose stories you never hear. And that's something that we, alongside the many people who opened their hearts to us, aim to change.

Yet a lot of what we found was heartening; we learned that people have created their own mourning and grieving rituals to commemorate their losses in the absence of societally proscribed ones. This ad hoc effort includes the making or buying of totems, and there's a growing online marketplace devoted to jewelry, keepsake boxes, and other talismans that intend to make the intangible tangible.

We want to note that this is not a book about the partners of people who suffered pregnancy loss. It's not that we don't appreciate and love them and recognize they also suffer from this mess, but we felt there was already too much ground to cover with the experiences of the pregnant person. We're focused on the bodies giving birth and being legislated while giving a subtle, supportive high five to the partner who experienced a loss too.

This is also a secular book. This space is dominated by a mostly Christian outlook, and we wanted to talk about it in a more societal way. We mention religion when those we interviewed talk about their personal observance, but it was important to us to carve out a temporal space. (Most of the religious people we interviewed also created secular rituals in their remembrance.)

Just as no two children have the same parents, as the saying goes, no one has the same experience with each pregnancy. Every birthing parent is entitled to compassion for every pregnancy, whether it's a seamless nine months that ends with a healthy baby, a devastating miscarriage after years of infertility, or an abortion that brings great relief. There is no inconsistency in the same woman feeling unconflicted about her abortion at nineteen, then relieved by a miscarriage that came too soon after her toddler, only to be devastated by a miscarriage a few years later, and then overjoyed to have her tubes tied. Nor is there any inconsistency in running a gamut of emotions within one pregnancy.

Pregnancy encompasses a vast gray area of experience that has been jammed into black-and-white definitions, which has led to worse outcomes for women medically, politically, and psychologically. Our hope is that in discussing every facet of pregnancy loss—with medical experts, legal experts, historians, linguists, marketers, therapists, grief counselors, activists, and pregnant people who know their own bodies—we can bring it all back together under one umbrella and help envision a system of compassionate care for those who experience pregnancy loss of any kind. A system that recognizes that the person giving birth— their physical and mental health, their grief, their right to choose a path for their own life—matters.

PART I

How We Got Here

CHAPTER ONE

There Are No Words

The Inadequacy of the Language for Pregnancy Loss

Nobody throws a fetus shower.

And most of us understand exactly why. Fetus is a medical word, devoid of any emotion. But baby? Now that's evocative. Baby connotes a sentimental connection—they have sweet little faces and wear duckling onesies. Intent matters too. Showers are thrown in anticipation of welcoming a child; the word *baby* is doing a lot of the emotional work of what the pregnancy means to you. No one walks around with a registry laser thinking, *boy, that complicated Swedish wrap carrier will be great for my fetus when it (fingers crossed) turns into a baby.*

But what's considered a baby? An infant that has emerged from the womb? A fetus past twenty weeks gestation? Whatever's brewing up when the stick turns pink? Or that embryo you are rooting to make it to day five blastocyst at the IVF lab?

Part of the reason we struggle to talk about pregnancy loss

is we just don't have the words—the literal building blocks of language—for it. And the words we do have are either strictly clinical or infused with stark political baggage. It's a rhetorical mess even before it's an emotional one. The clinical and colloquial words used to describe pregnancy and pregnancy loss fail us because they're not designed *for* us, even though they are *about* us.

It certainly doesn't help that the language is built around our very narrow societal notions of pregnancy and loss: mothers should sacrifice everything, pregnancy loss is a failure, and abortion is unthinkable.

Fetus, Baby, Soldier, Spy

The problem starts at the beginning, because we don't agree on a beginning. Many Christians think life begins at conception, a notion that has creeped into jurisprudence as well. Despite common parlance, there is no "moment" of conception. A sperm and egg fuse, but this is a process, not instantaneous. (We were trying to remember why we thought of conception as a sperm invading an egg like a hostile takeover. Was it from sex ed? Catholic school? Nope. Turns out it was the not-so-timeless *Look Who's Talking* series. In the first movie, a Bruce Willis–voiced sperm burrows its way into a silent egg. In the second movie, a John Travolta–voiced sperm fights his way past a diaphragm and says, "You know why I'm here. Give it up. Lemme in, baby," while the egg says, "Shoo! No! Stop doing that! *Ow*." Big time yikes.)

In actuality, it's all more cooperative than that. As the egg moves down the fallopian tube, the sperm is drawn in by a uterine contraction that controls the speed of the swimmers, the tube changes the composition of the incoming sperm to make it possible for the lucky winner to fuse with the egg, and the egg, it is now thought, chooses its favorite sperm. Then the two cells' membranes dissolve so they can "spoon." How about that? The "violent penetration" of a passive egg by an active sperm, or a male conquering a female, is just another story we tell.

Once the sperm and the egg fuse, they become a zygote. The dividing zygote turns into a blastocyst as it travels, and about fourteen days after the initial fusion, the blastocyst attaches to the uterine wall, and the cells start to differentiate into the building blocks of body systems. From week three to about week eight, this is known as an embryo. Which of these processes is the "moment" that would activate personhood? (Incidentally, most abortions and miscarriages happen in the embryonic stage, the vast majority in the first trimester—92.7 percent and 80 percent, respectively.)

Medically, these are approximate biological and developmental stages that aren't magically activated at a certain number of weeks. From the ninth week of gestation until birth, medicine calls it a fetus, but there isn't some rollover at 12:01 a.m. that announces "it's fetus time!" with confetti and fireworks or even a biological structure to check off the list, like a certain stage of the nervous system completed. It's all more arbitrary and fluid than most people realize. To add even more gray into the mix, what we call six weeks pregnant is really only four weeks along, because the weeks are counted from the last missed period, not embryonic development. (Is it any wonder that all this is a hot mess?)

Humans are notoriously inefficient reproducers—most zygotes don't make it to live birth—but let's say it all works out. Blastocyst implants, urine test reveals rising HCG. What are you calling it? That probably depends on your state of mind.

Embryo and *fetus* are both clinical words. *Baby* is a word that's part of every person's experience—there is a flood of affectionate associations and very few medical ones. Sociolinguists call these differences "registers," and people tend to communicate in the same register. These are the academic terms for something we do unconsciously—why you would be unlikely to say, "Smell ya later, Mr. President" while receiving a medal of honor. But the formality is just part of the problem. We also want to use emotional words to match emotional situations. It's much easier to connect with a personal essay written by a "cancer survivor" than a "human who was once diagnosed with papillary thyroid microcarcinoma." Same with pregnancy, which is nothing if not personal. It's hard to talk about feelings (emotional register) with impersonal or medical language like *embryo* or *fetus* (clinical register). "I'm super jazzed about my fetus!" just doesn't land right.

Sociolinguist George Lakoff talks about how this plays out in the political realm in regard to the abortion debate: "whereas 'cluster of cells,' 'embryo,' and 'fetus' keep discussion in the medical domain, 'baby' moves the discussion to the moral domain. The issue of the morality of abortion is settled once the words are chosen." The modern Supreme Court, in decisions pertaining to abortion, referred to a woman seeking an abortion as a "mother" and described the fetus as a "child." That's hardly an accident. Politics, of course, benefits from stark, black-and-white contrasts.

Another problem is that American English doesn't have a good word for a prebaby entity with some emotions attached to it. Linguists call this a lexical gap—when a culture has the concept but not the words to describe it. (Another example of a lexical gap in English is that we use sister-in-law to describe both your brother's wife and your spouse's sister, while other languages have different words for each.) While a preborn baby and a born baby might be different concepts, we really only have *baby* and *fetus* to work with. These aren't quite synonyms and also don't exist in the same register. Those who feel connected to their pregnancies really have no other option than to default to *baby*—a strong tendency regardless of personal politics. People who are more tentative about their pregnancies are still unlikely to use *fetus* and err more on the side of calling it "the pregnancy," referring more to the state of their body than the potential of what's inside.

We asked some of the people that we interviewed for suggestions, most of which were offered with a laugh. *Praby* (prebaby), *betus* (combination of baby and fetus), and, maybe our favorite, *feeby*. None of these seem likely to catch on. (Gretchen, stop trying to make *feeby* happen.)

Language choices, though they seem benign, are indicative

of a lot of intent and emotion. So in a culture where we have "no common agreement about the nature of life in the womb and no word for beings who are lost in pregnancy through miscarriage, stillbirth or abortion," the ones we choose—and those that get ascribed to our situation whether or not we're on board—affect how the loss is perceived.

Many people feel invalidated when medical professionals use the words *fetus* or *embryo* after a loss. It makes them feel discounted, like the meaning they assigned was foolish or not real. Therapists, doctors, and other medical providers are encouraged to use reflective language and take their cues from the patient. If the patient says "baby", you say "baby." Kiley Krekorian Hanish, the founder of Return to Zero: Hope, a nonprofit that provides support and resources for those who have experienced pregnancy loss, infant or toddler death, or loss through surrogacy or failed adoption, says it's important to check in first. "We recommend that providers don't use the term fetus and instead ask parents what they want to call their pregnancy," Hanish told us. "Some people will refer to it as a pregnancy, others a baby. It's important not to assume and use the parents' language as a guide."

For instance, people who have recurrent loss don't necessarily say baby. They often try to stay detached until they have a successful delivery in order to protect their own feelings.

Many of those we talked to struggled with the vocabulary available to them. Orlando-based Kelsey Garcia-Abdin has experienced a series of early pregnancy losses, miscarriages, and a failed IVF transfer.

"Terms like 'products of conception' downplay a family's loss," Garcia-Abdin said. "I struggle with how to talk about my embryos," she went on. "A lot of people have trouble seeing that embryo as a baby, but for me, that's all I see. I have such a strong connection to them because I had so much hope that they would be born. Their story is that they didn't get to grow."

Memphis-based Michelle Goldwin Kaufman's daughter Maya was delivered by emergency C-section but suffered a hypoxic brain injury that prevented her from breathing and swallowing on her own. Kaufman and her husband decided to withdraw life support. "I don't know what category she falls into exactly. She was almost a stillborn, but they were able to resuscitate her. She lived in the NICU for one week. It was such a roller coaster."

Ohio-based Katie N., who terminated her pregnancy after her baby received a fatal diagnosis, said she has thought a lot about the language of loss since her baby died. "We definitely talk about Nova as our baby. Fetus is a weird word. Baby sounds more loving, and that's what I want to use, even though my politics would dictate that I say fetus."

It came up repeatedly in our interviews that abortion rights supporters felt hemmed in by the terms of the political debate, like they couldn't mourn their miscarriages. They didn't want to fuel conservative arguments against abortion by expressing sadness over their loss when they supported abortion at the same number of weeks. Many view this as a failure of the abortion rights movement, including feminist anthropologist Linda Layne, who said the pro-choice crowd ceded ground to the antiabortion movement by refusing to acknowledge that miscarriage makes some people sad for fear of validating the legal notion of personhood.

We've only been thinking about pregnancy this way for about forty-five years, as we'll talk more about in the next two chapters. And it's pretty undeniable that the modern iteration is greatly influenced by the terms set out by conservative politics, which may rankle abortion rights supporters. But here's the thing—we can talk all day about what influences the way we perceive pregnancy: brutal politics, misogyny, unattainable motherhood perfection, extreme baby-centric consumerism, American bootstrap notions of success, scientific advances. And it is interesting and infuriating and true. But the person who lost a pregnancy is unlikely to care about any of that when they are personally grieving. This failure to meet the moment and create a new language and framework for loss leaves actual pregnant people adrift.

Did I Have a Miscarriage?

Colleen couldn't figure out what to say when her baby died at around twenty-four weeks. Was it just a bad miscarriage? A six-month loss felt different from a six-week loss, she thought, but many in her family wanted to call it a miscarriage because anything more made them uncomfortable. Stillbirth seemed uniquely bad. But a miscarriage, those were common enough. You could bounce back from that without much fanfare, right? In the United States, generally any loss after twenty weeks is considered a stillborn (some hospitals vary on that categorization). She'd been well into her second trimester when the baby died, but she was not nearly as far along as others who had full-term stillbirths at thirty-eight or forty weeks. And she didn't deliver; she had a two-day medical procedure known as a "dilation and evacuation." Did that matter? Should she be calling what she'd done an abortion? She went to an abortion clinic after all. And was she supposed to call it a baby? She thought so—it sure *felt* like one—but did she deserve to use that word?

Rebecca always called her twenty-week loss a stillbirth. The sonogram revealed that he was dead, she labored, and she was in her second trimester when it happened. Someone, probably one of the nurses, must have used the word first because it's hard to blaze a rhetorical trail while actively experiencing a trauma. Delivering, holding the baby, and memorializing him didn't seem to fit the word *miscarriage*. When her twins died a year later, she called it an "induction of terminally ill twins." It was accurate and gave all the pertinent info without inviting too much commentary. But it also offered linguistic cover that it was a societally acceptable loss. It wasn't until she and Colleen began researching this book that she learned the phrase TFMR—termination for medical reasons. She texted Colleen, "This is me! I didn't know it had a name."

After the *Dobbs* decision came down, she started to think more about the terminology. Was it an abortion? By medical definition, yes. By common American parlance—maybe? Yes? Some in Rebecca's own family vehemently disagree with this and say, "I do not consider what you had an abortion." Why not? Because it wasn't a dilation and evacuation (D&E)? The distinction is usually because they understand the reasoning—the twins were terminally ill. But let's be real. It's also because she was married, already a mother, and her babies were desperately wanted. She wasn't the imaginary harlot of antiabortion propaganda. (The wanted versus unwanted categories of baby represent an unfortunate hierarchy in who is deemed worthy of sympathy and choice, a "good loss" versus a "bad loss." More on this later.)

So many women we interviewed talked about their dissatisfaction or confusion about what description applied to them. Chicago area–based Jess C. lost a pregnancy at eighteen weeks and five days, due to a likely trisomy. "At that stage of pregnancy, it's just called a late miscarriage, but I delivered a stillborn. I had a child wrapped in my arms. I kissed his head, exactly like when I had kissed my daughter's head. And that broke me."

Boston-based Margaret P. goes back and forth. "I talk about it sort of euphemistically and call it the loss," she said. "When I'm feeling stronger and want to put a fine point on it, I will say it was a stillbirth. But I still haven't told many people that I experienced a stillbirth. Sometimes it's painful just to even say it." New York–based Nicole O., who ended her pregnancy for medical reasons at seventeen weeks and also experienced a nine-week miscarriage, said, "I don't even identify with miscarriage. I don't like that word. My babies died. Both times, my babies had to be removed from my body. Lost is too casual or something, like 'oops, I lost my baby.' No. My babies died."

These feelings are unsurprising given how misunderstood all these loss categories are and the fact that most people don't even realize that the list is so extensive.

A common misconception of miscarriage is that it's rare, and you find out because of bleeding at home. You get a heavy period, maybe you have a D&C, but overall, it was nature taking its course, and sometimes these things just happen. You should be sad, but not for very long, with a sidecar of some guilt and shame, but keep it mostly to yourself and then have another baby.

Sure, that's one possibility. But you could also take a morning-after pill before the zygote even had a chance to implant and never think about it again. You could get a positive pregnancy test and then have a period the following week. You could have a successful IVF transfer that peters out before eight weeks. You could go to a ten-week ultrasound and find the embryo never developed (a missed miscarriage) and need to take a pill or have a D&C. You could bleed at home at ten weeks, trying to assess if what's in the toilet amounts to the equivalent of two pads of blood or is just cervical bleeding and the pregnancy is fine. (You really haven't lived until you've peered over a toilet with your partner to decide whether you have had a miscarriage, as Rebecca did numerous times.) You could bleed at home and pass a fetus into the toilet at fourteen weeks. You could need a D&C at sixteen weeks. Sometimes the loss is definitive, and sometimes the heart rate is slow, gets slower, and then disappears. You could terminate a much-wanted pregnancy after a twenty-week ultrasound reveals a life-limiting diagnosis. You could deliver too prematurely for the baby to survive. You could deliver a stillbirth at the hospital. And this isn't even a full list.

The treatments for abortion and miscarriage often overlap. A loss before twenty weeks is medically called a "spontaneous abortion." Some that we spoke to reported being shocked to see the word *abortion* in their medical charts and wanted it removed, because they felt they'd had a miscarriage.

"If I tell somebody they're experiencing a spontaneous abortion, all they hear is abortion," said Dr. Sarah Prager, an ob-gyn and professor of obstetrics and gynecology at University of Washington, who coauthored the guidelines on miscarriage management for the American College of Obstetricians and Gynecologists. "And because abortion is so stigmatized, that feels bad to them, but that's the medical word for it. If they get a bill, it will say spontaneous abortion or inevitable abortion. You have to have the word 'abortion' because there isn't a code for pregnancy loss. It doesn't exist."

That means whether it's a voluntary or spontaneous abortion, whether it's for after a miscarriage, for a fetal anomaly, for the mother's health, because she cannot be pregnant right now, wanted or unwanted—it's all medically an abortion.

Medical coding causes limitations in how doctors can describe a loss in the charting, because there just aren't enough codes to encompass the many possibilities.

"It would be incredibly helpful if there was a diagnosis that I could officially pick," Dr. Prager said. Then, she could denote how she managed it—a spontaneous loss that needed no intervention, medication management to pass the tissue, or a procedure. "I don't have the ability to do that because those codes don't exist," Dr. Prager told us. The code would be helpful medically because it would provide more information, but it would also bring some clarity to the patient.

A miscarriage before twenty weeks can be treated with medication, by inducing labor, or with a surgical procedure known as a D&C (dilation and curettage). A D&E (dilation and evacuation) is the medical protocol for early stillbirth between twenty and twenty-four weeks—the same procedure used for 95 percent of second-trimester abortions, or a patient may deliver. Most stillbirths at or after twenty-four weeks involve childbirth, but not all, like Colleen's. Most people don't realize that third-trimester abortions—those twenty-eight weeks and after, which are almost always for a fetal anomaly or a threat to the mother's life—also involve giving birth to a dead fetus. The only difference is the fetus's heartbeat is usually stopped by a euthanizing injection before induction, followed by suction and aspiration for remaining tissue. Most states ban abortion after twenty-four weeks, but Colorado, Maryland, and New Mexico allow it throughout, so later-term clinics exist in those states.

That's complicated enough. But the procedure referred to as a D&C? It's more colloquial than accurate.

This procedure, used for abortion and miscarriage, is also used to treat fibroids, polyps, and postmenopausal bleeding. "But in my career, I don't know that I've ever done what's considered to be a D&C [for a miscarriage] because D&C stands for dilation and curettage, meaning using a sharp curette," Dr. Prager told us. "For decades, the recommendation has been not to use a sharp curette in spite of the fact that many people still do because it is more damaging to the uterus."

Instead, practitioners use a cannula or do a vacuum aspiration procedure that clears the uterus without any scraping. "I can write all that out in the documents, which I do. But it all creates confusion," Dr. Prager said.

Just to recap: the procedures that clear out the uterus for miscarriage and abortion are the same, something most Americans don't realize, and the physical experiences are often exactly the same. Early abortion and early miscarriage are often managed with medication abortion or a procedure. Later pregnancy losses and abortion, which are both rare, often involve the same procedures and induction of labor. But the medical code of D&C does not describe the standard of care or, in most cases, what is actually being performed.

Confused yet?

Chrissy Teigen was.

Confusion with Real-World Consequences

In 2020, Teigen, a model, author, and TV host, lost her third child, Jack, at twenty weeks gestation due to a partial placental abruption. She went viral with a social media post featuring photos of her anguished weeping while receiving an epidural before delivery. She called it a miscarriage at the time. Two years later, she changed the vocabulary she used to talk about it.

"Let's just call it what it was: It was an abortion. An abortion to save my life for a baby that had absolutely no chance. And to be honest, I never, ever put that together until, actually, a few months ago," she said in 2022. This reframing was met with scorn by antiabortion groups and lawmakers who said Teigen was flat wrong. The Catholic, antiabortion LifeNews.com ran a story with the headline "Chrissy Teigen's Miscarriage Can't Be an Abortion, Because Abortions Purposefully Kill Babies." These organizations and antiabortion medical groups and doctors distinguish an elective abortion ("for social or personal reasons") from medical treatment, like that for an ectopic pregnancy. As law professors Jill Wieber Lens and Greer Donley wrote in the *Vanderbilt Law Review*, "according to this line of attack, miscarriage involves 'a mother who wants a child and loses it' while abortion involves a child 'brutally dismembered and killed.'" The difference isn't medical—it's rhetorical and based on perceived intent.

On his podcast, antiabortion Senator Ted Cruz, a Texas Republican, said Teigen's procedure was a miscarriage because it saved her life. So is an abortion a miscarriage when it saves the mother's life? Is it a miscarriage when it's for a wanted baby that would otherwise be welcomed without a maternal complication or life-limiting diagnosis? You see the problem. Who decides? (Hopefully not Ted Cruz.) Writer and historian Daniela Blei put a fine point on it: "From a medical perspective, miscarriage and abortion are the same, even if the language we use and the emotions associated with the two experiences are not. One key difference: Talking about your miscarriage won't get you death threats."

The language and the laws have led to confusion in states with abortion restrictions, which for the most part consider the act an abortion only if the woman or her doctor ends the pregnancy and offer exceptions for "dire medical situations." Sometimes, like in Louisiana law, this category is referred to as "medically futile" pregnancies. But some of the laws include a list of diagnoses, and certain anomalies are so rare, they wouldn't be on there. And most states (so far) have exceptions to save the life of the pregnant person, but doctors under threat of legal repercussions are unsure what qualifies as life-threatening or lifesaving and have to consult with hospital lawyers and not solely their own medical judgment. Texas's ban specifies that a procedure is "not abortion" if it treats a miscarriage, but Arizona and Wisconsin do not. The threat of prosecution makes the differences opaque.

A spate of news stories since the Supreme Court overruled *Roe v. Wade* have shown women denied D&Cs after miscarriages or to end pregnancies with a fatal fetal prognosis. The American Medical Association has described this patchwork as "chaos." Antiabortion lawmakers and activists blame doctors for this confusion, but doctors in return say it's the laws that are unclear. Both sides accuse the other of being disingenuous—a fight that continues while people's lives hang in the balance. As journalist Christina Cauterucci wrote, "if the architects of these bans had wanted the 'medical emergency' exceptions to be easily intelligible—if they'd wanted them to be used at all—they would have written them broadly enough to allow for medical discretion and included a clear and exhaustive list of conditions covered."

When abortion is deemed a character issue rather than a medical procedure, then there's a societal narrative of who is deserving—a so-called blameless abortion. This usually only includes victims of rape or incest or a pregnant person whose life is in danger from medical situations like ectopic pregnancy, preeclampsia, or a cancer diagnosis or who needs a D&C to clear out remaining tissues from a missed miscarriage. But what about someone who is impoverished, can't handle more children, has depression, is in an abusive relationship, doesn't want to be a parent, or has a child with a fatal diagnosis, a life-limiting one, or a diagnosis that isn't fatal but would require the complete upending and possible bankruptcy of the family? Morgan Nuzzo, a certified nurse-midwife and cofounder of Partners in Abortion Care, an all-trimester abortion clinic in Maryland, wryly repeated a trope about anti-choice people who get abortions: "the only moral abortion is my abortion."

"I resist modifiers for the word abortion," Dr. Prager said. "People talk about induced abortion or indicated abortion or elective abortion. And I personally think, as do many of my colleagues, that every single abortion is indicated. They're indicated for different reasons. Somebody with a devastating fetal diagnosis, who chooses not to continue the pregnancy as a kind thing to do to that fetus, feels like a loss to that person. That's an abortion. Somebody who doesn't have money to pay for another child and is thinking about the children that they already have. You know, they equally are considering this to be an act of kindness to the pregnancy, to their family in general. They are experiencing a loss and also an abortion. I don't see it as all that different from someone who goes to the doctor and is told this fetus doesn't have a heartbeat anymore. It's all loss."

This brings us to terminations for medical reasons (TFMR), which illustrate the problem inherent in the good loss/bad loss and wanted/unwanted dichotomy baked into so many of our common pregnancy perceptions. The "wanted" pregnancy, if lost, still retains its virtue—sometimes even if that wanted pregnancy ends in a medical termination. (Especially if it conforms to the sadness the story demands.) This is a simplification because plenty of people we interviewed had been relieved by miscarriages or felt devastated by their termination but didn't regret it. The "hierarchy" of loss came up repeatedly in our interviews, not just with TFMR patients but with those who had stillbirths and miscarriages as well. Just being a part of the loss community made them aware of the imaginary rankings of who got to be sad, who was "bad," and which losses were "acceptable."

"There is definitely a nuance between wanted and unwanted," said Katie N., a TFMR parent based in Southwest Ohio. "The fact that we try to separate those, like if you terminate a wanted baby for a medical reason, then it's noble, but if you couldn't raise the baby at that time in your life, it's shameful and you shouldn't have that power. Those things go together. So much of this is worry or outright anger that women have that power."

There aren't statistics broken out on how many abortions are TFMR related, as they could occur at any trimester, but they are most likely after genetic tests reveal issues and after the twenty-week anatomy scan. Abortions after twenty weeks account for less than 1 percent of abortions.

Nuzzo says TFMR patients aren't "special," meaning that her clinic offers the same care and services to everyone who comes in, including the option for keepsakes and cremation. "There are two types of people who have later abortions. One is that something has gone wrong in their life medically with either their health or the pregnancy's health," Nuzzo told us. "Then there is a group of people who have a social indication, and guess what? Something in their life has gone seriously wrong."

Alison Dreith, director of strategic partnerships for the Midwest Abortion Coalition that helps people travel to, from, and within the Midwest to access abortions, says her organization does not ask patients for their reasons for needing an abortion because "it's none of our business." The organization consciously refuses to engage in the hierarchy.

"We need to talk about abortion in nonshameful, nonstigmatizing ways, which means that talking about your support for abortion should never have a 'but,'" Dreith said. "Not I support abortion but only until this or only if that. Abortion is needed and wanted at all stages of pregnancy for a long list of reasons."

Sabrina Fletcher, a TFMR doula who offers virtual support,

dislikes the tendency to rank. "Sometimes I don't even like that we have the acronym," Fletcher told us. "It feels like we're hiding between four little letters. It says we had to choose abortion, but we also want it to be seen as pregnancy loss. It's a different kind of abortion, but I don't want to fall into a moral or ethical hierarchy. My TFMR was OK, but your abortion for whatever other reason is not. I don't allow that sort of talk in my social media spaces."

TFMR itself is a newer acronym, and medical terminations are also sometimes called compassionate inductions or thera-peutic abortions. "I don't think most people have heard of it until they fall into the category themselves," Jane Armstrong, a Texas-based perinatal mental health therapist who works with TFMR patients, told us. "It's not a medical term. It's something that has come up from parents who have been through it, finding each other online, and building communities around it. You won't find it on anyone's chart."

Those patients created a community in part because they didn't quite fit in the stillbirth or miscarriage support groups and wanted to find others in their own category. They felt like an island unto themselves that didn't fit into either political camp or, in many cases, felt like they couldn't openly talk about their decision.

Fletcher, who became a bereavement doula after terminating a pregnancy in the early second trimester, said "both political sides feel invalidating" to TFMR people. "Pro-choice language like 'ball of cells' doesn't fit, and pro-life stances say you're a bad person for choosing to terminate. Pro-lifers focus on the emotions, and the pro-choice side seems to counter it by saying, 'I don't have these emotions.' None of that works. I got an abortion, yes. And I also grieved a very wanted and loved baby. That's a pregnancy loss experience we don't really have language for."

Even the word *choice* can be troublesome. North Carolina–based Heather Pew, who terminated after a twenty-week scan revealed her son's brain didn't divide into two hemispheres, chafes at the word. "Did I really choose it? I didn't really choose to lose my son," she said. "I chose not to let him die in pain."

These patients are also torn on whether to use the word *abortion*. Ann Arbor–based Margot Finn, a moderator of the Facebook group Ending a Wanted Pregnancy since 2015, traveled to Colorado for her twenty-nine-week abortion in 2014 after her daughter was diagnosed with lissencephaly, a rare brain abnormality. "Some in our group say, 'I didn't have an abortion, I had a termination or induction,'" Finn said. "But people have come to accept the term more, and we in the group work to help people accept it. They don't have to use it if they don't want to, but most of us do use the word abortion to describe our loss."

Many who terminate for medical reasons say it was a miscarriage. Rebecca S., who lives in the Washington, DC, area, terminated in 2022 when her son had numerous anomalies, including severely damaged kidneys and undeveloped lungs. "I had to sit there for every kick that I felt and knew he wouldn't survive," she said. She decided to induce before the twenty-fourth week, when it would be legal in Virginia, so she could deliver at the hospital she knew rather than go to a clinic elsewhere. "Even now, very few people know that I terminated. I framed it like I was having contractions the weekend before I was getting induced," she said.

Yvette, who ended her pregnancy in the second trimester, wondered why she didn't speak up more about terminating her much-wanted pregnancy. "I'm really not ashamed of it, and yet I want to protect myself from I'm not sure what. Questions? Judgment? I guess my feelings are still so tender I just can't take that on too."

Nuzzo, of the Maryland all-trimester abortion clinic, said many of her clients struggle with this. "One of my canned phrases for patients who need to be protective about how they describe their procedure, and this works for medical anomalies and not: 'I lost the pregnancy, and I don't want to talk about it.' Anyone who challenges that is an asshole. It shuts it down fast. And it's not a lie."

Since the Supreme Court decision to overturn abortion protections, the landscape has shifted under the feet of those who received therapeutic abortions, the historical term for TFMR. Many spoke about their phone blowing up the day a draft Supreme Court opinion leaked as friends and family who knew about their medical termination offered sympathy or tried to warn them to stay away from the news. Some speak about it differently in the wake of that decision, now using the word *abortion* more deliberately or being more open about the circumstances of their loss.

Seattle-based Malina W., who had a medical termination

at eighteen weeks when her baby didn't develop kidneys, said, "The word abortion was hard for me. I felt ashamed. I called it a surgery. I didn't call it an abortion until after *Roe* fell, and I had healed enough from that experience. I was disgusted by what happened in our country, and I felt a moral obligation to say I had an abortion and not use coded words. For my own personal sense of integrity, I had to stop feeling ashamed."

Laura T., who lives in the northern Chicago suburbs, had two young sons when she got pregnant with her third child. At twenty-one weeks, she found out the baby had anencephaly and would not develop a nervous system, brain, or skull. At twenty-three and a half weeks, she terminated in Chicago rather than her local hospital so no one in her hometown would know. "Being so visibly pregnant and then not, people kept saying, what happened? I said I lost the baby. That became the narrative, and we moved on. Because I knew I could not handle judgment on top of my grief. Even though I knew they were wrong, I couldn't do it."

She terminated fifteen years ago. The day of the *Dobbs* leak, she was at a funeral for a friend's mother who had ten children. "I realized, when I die, no one would talk about my third child because no one knows, and I won't be a mother who had a daughter, and I won't be a mother who lost a child. And I knew it was time to start sharing my story," she said. She told her sons, then eighteen and twenty, who were shocked and saddened. Her youngest visited her daughter's grave with her.

"I'm not compartmentalizing anymore. You're either in or

you're out," she said. "I'm not pretending your judgment has merit. I'm like, fuck it, my child didn't have a head. Is that hard for you to hear? You think it's harder to hear than to experience? Grow up. I'm not interested in coddling or softening the blow for you."

Judged by Jargon

Political language is limiting enough, but there is also a huge disconnect between medical jargon and the emotions of the experience that many of those we interviewed mentioned as an additional source of stress and confusion.

In early losses, the pregnant person will pass what doctors often call "products of conception"—the embryo or fetus and placenta. Many women reported being confused and even insulted by that term, particularly those who had miscarriages at home and saw the viscera in the toilet. Cleveland-based Brittany, who runs the Instagram account Understanding Heart, directed toward bereaved parents, said her son, who she miscarried at ten and a half weeks, was "more than just some 'leftover tissue' or 'products of conception' or 'worst period ever.' He is, and always will be, so much more."

Kristen Swanson, former dean of the Seattle University College of Nursing, is renowned for her work on pregnancy loss. Back when she was a doctoral student pursuing a PhD, one of her assignments was to enroll in and evaluate the process of going through therapy. She had just had a C-section, so she chose to complete her assignment by joining a cesarean birth support group. She attended the first meeting with her six-week-old son in her arms, where the guest speaker, an obstetrician, was talking about miscarriage.

"He was using words like 'spontaneous abortion' and 'products of conception.' And the women in the room, when they were asking questions, they were using words like, 'my baby, my little one' and were talking in loving terms," Swanson told us. "The obstetrician was talking about the actual and potential health problems of spontaneously aborting the products of conception. And they were talking about the human response to losing a baby they wanted. I was so struck with the two different languages to describe the same phenomenon." That inspired her dissertation about what women go through when they miscarry.

Many of the terms about pregnancy have roots in paternalism and sexism or, in the case of geriatric pregnancy, just seem unnecessarily rude. (Geriatric pregnancy used to refer to anyone pregnant at thirty-five or after, an age chosen in the 1970s at which the risk that an amniocentesis would harm the fetus was roughly equal to the chance of the fetus being born with Down syndrome—a calculation that is no longer true with screening advances.) *Geriatric pregnancy* gave way to *advanced maternal age*, and in 2022, the American College of Obstetricians and Gynecologists said the preferred terminology is now "pregnancy at thirty-five years or older," or just indicating the age of the patient.

Other terms people repeatedly brought up include *incompetent cervix*, when the cervix dilates before the end of the pregnancy, which, depending on the week, results in miscarriage, premature birth, or possibly perinatal loss. (This is how it is medically coded, so it's going in the chart even if the doctor uses sensitive language.) An incompetent cervix can be remedied if caught in time with a cerclage, basically a sewing together of the cervix, until full term. *Hostile* or *inhospitable womb* sounds like a bad motel with a one-star Yelp review. ("I wish I could give this place zero stars.") *Habitual aborter*—repeated miscarriages—is a real gut punch. Like your vices are smoking, gambling, and miscarrying. (This terminology is being replaced by *recurrent miscarriage*.) Labor "fails to progress." Ovaries "decline" and follicles "fail" to reach ovulation. This language has a long history. It used to be taught that "menstruation is the uterus crying for lack of a baby." Woof.

Central Washington–based Lacey M., whose TFMR inspired her to start training as a postpartum and bereavement doula, told us, "The language we use to describe women's bodies has in part brought us to where we are today—the building blocks of how the system treats us like garbage."

The gendered nature of it is undeniable. A guy with testicular cancer isn't told he has "a broken scrotum." Some of those we interviewed had gone through fertility treatments and talked about their male partners being treated with kid gloves if they were a factor in the infertility, with much less care given to the language and feelings when a finger was pointed in her direction.

These terms, sexist and rude though they may be, have real-world implications that lead to patient confusion and worse care.

A 2018 study found that stigmatizing language in a patient chart can contribute to negative bias toward the patient and can lead to treating pain less aggressively—something that has been a significant bias in treating people of color.

The pregnancy app Peanut teamed up with linguists and medical professionals in 2021 to create a glossary of more neutral language. (Some suggestions include replacing *incompetent cervix* with *early cervical dilation, infertility* with *reproductive struggles, lazy ovary* with *early ovarian decrease, products of conception* with *pregnancy tissue,* and *incompatible with life* with *life-limiting diagnosis.*) So far, these haven't caught on in the medical community. Lazy ovaries and incompetent cervixes still abound.

Another problem with medical jargon that was brought up repeatedly in our interviews was the euphemisms that left patients unsure about what was happening or what to expect. Pain is subjective, so telling a patient they may experience pain doesn't help articulate what's coming. Pregnant people we interviewed said they were confused by phrases like "you'll pass some tissue" or "it's like a period" after a miscarriage when they ended up feeling like they were going through labor. They said, "I honestly didn't know if I was dying or overreacting," "Do male doctors think that's what a period feels like?" and "That was labor, not 'passing tissue.'" This was common among those who had natural miscarriages and those who were prescribed misoprostol after a missed miscarriage. They weighed how bad was bad enough, how much blood was too much blood, how much pain was too much pain. They had no idea if what they were experiencing was normal because they had been told it would be like a bad period. Overland Park–based Ashley B., who has had recurrent miscarriages, lost one pregnancy at fifteen weeks and three days. "I didn't know I had been in labor for about two and a half days. Anybody who says it's like period pains is wrong."

Another source of confusion among those we interviewed were the polite terms for death. "Nature took care of it," "fetal demise," or "no fetal cardiac activity" often didn't penetrate the trauma of the moment. They couldn't process what was happening until the third or fourth time the words were repeated. Rebecca remembers when she was at the twenty-week ultrasound that revealed her stillbirth, the sonographer said, "There's no heartbeat." And she said, "Oh, I'll move" and shifted her belly. It didn't sink in until the doctor said "died."

"People need to hear the word 'died.' You have to say, 'I'm sorry, your baby died.' They told me, 'I'm sorry, there's no heartbeat.' I thought, well, open me up, get her out, and start her heart," said Boston-based Nneka Hall, who now is a full-spectrum doula and a pregnancy and infant loss awareness advocate who focuses on infant and maternal mortality within the Black community after having a stillborn daughter. "But death, death is final. You start to register what's happening. People gasp when I say that in my training. But you have to say the words. If the patient doesn't hear it, the brain will think there's still hope."

We find it inconsistent that much of the pregnancy loss language is judgmental and accusatory until it involves a death, and then it's all euphemisms and tiptoeing. Does America hate death more than it loves blaming women? Tough call.

You're Being So Heteronormative Right Now

Every queer person we interviewed had a story about being pregnant in a heteronormative space. Forms that say husband instead of partner, doctors and sonographers who say "Where's Dad?" when they walk in the room despite a female partner sitting there. "It's heteronormative assumption after assumption," said Sacramento-based Ashley P., who did reciprocal IVF with her wife. (Ashley's eggs were harvested and fertilized, and her wife, Jodi, carried their children.)

Tina Mody and her wife, Bella Mody, founded the nonprofit Maya's Wings after they lost their daughter to miscarriage at sixteen weeks. They want it to be an inclusive source for navigating IVF and working toward eliminating preventable pregnancy loss. "There is a complete lack of recognition for the other parent. There was a lot of scrutiny of 'where's the father?' There is no father. And this is in Portland," Tina Mody said.

Another story we heard repeatedly was after a loss with one gestating partner in a same-sex couple, they were told some variation of "well, you can try again with this one next time," pointing to the other partner, like it was a silver lining to have another set of eggs and a uterus, without knowing any of the medical, emotional, financial, or circumstantial decisions behind why those choices were made in the first place. One couple was told this with a bit of a chuckle—at their D&C appointment.

Some couples mitigated this by researching IVF clinics, ob-gyns, and hospitals that had inclusive reputations, but insurance doesn't always make accessing those possible, if they can be found at all.

Language is an obvious challenge for transmasculine or nonbinary pregnant people, who face being misgendered on intake forms and sometimes on the outside of the building—"women's birthing center." The American College of Obstetricians and Gynecologists has taken steps to remove gendered language from its documents. Family Equality, a nonprofit that advances equality for the LGBTQ+ community to build and sustain their families, also advocates for avoiding misgendering in the patient room, intake paperwork, and educational materials. The language is a start, but that respect also has to translate to the care trans, nonbinary, and queer patients receive.

The American Civil Liberties Union and the CDC have been phasing out "pregnant women" in favor of "pregnant people." Many doctors and academics we interviewed suggested using more specific language: pregnant women and transgender men. We use variations of "pregnant person" and "birthing parent" a lot in this book because we want to be inclusive of the pregnancy loss experience. (A book that's about feeling alone shouldn't make even more people feel alone.) Our goal is to talk about the experiences everyone has had with pregnancy loss while also recognizing that much of the current restrictions are predicated on misogyny.

Transgender studies scholar Paisley Currah advocates for "a transgender feminist approach that is not gender neutral—that dares to identify asymmetry when it sees it," so as not to lose "important historical and analytical frameworks" for seeing an issue like abortion restrictions "as part of a war against women." The patriarchal control of women's bodies matters in the context of much of women's health and pregnancy loss—some of the same issues that are currently at play in attempts to limit gender-affirming care and outlaw trans bodies. These are intersectional battles.

Maryland-based Catherine and her partner, a trans man, made their family through IVF. "Growing up and living in the culture of assumed heterosexuality, reproduction seems like a loving, spiritual thing. In my experience, it has been the most medicalized, legalized process that I've ever undertaken," she said.

Catherine delivered their first daughter by emergency C-section. This was followed by a twelve-week miscarriage. In her third pregnancy, she was six months along when she got a relatively mild case of COVID during the omicron wave, but it caused sudden acute onset preeclampsia. Her second daughter was delivered by C-section at twenty-four weeks, six days gestation. The baby was responsive and held their thumbs, but she died after three days.

"It probably wouldn't happen again, but if it did, it could be just as bad," Catherine said. "We just felt like I can't try anymore. It was the right decision, but it was a source of grief."

They had six embryos left. Her husband has been on testosterone for eighteen years but has a uterus and wanted to try. They found a trans-competent fertility clinic and gave it a shot. "The science on this, as with all fertility, is thin. It's even thinner because there just isn't research on trans men and pregnancy. It's all basically a shot in the dark," Catherine said.

He went off testosterone and had a cycle, and then they started to monitor the hormones and lining. The first two transfers failed, they tried a "fake" transfer cycle without an embryo to test the tissue, and then the third embryo transfer was successful. They weren't far out from the positive test when he was diagnosed with an ectopic pregnancy.

"We were like, our friends are going to be really tired of telling us that they're sorry," she said. "We've crossed out so many things on the bingo card."

After one more failed transfer, he gave birth to a healthy child in 2023.

There is very little research on trans pregnancy, and trans loss is an even smaller subset. Carla Pfeffer, director of the Consortium for Sexual and Gender Minority Health at Michigan State University, has studied pregnancy loss specifically in the trans community and conducted a small study that included trans pregnancy loss in the United States, Canada, Australia, and Europe. Some of the unique issues for trans and nonbinary people included an extra layer of worrying about testosterone. "While some talked about [the loss] as devastating, others found positive meaning, because their bodies were capable of getting pregnant," she told us. Some in the study received compassionate care but overall had very little support "in the hospital or loss support from friends or family members," she said. "There was a lack of understanding of what it's like to miscarry among those groups."

Perhaps that is what we really need the language for—telling our own stories. Language evolves, as all languages do, over time and to better fit the age in which it is needed (we gave up on saying crunk, right?). But if the words we have are woefully inadequate for an outsider to find us, then maybe we most need them to find ourselves.

CHAPTER TWO

How to Make an American Baby

The Modern Resonance of Reproduction in Earlier Eras

For most of history, childbirth was the same old story: women were frequently pregnant but often trying not to be, birth could be very dangerous, and abortion was attempted and achieved through various rudimentary methods. (Abortion was referenced in ancient Egypt, Greece, and Rome. It is age-old and evergreen.) Markedly, the whole continuum was female—a birthing woman was attended by a female midwife in a room full of female relatives and friends. (What's the opposite of a sausage fest? It was that.)

And it stayed that way until reproduction became about control, capitalism, and fears that the number of white babies was being outpaced by immigrants, Catholics, and people of color. When slaveholders profited from Black children, that reproduction was encouraged. When there was no longer a white capitalist profit to it, there ensued a long trail of eugenics and forced sterilizations on people of color.

It's not a pretty history.

In some ways, reproduction in America has been stripped back to basics, but we don't find ourselves suddenly reliving a colonial life. We would argue it's more perverse in some ways because the advances in medicine are available, but they're being withheld. Like the *Back to the Future* timeline where Biff Tannen runs a dystopian Hill Valley, we're going back to a place we never really were.

The current moment seems to have taken the worst components from America's reproductive past while also withholding the medical advances that saved lives or that gave pregnant people any kind of control over their own bodies and futures. So how the hell did we get here?

Let's back up to our beginnings. A married woman in colonial America (which spanned the seventeenth and eighteenth centuries) would spend most of her life childbearing and childrearing. Women were expected to be fruitful and multiply, and a lady with a bunch of kids would be admired for doing her job to populate a nascent America. White women typically married in their late teens or early twenties, nursed each child for a year or two before becoming pregnant again, and gave birth roughly every eighteen months to two years until menopause. They were likely welcoming grandchildren while still giving birth themselves. (Exhausting.)

Colonial women were playing a numbers game; most

experienced five to ten pregnancies to end up with between three and eight surviving children because so many ended with miscarriage, stillbirth, and infant death. Nearly one in five children died in the first year of life. Yet the idea of grieving a miscarriage would have made no sense to them; they were worried about survival, for themselves and their children.

The experience of giving birth during this time was communal and exclusively female. It was also one of the only places where women had ultimate control (well, as much control as nature would allow), as historian Judith Walzer Leavitt wrote in *Brought to Bed*. Her friends, neighbors, mother, and sisters (if they could get away from their own duties and childcare—an unmarried sister was ideal) would create her "lying in" chamber where they'd all stay together during prelabor, labor, and a bit into the postpartum period to help with cooking, cleaning, and childcare. The word *gossip* derives from the British "god sibs" or godparents. All these ladies descending onto the home for very frequent births? Godsibs. Gossips.

The follow-up to the lying-in period (the immediate postpartum weeks to months, depending on how rough the delivery) was followed by a "groaning" or "birthing" party, when the mother would cook a meal of appreciation for those who helped her. In *Celebrating the Family*, historian Elizabeth H. Pleck described this as "part of the cradle-to-grave system of emotional support among women." The support part was great. How soon that grave could come calling was not.

Birth was often dangerous. Approximately one in thirty

women could expect to die in childbirth or because of postpartum complications, and women were more likely to die in the prime of life than men. Cotton Mather warned in the early eighteenth century that conception meant "your Death has Entered into you." (Rude.) Pregnant poet Anne Bradstreet, a resident of the Massachusetts Bay Colony, wrote a poem to her husband that read in part, "how soon, my Dear, death may my steps attend." (Bradstreet died in 1672 at age sixty after bearing eight children, so she skirted the danger.) Thomas Jefferson's first wife, Martha, died in childbirth, and his daughter Maria died after delivering her second child. Sam Adams's first wife, Elizabeth, died soon after giving birth to a stillborn. Though some historians do not think childbirth deaths were as prevalent as feared, it's fair to say that all colonists would have known someone who died from childbirth complications.

Infants, children, and birthing women were often imperiled by the realities of colonial life, and pregnancies too close together could leave a woman weak, still suffering from injuries and infections from childbirth before the next round. Babies would often fail to thrive when born to physically exhausted women or if they were weaned too soon when their mothers became pregnant again. There is much evidence that women would have been very aware of the dangers of back-to-back pregnancies. In her letters, Abigail Adams lamented her daughter Nabby's repeated pregnancies, called her sister Elizabeth "foolish" for starting "a second crop" of children at forty, and welcomed the news of a young relative's miscarriage in 1800.

Contraception was minimal. But colonial mothers consistently achieved two-year spacing between children through a combination of coitus interruptus (otherwise known as the pullout method) and breastfeeding, which is not reliable but can sometimes suppress ovulation. (Less so when rampant infant death would end lactation and start the cycle over sooner.) Prolonged breastfeeding was sometimes accompanied by abstinence, which was not always a popular option within the marriage. Alexander Hamilton grew impatient with his wife, Eliza, in 1802 and wrote, "I shall be glad to find that my dear little Philip is weaned if circumstances have rendered it prudent. It is of importance to me to rest quietly in your bosom." (See the musical *Hamilton* for further evidence of that guy's inability to say no to this.) There isn't a lot of data on how often any of these methods were used, as a proper gentleman would be unlikely to note in his diary that he interrupted his coitus. And we don't have a lot to go on from women in this era; not all could read or write, and their records were scarcer and similarly concerned with propriety.

Colonial Americans would have understood pregnancy completely differently than we do now. There was no definitive test, no medical way to confirm a pregnancy—it all came down to a woman knowing her own body. She may suspect it when she was tired, had sore boobs, and missed a period or two, but there were many potential causes of irregular and late cycles in a time of rampant illness, not to mention a bone-weary life of constant childbearing, childrearing, and incessant chores. She wouldn't know for sure that she was expecting until quickening, around sixteen to twenty weeks. Most American laws during this time were based on the English common law, which distinguished between being "with child" and "with quick child," when it all became official. (A woman could be prosecuted for an abortion when she was "with quick child," but such prosecutions were rare, even among the Puritans. And those guys would whip scofflaws who skipped church. They weren't exactly known for being laid-back.)

Lara Freidenfelds, a historian of health, reproduction, and parenting in America, wrote in her book *The Myth of the Perfect Pregnancy* that "women mostly tried not to be pregnant, at the same time that they wanted a family. They expected that their wanted children would result from pregnancies they had in fact tried to avoid."

Early miscarriage doesn't look much different from a missed period, so a woman may never have known she was pregnant at all if she lost it before the fourth month. But if she had some pregnancy symptoms and maybe bled with some heavy cramps, she might call it a "mishap," "miss," or "abortion," all of which were synonyms. Pregnancies lost further along resemble coagulated blood or lumps of tissue, and especially in an era before embryology or the stages of fetal development were understood, a fetus was reported to look "ill-formed and alien" when compared to a full-term infant. (Even now, plenty of people squint at a twelve-week ultrasound and acknowledge it looks more like a tadpole than the star of a diaper commercial.) Historian Barbara Duden noted that until the late eighteenth century, illustrations of the unborn showed a little man dancing in the womb or a full-term infant drawn smaller. Women at the time would have considered the passed tissue to be the beginning materials for the pregnancy that just didn't properly "cook" into a baby.

Miscarriages only became worrisome if she had a lot of them and few or no children. They were not generally dangerous and often passed without much more fanfare than cramping and a heavy period. But very much like today, there was a possibility of hemorrhage or sepsis if she didn't expel the materials of conception, and without modern antibiotics or procedures to help, she could sicken and die within weeks. A 1766 obituary in the *South Carolina Gazette* reads "of a miscarriage of twins, on the 10th instant, died here, and the 24th year of her age, one of the most pious and accomplished young women in these parts."

Stillbirths were much more common than they are today because there were so few safe options for intervening in prolonged labor. But it's important to note that at this point, the woman's life was always prioritized over any individual pregnancy, at least in part because a premature infant almost certainly would have died without the interventions we have today. Many old American cemeteries have gravestones marking a stillborn buried with his or her mother, both dead in childbirth.

The attitudes around all this were so different from what they are today. In a culture where pregnancy wasn't real until quickening, "there was no obvious moral distinction between intervening before or after conception." Abortion, miscarriage, stillbirth, and pregnancy were all part of the same continuum. Herbal remedies at the time were known to help with all sorts of "female" complaints. British herbalist Nicholas Culpeper's book *The English Physician*, the first medical book published in the colonies (really just a list of folk remedies), included six to twelve herbs he believed would cause an abortion. Those best known would have been savin, rue, tansy, and pennyroyal. (Fun fact: the Nirvana song "Pennyroyal Tea" refers to this. In Kurt Cobain's unused liner notes published in *Journals*, he wrote, "herbal abortive…it doesn't work, you hippie.") Tansy was also thought to help with fertility, a dual purpose that was "neither uncommon nor illogical in folk medicine."

These natural abortifacients, or substances that induce abortion, were far less efficient, predictable, reliable, or safe than medications we have today. The idea here was that if a woman wanted to get pregnant, try to bring on a period! And if she didn't want to be pregnant, try to bring on a period! These herbal inducements were relatively easy to get, and they often worked. "But it wasn't like, 'I now need an abortion. I shall go harvest my herbs,' and it would be just like taking misoprostol," Freidenfelds told us, referring to a medication used in both miscarriage and abortion. "It was more like, 'I'm late. I'm going to drink this tea to help my cycle come back.' And it seemed to have worked sometimes to induce miscarriage."

It was so common and such a nonissue that in 1748, Benjamin Franklin added a recipe for an at-home abortion to an adapted British manual called *The Instructor* for the colonies, general instructions for how to do a little bit of everything, including math, writing letters, and caring for horse hooves. "Abortion was so 'deeply rooted' in colonial America that one of our nation's most influential architects went out of his way to insert it into the most widely and enduringly read and reprinted math textbook of the colonial Americas—and he received so little pushback or outcry for the inclusion that historians have barely noticed it is there. Abortion was simply a part of life, as much as reading, writing, and arithmetic," author Molly Farrell wrote on Slate. Abortion, she argued, is originalism.

Slavery and Reproduction

Black women today are at greater risk of experiencing stillbirths and miscarriages as well as dying from pregnancy and childbirth complications than any other American demographic. Overall, they receive poorer medical care, and their complaints are less likely to be believed. That didn't arise out of thin air; it's the result of deeply entrenched racism that dates back to the very founding of the nation.

The first enslaved people arrived in the colonies in 1619. In 1808, Congress ended America's participation in the international slave trade but, of course, not slavery itself. Plantation owners could no longer kidnap slaves from abroad, so the slave population had to grow domestically. This, coupled with the expansion of cotton production, intensified the coercion and interference in enslaved women's reproduction, and from 1807 to 1860, the number of enslaved people in the United States increased from just over one million to more than 3.9 million. Children born to enslaved women were slaves regardless of paternity, which legal theorist Dorothy Roberts describes in *Killing the Black Body* as one of slavery's "most odious features: it forced its victims to perpetuate the very institution that subjugated them by bearing children who were born the property of their masters." Thomas Jefferson, founding father and Virginia plantation owner, wrote that "a woman who brings a child every two years is more profitable than the best man of the farm." It's worth remembering that the man who authored the rhapsodic underpinnings of American freedom owned more than six hundred slaves in his lifetime, including Sally Hemings, whom he first impregnated when she was sixteen.

Childbirth and pregnancy were so much worse for enslaved women, and the persistence of the variants on this racist history is horrifying. These women experienced pregnancy amid an environment of extreme fieldwork, poor nutrition, miscarriages, stillbirths, and infant deaths in addition to dangerous births and the risk of childbirth injury. Prenatal care would have come from Black "granny midwives" who offered comfort, advice, and herbal remedies. Some slaveholders might reduce a pregnant woman's workload closer to her due date, but many worked a pregnant woman until the moment she went into labor and sent her back to the field the next day. Birth isn't exactly something you can bounce back from in one day. Or maybe not even twenty depending on the labor. (You know that oft-repeated phrase "women used to give birth in a field" that is somehow supposed to be reassuring, like birth is no big deal? We couldn't get confirmation if this phrase is rooted in American slavery or European peasantry, but regardless, giving birth in a field is demonstrably bad. This expression both minimizes the pain and physicality of childbirth and valorizes self-sacrificing for capitalism. Let's stop perpetuating it.)

Pregnancy was unlikely to give her any reprieve from punishments, and some slaveholders devised a way to discipline a pregnant woman by digging a hole to accommodate her stomach while she lay on the ground to be beaten and whipped. Most academics working on women's reproductive health today cite the rising importance of the fetus over the mother as a backlash to the women's movement of the 1960s and 1970s and the post-*Roe v. Wade* antiabortion movement, but legal theorist Dorothy Roberts argues that whipping pregnant slaves while digging out space on the ground for her belly "is the most powerful image of maternal-fetal conflict I have ever come across in all my research on reproductive rights. It is the most striking metaphor I know for the evils of policies that seek to protect the fetus while disregarding the humanity of the mother." Miscarriages and stillbirths were rampant. The infant mortality rate for enslaved babies in 1850 was twice that of whites, with fewer than two out of three Black children surviving to age ten, usually from malnutrition and disease. An enslaved women would not have been much troubled by miscarriage either, unless as with white women, she was unable to produce live children—though that had different implications for her life.

Enslaved women were often separated from their children as they worked, if they were allowed to live with them at all. Frederick Douglass said, "I do not recollect of ever seeing my mother by the light of day." His mother, Harriet, was sold when he was an infant, and she would walk twelve miles to see him after a full day's labor, visit with him, then walk twelve miles back and work. She died when Douglass was seven. (Go ahead and stop to weep. We'll wait.) Slaveholders would break up slave marriages if no children came about or, more likely, the childless woman was sold off to another plantation, but part of the trap was that she was less likely to be sold and separated from her loved ones by continuing to reproduce. Slave owners also used children as pawns to prevent enslaved women from running away. Because of this, "far fewer enslaved women than men escaped—only 19 percent of the runaways advertised in North Carolina from 1850 to 1860, for example, were women. The same pattern was common throughout the South." Childbearing—separate from physical dangers—was emotionally fraught, to say the least.

They were also trying not to be pregnant, which would have included attempts to "bring on their menses" with cotton root, the preferred abortifacient for the enslaved because it was easy to get and could be chewed or brewed into a tea. As Marie Jenkins Schwartz poetically wrote in *Birthing a Slave*, "the fortunes of slaveholders rested on the portion of the plant that grew above ground, the destiny of women on the part below." Slave owners and some white physicians may have suspected the use of herbs, but it's hard to know how prevalent this was, especially against the backdrop of an environment so ill-suited to a healthy pregnancy.

Victorians, Racism, and the New Field of Gynecology

At the same time, the culture around mothering and child-birth was evolving for white, middle- and upper-class native-born women who had the luxury of being able to change their attitudes. Enter the Victorian sensibility. The colonial era had been a mostly agrarian system where it was all hands on deck to keep the family economy going. But the Victorian era was marked by separate spheres—men started to work outside the home and were in the public sphere, while the ladies stayed home in the private sphere. This privacy extended toward pregnancy. Colonials referred to pregnancy as being "big with child," "fruitful," and sometimes even "lusty" because that fertility was her duty, her cache in society—something to be out and proud about. That attitude had reversed by the Victorian era, when pregnancy was called "confinement" because it was literally considered obscene for a woman to be seen in public with a pregnant belly. Why obscene? Because it was obvious evidence that she had sex at least once. Apparently, everyone would have dropped their monocles in Victorian streets by seeing a big belly go by in a petticoat. It sounds ridiculous now, but this confinement had very real consequences in keeping women isolated.

These Victorian mothers were the first to have children as

their primary companions at home, and with fewer children to care for (and, for upper-class women, servants to take over household tasks), it all added up to smaller and more emotionally intense families. This kick-started the idea that mothers should devote their lives to their children. And though it started in the upper classes, it would eventually trickle down to the rest of American culture and change the family model forever, inventing our notion of childhood. ("Happy Birthday to You" was introduced in 1893, Halloween became gentler and more child-centric toward the end of the century, and Christmas transformed into a holiday where parents could buy presents without seeming to spoil their children.) That doesn't sound so bad, right? But a side effect of these smaller families—the average number of children dropped from 7.04 in 1800 to 3.56 in 1900—contributed to white supremacist fears of losing ground to immigrants, people of color, and Catholics. That would lead to clamping down on reproductive rights later in the century.

All these societal and cultural shifts were happening against the backdrop of the changing medical profession. From 1600 to the mid-1850s, anyone who had healing skills was a "doctor." It simply didn't exist as an accredited profession. But "regular" doctors looked to professionalize the field. (This is what they called themselves, and we all know it's never cool to give yourself a nickname. They did it to differentiate from the lay healers and midwives they deemed "irregulars," or quacks, but "I'm regular" is a weird brag.) Regulars were usually middle- to upper-middle-class white men who had some stamp of training, though it wasn't standardized and was from schools often characterized as "diploma mills."

These regulars started to turn an eye toward childbirth to expand their purview. Healing up until this point was a mostly female field, and childbirth was entirely female, whether it was through midwives, lay healers, or a mother at home attending to her family. Men weren't part of the baby-delivering equation at all. So why the sudden interest? Money, of course. Barbara Ehrenreich and Deirdre English argue in *For Her Own Good: Two Centuries of the Experts' Advice to Women* that medicine was becoming "a thing to be bought and sold." Healing was female when it was a community enterprise, based on relationships; once healing became a commodity, it was male. Childbirth in the early part of the century was still taking place in the home, and it was what first brought the doctor into the family. Getting a foot in the door for the rest of the family's medical needs "meant developing a working relationship with the birthing woman and her female friends and relatives who attended the delivery along with the physician." That is to say, deliver her baby and have a family of patients for life. Doctors started to slowly shove midwives out of that position, starting with upper-class patients.

But why was this upper-middle-class Victorian woman so willing to jettison the female-centric birthing system that had existed for centuries in Western culture? Because she was really afraid of dying in childbirth, and those who could afford to were hunting for a safer, less painful birthing experience. The hope was that doctors could offer some relief (chloroform began to be used around 1847, though not widely) and use medical intervention to improve outcomes. But the regulars weren't very good at it—just winging it as they learned—and the "frequent misuse of forceps" (large metal objects that resemble salad tongs and are used to help a baby out of the birth canal) and "variation in skill" of the doctor "did not, on the whole, increase women's chances of survival."

This medical push into gynecology was nowhere more evident (and dangerous) than on Southern plantations. Enslaved women were mostly tended to by Black midwives who would deliver all babies—Black and white—in rural areas, and they were much less interventionist than the doctors who would be called in for a difficult delivery or prolonged labor. Regardless, the doctor would have been treated as the expert, despite the fact that most saw their first live births in the slave quarters, with the midwife dismissed as uneducated despite her vast practical experience. In fact, doctors were much more likely to do harm with their "heroic measures," which in the beginning of the century would have included bloodletting and laxatives, moving as the century wore on to forceps and sticking their hands inside the womb, none of which tended to be lifesaving and often introduced fatal infection. When slaveholders called a physician, the slaveholder rather than the woman was the client, so it is unsurprising that enslaved women, seeing the invasive treatments and poor outcomes, remained devoted to their own midwives and came to dread the intervention of doctors. This is also part of the history that would make later generations afraid of medical care.

This inevitably brings us to J. Marion Sims, the so-called father of gynecology. (Sigh. This guy.) He supplemented his Montgomery, Alabama, practice by working as a plantation doctor, which was how he came to learn about vesicovaginal fistulas, a birth injury that tears an opening between the bladder and the vagina, leading to urinary (and possibly fecal) incontinence, which brings on frequent infections, discomfort, and an overwhelming smell that leads to social ostracism, all of which made subsequent children less likely. The condition isn't fatal, but it is pretty miserable. Anarcha, a girl of only seventeen, had the first fistula Sims had ever seen. She had labored for three days in her first birth on the Westcott Plantation, which probably resulted in a stillbirth. (No records exist to say one way or the other.) She could no longer control urination or bowel function, and Sims decided to devote his life to finding a cure. He was not concerned about the enslaved women per se but the middle- and upper-class white women he hoped to treat once he mastered a fix.

By 1845, enslaved women Anarcha, Betsey, and Lucy were living and working at Sims's Montgomery hospital among a group that included other enslaved people loaned to Sims and those he owned himself. According to the 1850 census, he claimed seventeen slaves, twelve of whom were female. He had them on a "rotational work and healing shift" where some recovered in the hospital while others worked on the farm, in his home, and in the hospital as his nursing assistants. Their duties would have included cleaning and dressing wounds, aiding in the techniques, and holding women down as they were operated on without anesthesia. They were given opium during recovery but not during the operations, which author and medical ethicist Harriet A. Washington says was probably more about controlling behavior than pain because addiction "weakened their will to resist repeated procedures." (Just to recap, these enslaved women would split their time between backbreaking labor, raising Sims's children, working as surgical assistants, and being unwilling, unanesthetized surgical patients. Oh, and until very recently, Sims was lauded for his medical contributions. There was a *statue* of the guy erected in Central Park, facing the New York Academy of Medicine, until 2018.) These surgeries would have been truly excruciating, and the stitches would become infected and reopen each time until he finally "perfected" the procedure. Sims notes that during one surgery where he yanked away a sponge that adhered to Lucy's bladder, she nearly died, and her "agony was extreme."

Like other slaveholders, Sims subscribed to the commonly held racist belief that Black people don't feel pain in the same way as white people. These dangerous falsehoods about a difference in pain thresholds persist and continue to cause harm. Anushay Hossain wrote in *The Pain Gap* that a 2016 University of Virginia study found that some doctors still believed that Black people have thicker skin and are less apt to feel pain. There's a direct line from this era to today, when Black women are still less likely to be believed, their pain more often dismissed.

Sims's white physician apprentices who held the women

down quit within a year, because "they could bear neither the bone-chilling shrieks of the women nor the lack of progress any longer." These guys left because they couldn't handle *watching* the brutal surgeries; Anarcha, Betsey, and Lucy lacked the option to quit being the patients. Anarcha underwent a staggering thirty surgeries in just under four years—all without anesthesia. In June 1849, the silver suture technique finally repaired one of her fistulas. It is not known if Sims repaired the remaining tears or even if Anarcha ever found long-term relief. (The procedure Sims is so famous for didn't really work, according to his associate Nathan Bozeman , who said that less than half of those Sims treated were cured.) Sims's mission accomplished, the enslaved patients would have been returned to their masters, and there was a high likelihood that a subsequent pregnancy would have reopened the wound. Anarcha, Betsey, and Lucy did not have an opportunity to leave records of their own, and almost all of what is known about them comes from Sims's self-aggrandizing autobiography, *The Story of My Life*. The historical record of the women mostly disappears after they left Sims's hospital. But they were publicly recognized not that long ago with three towering statues, the Mothers of Gynecology Monument Park in Montgomery, erected in 2021. The J. Marion Sims statue that stood for nearly one hundred years, meanwhile, was removed from Central Park, and the plaque now bears the names of Anarcha, Betsey, and Lucy. (Two other Sims statues remain, in South Carolina and Alabama.)

Doctors had pushed their way into the birth experiences of

enslaved women without their permission and upper-class white women with their consent. Immigrant women still preferred midwives from their own country who knew their customs, but even that was about to change. Unprecedented immigration into cities in the latter half of the nineteenth century during the Industrial Revolution often left the poorest and most isolated women with no choice but to give birth in charity hospitals. They lacked a social network of female friends or relatives, not to mention money to pay a midwife, so there were no other options.

Sims moved to New York after publishing his paper on fistula repair and enjoying a stint as the toast of Europe. In 1855, he helped found the Woman's Hospital of the State of New York, a charity hospital where doctors were rough with the immigrant and working-class women and women of color who were its main clientele. The doctors were much more likely to insert their (likely unwashed) hands or metal instruments into the womb, and Sims continued to experiment—this time on poor Irish women who left Ireland in droves during the Great Famine, who were also subjected to the same nonsensical and harmful ideas about higher pain tolerance.

These charity hospitals provided care, yes, but it's impossible to ignore the fact that they were also about access to bodies for practice—living and dead. More bodies meant more time for doctors to use their skills. In a time when medical schools were proliferating and there were laws restricting the study of human cadavers, bodies for dissection were poor, Black, or enslaved and donated (a requirement of a charity hospital) or stolen from (usually Black) graveyards. This access to bodies is also why all early gynecologists were Southern: Kentucky-based Ephraim McDowell, father of the ovariotomy, and Louisiana-based Francois Marie Prevost, father of the C-section, also operated on enslaved women. (Julius Caesar was not, in fact, born by cesarean, because his mother, Aurelia, lived to advise her grown son, and no woman could survive a C-section in ancient Rome. Julius was shot out of a standard vagina.)

The Medicalization of Miscarriage

This lack of access to medical specimens is what fueled the "medicalization of miscarriage." Until this point, miscarriages usually occurred at home, but the proliferation of charity hospitals meant they were happening more often in a medical setting. "The fetus served as a handy stand-in for the cadaver," historian Shannon Withycombe wrote in *Lost*, her book about nineteenth-century miscarriage. Access to human tissue intersected with the budding field of embryology. Doctors and scientists were finally understanding the basics of mammalian reproduction, that sperm and egg met to start development. (A baby had previously been thought to be just one of many possibilities of a pregnancy— what they thought were misfires between "seed" and "blood," sometimes called "fleshy morsels" and "useless beings.") Fetal tissue began to be displayed in jars around doctor's offices, museums, and labs across the country. Male doctors were trying to establish the medical profession in part by engaging with science in a way they felt midwives and "irregular" doctors were not. "They could say, midwives know nothing about science, but I do, and I even have this physical specimen in my office to prove it," Withycombe told us. Most people would not have considered the products of miscarriage to be a child, and the fetal remains would have been collected from hospitals.

Meanwhile, women would still be relying on "misses" to keep their families smaller. Withycombe studied the personal letters and diaries of women of this era, which did not reveal any trace of the guilt or shame associated with modern miscarriage. Instead, her subjects expressed a variety of emotions— relief, grief, frustration, and even happiness. Interestingly, at a time when women were told their sole duty in life was to have children, "when that enterprise failed in the form of miscarriage, no one blamed the woman, least of all herself." Those, she wrote, are twentieth-century notions.

Contraceptive use became much more commonplace in the nineteenth century. Literacy rates skyrocketed to up to 90 percent by 1850 among American-born white people, and advances in printing and transportation meant there was a proliferation of reading material available, including health manuals. The upshot? People could read about sex and contraceptives without having to rely on family and friends to give them the scoop. (A scoop that was harder to obtain for women, particularly at a time of such relentless decorum. Your dowager aunt was unlikely to hand you a diaphragm.) Also, advertisements for contraception and abortion-inducing services were widely published in newspapers, magazines, and mail-order catalogs, often under "female complaint" and "feminine hygiene," among many other euphemisms. There was a veritable smorgasbord of devices to try—diaphragms, condoms, douches, and abortifacients among them—which although available through doctors and pharmacists primarily became a mail-order business to allow for anonymity. None of these methods would be considered reliable by today's standards, but even a rate of 50 percent was significant at the time. These, combined with traditional abortifacients, miscarriages, and traditional child spacing would, taken together, keep the number of pregnancies down. "It doesn't have to be super reliable to change from having a family of seven kids to a family of four," historian Freidenfelds told us.

There was also a lot of easily accessible, legal abortion. (Most people still believed that pregnancy wasn't official until quickening, so intervening before then wasn't an issue.) If other methods failed, women could always turn to an instrument abortion, a D&C surgical procedure. And it was widely used, with an estimated one out of every five to six pregnancies being willfully terminated by the 1850s. (In the United States in 2020, one in five pregnancies ended in abortion, according to the Guttmacher Institute. Even though the nation's population is now almost fourteen times larger—23.1 million in 1850 to 330 million in 2020—the average rate did not change.) By the mid-nineteenth century, abortion was a business. Middle- and upper-class women would have been able to get surgical abortions at home through their family doctor, with whom they already had a relationship (and whose livelihood depended on doing what they asked). Women in major cities would have been able to find abortion practitioners through word of mouth or ads in pamphlets and newspapers. Immigrant and working-class women were more likely to go to midwives, who charged about half as much as doctors for both birth and abortion. In addition to perennial reasons for not starting a family—personal finances, relationship status, etc.—it was certainly part of the calculation that pregnancy and childbirth could be more dangerous than having an abortion given the high maternal mortality at the time.

This permissiveness didn't last long. Starting in 1857, just nine years after its founding, the American Medical Association moved to prohibit abortion with a campaign led by Dr. Horatio R. Storer, who was against both abortion and contraceptives with near equal zeal. Doctors were by far the most vocal antiabortion activists in the nineteenth century, and historians ascribe different motivations. Some say it was to consolidate professional power and push out competitors, mostly homeopaths and midwives, who had helped women with both childbirth and abortions for centuries. But there's no question that Storer and many other activists against abortion and contraception were also anti-feminist. (Storer blamed newfangled ideas about women's rights for the increase in abortions and equated a childless marriage to legalized prostitution.) It's also likely that restricting contra-ception and abortion was about limiting "the means by which women could avoid childbearing and domesticity." An opinion of the American Medical Association's Committee on Criminal Abortion in 1871 read, "she overlooks the duties imposed upon her by the marriage contract." (Pretty unambiguous.)

In Susan Faludi's groundbreaking feminist work *Backlash: The Undeclared War against American Women*, she argued that the antiabortion campaign was a backlash to the first women's convention in Seneca Falls a decade earlier in 1848. The convention brought together women who were fighting for suffrage, temperance, abolition, and "voluntary motherhood"—they wanted the right to occasionally refuse sex with their husbands. "Perhaps it is inevitable that even the most modest efforts by women to control their fertility spark a firestorm of opposition," Faludi wrote. "All of women's aspirations—whether for education, work, or any form of self-determination—ultimately rest on their ability to decide whether and when to bear children."

Critics were also concerned that births among white, nonimmigrant women were demonstrably declining at a time when immigration was exploding. In other words, one of the major objections was about *who* was having abortions more than the abortion issue itself. Nativist white men didn't want to lose political, economic, and cultural power to European and Catholic immigrants, let alone people with brown skin. Storer asked white Protestant women of the expanding western territories, "Shall [these regions] be filled by our own children or by those of aliens? This is a question our women must answer; upon their loins depends the future destiny of the nation." (Any mention of the word "loins"—in particular what depends on them—doesn't portend anything good for women.)

And this, maybe, is the most American lesson: abortion "has always been a contest not only over women's reproduction, but also over the reproduction of political power—because in a (putatively) representative democracy, power is a function of population." The latter-day assault on abortion is similar: "the wider move to reclaim the 'commanding place' in society for a small minority of patriarchal white men."

Restrictions started to proliferate. When abortion had been readily accessible, between 1821 and 1841, there were laws in ten states that outlawed abortion, but not until after quickening, which was consistent with earlier regulations. These early laws were really more about protecting women from poisonous abortifacients rather than instrument abortions, because "quack" medicines had unlisted and unregulated ingredients. (This was the era of snake oil, after all.) But between 1860 and 1880, quickening was eliminated as an underpinning of legality, and abortion became prohibited at any point in pregnancy. This was a complete departure from how abortion had been regulated since the first Puritan settlements. "Almost all states got rid of quickening and changed it to say 'from the moment of conception,'" Withycombe told us. "It lost its legal power as well as something that marks a definitive pregnancy."

It's hard to overstate how different this would have been from any previous understanding of pregnancy. Doctors had started to insist that conception made the baby "real," not quickening.

Many of these doctors were also religious and talked about "ensoulment" as conception rather than quickening, Freidenfelds noted. "They insist there is no scientific difference between conception and birth that quickening would signify. It's just the woman's experience, and that doesn't count," Freidenfelds told us. As body historian Barbara Duden wrote, "without her own witness, no woman was definitely pregnant. For at least two thousand years, the annunciation of quickening took place in her own secret parts." That secret was no longer of any consequence. Doctors, irritated that women continued to believe in quickening, took pains to dismiss it as meaningless folk medicine in lecture circuits, in journals, and to their patients.

By 1900, every state had passed a law forbidding the use of drugs or instruments to procure abortion at any stage of pregnancy unless it was to save the woman's life. Whether she qualified as being in mortal peril was determined, of course, by a doctor. (And now, in many states, by a doctor in consultation with a lawyer to avoid punishments for making the wrong call.) As historian James C. Mohr wrote, in a span of about twenty years, the United States shifted from a country with no abortion laws to one that almost entirely prohibited it.

Why was this so successful, so swiftly? In large part because the nineteenth century, particularly the latter half of the century, had produced the fastest, most dramatic changes to American life that had taken place up to that point. The nation went from agrarian to industrial; the Civil War literally tore the country in two; slaves had been freed, and the Jim Crow backlash moved to contain that newfound freedom; the railroad pushed settlement farther into the United States but also pulled families apart as it became easier to move; nearly twelve million immigrants arrived between 1870 and 1900, the largest influx to date; medicine was establishing itself as a "science" that could (possibly) keep death and illness at bay; and women had obtained a slight modicum of reproductive freedom and were trying for more—including temperance and suffrage. Immigration and industrialization weren't going to be reversed, but those in charge were rattled and doing their best to halt changes that threatened their dominance. One way to do that was to assert their sole control over women's reproduction, which included limiting abortion unless they deemed it necessary. Now that upper-class Anglo doctor was in charge of who could end a pregnancy. He commodified doctoring, pushed out the competition, outlawed most abortion, and then made himself the decider on who was worthy of one. A momentous half century for a guy worried he was being crowded out by immigrant masses and ladies with pesky rights.

By the late nineteenth century, the American Medical Association started categorizing pregnancy and childbirth as medical conditions to be managed and controlled by doctors. Philosopher Iris Marion Young wrote, "once women's reproductive processes came within the domain of medicine, they were defined as diseases... Being female itself was symptomatic of disease." Similarly, by the 1880s, doctors began describing miscarriages as "serious and risky," a change from natural miss to pathology. Rather than waiting for miscarriages to pass, doctors started "clearing out the uterus" by using a finger, metal instruments, and sometimes spoons, which by 1899 were commodified in medical instrument catalogs as curettes.

Which demon was left to slay? Contraception. How we view pregnancy loss today has a lot to do with contraception—the ability many of us have to choose not to be pregnant. The man who went after this with messianic zeal was postal inspector and anti-vice crusader Anthony Comstock, who was lampooned in his day as a "mutton-chopped buffoon." (Buffoonery is still a ticket to rule in postmillennial America. Mutton chops optional.) His dislikes included pornography, urbanism, abortion, masturbation, gambling, prostitution, and "anything that created impure thoughts in otherwise innocent minds." (Wouldn't want to ruin a promising young man's future, after all.) His backers included the richest and most powerful families in New York City, who encouraged his dogged efforts in lobbying Congress to pass anti-obscenity legislation. The Comstock Act passed in 1873, a sweeping law that included abortion and birth control, making it illegal to send contraceptives—or information about them— by mail. (Sound familiar? We're still here. Various lawsuits that invoke the Comstock laws threaten access to abortion medication mifepristone by mail.) Some states went beyond the federal regulations, punishing both the recipient and the senders with prison and steep fines.

The Comstock laws were mitigated by some court decisions in the 1930s but not overturned until a series of Supreme Court decisions in the 1960s and '70s. After couples finally had access to semi-reliable contraception, it disappeared again for nearly one hundred years.

The rhythms of reproduction that had marked birth for centuries were upended by the late nineteenth century. Women lost their authority as both the pregnant person and the one attending a delivery, and a new era of restriction overseen by the ruling class was instated and would remain mostly unchanged until the 1960s. As we'll see in the next chapter, these changes influenced not just care but also the notions of motherhood that have implications today.

CHAPTER THREE

Hey, We Might Actually Survive This

Medical and Social Advances in Pregnancy

By the early twentieth century, Americans on the whole were healthier and living longer, but newborn and maternal mortality rates remained high. Infant mortality in particular was considered an "appalling and outdated travesty" in an era of burgeoning science and technological advances. (Depressingly, it remains a problem to this day; our infant mortality rates are still abysmal compared with other developed countries; the United States ranks thirty-third out of thirty-eight.)

Prenatal care, which can improve outcomes for both mothers and babies, didn't really exist in any formal way, and maternity care reformers set out to educate mothers about lying-in conditions, nutrition, and childrearing. In 1912, the Children's Bureau—the first female-led federal agency—was established and published two pamphlets: *Prenatal Care* and *Infant Care*.

Most parents still did not have regular access to doctors, but 1.5 million copies of *Infant Care* were distributed to women from every region, class, and educational background—the closest thing to a standard of care that had ever been mass produced. The Children's Bureau answered letters from mothers who wrote in for advice about parenting and breastfeeding, though the agency was not legally allowed to respond to queries about birth control despite the desperate entreaties of women who wanted it. A Mrs. E.S., a married mother of three in Kansas, wrote, "Why can't We poor people be given Birth Control as well as Dr's & the Rich people... We need help to prevent any more babies."

At the same time, the early decades of the twentieth century saw a wider embrace of the belief that children were precious primarily for the emotional satisfaction that they brought their parents, a departure from when they were an essential part of a household economy and when childhood death was rampant. The move from fatalistically waiting to see if a child would die to focusing on child development happened "within less than a generation." The "joy" of parenting was born. Miscarriage was still unlikely to be mourned at this stage of American life, but a cultural shift toward cherishing the child would set the stage for that to develop later.

The Children's Bureau helped push forward the Sheppard-Towner Maternity and Infancy Protection Act, which passed in 1921. Through this act, the federal government matched state funds for use in infant and maternal health, provided funding for public health nurses, and briefly funded public health clinics for poor women and children. It was the only federal program of this nature until the 1960s. It's especially a bummer, then, that such a groundbreaking program was used by many states to eliminate and outlaw midwifery. Basically, the law required that midwives be licensed, which was an expensive and complicated process and harder to obtain for those not trained at "regular" medical schools.

Midwives were the ballasts of a support network, particularly for immigrant, Black, and Indigenous women. They were spread across the United States—Black granny midwives in the South and rural mountain eras, Hispanic midwives in California and Texas, and *sanba* midwives in Hawaii and the Pacific Northwest serving Japanese communities. These communities were reluctant to give up their midwifery care, and the midwives were equally reluctant to leave their field. They were deeply ingrained in the "community and culture" of their patients, from speaking the mother's language to knowing cultural rituals for greeting the baby, disposing of the afterbirth, or laying a dead infant to rest. But they lacked formal training, legal recognition, access to the hospital settings that were increasingly necessary for childbirth, and any unity or ability to organize with one another due to distance and cultural barriers.

Undeniably the most impacted by the licensing movement were granny midwives. They were "less likely to be literate, less likely to be formally educated, and, because they lived and worked in rural areas, less likely to have access to the registration offices that would allow them to continue to work legally." This movement to delegitimize midwifery rose alongside Jim Crow laws, Hossain argues in *The Pain Gap*, with doctors and health officials linking midwifery to high rates of infant and maternal mortality as well as "illiteracy, carelessness and general filth." A reliable, safe, supportive system of care was dismantled by politics, racism, and capitalism.

Moreover, doctors were also less willing to sit around "watching a hole" (as one doctor put it) so were more likely to intervene to get the show on the road. The care, nurturing, and personal relationships that had previously marked childbirth were on their way out. Midwives were banned from hospitals, and by 1950, 88 percent of women gave birth in hospitals. That, combined with the barriers that had been erected in the nineteenth century to prevent healers, midwives, women, or anyone of color from scooting over into medical school, meant that birth was officially taken over by white, male physicians. Fait accompli.

Around this same time, the controversial birth control pioneer Margaret Sanger made her mark. She credited her awakening to the movement to her mother, who had eighteen children in quick succession, which Sanger blamed for her death at age fifty. Another inspiration was Jewish immigrant Sadie Sachs, whom Sanger nursed through the complications of a self-induced abortion in a Hester Street tenement in New York. Sachs had asked for contraception, and her doctor's pithy rebuff was to tell her husband to "sleep on the roof." Sachs died of sepsis as the result of the abortion in her mid to late twenties. Whether Sadie really existed or was a composite, maternal mortality was undoubtedly a grim reality in the urban ghetto due to a lack of prenatal care, poor conditions, and a high incidence of criminal (unregulated) abortion. Abortion, though illegal, remained prevalent, particularly among non-English-speaking immigrants who had trouble getting contraceptive access or information.

Nativist fears of "race suicide" grew up along with the nascent birth control movement. Upper-class white Protestant women were still the most likely to use contraceptives or abortion to keep their birth rate down, in part because their race and class privilege afforded them safe access through private doctors. The average number of children born to a woman who survived to menopause fell from 4.24 in 1880 to 3.56 in 1900 to 3.17 by 1920. Former president Theodore Roosevelt published an article in *Metropolitan Magazine* lamenting that the birth rates of Harvard and Yale men were declining and "the country's best stock was dying out." He was very interested in the "right kind" of children and claimed that "intentional childlessness" made Americans guilty of being "criminals against the race." (Sheesh, we should probably remember this guy for more than teddy bears and national parks.)

But Sanger also thought birth control would allow married women to be free from the "oppression of compulsory motherhood." She opened her first birth control clinic in 1916 in Brooklyn to directly challenge the Comstock laws and posted handbills in English, Yiddish, and Italian promoting the benefits of contraception over abortion. Sanger, like most in the contemporary birth control movement, eschewed abortion and contrasted the "danger of abortion to the safety of contraceptives." She was arrested repeatedly for distributing contraceptives, which made her a celebrity in her time, and she spent her stints in jail educating other inmates about birth control. In 1928, she published *Motherhood in Bondage*, a collection of letters she received from people wanting to avoid pregnancy. In addition to begging for contraceptive information to limit the size of their families also frequently cite incessant miscarriages, which women feared would eventually kill them. One mother of four wrote, "I get pregnant every two or three months, and in [a] few weeks miscarry. I realize it is killing me—soon I'll be gone and then who will see to my little children?"

Sanger worked tirelessly to bring birth control to rich and poor women alike, and she founded the American Birth Control League in 1921. However, the American Eugenics Society was founded in 1923, and the two would repeatedly overlap over the coming decades as birth control became wrapped in eugenics, a discredited, racist pseudoscience that promoted elevating a so-called superior Nordic race and eliminating the "unfit" through birth control, sterilizations, immigration quotas, pushing Native Americans onto reservations, and laws against interracial marriage. In fact, Nazis credited America's brutal eugenics policies as inspiration for the Holocaust. The Supreme Court signed off on eugenics in an eight-to-one decision in *Buck v. Bell* in 1924. Thirty-two states passed sterilization laws, and sixty thousand known operations occurred. The victims were mostly poor, people of color, immigrants, Native American people, the mentally ill, and others who weren't the blond, blue-eyed "ideal." It was common knowledge among Southern Black people that women were routinely sterilized without their consent and for no medical reason—nicknamed "Mississippi appendectomies."

Sanger espoused eugenic ideas in her writing, and historians have surmised that she aligned herself with this despicable (but popular) movement in her quest to spread her own message. The why is less important than the result: the long tail of sterilizations in America—and deciding who could have children and when—had its roots in the intersection of birth control and eugenics. Planned Parenthood now includes a page on its website denouncing "Sanger's racism and belief in eugenics."

Birth control has always to some extent been about who is allowed to control fertility. That through line remains consistent today.

Living to Tell the (Still Pretty Sexist) Tale

The Great Depression saw a precipitous drop in the birth rate, to 2.9 by 1930 from 3.56 in 1900. While that was a continuation of a longer trend, the financial hardships wrapped up in the Depression trapped families under circumstances of extreme economic pressure. Keep in mind the realities of the time: unmarried women were routinely fired because jobs were supposed to go to men. (Her income was often dismissed as "pin money," which had earlier been shorthand for money used for small luxuries.) This dismissiveness was an excuse to pay her less than men for the same job. With men in and out of work, many couples literally could not afford to get married. This did not translate, of course, to celibacy. But if an unmarried woman had a baby, she would lose her job. If she carried to term, there were fewer people adopting children because everyone was in dire financial straits. Married women with children found it impossible to afford another child. Women in all these circumstances turned to abortion, and there was a massive upsurge in abortion rates for both working- and upper-class women.

"Therapeutic" abortions, which were abortions that doctors felt were necessary for the health of women, were narrowly available—usually for women with tuberculosis. But doctors during this time allowed for abortions for "social consideration" like extreme financial difficulty—a qualifier that would not last much longer than the Depression. They were rare, though, and mostly available to white women. So it's no surprise that doctors saw "a continuous stream of patients needing emergency care as a result of illegal abortions," including sepsis, uterine perforations, hemorrhage, and mutilation of other organs. These injuries resulted from self-performed abortions with crude tools or with dangerous techniques or from those performed by untrained practitioners. (Unregulated, cash-only businesses tend to be dangerous.)

Nearly fifty years after they were first passed, a portion of the Comstock laws was overturned in a fight picked by birth control advocate Dr. Hannah Mayer Stone. Doctors were now allowed to distribute contraceptives for medical purposes—but only to married women. It just barely chipped away at the ban, but it was something. Contraceptive manufacturers, with condom makers in particular doing brisk business, were netting hundreds of millions of dollars in profits by 1938, and women accounted for more than 80 percent of contraceptive sales, usually for diaphragms and foam. It wasn't all necessarily safe though. Lysol—yes, the household cleaning product—was the most popular douching agent during the Great Depression. It was "widely advertised as an antiseptic, disinfectant, and germicide, 'invaluable for personal hygiene,'" a euphemism that would have been understood as birth control at the time. Truly, a miracle product. (PSA: Never douche with anything, for any reason, no matter how many mothers on sailboats during 1980s commercials told you it was a good idea. Especially not with a corrosive cleaning agent that, yeah, probably does kill sperm, along with a whole lot else.)

The economic reality of the Great Depression, when many parents couldn't afford to feed the children they had, "solidified public sentiment in favor of access to contraception." It's interesting, and feminist historians have clocked it as likely not coincidental, that when birth control went from something she might need to fulfill her dreams or assert independence to something she needed for basic survival, it mostly dodged the backlash that had marked previous access.

After World War II, maternal mortality (from all causes) dropped dramatically. This was mostly due to the widespread use of antibiotics and blood transfusions, which combated infections and hemorrhage. This was a watershed moment for childbirth in America—a woman was more likely to survive childbirth than any previous generation in the nation's history. Her children likewise were also probably going to survive into adulthood. This was taken for granted rather quickly, given what a new development it was. Suddenly, pregnancy and childbirth had a reassurance of relative safety that American women had never before experienced. And that led us to where we are today, with the idea that because many of us choose pregnancy, everything can and should be just fine.

This optimism about science extended to miscarriage. Articles about miscarriage started to appear in popular magazines in the 1940s and focused on reassurances that a woman who had a miscarriage would eventually be a mother, wrote historian Leslie J. Reagan in a 2003 issue of *Feminist Studies*. She wasn't blamed for it, and conventional wisdom rather "exuded confidence in medicine's abilities to give all women babies"—as long as she followed expert advice, of course.

The birth process had also radically changed. A hospital birth at the time would involve a full perineal shave, enema, sterile drapes, instruments such as forceps, procedures like episiotomies, and a doctor who would blow in for the main event while nurses tended to the patient before and after delivery. She likely would have labored in a large maternity ward, alone, which some women called "assembly line births." She possibly wasn't even conscious. During this era, doctors sometimes also gave women a combination of Demerol and scopolamine that put them into a so-called twilight sleep where their bodies thrashed violently, but they remembered nothing. Forget the communal female births of old. Now many women weren't even trusted to be *conscious* for their childbirth. Some woke up to find their baby had died, either as stillbirth or soon after birth, and would have had no idea what had even happened. If the baby lived, the mother would have been separated from him or her during the long recovery period, which she was advised to spend in bed.

Black doctors, meanwhile, weren't allowed to treat their patients in a hospital; they had to transfer them to a white doctor. There weren't enough hospitals where Black people could be treated, and the segregated "Negro" floors of hospitals compressed people with all manner of maladies into one place. A laboring woman would be on the same floor as those suffering from kidney stones and heart attacks. According to Jenny M. Luke in *Delivered by Midwives*, there were 112 hospital beds in Mississippi for a Black population of one million and eighteen thousand people for every Black physician in 1942. White doctors felt no compunction to see Black patients and feared they'd lose their white patients if they did. Birth had moved to hospitals, but hospitals weren't accommodating Black patients or the doctors who would serve them. The government had forced midwives out only to replace them with almost nothing.

An Idealized Time That Never Really Was

The 1950s are often idealized by the American political right as a time of patriarchy, female subservience, and economic security. The decade was remarkable because it was an outlier— all the trends characterizing the rest of the twentieth century suddenly reversed themselves. For the first time in more than one hundred years, the age for marriage and motherhood fell, fertility increased, divorce rates declined, and women's degree of educational parity with men dropped sharply, all documented by Stephanie Coontz in her seminal book *The Way We Never Were*, where she argued that the 1950s are more important for what they symbolize than for what was actually true at the time.

The birth rates rose for all social groups with "remarkable conformity," Elaine Tyler May wrote in *Homeward Bound*. Women married young (younger than they had since the colonial era), had an average of at least three kids in a few years, and completed their families by the time they were in their late twenties. These women had far more children than their Victorian grandmothers, and the number of babies, well, boomed in the postwar period, from roughly 1946 through 1964, as did the cultural expectation that women should devote their lives to their children as their American identity. Childcare absorbed more than twice as much time as it had in the 1920s, and the amount of time women spent doing housework increased, despite labor-saving appliances. Her life was supposed to be chores, childcare, and her husband. (She couldn't have credit cards in her own name, establish her own residence, or serve on a jury, so that left cooking, cleaning, and perfecting noodle casseroles.)

Mothers were told they had to parent right or risk damaging

their children forever—either by being frigid or overindulgent, with most social ills traced to mothering one way or another, including juvenile delinquency, alcoholism, and homosexuality, which at the time was considered a perversion. J. Edgar Hoover even blamed communism on neurotic moms, and cold "refrigerator mothers" were responsible for mental health problems and the relatively new diagnosis of autism. It was a no-win scenario. Women were neurotic or even schizophrenic if they weren't fulfilled by motherhood, and electroshock treatments were often recommended for women who sought abortions because not wanting a baby was an emotional disturbance.

An early miscarriage or two was accepted by a woman and her doctor, "as long as some of her pregnancies resulted in children." She didn't even see a doctor until she missed two periods, so if she miscarried before then, she was just "late." The miscarriage may not have been as welcome as in earlier eras, especially because big families were the norm and everyone's survival was much more assured, but historian Freidenfelds explains that it wasn't greeted with dread or a sense of tragedy either. It landed more in the category of "unwelcome disappointment."

Freud, that old pal to women, believed having a baby was merely "fulfilling a wish" on the part of a mother, so its death could be remedied by having another one. (We're not sure whether the doctors who tell grieving women "You can just try again" read Freud, but it sure sounds like it.) Furthermore, as Julia Bueno details in *The Brink of Being: Talking about Miscarriage*, it was thought that a mother would recover best for another pregnancy by being kept calm and not seeing the baby who had died, because a "healthy grief" involved cutting ties with those who were lost. Sedating women in these tragic circumstances was also frequent in a futile attempt to help her forget. And here's more Freudian fun—psychiatrists began to suggest that women miscarried because they were "neurotic and carried unconscious animosity toward pregnancy and motherhood."

Although the reasoning may have been tweaked, this concept of feeling responsible for pregnancy loss would sound familiar to modern-day pregnant people. In fact, our contemporary interpretation of pregnancy loss being an aberration can be pegged "somewhere between 1940 and 1960," historian Withycombe told us. "It's very much wrapped in obstetricians pushing a narrative that we now know so much about birth, you should never have a miscarriage or a stillbirth. Women were hearing this message through public health programs and doctors that American medicine is so great that these losses shouldn't happen. And if it did, she must have screwed up." Except, of course, we don't know for certain why most miscarriages or stillbirths occur, even today.

Unmarried women had limited routes to obtain birth control (which wouldn't be legalized until 1972). Heavy petting paired with the generous back seats of Chevys had consequences—teen birth rates soared to levels that *have not been equaled since*. In 1957, ninety-seven out of every one thousand girls aged fifteen to nineteen gave birth, compared to only fifty-two of every one thousand in 1983. And the proportion of white brides who were pregnant at marriage more than doubled. In other words, the teens were pregnant; they just were also married off in greater numbers. They were pressured to put their babies up for adoption too. Ann Fessler compiled oral histories of the women who gave their babies up from 1945 to 1973 in *The Girls Who Went Away* and wrote, "almost every graduating class had a girl who disappeared." Many women Fessler wrote about were haunted by the coercion. (Choice and agency, as it turns out, are important for many reasons.) White, unwed mothers who couldn't (or wouldn't) be married off were shunted into maternity homes and told to give up their babies and move on. (They didn't have much ground to object—an unmarried pregnant woman would be expelled from school or fired from her job.) Maternity homes were segregated, and Black families were much more likely to absorb the baby into the extended family. Women escaped the stigma of unwed motherhood, and the baby, they were told, would benefit from being raised without the stigma of illegitimacy.

Abortions remained illegal and only available through a two-tiered system divided by race and class. Wealthy and middle-class white women had access to referrals for safe (though still illegal) abortion providers. This same demographic could sometimes get legal, therapeutic abortions because they were more likely to have a physician willing to go to bat for them and provide a medical argument for why the abortion was needed to a hospital board. The means by which to obtain them were haphazard, and some hospitals had quota systems of abortions to live births. Psychiatric conditions became an indication for a therapeutic abortion, and by the 1960s, it was known that if a (white) woman "found the right psychiatrist and said the right words," it just might work. (Those words, according to a 1967 article about abortion in New York City were "If I have this baby I'll kill myself.")

Dr. Alan F. Guttmacher, former president of Planned Parenthood and namesake of the reproductive health and rights policy organization, wrote that 85 percent of the abortions performed at Mount Sinai Hospital in New York City in the mid-1950s when he was chair "at least bent the law, if they did not fracture it." But hospital therapeutic abortions were generally uncommon. In the 1950s, roughly 250,000 to one million women per year sought illegal abortions, and these were responsible for 40 percent of all maternal deaths. In 1953, Alfred Kinsey, the pioneering scientist who studied sex, reported that among his sample, 24 percent of the married women had abortions by the time they were forty, and nine out of ten premarital pregnancies ended in abortion, most illegal. More evidence that outlawing abortion doesn't decrease abortion, it just makes it more dangerous.

Poor women and women of color almost never received hospital abortions and took their chances on an unregulated black market where some practitioners were skilled and some were inexperienced and dangerous. Some were doctors, and some were bartenders who knew there was money in it. Some practitioners sexually harassed and verbally abused the women, who could be blindfolded and driven to a secret place where an unseen person performed the abortion. It was a scary system of extreme vulnerability. In New York City between 1951 and 1962, illegal abortion-related deaths of women of color doubled. In Cook County Hospital in Chicago, the number of illegal abortion-related complications treated rose from one thousand per year in 1939 to over three thousand per year in 1959, which would have included self-induced complications like bleeding and infections.

Why the prevalence of abortion in a time marked by its childbearing? More women entered the workforce, and they would often lose their jobs or be expelled from school if they remained pregnant. Many employers had mandatory leave requiring women to leave work at a certain month of pregnancy, whether or not she was still capable of working, and there was no job held for her afterward. These laws were an outgrowth of the Victorian notion that a visible pregnancy was obscene, and it wasn't until 1952 when a pregnant Lucille Ball appeared on *I Love Lucy* that views started to change. (It seems completely insane that it took a television show to reverse a century-old prudishness, though not entirely. Lucy and Ricky still had separate beds.) But the reason abortion rates rose was because of punitive workplace policies where a pregnancy could jeopardize a woman's job and education, which meant she couldn't incorporate a child into her life as easily as a woman in the early twentieth century could. By the 1950s, historian Leslie J. Reagan wrote, the economy, education, and gender norms created a need for abortion.

In the following two decades, the overlap of these three new trends—mother and baby surviving childbirth, pregnancy hampering women in the workforce, and the legalization and availability of birth control and abortion—would change everything about the American experience of modern pregnancy and pregnancy loss.

CHAPTER FOUR

Modern Miscarriage

How Birth Control, "Choice," and Home Pregnancy Tests Transformed Pregnancy Loss

I f we were to create reproductive amalgams for the years prior to 1960—kind of like American Girl dolls but pregnant and way more likely to die—their bios would be pretty grim for most of those eras.

Meet Elizabeth! She's a colonial mother who was pregnant twelve times from her marriage at age twenty-four until menopause at forty-seven. She had three miscarriages, two babies died as infants, and three more children died before age fifteen. She survived childbirth, but her sister, Sarah, did not. Will she collapse from exhaustion before she gets to see the new America that excludes her from its much-touted liberty?

Meet Clara! She's a Victorian mother who stayed indoors during her last trimester of pregnancy because her big pregnant belly was too obscene for public eyes. She used a variety of contraceptives and had a safe, accessible abortion to keep her family size down to four children. She mourned deeply and wore black for years after her daughter died at age eight. Will her doctor cause untold pelvic damage with the forceps he's not quite sure how to use?

Meet Dorothy! She's a teacher in the Great Depression who can't marry or become pregnant because either would cause her to be fired from her much-needed job. She can't access any other contraceptives or a safe abortion. Will that Lysol she's using to douche cause a deadly infection or just burn the delicate tissues of her nethers?

Meet Barbara! She's a 1950s woman who experienced safe childbirth with all six of her children—all of whom survived into adulthood! She had a couple of miscarriages but put them out of her head when more babies came and continued to have dinner on the table by the time her husband came home from the office. Will her access to personal fulfillment be as limited as her access to contraceptives and abortion?

Well, it's time to get a load of Susan! Outfitted in bell-bottom jeans and a floral wreath headpiece, she comes with optional accessories: peace sign necklace, granny glasses, and a little packet of birth control pills. Susan! can reliably prevent pregnancy, open her own bank account, and, if all else fails, have a safe, legal abortion. Will women have it all forever in an arc ever bending toward justice?

We know that's a hard no. But now we're going to get into how this one hopeful era of reproductive control landed us where we are today—at one of the bleakest moments in

American reproductive history. When Elizabeth! was endlessly pregnant and women were dying in childbirth, there really were no other options. Women giving birth before the 1940s were at the mercy of their wombs because of lack of access to reliable contraceptives, tough living conditions, and no antibiotics and other medical advances. The medicine simply didn't exist to save her or her children's lives.

Now, restrictive abortion laws in about half the states are strangling access to reproductive care for those experiencing miscarriages, stillbirths, and terminations for medical reasons. Pregnant people are living in a world we haven't seen in half a century, and in some cases, it's worse. Increasingly, women are arrested when they have a miscarriage or stillbirth. A bounty law in Texas inspired by the Fugitive Slave Law of 1850 enables private citizens to sue anyone who "aids or abets" an abortion after six weeks, and they can collect a $10,000 award. Doctors can be charged with a crime for performing an abortion to save a woman's life. And because the laws are so murky around when doctors can step in, some just don't want to take the chance. A survey in 2022 by the Texas Policy Evaluation Project, for example, found that some doctors, while they avoided abortions, instead performed a more invasive "hysterotomy, a surgical incision into the uterus, because it might not be construed as an abortion."

Before abortion protections were codified and then stripped, the life and health of the mother—her future fertility and the survival of her living children—was prioritized over any individual pregnancy. Now, there's a growing movement in some states to regard the fetus as a person with the same legal rights as the mother.

All that to say it would have been hard for bell-bottomed Susan to imagine how royally fucked her granddaughter Emma! was going to be.

Much of the backslide in reproductive rights is rooted in their unprecedented expansion in the 1960s and 1970s, which changed everything about pregnancy for American women. The proliferation of the birth control pill after 1960 and the legalization of abortion by the U.S. Supreme Court through the decision in the *Roe v. Wade* case in 1973 meant prevention could be reliable and an unintended pregnancy could be legally terminated. In the words of feminist author Katha Pollitt, "it changed how women saw themselves: as mothers by choice, not fate."

Prevention and "control" contributed to a narrative that all kept pregnancies were wanted pregnancies, wrote Jessica Zucker, a psychologist who started the "I Had a Miscarriage" hashtag on Instagram and wrote a book of the same name. This, combined with medical advances that translated to greater survival for both mother and baby, led to the idea that all planned pregnancies should be successful. (She "chose" this, and therefore, it should turn out fine.) Control it, plan it, see it through to its inevitable conclusion of a successful birth and a child who outlives the parent. Impossible across an entire population but a clean little story if you're lucky.

This had a profound effect on the perception of miscarriage

and loss. No longer was a miscarriage just nature taking its course—it was a mother failing. This sense of failure made Americans more secretive about their losses, and that secrecy made loss invisible. The emotions we now associate with miscarriage, stillbirth, medical terminations, and to some extent perinatal loss fully took root: guilt, shame, and blame.

Birth Control and Women's Libbers

Put on that San Francisco sound as we welcome the dawn of the age of the birth control pill, which was approved by the U.S. Food and Drug Administration in 1960. Before this, almost all contraceptive practices were related to the act of sex—withdrawal, condoms, diaphragms, and sponges. Historian Elaine Tyler May wrote in *America and the Pill*, "for the first time, a method of contraception separated birth control technology from the act of sexual intercourse and was nearly 100 percent effective." It didn't require any cooperation from (or even the knowledge of) men. When the pill was approved, it ramped up quickly, and "practically every woman had at least tried it," historian Lara Freidenfelds told us. Many used it for only a few years because early formulations blasted women with hormones and had numerous side effects, but that didn't detract from the revolutionary nature of an effective, female control that had hardly existed for American women up to that point and certainly not all at the same time. Sure, the pill couldn't guarantee sex without consequences— sexually transmitted diseases were still in the mix—but for the first time, women could have sex divorced from pregnancy. (Hot damn!) Plus, it turns out those large 1950s families and Jell-O salads weren't the key to happiness. Betty Friedan's *The Feminine Mystique* kicked off the women's movement with the simple question *Is this all?*

The pill put control into a woman's own hands. A woman before the 1860s may have had "knowing," maybe a kind of mystical, liminal experience of pregnancy, but certainly no power. Feminists expanded on that newfound empowerment by kicking off the women's health movement, gathering abortion, pregnancy, sexuality, childbirth, rape, menopause, and mental health under its mantle, with the best-known result being *Our Bodies, Ourselves*, published by the Boston Women's Health Book Collective in 1970. (If you know anything at all about this book, it's almost certainly that it encourages women to stand on top of a mirror to look at their own vaginas.)

This newfangled power and control naturally influenced the abortion debate—if she could handle the responsibility of the pill, then she should be making decisions about her own body, a departure from the reigning argument of the previous one hundred years that only professional doctors (and their therapeutic committees) could handle abortion decisions "objectively." Women came out of the shadows and publicly spoke about their illegal abortions at speak-outs to erase the stigma, ending what sociologist Kristin Luker called "the century of silence." By 1969, NARAL (the National Association for the Repeal of Abortion Laws) and the National Right to Life Committee had both been formed. The positions were staked. Neither side had any idea what was coming.

The common understanding of abortion—and who should be allowed to get one—started to change through a series of high-profile cases. In 1962, the host of *Romper Room*, Sherri Chessen (sometimes called by her married name, Finkbine), was pregnant with her fifth child when she took a sleeping pill her husband had picked up in Europe. It turned out to be thalidomide, a dangerous drug that had been linked to shortened limbs, brain abnormalities, miscarriages, stillbirths, and infant deaths overseas. (Americans were largely spared the horrors of thalidomide because FDA reviewer Frances Oldham Kelsey did not think the clinical trials showed it was safe enough.) Chessen's hospital board turned her down for a therapeutic abortion because it wouldn't preserve her life (and the board got spooked when the press got wind of her petition), so she went to Sweden for the procedure, where it was revealed "the fetus was so deformed that it would not have survived." When she returned home, she lost her job, the Vatican openly condemned her, and calls and letters dogged her for a long time. (A pre-social-media public pile-on.) Her case garnered a lot of national attention, and 52 percent of Americans supported her abortion. (This has been consistent for more than sixty years: most Americans, when actually asked, approve of some form of abortion.)

Soon after, the rubella (German measles) epidemic in 1962–63 afflicted eighty-two thousand pregnant women in their first trimester. The American College of Obstetricians and

Gynecologists estimated that as many as thirty thousand babies were born dead or died in infancy, and another twenty thousand suffered from severe abnormalities. Rubella became one of the grounds for granting a therapeutic abortion, and that, along with Chessen's case, primed the public to be more empathetic toward abortion and to see there were many reasons a woman might seek one. These cases—known today as terminations for medical reasons—still earn the most public sympathy.

This turn in public opinion was already well underway among the medical community. Doctors, who had been instrumental in making abortion illegal in the 1860s, were equally consequential in the push to loosen and reform abortion laws by the 1960s.

Physicians were seeing firsthand the devastating consequences of self-induced and botched abortions—women coming to emergency rooms with pierced uteruses, deadly infections, and butchery performed by illegal practitioners. By 1967, a survey by *Modern Medicine* magazine showed 87 percent of American doctors favored a liberalization of the country's antiabortion policies, with doctors and women alike frustrated by the discriminatory and dangerous system. Part of the reason this was successful in swaying public opinion was it portrayed women as victims, a damsel-in-distress tale that was "palpable to the white middle-class majority."

Abortion laws have usually rested on a cultural ideal of who is deserving of this care, whose tragedies matter. Today, restrictive abortion laws that only allow for exceptions for rape or incest show hostility toward those who do not meet "the socially accepted role of victim." (The antiabortion movement also used this tactic in the 1980s by purporting women were as much the victims of abortion as fetuses. More on this later, but "woman as victim" has always played in America, and the proliferation of modern-day true-crime podcasts shows that not much has changed.)

The Seismic Shift of *Roe v. Wade* (or: Richard Nixon Needed a Win)

In the run-up to *Roe*, abortion was illegal but not necessarily political, at least not in the way we know it today. This change was kicked off by a cynical, political choice made by everyone's favorite not-a-crook, former president Richard Nixon. During his presidency, he oversaw an expansion of federal family planning and required military bases to perform abortions for military members and their families. This wasn't even controversial. But facing a tough reelection in 1972, he reversed course. Senator Ed Muskie, a leading contender for the Democratic presidential nomination, denounced legal abortion. Nixon feared losing conservative Catholic voters (the Kennedy family really left a psychic mark on this guy), so he announced himself to be opposed to "abortion on demand," overturned his own military policy, and condemned a groundbreaking report *that he had commissioned* that concluded that abortion should be legal. (Only Nixon can go to China, but selling out women for political gain is for everyone.) Nixon had discovered a way to siphon off conservative voters who may otherwise have voted for Democrats for economic reasons—a position he stuck with even when his opponent turned out to be George McGovern. (Nixon won.) This would have lasting consequences, to say the least. Do you feel a certain way about abortion and by extension miscarriage because of Nixon? Not entirely yes. But not entirely no.

Before *Roe* was decided in 1973, the Supreme Court warmed up with a series of landmark cases regarding reproductive rights—gateway cases, if you will—that erased the last vestiges of the Comstock laws. In 1965, the U.S. Supreme Court granted married couples a right to birth control without state interference. Impediments to birth control were many—married women needed prescriptions for diaphragms. (The health clinic at the University of Illinois in Chicago insisted on seeing a marriage license before providing birth control.) Then in 1972, the Supreme Court struck down a Massachusetts contraception ban for unmarried individuals. The birth control pill that had been available since 1960? Well, now even single ladies could legally access it with few impediments. (You owe knowing if you're a Samantha or a Charlotte to this landmark case.) Just one year before *Roe v. Wade*, birth control was a guaranteed American right for anyone, regardless of marital status.

And now we've arrived at the main event. In 1973, *Roe v. Wade* was decided in a seven-to-two decision that declared that abortion should be free from government intrusion under the right to privacy. *Roe* required that each state make abortion legal until viability (which then was roughly twenty-eight weeks), and laws that had stood for one hundred years were voided. Though it is next to impossible to believe now, Justice Harry Blackmun hoped the *Roe* decision he authored would de-escalate the abortion debate, because recent Gallup polling showed more than two-thirds of Americans thought abortion should be left to a woman and her doctor. Abortion and birth control were now legal, safe, and reliable—a trio that had never before been true of both abortion and contraceptives at the same time. For the first time a woman could control whether (and when) she got pregnant. And if she was and didn't want to remain so? She could access an abortion.

Roe v. Wade was a watershed moment in American history and *the* watershed moment in American reproductive history. Metric tons of ink have been spilled on the mechanics of the *Roe* decision, so forgive us for boiling down this historic moment to the elements relevant to our cultural attitudes about pregnancy loss. First, *Roe* set out the trimester framework that still governs access in the states where access remains. In the first trimester, most abortion restrictions were deemed unconstitutional. In the second trimester, states could regulate abortion only to advance patient health (something that would later be tested and manipulated with restrictions like requiring parental permission), and the state could only prohibit access after viability— when a baby could survive outside the womb, put somewhere between twenty-four and twenty-eight weeks. (Viability has been a constant source of debate as medical advances allow more premature babies to survive—a record broken in 2020 when a preemie born at twenty-one weeks survived. Antiabortion activists have argued that if a baby can survive in neonatal intensive care, abortion shouldn't be allowed at that gestational age. But does viability mean survive or thrive? Does it mean live for one, five, or twenty days? You see the conundrum.)

Public health experts estimated in the mid-1970s that approximately the same number of abortions were being performed in the United States after legalization—between one and two million a year—but the death rate plummeted from sixty to eighty deaths per one hundred thousand cases in the decades prior to legalization and sank to 1.3 by 1976–77 due to the decline in self-induced abortions, a truly astonishing decline in mortality. Legal abortions before sixteen weeks were now safer than any alternative, including continued pregnancy and childbirth. Women had more economic, social, and sexual freedom than ever before. They could build careers, delay marriage and childbearing, or never do them at all. Sisters were doing it for themselves! But the backlash was almost immediate and never-ending.

For three short years, access to abortion was relatively equally accessible, covered by insurance, and safe. But the rights granted under the *Roe* decision were chipped away with the passage of the Hyde Amendment in 1976, which made it illegal for Medicaid (the nation's public health insurance for low-income Americans, a program then only a decade old) to cover any abortions that were not medically indicated to save the life of the pregnant person. This is the only legal medical service for which this qualifier is included—no one's hernia surgery is denied because it isn't lifesaving. The Hyde Amendment has been reaffirmed every year since, though it now includes very qualified exceptions for rape or incest and possibly the health of the mother *if two doctors agree.*

This is the part of *Roe* that many people don't know or at least don't fully appreciate. The two-tiered system of abortion that had existed since the nineteenth century returned just three years after it was overruled. As many reproductive justice advocates have said, poor women were living—and have lived—in a post-*Roe* reality since 1976. Because those seeking abortions post-*Roe* were more likely to be young, poor, unmarried people of color, legal historian Mary Ziegler wrote that "limiting access for the poor promised to force a major decline in the abortion rate." *Roe* had not guaranteed a right to the procedure—a woman still had to find a provider and pay for it—and the high inflation of the 1970s had caused a marked disdain for the "welfare state" that was racialized through political propaganda. Antiabortion groups (and plenty of others) blamed a woman's inability to pay for abortion on her own bad decisions and poverty. Those who could afford abortion had a "choice"; low-income women did not. (And remember, low-income people of color were already disproportionately sterilized without their consent.)

Women's health activists of color bristled almost immediately against choice-based feminism, and in the 1990s, twelve Black women developed the concept of reproductive justice, which broadened the movement from being just about abortion to include the right to bodily autonomy, to decide when and whether to have children, and to parent their children in safe, healthy, and sustainable communities.

The Hyde Amendment had a long tail. It enshrined subsequent restrictions on federal funds for abortion to prohibit access for Indigenous women, federal employees on government insurance, Peace Corps volunteers, Washington, DC, residents, military personnel, veterans and their dependents, federal prisoners, and those in immigration detention facilities. As of 2023, the Hyde Amendment is in effect across thirty-four states and the District of Columbia while sixteen states use their own funds to pay for abortion under Medicaid. In 2019, that amounted to about 7.5 million American women, 3.5 million of whom are low income. Diana Greene Foster, the author of the revelatory abortion work *The Turnaway Study*, noted that by 2014, this may have resulted in as many as a quarter of women who wanted an abortion carrying an unwanted pregnancy to term. For the three-quarters who do obtain an abortion anyway, Foster wrote, "the result of not covering it via public or private insurance is that abortion is delayed to a point where the fetus is more developed and the procedure is more difficult." Those affected can pay for abortion services privately, but costs as of 2023 can range from $580 for an abortion pill at Planned Parenthood to a couple thousand for a first- or early second-trimester abortion, up to $23,000 or more in cash for a third-trimester abortion in one of a handful of private clinics equipped to provide them. The price tag can be crushing, especially when travel, childcare, and lodging are heaped on top. (Keep in mind that nearly six in ten Americans cannot afford an unexpected $500 expense.)

The Forever Wedge Issue

It's hard to imagine now, but before the 1980 election, neither political party had staked out a definitive abortion position, and the makeup of antiabortion and abortion rights coalitions had been more fluid, with Democrats and Republicans in both camps. It was also a new concept in the 1970s that "pro-life" was a religious position and "pro-choice" a largely secular one. As we saw, Catholic clergy in the late nineteenth century had settled on a "no abortion, no matter what" position, and they didn't have much more patience for contraceptives, but lay Catholics had a more nuanced understanding. Dr. John Rock, for instance, who helped develop the pill, saw no conflict between his devout Catholicism and his support of birth control.

After Nixon's reelection in 1972, the Republican Party started its shift toward a focus on "family values"—an emphasis on heterosexuality, marriage, and stay-at-home moms and opposition to homosexuality, divorce, and abortion. (The divorce rate more than doubled for women in the United States between 1960 and 1980. Starting in the 1960s, women were allowed to open their own bank accounts, and in the 1970s, they were allowed to have credit cards in their names. That doesn't feel like a coincidence.) On a parallel track, attorney and conservative activist Phyllis Schlafly, who worked to defeat the Equal

Rights Amendment, was connecting the dots between women's changing societal roles and abortion. In a 1972 essay, she wrote that "women's libbers" were "anti-family, anti-children and pro-abortion." Paul Weyrich, an architect of modern conservatism, was testing abortion as a campaign issue with evangelical Christians, and wow, did that have traction. Around the same time as *Roe*, segregated white Christian schools lost their tax-exempt status and were no longer able to dodge *Brown v. Board of Education*. A lot of various anxieties about the sexual revolution, the feminist movement, and racial integration were channeled onto *Roe*. It was no longer just about abortion. It was a series of issues linking arms to form an entire political identity.

The religious coalition that joined forces against abortion was formed in 1979. Before then, the movement had been mostly Catholic. Catholics, Christian evangelicals, and Mormons—three religious groups that hadn't been terribly fond of one another if not outright hostile—were united by Jerry Falwell into the "Moral Majority," a new coalition formed for the express purpose of motivating evangelicals to vote. (Nothing brings people together like a common enemy, and there are few enemies more Biblical than "Woman.") The newly formed religious right fundraised like hell, and the 1980 election was the first time antiabortion and abortion rights groups invested significant amounts of money in a presidential campaign.

That campaign? Ronald Reagan, a former abortion rights supporter, and his running mate, George Bush, also a formerly staunch reproductive freedom advocate, ran as a "pro-life ticket" on a platform that also capitalized on the "stagflation" of the late 1970s. Being antiabortion was how evangelical Christians justified supporting Reagan over incumbent Jimmy Carter—*an evangelical Christian*. Formerly Democratic southern whites and northern white Catholics helped deliver a decisive victory to Reagan—he won a staggering forty-four states and a 9.7 percent vote margin. Their success made the Republican party officially the antiabortion party or, in their own parlance, the Party of Life. The abortion debates as you know them were formed.

The movement's original goal was passing a constitutional fetal life amendment, and when that didn't pan out, the movement focused on limiting access, emphasizing fetal life, and moving the argument toward (debunked) claims that abortion had dire emotional and physical health costs for women and families. The new strategy was to change hearts and minds and focus on the laws later. And, in the meantime, build a Supreme Court that would overturn *Roe*. You gotta hand it to them—they played the long game.

Home Pregnancy Tests and Modern Miscarriages

The final major shift that really influenced the new perception of pregnancy and loss was the over-the-counter pregnancy test, which was approved by the FDA in 1976 and began to be widely marketed and available in the following years. In 1978, readers of *Mademoiselle* saw an ad for a "private little revolution"—a home pregnancy test. Sarah A. Leavitt, associate historian of the office of National Institutes of Health history in 2006, collected oral histories of Americans' experience with pregnancy tests. In Leavitt's analysis, a home pregnancy test allowed women to reclaim some of the personal autonomy and feminine knowledge that had been stolen by the medicalization of birth. (A truly incredible fact she shares in her research: director David Lynch directed an advertisement for Clearblue Easy in 1997 because "it involves the psychological torture of a beautiful young woman." There's a lot to unpack there. Laura Palmer by way of Clearblue Easy.)

Maybe women reclaimed some of the intimate "knowing" that the eradication of quickening had erased, but home pregnancy tests also brought us closer to our present moment because they could find out about a pregnancy much earlier and possibly be aware of a miscarriage they otherwise might not have known about. "[Miscarriage] took on an increasingly tragedy-laden language in the late 20th century that it had not carried earlier. Pregnancy tests have contributed to this change by relocating the time frame of pregnancy identification and making early information of nonviable pregnancies more widespread," Leavitt wrote. Pregnancy tests made invisible miscarriages visible. This changed the way pregnancy was discussed, framed, and encountered on both a narrative and experiential level.

Miscarriage and stillbirth were brought to public attention because of two developments around the environmental justice movement in the 1970s. Love Canal, New York, resident Lois

Gibbs convinced her neighbors to help research the effects of living atop a former chemical dump and uncovered higher than average rates of miscarriage, stillbirth, and crib deaths. In the case of miscarriage, a 300 percent increase. Then Bonnie Hill, a western Oregon teacher who miscarried in 1973, uncovered links between an herbicide sprayed in the nearby national forest to rising miscarriage rates. The EPA eventually banned the chemical, which was derived from Agent Orange. But the focus on miscarriage as a community ill or even just evidence of corporate malfeasance was short-lived. Merely a pit stop on the way to the blame paradigm.

Miscarriage completed its metamorphosis into an issue of individual responsibility by the early 1980s. Popular and health media "reported on the hazards posed by individual behaviors— particularly consumption of coffee, alcohol, illegal drugs and tobacco—to fetal development." (Think how different this focus was from the 1950s, when women would balance ashtrays on their pregnant bellies to keep their hands free for a cocktail—an actual photo Rebecca's former gynecologist had of her own mother.) Yes, the official word from the medical community and even most mainstream publications aimed at women was "it's not your fault," but the growing focus on the fetus, the seemingly limitless nature of science that made IVF possible (Louise Brown, the first so-called test tube baby, was born in 1978), and coverage of all the ways women could endanger their baby were starting to tell a different story. It's unsurprising that guilt, shame, and blame became the accompanying emotions.

Something else was at play here too. Because the home

pregnancy test allowed women to find out they were pregnant earlier than ever before, they now also had the means to make decisions earlier than ever before. This was true since the late 1970s but accelerated after 2000, when the morning-after pill became available—she didn't even need a doctor's appointment to end the pregnancy. Now, two-thirds of abortions take place before the eighth week of pregnancy, according to the Guttmacher Institute. What does that have to do with miscarriage? Historian Freidenfelds lays out the gymnastics at play here in *The Myth of the Perfect Pregnancy*: with women aborting earlier, a "substantial proportion of abortions represent what would have been miscarried pregnancies in a previous generation," meaning that a greater proportion of miscarriages are happening to "wanted" pregnancies. A so-called unwanted pregnancy is terminated before she even has a chance to miscarry—she's intervening before nature can—so miscarriages are no longer evenly spread among all pregnancies. This reduces the number of "oh, phew" miscarriages and tips the balance to affect proportionally more "wanted" pregnancies. See what we mean? As miscarriages lost their status of providing occasional relief in a world without reproductive control, they moved into tragic territory in a world with it. (Science giveth, culture taketh away.)

In the 1980s, miscarriage was solidly in "personal tragedy" territory. This was due in no small part to the antiabortion movement being highly successful in changing the narrative on abortion, and it seeped over into miscarriage. For example, "precious feet" pins were the symbol of Catholic pro-life campaigns. Decidedly religious with a side of political mission. Religious hospitals started using footprints on their miscarriage literature, and now they are common across secular hospitals as well. (Inked footprints are routinely now given as a keepsake to parents who lose pregnancies far enough along for it to be possible.) Support groups (mostly among white and middle- and upper-class parents) started to focus on women's grief in the 1980s.

Historian Leslie J. Reagan cites an example of the creep of antiabortion language in a hospital that encouraged those who survived potentially fatal ectopic pregnancies to remember and mourn the loss of their "babies" at a bereavement ceremony—"the sympathy offered by this medical institution teaches women to think of ectopic pregnancy as a life lost rather than a life saved—their own." (An ectopic pregnancy cannot under any circumstance grow into a healthy baby.) This doesn't mean that a pregnant person shouldn't grieve their miscarriage or ectopic pregnancy, shouldn't cherish the footprints of their stillbirth. Many do. But the culture of the antiabortion movement has undeniably permeated the culture of miscarriage.

And the implications of that—in particular the ubiquity of the fetus—have loomed large.

CHAPTER FIVE

The Puppetry of the Fetus

How Images of the Unborn Redefined Abortion and Miscarriage

I n fourth or fifth grade, our school choir went on a field trip to Chicago's Museum of Science and Industry to sing carols. During nonperformance hours, we would dare one another to dart in and look at the creepy fetuses in the Prenatal Development exhibit, taking turns to gape at the floating "babies" in jars. There was no goal to this game or even a badge of honor for having done it. Just a bunch of tweens screaming and giggling their way through a museum. (This would have predated the Catholic school Family Life sex education course that illuminated nothing and left a years-long trail of confusion.)

This exhibit is one of the oldest science displays in the United States. The twenty-four embryo and fetal specimens were collected in the 1930s by Dr. Helen Button through local hospitals when the Great Depression was leading to especially bad pregnancy outcomes. These are the very same ones as those originally displayed at the 1933 World's Fair in a booth sponsored by the Loyola University School of Medicine, which donated the specimens to the Museum of Science and Industry in 1939. (The museum, coincidentally, is housed in one of the only remaining buildings from the 1893 World's Fair.) The museum has displayed this collection since 1947, though for a time, they were the wax models. The real deal has been in the mix for our lifetimes.

Rebecca, still local, returned in 2023 to visit the exhibit for the first time as an adult who had figured out the miracle of life for herself—for better and for worse. She had assiduously avoided it since age eleven despite visiting the museum many times since. The fetuses were tucked into a corner of the top floor You exhibit, which demonstrates how all parts of the human body work. The specimens are now displayed in a very dark gallery, which a placard notes is to "allow for quiet reflection." The darkness makes it more somber than it had been when we were kids, and everyone was speaking either in hushed tones or not at all. It felt funereal—more sad than creepy, more open casket than sideshow, but the lighting and the glass-fronted cases allowed for Rebecca and her oldest son to see their own reflections superimposed on a twenty-eight-day embryo (a webby clump of material), a twenty-two-week-old fetus, and a thirty-eight-week stillbirth. "It's like the Vietnam Memorial," her then twelve-year-old son said. "We can see us."

Since at least the 1990s, the exhibit has displayed some variation of the following disclaimer: "To the best of our knowledge, all failed to survive because of accidents or natural causes. Dr. Button obtained the parents' permission to use these specimens as teaching tools." It sure seems like this "scientific" exhibit had to hedge its bets against the antiabortion movement, which would want to know if any of the abortions were induced.

Rebecca and her son clocked the gestational ages of their family's losses, the sizes a surprise to him but not to her. He was about the same age we had been when we first encountered the exhibit. This time, there was no running, no giggling, no dares. The familial connection had made that impossible. This time, there was a personal relationship with fetuses—a relationship that would itself have been odd, if not unthinkable, to parents at the time the specimens were collected.

The fetus holds a strange place in American culture because it affects so much about perceptions of miscarriage and abortion politics. The ubiquity of it as a symbol—both of the "pro-life" political movement and as a totem of the officiality of an early pregnancy—picked up steam in the early 1980s as the use of sonograms proliferated, allowing more people to see their growing babies. This visual language had a huge influence on how our society talks about pregnancy. As cognitive linguist George Lakoff wrote, "frequency of language use and imagery matters. The more frequent the language use or imagery, the more strengthening occurs." There have been few images more pervasive in the late twentieth century than the fetus, which has permeated every element of the pregnancy experience. In the nineteenth century, they were merely unsentimental specimens in jars at a doctor's office. Today, there's a panoply of fetus paper-weights, earrings, and resin dolls available on Etsy. How did that happen?

As we discussed in previous chapters, fetuses made their public debut as scientific specimens in the mid-1800s, leveraged as proof of being a man of science among the budding doctors of the day. The fascination with what was actually inside that mysterious belly and what it said about humans got a boost at various world's fairs, the closest thing to mass culture in this era.

The first public fetal display of note was in 1893, at the World's Columbian Exposition in Chicago. (Yes, the one from *The Devil in the White City*. It was a big fair, and not every-thing has to be about handsome psychopaths with murder chutes.) German artist-scientist Friedrich Ziegler exhibited three-dimensional wax models of developing organs and animal and human embryos that were scientific and "not particularly humanized," which later became a hallmark of fetal depictions. He won the fair's highest prize. At the 1933 Century of Progress International Exposition, again held in Chicago, twenty million visitors ambled through the Hall of Sciences to view embryos and fetuses ranging from a few days to nine months.

In 1939–40, at yet another world's fair, an exhibit called the Birth Series sculptures was displayed in New York City, wax models that traced human development from fertilization through delivery. They were created by Dr. Robert Dickinson, an obstetrician-gynecologist and the leader of the Planned Parenthood Federation of America, and sculptor Abram Belskie.

The sculptures depicted something no one had ever seen—"what happens inside a pregnant woman's body from the moment of fertilization through the process of delivery."

Most previous knowledge of in utero development had been derived from pregnant cadavers and the fetal remains of miscarriages, abortions, and hysterectomies. These sculptures, admired for their beauty and reverence, were created by taking thousands of X-rays of pregnant women as they delivered their babies. (Yeah, we know. Not great. But X-rays of pregnant women were routine until 1956, when Dr. Alice Stewart raised the alarm that they could harm babies in utero.)

These sculptures were idealized—pale white in their original form, sans blood or gore, with nary a conehead misshaped by a birth canal—depicting a seamless journey from fertilized egg to birth. Though Dickinson's practical experience made him aware of pregnancy complications—which was why he was an abortion and birth control advocate in the first place—the world's fair was a time to hit the highlights. These sculptures were such a departure from the inert, jarred specimens kept in universities, doctor's offices, and other hallowed science-y places because they told a story for the first time, argued Rose Holz, associate director of the women's and gender studies program at the University of Nebraska. "The story of in utero development became a romantic one, with a humanized fetus whose story began at the moment of conception and culminated in the birth of a sweet and innocent child," Holz wrote. Bonus exhibits featured rotating plaster depictions of the famous (at the time)

Canadian Dionne quintuplets in the uterus and three sets of twins depicting "see no evil, speak no evil, and hear no evil." We can't know for sure, but this was likely the debut of the "adorable" fetus.

The Comstock Act still severely limited access to "obscene" information, including sex ed, so this was the first time most visitors had seen anything like it. The sculptures attained even broader reach when they were mass produced in photographs and manuals to educate the lay public, school children, and medical professionals around the world, one of which, *Birth Atlas*, was in print until the 1960s.

Despite their cultural impact at the time, the Dickinson sculptures have been largely forgotten, pushed aside by Lennart Nilsson's gorgeous series depicting fetal development published in *Life* magazine in 1965. The cover photo was captioned "living 18-week-old fetus inside its amniotic sac," and its hands were resting under its chin in contemplative fashion. (If you're keeping count: adorable fetus #2.) And that caption is true—of the cover photo, which was shot with a camera on a scope alongside an amniocentesis procedure. But the rest of the photos were taken of embryos and fetuses removed from dead people or during medically indicated abortions like ectopic pregnancies. Every other one was dead—or at least never alive—but he rendered the surroundings as black backdrops to suggest a womb. In the book *Pregnant Pictures*, authors Sandra Matthews and Laura Wexler suggest the photos had so much resonance in the cultural imagination because the cover in particular looks like the child at the

end of Stanley Kubrick's 1968 movie *2001: A Space Odyssey*—
another cosmonaut-like fetus making its mark on the cultural
imagination during the space age. The Nilsson photos have been
subject to much feminist discourse because the fetuses "fly solo:
there is no sense of a womb cocooning these bodies, apart from
an umbilical cord drifting off into the distance, like an astronaut
attached to its mothership." The fetus was alone in his watery
home. The mother? Not pictured.

Life magazine's print run of eight million copies sold out
within days, and it was later adapted to an educational book
A Child Is Born, which followed a young couple through
their pregnancy with accompanying photos of the developing
embryo. It sold over fifty million copies internationally. "The
'beginning of life' sequence Nilsson sold to the press and the
textbook publishers showed mainly corpses," wrote body historian Barbara Duden. Kind of mind-blowing.

These images contributed to the sentiment that the fetus—
something previously considered to be completely related to
the mother (you know, because it was inside her body)—was
separate from her. It helped usher in the idea that the fetus was
a baby.

Though she didn't match Nilsson's cultural reach, childbirth
education advocate Geraldine Lux Flanagan wrote the book *The
First Nine Months of Life* for new parents, which was featured in
Look magazine in 1962. She wanted to feature photos of living
fetuses, which were hard to come by, so she used those taken by
neuroanatomist Davenport Hooker between 1932 and 1958,

who studied fetuses by asking doctors to perform therapeutic abortions by hysterotomy (basically a C-section) so the fetus would be surgically removed intact. The fact that these films and still photos were taken as the fetuses died (too premature to live) or that they came from therapeutic abortions—well, none of this is mentioned in the book.

Nilsson's and Flanagan's works weren't the first to bring embryos and fetuses to a broad audience, but the difference, Lynn Morgan wrote in her (ahem) seminal work *Icons of Life*, "was that the new imagery claimed the fetuses were alive." A fallacy from the start, because those pictured were already dead or doomed. The switch from specimen to person in the cultural imagination—the "cult of fetal personhood"—is usually attributed to Nilsson's photos and their astronomical reach. From then on, most visual imagery ignored the two trimesters where the fetus literally cannot live without its mother. "From their beginning, such photographs have represented the fetus as primary and autonomous, the woman as absent or peripheral," wrote political scientist Rosalind Petchesky. This imagery has had a profound effect on how we view both pregnancy and loss.

The fetus was now a stand-alone fella. But there was another important change. Just like the Dickinson sculptures, most renderings going forward erased any sort of complication, either in the woman's life or the health of the pregnancy, instead "depicting a single, ideal path directly from conception to baby." A path that would not have been taken for granted just a generation prior and which still isn't happening for up to 20 percent of pregnancies. This same seamlessness was portrayed in the 1983 special *The Miracle of Life*, the most watched *Nova* documentary ever made, which was photographed by (wait for it...) Lennart Nilsson. A generation of children, us included, got their first eyeful of the bloodbath of a vaginal delivery via the same network that brought them *Sesame Street*. The film whips through human development in under an hour: ovary spits egg into fallopian tube, sperm exits penis, egg and sperm fuse, zygote implants, with accelerated fetal development to vaginal birth. Efficient but eliding the long months of the pregnancy experience, with little mention of the ones that don't end with a living baby.

Many scholars and feminists peg the final development in the separation of fetus and mother to ultrasounds, which allowed doctors to "bypass pregnant women's self-reports in favor of a 'window' on the developing fetus." A redux of kicking quickening to the curb, twentieth-century style.

By the 1980s, sonograms were a near-universal diagnostic tool that made the fetus more visible to both parents and the doctor. Sonograms "altered the relationship between a pregnant woman and her fetus, and also between the fetus and the public." And it's not hard to see why. A photograph on the cover of *Life* magazine was cool at a moment when science seemed limitless, but a photograph of the fetus inside *your* womb? *Your* baby? The one that the sonographer personifies by saying "he's shy today" or "she's waving at you"? It's harder to stay casual and detached about that.

This relationship has been both weaponized and oversimplified. The term *bonding* had been coined in the 1970s to refer to a mother bonding with her newborn but began to be applied to ultrasounds in 1983—first used in the context of persuading women ambivalent about their pregnancies not to abort. Though "bonding" via ultrasound is hardly universal, states continue to rely on this as a means of dissuasion (or punishment) in limiting abortion by adding stipulations for repeated ultrasounds before being allowed to terminate. And it's also a reason why we grieve miscarriages so hard—we've been culturally digesting all this for decades.

There's an inherent dissonance with sonograms. Yes, they can be exciting glimpses into the womb for an expectant parent, but they're primarily a medical diagnostic tool to see if there are problems with the developing fetus—"for most of which medicine has no treatment to offer other than the option of selective abortions." It's interesting that sonograms are so promoted as a means of connection, of excitement, of proof that the fetus is a person but came up in nearly every single one of our interviews as a source of trauma for those who lost pregnancies. They described going in happily, wanting to get more pictures of the baby, and then the feeling of terror when they realized something was wrong. The sonographer got quiet, or they didn't hear a heartbeat, or the screen was turned to show them severe anomalies or evidence that the fetus had died. This fear remained in every pregnancy thereafter, this glimpse into the womb having revealed loss before. There's no guarantee that a pregnant person will experience the reassurance—or even the connection—an ultrasound is supposed to provide.

Photography, sonograms, and politics all converged in the 1980s to give the fetus a new identity—as a symbol. The scientific accuracy of the nineteenth century fetus gave way to a stylized one. The fetus of antiabortion propaganda often appears larger and more Gerber-like than is developmentally accurate when it serves one purpose but dismembered and gory for protest signs when it serves another. Either way, the fetus is an innocent—an undemanding, silent entity upon which to superimpose meaning. Most people who came of age in the 1980s (and after) first encountered a fetus not in relation to a loved one's or their own pregnancy but through antiabortion billboards and campaigns—a cutesified fetus accompanied by a political and/or religious message that abortion "stops a beating heart." (Yeah, about that. At six weeks, it's neither a fetus nor a heartbeat. Discuss.) Heartbeats can be detected on fetal doppler at around five to six weeks of pregnancy, but it's an electrical impulse in what will eventually become the heart. It's not a cardiovascular system—the heart forms around week ten. "Fetal heartbeat" is not a clinical term, but it has been a wildly successful political one that has permeated descriptions of a baby's heartbeat on BabyCenter, in *What to Expect When You're Expecting*, and, until 2022, even by Planned Parenthood.

This new identity for the fetus was decidedly Christian. In Judaism, the fetus is a person only when the baby has taken its first breath. In Islam, it's after 120 days of gestation. Hindus don't conceive of life in the same way with a beginning and an end—conception and death are not the boundaries of life. The Catholic position changed from initially stating personhood was forty days after conception for a boy and eighty for a girl (side-eye) to updating to personhood at conception in the nineteenth century.

Even if you've never heard of it, a lot of perceptions around the fetus come from a 1984 antiabortion propaganda film, *The Silent Scream*. Political scientist Petchesky called it a "medieval morality play" with the fetus being called "the victim," the cannula a "lethal weapon," and the "silent scream" accompanied by a fever pitch of music. The storytelling that had been so effective in the Dickinson sculptures was being deployed in a different way. Former abortion provider/now antiabortion activist Bernard Nathanson narrates the abortion procedure on a twelve-week fetus, and as historian Johanna Schoen wrote, "the power of the images lay less in what viewers actually saw and more in what Nathanson told them they saw." A fetus "the size of a lime is made to look as large as a toddler," and the entire premise relies on the misinformation that the fetus can feel pain at twelve weeks, which has been debunked numerous times. (According to the American College of Obstetricians and Gynecologists, science has established that the fetus doesn't have the capacity to feel pain until after at least twenty-four weeks gestation, when the central nervous system has formed. When just 0.9 percent of the procedures are performed.) But its reach was significant. President Reagan screened it in the White House, the National

Right to Life Committee mailed it to members of the Supreme Court and Congress, and parts of it aired on most major networks. It was "cultural representation rather than medical science," Petchesky said in her analysis, geared to the result of making abortion unthinkable. As Ziegler wrote in *Reproduction and the Constitution in the United States*, "if popular culture recognized fetal personhood...abortion rights would look more and more incongruous."

Perhaps to the surprise of no one even glancingly familiar with a parochial education, fetal identity intersected a lot with our young lives. "I'd never really thought about it before, but our childhoods were actually pretty fetus-y," Rebecca said to Colleen. This included Right to Life leaflets papering the bulletins at church, *Horton Hears a Who*-esque commentary that "a person's a person no matter how small," and yes, being shown *The Silent Scream* in eighth grade. Colleen has very little memory of it, and Rebecca remembers being more confused than horrified. (Here's one of the many downsides of abstinence-only education: if you don't even really understand how the fetus gets in there, you don't sweat the details of how it gets out. Birth, miscarriage, abortion—it's all a mystery.)

The directions were explicit in the antiabortion text *Closed: 99 Ways to Stop Abortion*, where Joseph Scheidler, considered the "godfather of the anti-abortion movement," gave specific instructions about "controlling" abortion language, instructing those who spoke to the press not to use the word *fetus* but rather *baby* or *unborn child*. "You don't have to surrender to their vocabulary," the manual reads. "They will start using your terms if you use them." The Ku Klux Klan had pulled off a similar rhetorical move by reframing racism as patriotism.

Legal scholar Jill Wieber Lens, who studies stillbirth, told us that Americans rarely hear the word *fetus* outside abortion— and that's on purpose. This framing is extremely effective. In 2007, the Supreme Court upheld the ban on an infrequently used intact dilation and extraction procedure that was mostly performed when the health of the mother was at risk or to allow for autopsy of fetal anomalies. *Partial-birth abortion* was never a medical term, but it sure made people feel feelings. Researchers Adam F. Simon and Michael Xenos studied reactions after people read manipulated news stories: one group used the word *baby*, one the word *fetus*, and one a mixture of the two. "Changing the 'fetus' mentions to baby either halfway or completely resulted in an increase in support for the ban."

All this is to say that many historians call the fetus "an engineered construct of modern society." From the nineteenth century until the 1960s, the fetus wasn't a separate entity and wasn't really considered with sentiment or affection, at least not outwardly. A pregnant person may have had feelings about the baby growing inside them, but those weren't publicly broadcast. Starting with changes after *Roe*, the fetus became imbued with libertarian notions of individual identity, not "a being" in process.

"Fetal imagery became part of our ritual and emotional life around pregnancy, amped up through pro-life politics and pregnancy apps," historian Lara Freidenfelds told us. The week-by-week updates through BabyCenter emails track the growth of the fetus and are part of the pregnancy journey that people enjoy—for as long as things go well. But it's a little strange to be cheered by a sketch or photo of an alien, stylized fetus sent to your inbox.

"We sentimentalize images that our grandmothers would have found bizarrely, scientifically medicalized," Freidenfelds told us. "Picture it this way—if somebody showed you an X-ray of your loved one's skeleton that they were going to use in an 'In Memoriam' tribute, you would be horrified. But people publicly share their sonogram photos all the time."

The downside here is that because the narrative around pregnancy is increasingly focused on the fetus, the pregnant person matters less and less. This is ideological work that took decades to achieve in culture, politics, and the law—that the embryo or fetus is a "'person' with its own interests, rights, and life completely separate from a woman's pregnant body." All that led to a culture where a missed period is a "pregnancy," what's inside is an "unborn child," abortion is a "moral failure," and a miscarriage is a "mother's failure." Tidy work for half a century.

Abortion as an Island

The final change that brought us to where we are today was the push to silo abortion care from healthcare. In the decade after legalization, abortion began to calve off the healthcare iceberg, floating away out on its own. What caused this break so soon after public opinion, even a majority of religious Americans, had supported legal abortion? So soon after doctors had heavily campaigned against the dangers of illegal abortion?

The answer is political and rhetorical, and both strategies were quite deliberate. The antiabortion movement successfully reframed abortion in a way so enduring that it still affects the way we talk about it. (It is no more evident that how, before the end of *Roe* protections, pregnant people could go to any old hospital for a D&C after a thirteen-week miscarriage but would only go to a specific abortion clinic to have an abortion at thirteen weeks. Even though the procedure performed is the same.)

The political camps are *pro-life* versus *pro-choice*. Both sides emphasize the *pro*, which is more mentally appealing than being *anti*. It just works better as a rallying cry. More importantly, each side offers its own frame around which to think about not just abortion but all pregnancy, including run-of-the-mill healthy pregnancies and miscarriages. Each opts to emphasize a different identity: one a woman's choice, the other an embryo or fetus's life. *Life* and *choice* are not actually opposites in common parlance but are diametrically opposed in abortion policy. The opposite of life is death; the opposite of choice is force. (You probably already knew that because both political sides have leveraged those true opposites to further erode any gray areas.) Pro-life activists accuse their opponents of being pro-death, murderers. Pro-choice activists accuse their political opponents of being pro-forced birth. The volume is always at eleven.

This strategy was no accident. As Susan Faludi laid out in *Backlash*, the New Right of the 1980s deliberately shifted gears to a new "linguistic strategy." Instead of being antiabortion, anti-women's lib, anti-women's work, they became "pro-life," "pro-chastity," "pro-motherhood." The New Right itself became "pro-family." It's not hard to see why that would work. And work it did. Paul Weyrich, the man who orchestrated the coalition that delivered Reagan his victory, formerly had no option but to stake out his position as anti-women's liberation. After this semantic switcheroo, he could "refer to his nemesis as the anti-family movement." As Faludi wrote, "this Orwellian wordplay not only painted the New Right leaders out of their passive corner; it also served to conceal their anger at women's rising independence" by claiming to "march under the banner of traditional family values."

This is a great example of the concept that sociolinguists call "framing" to explain the effect language and ideas have on our brains. Lakoff's titular famous example is "if I tell you 'don't think of an elephant!', you'll think of an elephant." The right, in the above example, successfully changed the language rather than negating the frame. Pro-family instead of anti-woman. Everyone loves families! Not everyone wants to be anti-woman. The language shift was so successful that it painted abortion rights supporters into a corner, where they continue to use the language and framing of the antiabortion side. (The opposite rarely happens.) The sociolinguists and linguistic anthropologists we interviewed study the way society shapes the way we talk and how the way we talk shapes society. People learn about the world by how culture lays it out for them, so whatever the dominant discourse about pregnancy or miscarriage or abortion is tends to shape our habitual thoughts about the world. It doesn't constrain it necessarily, but it wears a groove. Antiabortion activism has been wildly successful—and downright relentless—in wearing a groove.

Pro-life allows for only one acceptable outcome—no abortions. The answer may be authoritarian, but it's simple and clear. "It's effective politically to talk about it in black-and-white language," said Jane Armstrong, a perinatal mental health therapist who works with patients who have terminated for medical reasons through her practice Both/And Therapy. "They say you're murdering babies. There's nothing you can come back with that's as brief or easy to fit on a campaign mailer. Even it being two sides of a debate is reductive. It's such a spectrum of experience."

The pro-choice position is inherently more chill because it allows for a lot of possibilities—choose among them, fair liberal, while eating avocado toast in your decadent urban ivory tower. Allowing for many possibilities means it is hard to offer a simple, clear explanation. Anat Shenker-Osorio, a progressive political consultant, said the pro-life movement is "constantly providing a role for the audience. They're directing their audience to be the hero. They're directing their audience to 'save babies,'" she told Slate in 2022. "In contrast, for a long time, the job of the listener on the 'pro-choice' side was to mind your own business.

It was to stay out of it." You can see how one is stronger than the other as an argument, even if you vehemently disagree with the underpinnings.

For a brief moment in the 1970s, abortion wasn't shameful or taboo. Women spoke about their abortion experiences, felt empowered by their decisions. But the antiabortion movement was persistent in its framing, and many have argued that the abortion rights movement lost ground by ceding to it, both by not counteracting a frame that pits fetus against mother and by staking out a position that abortion should be "safe, legal, and rare" with an emphasis on rare. "We hear endlessly about rape victims, incest victims, women at risk of death and injury, women carrying fetuses with rare fatal conditions—and make no mistake, those girls and women exist and their rights need to be defended, because the laws now being passed in many states will harm them greatly. But we don't hear much about the vast majority of women who choose abortion, who are basically trying to get their life on track or keep it there," feminist Katha Pollitt wrote in *Pro*. By the late 1980s, just a decade after legalization, historian Johanna Schoen wrote, "in public discourse, women and abortion providers had lost the argument for abortion as a positive good that helped women gain control over their lives." This contributed to the view that the only acceptable loss was one that a woman felt bad about—an attitude that spilled over onto miscarriage—and it "publicly silenced those who felt good about receiving and providing abortions." Stigma is a powerful tool of social control, and it was masterfully executed.

The antiabortion movement drew a violent fringe, using the idea of the fetus as a "child" and the women seeking the abortion as "murderers" as an excuse to justify violence. Abortion rights supporters set up clinics meant to offer abortion care to everyone when hospitals were restricting the procedure and refusing to perform it. (In 1973, 81 percent of abortion providers were affiliated with a hospital. But by 1979, it had dropped to 56 percent.) But this separation also made them an easy target. Protesters posted outside abortion clinics and Planned Parenthood offices, often with photos of aborted fetuses. This had a considerable effect on making abortion taboo. After all, the prevention of murder was justified, valorous, even if it included clinic blockades, arson, assault, murder, and terrorizing abortion providers and their patients. Although there were investigations, newspaper exposés, and sometimes prosecutions of abortion providers in the nineteenth and early twentieth centuries, violence against them was a product of the 1980s and beyond.

At least eleven people have been killed in attacks on clinics and providers since 1993. The violence took its toll. As Schoen wrote, "the number of physicians willing to provide abortions fell for the first time since abortion had become legal, from the all-time high of 2,908 in 1982 to 2,380 a decade later to 1,819 by 2000, a drop of 37 percent." Kansas doctor George Tiller, a physician who provided abortions up to the third trimester, was assassinated in church in 2009. His motto was "trust women." Since Tiller, fewer and fewer doctors are willing to perform these procedures because of threats to their own lives, and now there are just a handful of all-trimester clinics across the country. In 2022 after the *Dobbs* decision, there was a sharp increase in violence directed against abortion providers and patients, according to a report from the National Abortion Federation, with threats concentrated in states that protect access.

Crisis pregnancy centers (CPCs) have proliferated since the 1980s. They masquerade as healthcare facilities but exist to dissuade and delay patients from accessing abortion and often contraceptives. They use deceptive practices, and patients are often unaware that they are not traditional healthcare facilities, which has led to cases like one in Massachusetts in 2023, where a woman lost a fallopian tube in emergency surgery after a CPC failed to diagnose her ectopic pregnancy. "Legitimate medical providers" would have diagnosed the ectopic and treated her with medication, usually methotrexate, before her situation turned more dangerous, her lawsuit contends.

Many of the people we spoke to were unable to end pregnancies with a grave medical diagnosis with their doctor or at their local hospital because of the religious affiliation of the hospital, state laws, or how far along they were. Many had to go to abortion clinics or travel out of state, and some paid for it by borrowing money from family or dipping into or eradicating their savings. Nearly all were stunned that their healthcare couldn't continue where it always had. Most who had to terminate at an abortion clinic described walking past protesters or being advised to come when they were less likely to be outside. "I called the morning of, and they said, we're lucky, there's no protesters outside right now," said Yvette, who ended her pregnancy in the second trimester because of a diagnosis she declined to specify. She had to go to a more affordable abortion clinic and pay out of pocket because she was on federal insurance that was affected by the Hyde Amendment. "I wanted to vomit. That had never even occurred to me as remotely possible. I was so upset about terminating this pregnancy, and that was an extra layer I hadn't even considered."

In 1992, the Supreme Court allowed states to restrict abortion as long as the restrictions didn't create an "undue burden" on the right to abortion and either protected the woman's health or the unborn. Antiabortion activists were off to the races, and many states passed targeted regulation of abortion providers (TRAP) laws, which required abortion clinics to basically become hospitals and added or expanded restrictions like twenty-four-hour waiting periods and requiring abortion providers to read inaccurate scripts, notify parents, and perform invasive transvaginal ultrasounds before the procedure. The new requirements were expensive, and many clinics were forced to close. Pregnant people had to travel farther and spend more money to find a provider, something that has only become harder today.

In an era when miscarriage was all about blaming the mother—it was her responsibility to keep that pregnancy safe— the consequences for low-income women and women of color went far beyond simply feeling guilty. They were disproportionately investigated and prosecuted for drug and alcohol use during pregnancy as child abuse. In 1990, the ACLU estimated that 70 percent of the prosecutions for prenatal abuse were targeted at women of color. Guilt and shame were privileges compared to prosecution.

As we draw closer to our present moment, it's impossible to detail all the political back-and-forth in reproductive rights in the space allotted. Since the late 1990s, women's healthcare has been marked by the whipsawing of regulations that oscillate with judiciary decisions and the political affiliations of presidents. The global gag order that Reagan instated that blocked U.S. funds to global organizations that provide information, referrals, or services for abortion in their own countries? Clinton rescinded it, Bush reinstated it, Obama rescinded it, Trump reinstated it, Biden rescinded it. And so on for many positions related to reproductive rights. You get the idea.

The Affordable Care Act, the most significant healthcare legislation since the 1960s, passed in 2010. The greatest expansion of healthcare in almost fifty years? Yeah, it includes the Hyde Amendment. Approximately one in four pregnant Medicaid users seeking to terminate end up carrying to term because they can't afford an abortion. The ACA also provided for the establishment of state-level health insurance exchanges, which half the states used to restrict abortion coverage in private health insurance plans. These restrictions frequently affect those terminating for medical reasons, which they find out when they call to schedule and hear they don't have coverage. And a 2014 Supreme Court ruling sought by Hobby Lobby stores allowed companies to deny birth control coverage to their employees under religious exemptions.

Some patients successfully fight the bureaucratic blockages to care, but even that fight takes time, energy, and sometimes connections. Julie Cohen, the Jewish Fertility Fund manager for Birmingham, Alabama, was pregnant with a daughter diagnosed with limb body wall complex, where her heart was outside her chest cavity and her spine was severely rotated. Cohen intended to carry until her baby died in utero or deliver her to term if she made it to forty weeks, but she found out at her sixteen-week appointment that due to the baby's development, a vaginal delivery would be impossible. "It seemed best for our family for me not to have to recover from a C-section with three little ones at home," Cohen said. She wanted to induce labor early. "It was fatal. There was no gray area with the diagnosis," Cohen told us. The University of Alabama at Birmingham Hospital agreed that the unequivocal diagnosis made it legal but said there was an insurance issue, and she might get a bill for $20,000. That's a lot of money for "might." Blue Cross Blue Shield of Alabama had the wrong copy of Alabama law and thought the procedure was only covered if the mother's life was at risk. "We're calling them every other day and fighting it, and they're saying it isn't covered because it's against the law. But my doctor wouldn't be able to do it if it wasn't legal," she said. She was able to leverage her contacts to find someone on the board for BCBS Alabama, and he helped her cut through the bureaucracy, a privilege she acknowledged. "What do people do if they can't fight it?" she said. Days later, she delivered her daughter, Adina, who lived for a few minutes before she died.

The Fallacy of Choice and Control

In our cultural minds right now, pregnancies are supposed to end with a child or an abortion. End of list. In earlier eras, historian Lara Freidenfelds wrote, the opposite of pregnancy was miscarriage (whether voluntary or involuntary). "After legalization, the opposite of 'pregnancy' was 'abortion,' and miscarriage became invisible, an event that simply was not supposed to happen." If a woman "chooses" to keep her pregnancy, then it should be successful. But it isn't just the antiabortion arsonists that have helped to erase the reality of pregnancy loss outside the doctor's office. Reproductive rights groups, in their efforts to safeguard access to abortion care, have also allowed discussion of miscarriage and stillbirth to wither, in part because of how complicated pregnancy loss is and how hard it is to combat all this "cute fetus" business. If one side has cornered the market on life and death, what's left for the rest of us who live in between?

The effect of this narrative it is that it changes the way the birthing parent thinks about the pregnancy. Once they decide to keep that baby, they are committed in not only practical terms but also mental terms. And thinking about the pregnancy as a "baby" rather than a "pregnancy"—a focus on the end result rather than the liminal state of being—also activates channels in their own brains in a way that wouldn't have happened prior to 1973. "Choosing" to stay pregnant must then end with a healthy baby. But this is a biological impossibility on a population scale.

Control came up over and over in our interviews, people who thought they did everything right and were shocked that medicine or their bodies or nature had failed them. They brought up how they had poured money, time, and discomfort into fertility treatments, thinking if they just worked hard enough, they would get that baby in the end.

This expectation of control is kind of bananas when you think about it. Plenty of Americans cannot access contraception or abortion, 45 percent of American pregnancies are unintended, up to 20 percent of known pregnancies end in miscarriage or stillbirth, and approximately one in six people worldwide are affected by infertility. Yet pregnancy is assumed to be "an easy, purposeful, and wanted condition." An unplanned pregnancy can certainly still be wanted (or unwanted but not interrupted), but the narrative centers around control, and an unintended pregnancy is a failure of control.

"The narratives our society has about pregnancy and family building are completely batshit crazy," said Jane Armstrong, the Texas-based TFMR therapist. "There's this assumption that it's easy to get pregnant, and as soon as you have a positive pregnancy test, you will have a living baby in nine months. We know the statistics, we know people have miscarriages, we know people have stillbirths, we really don't talk about anything connected to abortion—but we just pretend none of that is true. If we do talk about any of it, it's in the context of this very binary argument that puts these very gray circumstances into black-and-white language that does not serve anyone."

Even the experience of modern childbirth has been one of control—or at least an attempt at it. Since the late 1970s, fathers and partners have been expected to be in the room for the birth (control by ally). Since the 1980s, women have had access to amniocentesis, and other genetic screens have been added along the way, as well as the twenty-week anatomy scan that often reveals that all is well—or that it very much isn't (control of information). Parents have more prenatal details than ever and are left with vast gray areas and narrowing legal limitations to decide what to do about them. Modern-day women are usually not separated from their babies at the hospital (control of the baby), breastfeeding has a lot of support (control of feeding), and hospitals now encourage birth plans (control of the birth process), which can include everything from preferences on anesthetics to playlists (control of the goddamn ambient noise). Childbirth remains medicalized, but there are more options, and the parents (ideally) get to weigh in on whether to have an epidural and get more insight on why a C-section is indicated, and midwifery care and birthing centers are available to those who live near a hospital that offers them. The female-centric births of yore are long gone, but there are more birthing choices for those who can afford them.

"There's comfort in the narrative that medical science has gotten us to the point where we can control our pregnancies, we can prevent pregnancies, we have all this control," historian Shannon Withycombe told us. "But one of the unintended consequences of this is the idea that as soon as you see the blue line, you're going to have a baby at the end, and if you don't, there's obviously something wrong with you. The reproductive narrative in our country is so black and white, and most people, including politicians, believe this is pregnancy. Pregnancy equals baby unless a woman has an abortion, end of story. And it's so entrenched in our culture now."

This notion of control and choice has made society more suspicious of miscarriage, judgmental about pregnancy and abortion, and more perverse and inconsistent about who "matters" in a pregnancy. And as parents on individual levels try to control fertility and parenthood, the government has also sought to exercise control over who will give birth and under what circumstances.

PART II

Sick Mothers

CHAPTER SIX

Medical Mystery

Scientific Uncertainty That Comes from Ignoring the Right Questions

Bethany from Texas was sick. At an urgent care, doctors performed a CT scan and could find nothing causing her abdominal cramping and nausea. They sent her home. A few days later, her cousin announced she was pregnant, and Bethany started to wonder. Sure enough, a pregnancy test came back faintly positive. But she'd already had a kid, and this felt so different. She felt intense pain, and her hair was falling out in clumps. She called her ob-gyn, who said she didn't want to see her for a few weeks. But the pain persisted, so she went to a local Planned Parenthood where they determined there may be something off with the pregnancy; possibly it was ectopic. She called her ob-gyn back, who said she could see her, asked whether the pregnancy had been planned, and then gave her a blood test. Bethany assumed her doctor was testing for the pregnancy hormones, which are supposed to rapidly increase in the early weeks. Everyone at the office kept telling her that she was going to be just fine, and she'd see her little peanut soon enough. No one was listening to her about her pain or concerns, she said. She got a message that her test results were in, and when she opened them, she noticed she'd been tested for STDs, cocaine, and methamphetamine use.

"I'm African American, I'm coming to you because I'm in pain, and I'm telling you—we women have instincts, and I'm 'like something is not right,' and for her to test me for drugs… It makes me feel as if I was discriminated against," she told us.

To the nurses, she said, "This is crazy. None of my questions got addressed. I don't know what's going on with my body, and I feel in my gut something is off."

She was right. Over the next few weeks, she went to the ER and back to her doctor, shelling out money she didn't have in medical bills to get no answers—$4,000 by the time it was over. They kept telling her the pregnancy wasn't progressing, but they needed to wait longer. They talked over her pain, ignoring what she was telling them. Her eyes turned bloodshot, her head pounded, and her abdominal pain got so bad she thought she might be dying. Her doctor told her she was likely miscarrying, and it would pass naturally. She survived. Eventually, the pain subsided. But she felt confused and upset that she'd lost the pregnancy and angry the doctors didn't listen to her. They told her nothing after she miscarried. She had been anxious, sad, and also hopeful, because while no one had asked, she wanted her baby. She said while the physical pain is gone, her anguish is just kind of hanging around.

Bethany ran smack into the post-*Roe* healthcare universe, where women are struggling to figure out how to manage their bodies in places where they no longer have reproductive autonomy. But in order to appreciate how badly we treat people who suffer pregnancy loss—people of color in particular—we first need to understand how badly our healthcare system treats women in general. Women's mental and physical health has been ignored, minimized, and misdiagnosed for centuries—a tradition that long predates America. The ancient Greeks thought that women's illnesses were caused by their uteruses moving around in their bodies, and the cure for most of these ailments was, get this, sex with a man. (Some important stuff on gender equality was left inside Plato's cave, we guess.) The term *hysteria* —we know it from the adjective to describe a (usually female) person who is overly emotional or "hysterical"—was for a long time a catchall medical term used to diagnose a woman when she was physically or mentally unwell. (Abdominal twinge? Hysteria. Chronic pain? Hysteria. Sad feelings? Hysteria. Pretty handy.) This diagnosis was reserved exclusively for women, and it was a way to dismiss female pain without ever having to really get to the bottom of it. It was also a clear indication of just how little medicine understood the female body; the symptoms of hysteria also included headaches, hallucinations, loss of sensation, and even blindness. It's so dumb that it would be kind of funny, except traces of this myth persist today in how women are perceived and treated by doctors.

In 1849, Elizabeth Blackwell became the first woman in the

United States to be granted a medical degree. She was admitted to Geneva Medical College after the medical students thought her application was a joke and voted to admit her. (Hilarious! But not hysterical.) After more women entered the field, some care started to improve because they were around to advocate for their own gender in hospitals and medical schools. But the idea of women as fragile and weakened by their menses or the harsh world lasted a long while, from the antebellum South and Victorian perception of a damsel in need of a fainting couch on up to the neurotic moms of the 1950s (and there's still some of that lingering today). As of 2019, women make up roughly 36 percent of all physicians according to the Association of American Medical Colleges, and that same year, they made up 50.5 percent of medical school students, a majority, however slim, for the first time.

But much of the way we as a society have learned about the human body has come via men, as the doctors, scientists, and test subjects. And of course, that has led to some amazing medical advancements. Heart transplants, antibiotics, and blood transfusions have transformed medicine, and we're so much better now at understanding the ailments that plague us and how to treat them, whether inside a male, female, or intersex body. So yes, after centuries of clawing and begging (go back and reread the history chapter if you need to), women's health has improved. It's gotten vastly better if you're white and only partially better if you're not. Bump it up a notch if you're rich.

But even though medical care is categorically better than

when surgeons were digging around in human bodies with dirty hands and didn't understand that babies are not created by sperm joining menstrual blood, the truth is that science and medicine still know far less about women; they simply are not studied as much, even today. And that has implications for everything in female life, especially reproduction. This is not by accident. Women and people of color were systematically excluded from medical research until 1993, when the National Institutes of Health, the nation's medical research agency, finally warmed to the idea that maybe women and men were, you know, different in big ways and mandated their inclusion in clinical studies. Biomedical research, just to note, is imperative for the understanding of how medications affect the human body, for the collection and dissemination of data, and for deciding eventually how to dose medicine. Every device, every diagnostic test and technology and drug used was first tested in volunteers. The change came amid a major effort by doctors who pushed Congressional members to codify it.

Dr. Ruth Faden was among the members of a committee on the ethical and legal issues relating to the inclusion of women in clinical studies, and she compiled a report at the time for the Institute of Medicine, now known as the National Academy of Medicine, to convince the medical world it was necessary to include women in testing.

"When we were first advocating for the report, we used to say that women are not just men without penises," Faden told us.

It sure seems easy to grasp the notion that men and women

are different and therefore might turn up different scientific outcomes based on the same study and that their data would also be valuable. But for most of medical history, scientific research was based almost entirely on white men. Doctors and researchers eschewed women in part because women could become pregnant, and there are serious ethical considerations with pregnant research volunteers. But doctors also believed hormone fluctuations due to menstrual cycles might mess with their data sets. (Blame it in on the period! There's no actual evidence to support that, by the bye.) For people of color, systemic bias plus a (very understandable) mistrust in the medical world combined so that few people were included in studies.

So to be clear, *Seinfeld* was already on the air by the time scientists were ordered to include people of color and women in federally funded research. For a practical reason why this matters, consider this: many doses for common medications, including many antidepressants and even common painkillers like acetaminophen, are still largely calculated based on studies performed overwhelmingly on men. That means men and women get the same dose. And as a result, according to a 2020 study published in *Biology of Sex Differences* by University of Chicago and University of California, Berkeley researchers, women today are likely overmedicated and suffering worse side effects, like nausea, headaches, depression, weight gain, seizures, and hallucinations. Researcher Irving Zucker at Berkeley and University of Chicago psychologist Brian Prendergast analyzed data from several thousand medical journal articles and found that while women were given the same drug doses as men, they had higher concentrations in their blood, and it took longer for the drug to make its way out of their bodies, but not just because of weight differences. Women were found to experience adverse reactions nearly twice as much as men. The researchers believe it to be a widespread issue, but they ran into a problem trying to answer that question: not enough data.

"Unwanted side effects often remain unknown," the authors wrote. "Most of the data submitted to the FDA by drug companies are not publicly available and not subject to peer-review by the broader scientific community."

A 2001 Government Accountability Report found that eight out of ten drugs pulled from the market had greater health risks for women than for men. And in 2013, twenty-one years after Ambien was approved, the FDA released the first sex-specific instructions after women experienced significant side effects because men and women metabolize the drug differently. Pregnancy adds another complicating layer. As Dr. Katherine Wisner, an expert in perinatal psychiatry and pharmacology and an ob-gyn, put it, "pregnant women get sick, and sick women get pregnant." And doctors need to be able to know how to treat them. Pregnant women with cancer and severe epilepsy really can't be treated, says Nicole Woitowich, a biomedical scientist at Northwestern University Feinberg School of Medicine, and women with cancer are often just advised to have an abortion. Even the list of drugs without safety data in pregnancy includes antibiotics and common over-the-counter pills like ibuprofen. Not studying women isn't just annoying, it's dangerous.

The National Institutes of Health mandate has been somewhat successful over the past few decades; according to its data, between 2010 and 2020, roughly 57 percent of research participants enrolled each year were female. And in 2020, for example, there were 13.7 million people enrolled in studies, 7.5 million female. The statistics are not as good when it comes to race; people of color continue to be underrepresented.

And there's much more to be done. In 2022, Harvard Medical School investigators at Brigham and Women's Hospital reported in the journal *Contemporary Clinical Trials* that the participation of women is still lagging, and the number of women in clinical trials did not proportionally reflect how many women are affected by the specific diseases those trials are aiming to treat, especially in cardiovascular, psychiatric, and cancer-related illnesses. Researchers pored over data from both private and public clinical research studies from 2016 to 2019 and found out of 1,433 trials with 302,664 participants, on average 41.2 percent were female.

Women make up 60 percent of the patient population for psychiatric disorders but just 42 percent of trial participants, they found.

"Though there are overall improvements in the participation of women in clinical trials, they are still underrepresented in studies that they rightfully belong in," author and assistant professor of psychiatry Primavera Spagnolo said in a statement announcing the study.

In *Invisible Women: Data Bias in a World Designed for Men*, Caroline Criado Perez highlighted a February 2018 paper published in the *British Journal of Pharmacology* titled "Gender Differences in Clinical Registration Trials: Is There a Real Problem?" The paper's authors concluded that the problem was not "real" despite the fact that data was only available for 28 percent of drug trials, because women were included at 48 and 49 percent in phase two and three trials. Phase one represented only 22 percent female participants. Why is that an issue? Perez wrote, "According to the FDA, the second most common adverse drug reaction in women is the drug simply doesn't work, even though it clearly works in men. So with that substantial sex difference in mind: how many drugs that would work for women are we ruling out at phase one trials just because they don't work in men?"

A 2016 updated National Institutes of Health policy requires scientists to "consider sex as a biological variable" to receive grant funding, but the majority of researchers still are not analyzing data by sex. (Female scientists are much more likely to analyze their data by sex than male scientists, but they are not the majority in the field.) "When this happens, we have no way of knowing if males or females respond to treatments differently or if there are fundamental differences in the way they are affected by certain diseases or disorders—the differences get flattened by grouping the data together," wrote Woitowich.

If we don't know as much about women because we aren't studying them enough, it becomes a lot easier to overlook their medical problems. And dealing with the healthcare system while being female has deep emotional and mental side effects. In her book *The Pain Gap*, Anushay Hossain noted there are two major problems facing the medical system today. One is the "knowledge gap," because so much less is known about women's bodies and how disease affects them. The other is the "trust gap," which is "the tendency not to trust women and to dismiss their unexplained symptoms; to normalize, minimize, or attribute them to psychological causes."

Many people we interviewed described this to us—how they felt dismissed by the medical community or their symptoms were ignored, especially Black and trans patients. According to research from the Giving Voice to Mothers study detailed in 2019 in the medical journal *Reproductive Health*, one in six women reported experiencing mistreatment during pregnancy care. But that is only from women *reporting* mistreatment, so the figure is likely much higher. Mistreatment in this study included scolding or yelling, private information shared without consent, physical privacy violated, threats, physical or sexual abuse, and medical professionals ignoring or refusing requests for help.

Indigenous women were most likely to report experiencing one form of mistreatment, followed by Latina and then Black women, with white women least likely to report it. How they were mistreated varied by race too, the researchers found. Twice as many Indigenous and Latina women compared with white women reported that healthcare providers scolded them.

Rayna Markin, a psychologist and associate professor at

Villanova University who specializes in psychotherapy for infertility and pregnancy loss, said that some couples feel dismissed or invalidated by their medical providers when they suffer pregnancy loss, "even though experience shows it's so helpful to get support and empathy."

This happened to Chicago area–based Jen D., a Native American U.S. veteran, who said her doctors were nice right up until she lost her baby. Then her doctor treated her roughly as she labored with her stillborn baby girl, Olivia. When she asked if the doctor could go a little easier, the doctor yelled at her.

"I'm about to give birth to a dead baby. You think you can be nice to me?"

Katie N. ended her pregnancy after she and her wife got a shocking diagnosis; the baby had an open abdomen, deformed spine, and brain abnormalities and was not expected to survive. After it was all over, she felt "super let down by the medical community."

"Nobody checked up on me. Nobody was like, hey, you good? Not just physically but emotionally, mentally. My milk came in, and I lost it. I knew it could happen, but it felt like my body was betraying me," she told us.

She was never screened for depression. No one said "come back and check in." She was just dismissed. At least two dozen women told us this—that they weren't screened for depression, they weren't told about depression or anxiety as a side effect of miscarriage or stillbirth, and they weren't clear on what to do if they felt depressed. How sad was too sad?

Black, Latina, Indigenous, and Asian American women were twice as likely as white women to report a healthcare provider ignored them or refused to help them. Another group of researchers in 2022 studied how reproductive health decisions and care for Black women were impacted by racism. "Within the context of a historical and contemporary reproductive health care system, which devalues the reproductive health of Black women, participants in this study voiced personal and vicarious experiences of racism that triggered a need for self-protection through a variety of behaviors," the researchers reported. "The devaluation of Black reproduction is deeply ingrained in U.S. society, stemming from when the sexuality of enslaved Black women and girls was expressly manipulated and controlled. Participants' narratives reflected a tangible and omnipresent climate of racism within which participants experience reproductive health and health care."

Central Massachusetts–based Emy C. told us she had uterine fibroids—noncancerous growths that appear during childbearing years. They range in size from tiny undetectable specks to masses that can swell the uterus and leave a woman doubled over in pain. (They're very poorly understood, and it's not clear why some women get them and others don't, in part—wait for it—because they're not studied very much.) She was in intense pain, soaking tampons and getting yelled at during work for staying in the bathroom too long. She took herself to the emergency room a few times because her pain was so bad.

"I went once, and this doctor, this male doctor, said—and

this was kind of like what I got from people—he's like, 'It's probably just your new normal,'" she said after explaining to him the bleeding, the pain, the swelling, and inability to get through the day. "But it should be no one's normal."

She also suffered preeclampsia with her first child. When she became pregnant again, she tried to tell the doctors and midwives about her medical issues, but she told us that no one seemed to listen. She was losing weight, feeling sick, and knew something was wrong, but everyone kept sending her home. "I thought, if they're not worried, I guess I shouldn't be? They're the doctors," she said.

She eventually went into preterm labor, and it was only then she was diagnosed with preeclampsia. She delivered her son, who lived for fifteen days. She became gravely ill in the process but still sat by his side in the NICU.

"He was a baby. He had curly hair and eyebrows. And he was just so, so sick," she said. "And no one talked to me about the possibility of him dying. No one mentioned he was born so severely premature he might not leave the hospital."

Xaviera Bell, who was living in Raleigh, North Carolina, had been having an uneventful pregnancy until around twenty-one weeks, when she started to cramp and bleed. A sonogram had showed her son was measuring small, so her doctors changed his due date from August 20 to August 30, a change she didn't question at the time.

Now she knows that numerous medical studies have shown that Black, Hispanic, and Asian babies have a lower birth weight than white babies, with babies born to Black mothers measuring the smallest.

And she thinks that time was critical. "Those ten days cost my son his life," she said.

When she was checked, she was one centimeter dilated, a process that means labor is starting. She had what is medically called "cervical insufficiency," where the cervix opens too early and results in premature labor.

They sent her to the hospital for a cerclage, a procedure where the doctor places stitches to try to keep the cervix shut until delivery. But by the time she arrived, they told her it was too late. She would have to deliver or have a D&E.

She has since become a doula, and now she knows that some patients can go from twenty-three to thirty weeks with dilation without having to deliver as long as they have the help of drugs to delay labor. Her son was twenty-two weeks; had he been one week older, the hospital would have called the NICU when she delivered to try to save the baby's life.

"Maybe they could have prevented preterm labor for another week. Or a reevaluation of my original due date. All I needed were those days."

The March of Dimes 2023 report card, which judges the state of maternal and infant health in the nation, gave North Carolina a D-plus for its preterm delivery rate, which is 1.5 times higher among Black women than the rate among all other women.

"I always thought if I overachieve and I go to college and get a master's degree, I will be OK. I'll make a good income, and my kids will be fine. All of that is a lie," Bell said. "You can't check any of the boxes to make yourself safe if you are a Black birthing person. The checklist doesn't exist."

Listen, we spoke to so many caring and compassionate doctors, midwives, and nurses who are working in their own corner of the world to combat these systemic problems. Some have loudly sounded the alarm about worse medical care for all pregnant people as collateral damage of the overturning of abortion protections. But what we also know is there are fewer answers to medical questions about women because scientists aren't bothering to research (or analyze) the answers. The issues here are bigger than any individual medical professional or researcher. And the systems still in place were formed when attitudes about women, and in particular people of color, were predicated on sexist, racist, and dangerous assumptions, and those systems still make up the backbone of the medical world.

Medical advancements in pregnancy over the past thirty years are staggering. More people can become pregnant through medical interventions that have become more common, like IVF. We now have the tools to pick up on potential problems earlier in the pregnancy; surgeons can intervene and perform lifesaving medical procedures when the baby is still in the womb. A baby can survive earlier and earlier thanks to technological advancements. But pregnancy *loss*, not so much.

We don't understand why roughly 20 percent of known pregnancies end with miscarriage or why a baby suddenly dies in utero. Stillbirth is still shrouded in mystery. People of color are far more likely to suffer these complications, and the disparities just seem to grow. We don't know whether medicines are safe for pregnant people to take and rely instead on studies performed on animals to guesstimate. When it comes to pregnancy loss, there are very few answers.

Science, by the way, considers a woman's childbearing capability as a reason to exclude her from biomedical research, so just by having a monthly period, a woman can be eighty-sixed as a volunteer or made to take very specific contraception if selected for some kind of research program. (Meaning they're dictating whether she is taking birth control or other types of contraception.) And there's stigma when studying pregnant people, largely because of ethical concerns over exposing them and their fetuses to the risks of research. Those ethical concerns are legitimate, but it's really complicated. On one hand, the only way to understand pathology better is through study. Test subjects (today, at least) are all volunteers, and they're well advised of the potential concerns associated with their involvement in a clinical test. On the other hand, women and doctors alike are rightly concerned about doing harm to the fetus. There is a history here; in the late 1950s, 1960s, and early 1970s, a drug called thalidomide was given to pregnant women as a tool to treat morning sickness, and another called diethylstilbestrol, or DES, was prescribed to avoid miscarriages. But the drugs caused birth defects, many infants died after a few months, and the ones who survived were often born with missing limbs.

In 1977, the FDA recommended banning women of reproductive age in early-stage clinical trials—all women. "So regardless if you were pregnant or not, because you had a uterus and you *might* be able to get pregnant, you were excluded from research," Woitowich, the biomedical scientist at Northwestern University who studies the need for gender-inclusive research, told us. "It was like that for years, and the stigma of that lingers."

For example, pregnant people were excluded from the COVID-19 vaccine trials amid the pandemic, though they were found to be at greater risk for the virus than nonpregnant people. Numerous studies showed that unvaccinated mothers who had COVID-19 were significantly more likely to have preterm and stillborn babies. Women who are vaccinated during pregnancy and breastfeeding pass that immunity on to the baby. This information would help pregnant people make a personal decision whether to get vaccinated.

The National Institutes of Health fund a huge amount of research in the United States. They're particularly important for academic research that isn't going to make a lot of money for a private drug company. But among the institutes, there's nothing focused specifically on maternal health. The most closely aligned is the Eunice Kennedy Shriver National Institute of Child Health and Human Development, or the NICHD. In just the past decade, it's begun to study maternal health as uniquely important—not just a sidecar to child health. It's only been in the last five years or so that a focus has been put on studying pregnant women. The problem, of course, is the political storm cloud that makes even the most well-intentioned study tricky. (See also: Everything we've said about abortion.)

But Dr. Faden and others who have worked to advocate for the inclusion of pregnant people in medical studies for decades believe there are strong ethical reasons to study pregnant people, and that study does not have to rely on biomedical research alone. There's a lot of "ethically unproblematic" work out there to help fill the evidence vacuum about healthcare for pregnant women, Faden wrote in 2013. She cites, as an example, performing a simple blood test on pregnant women who are already taking medication and studying the effects of that medication. And a big, missed opportunity, she argued, was the National Children's Study in 2009 in which more than one hundred thousand women were followed during pregnancy and their kids studied for twenty years in order to understand the impact of a child's environment on health. The pregnant women were not the test subjects but just a part of the overall environment—the study focused only on kids.

"Pregnant people are not just women with big bellies. And the physiology of pregnancy has all kinds of implications for the metabolism of drugs and vaccines and for the natural history of certain diseases," Faden told us. "Until we fully come to recognize that and ensure that we try to get an evidence base in pregnancy that is as close as possible to the evidence base we have for people who are not pregnant, we are really treating pregnant people unfairly. So that's where we are now."

Medical research that involves the potential for risk to fetuses raises red flags among researchers and even patients. But, Faden and others argue, a controlled study environment where subjects are closely monitored is actually less risky, because there's so little evidence on how medications work with pregnancy. We're just guessing anyway, so why not guess in a safer environment where you're monitored more closely?

"In considering the ethics of trial participation," Faden and her colleague wrote, "we cannot forget context: if women are excluded from research, their only option may be to take medication in an uncontrolled clinical environment absent the data to inform dosing or safety considerations specific to pregnancy."

In 2015, the American College of Obstetricians and Gynecologists published a committee opinion titled "Ethical Considerations for Including Women as Research Participants" that sought to lay out reasons why women should be included more in clinical studies. In particular, it addresses the ethics around pregnant people. The committee found that pregnant women should be considered "scientifically complex," which has a much different connotation from how they are largely thought of now—"vulnerable." The committee argued that while there are ethical concerns over testing on pregnant women, including but not limited to consent and fetal development, there are also major ethical implications for *not* studying pregnant women.

The appetite to study these issues in a major way has only emerged in recent years. Hundreds of research projects are in the works, and advancements are happening—the FDA in June 2023 approved a blood test that can identify pregnant women at risk of preeclampsia, and the NICHD has a stillbirth working group, for example. The Biden administration in 2023 launched an initiative to help change how the United States approaches and funds health research for women, but that effort is only in business as long as someone politically aligned is in the White House. Meanwhile, stillbirth rates have changed very little over the last fifteen years; this isn't a new or emerging problem.

"We are beginning to understand that pregnancy has the potential to really affect long-term health outcomes. We should learn as much as we can about this," Woitowich told us. "If I'm going to the worst-case scenario, we live in a political environment where women's lives just don't matter as much."

But the absence of information breeds superstition and misinformation. Take the Greeks—that whole business about how a woman's uterus moved around and caused all her medical problems persisted for *centuries*. Part of it, of course, is because we didn't know much about the human body at that time. But the myth took hold and persisted even after medical advancements made our understanding exponentially better. Even when the science is right in front of our faces, we often ignore it. This has always been an issue, but the rise of the internet has made it so much easier to access complete nonsense that affirms our biases.

"This rejection of science is not the result of mere ignorance but is driven by factors such as conspiratorial mentality, fears, identity expression and motivated reasoning—reasoning driven more by personal or moral values than objective evidence," according to a 2022 study on misinformation and the human brain in the journal *Nature*.

Dr. Jamila Perritt, an ob-gyn, reproductive justice advocate, and president of Physicians for Reproductive Health, said part of the dissonance around reproductive care comes from doctors themselves, who have over the years held medical knowledge hostage while eschewing a person's own lived experiences. As an example, she mentioned medical journals, where scientific study is reviewed and published, are often behind a costly paywall.

"We, doctors, scientists, clinicians have essentially conspired to keep knowledge, research, and practices around reproductive health, including contraception, pregnancy, and the menstrual cycle, out of the hands of the community," she said. "Essentially, we have strategically organized to take that information away from our communities and then blame them for not understanding how their bodies work or not managing their own health and well-being in the way *we* think they should."

A very common refrain we've heard from loss parents we interviewed is this: doctors just don't know. About a variety of topics, from what to avoid during pregnancy to why their loss occurred. And that leaves pregnant people with some tough decisions to make. Do they go down a Google rabbit hole where it's sometimes impossible to recognize bad information? Do they take prescribed medicine and hope for the best? Do they exercise? Do they stay off their feet? Are they going to cause a miscarriage if they eat French cheeses? We are still only guessing. And doesn't science owe us more than that?

CHAPTER SEVEN

Nothing about This Is Simple

Miscarriage, Stillbirth, and Other Complications

Almost all the people we interviewed for this book told us they believed they'd done something to cause the unwanted end of their wanted pregnancies. Even Colleen felt like she wasn't welcoming enough when she found out she was pregnant, and that contributed to her loss.

"No matter how educated somebody is, no matter how many kids they've successfully been able to give birth to or the losses they've had, everybody is looking for the thing that they did," Dr. Katharine White told us. White is an associate professor of obstetrics and gynecology at the Boston University School of Medicine, runs a clinic for people suffering miscarriage, and is also the author of *Your Guide to Miscarriage and Pregnancy Loss: Hope and Healing When You're No Longer Expecting*.

"If they had only got care sooner. If only my doctor had taken my bleeding seriously," she went on. "'If only' gets a hold and won't let go. It is absolutely okay to grieve all of this, but like, let me at least take that burden off your shoulders. It doesn't matter what they would have done as soon as you started bleeding. It's just not your fault. I do a lot of this in my miscarriage clinic. Half of what I talk about are all the things that did not cause this loss. And how it is not your fault. It's very *Good Will Hunting*."

It's Common, But It Still Sucks

Some women have one miscarriage. Some have five or ten. People of color are at a higher risk for miscarriage than white women. And the pain varies widely, both physically and emotionally. Some experience bleeding and cramping they'd call a nuisance. Others are doubled over in pain for days. For some, it's heartbreaking. For others, it's a momentary sadness or even a relief. It's all very personal. The one thing miscarriages have in common is how common they are and how that fact makes exactly zero people feel better when it happens to them.

Margaret M. was in her late thirties when she decided she wanted to have children. She had spent much of her early thirties in the pursuit of advanced degrees. Like many of the people we spoke to, she assumed because she wanted to get pregnant, she could, and she started to get impatient when it didn't happen right away. When she had a miscarriage at roughly six or seven weeks, it deeply troubled her. "It was not a happy time," she told us. "I guess I didn't appreciate how common it was. I didn't realize that. Not that I would have taken it in stride."

Northern New Jersey–based Pamela Caine, who lost her infant son at thirteen days old in 1996, is the cofounder and executive director of Griffin Cares Foundation, which helps parents who have experienced pregnancy and infant loss. "Because of the trauma that the loss parent is experiencing, these memories are just locked in," she told us. "Healthcare providers are the leads in a video that's going to replay in this person's memory forever. What they say or do makes a big difference. They can use that moment to set someone on a path to healing by sharing options to give the parents some agency in a really out-of-control situation, or they can be the star of a traumatic memory."

South Bend, Indiana–based Krysta H. told us that she'd suffered two miscarriages. One she weathered at home, doubled over in pain and bleeding so much she worried she was hemorrhaging. The second time she became pregnant, she made it to ten weeks, and then there was no heartbeat during an ultrasound. This time, she opted for a D&C procedure. It was easier for her physically but not emotionally. "It was the picture of the tiny little fetus lying motionless at the bottom of my uterus," she told us. That was it on pregnancy for her; they decided instead to adopt. She couldn't handle any more feelings of failure and grief.

A D&C procedure is used for an abortion and miscarriage. We've talked about this already, but these procedures are *the same*. Every doctor we've talked to wants to make sure that you, dear readers, understand this. Because in the world we're inhabiting now, it's becoming more and more important as abortion restrictions limit what procedures can and can't be done.

"The issue, I think, and why confusion is the norm is that the procedures and medications that we use to treat pregnancy loss or miscarriage or fetal loss that someone did not choose are the same as treatments and medications that we use to treat and provide abortion care—which in this case means a pregnancy that ends because someone makes a decision to end it," said Dr. Lisa Harris, an ob-gyn who treats patients, runs a miscarriage clinic, and has been advocating for more than a decade for doctors to speak more publicly about miscarriage and abortion.

Modern Restrictions for Modern Times

Miscarriage treatment is now becoming ever more fraught as the United States moves to further restrict medical access under the umbrella of antiabortion laws. In many cases, people miscarry with no medical intervention, which was how it was done before we had the science to help it along. (But women also used to die a whole lot more.) One of the ways they got terminally sick was through an infection from unpassed tissue, which is why doctors started regularly performing D&Cs. Today, doctors are *looking* for signs of distress to intervene if necessary. Generally, when patients opt for a D&C, they report less pain, considerably less bleeding, and an overall less troublesome experience than when they miscarry at home, doctors told us.

Doctors have a lot of training in D&Cs, because they are a frequent and common gynecological procedure also used for fibroids, polyps, and postmenopausal bleeding. Where it gets trickier, procedurally and otherwise, is with D&Es, and some hospitals and doctors colloquially refer to a procedure after just fourteen weeks as a D&E because everything gets more complicated as the fetus grows, there's more tissue, and there is a higher risk of uterine perforation and hemorrhage. In a D&E, a person's cervix is dilated and then the fetal remains are removed with instruments, sometimes in pieces. The other option is labor and delivery, often among the other people in the maternity ward who are about to have a healthy baby. Labor, even induction, can take hours. Delivering is hard and painful. And then you must face the reality that your baby has died. (Of course, you must face that reality with a D&E too, but the patient is knocked out for the procedure itself.)

Many hospitals refer out to abortion clinics for D&Es, as happened with Colleen, because you want the doctor who has the most experience and does ten procedures a day, not occasionally. For that same reason, this training is endangered by restrictive laws because they're not folded into everyday care.

This is part of the unforeseen damage from the effort by 1970s feminists to make abortions more widely available. They were working to make quality care accessible, particularly as some hospital doctors refused to perform abortions in the days following the 1973 legalization. The idea was for clinics to provide the whole menu of care, from routine exams to abortions and prenatal care. But the result was that the procedure was siloed, performed mostly in clinics, and not routinely considered hospital or outpatient ob-gyn care. We call them "abortion providers," but we call our ob-gyns "doctors" or "midwives." Over the past fifty years, doctors too split into those who perform the procedures and those who do not. There is little discussion of abortion and miscarriage as part of the same spectrum, even though medically, the procedures can be identical.

The Accreditation Council for Graduate Medical Education formally reaffirmed in 2022 that ob-gyn residency programs have to make abortion training available, leaving programs in certain states in a precarious spot. "If they continue to provide abortion training in states where the procedure is now outlawed, they could be prosecuted. If they don't offer it, they risk losing their accreditation, which in turn would render their residents ineligible to receive specialty board certification and imperil recruitment of faculty and medical students." Teachers fear that arranging for out-of-state training could make them vulnerable to prosecution for aiding and abetting abortion in some states.

In states where abortion is highly restricted, doctors must weigh whether they may be criminally liable for performing a D&C if they didn't first diagnose the miscarriage, because perhaps the pregnant person had ended the pregnancy at home and then went to the hospital. In states with strict rules, if there's any cardiac activity at all, doctors are more hesitant to perform the procedure. The result is delayed care, which can be emotionally damaging at best, life-threatening at worst.

In Texas for example, one woman named Amanda told the *New York Times* that she went in for a routine D&C after a miscarriage, and the next year when she suffered another miscarriage, the same hospital denied her the procedure and sent her home with instructions to return only if she bled so much that she filled a menstrual pad more than once an hour. What changed? She doesn't know for sure, they didn't give a reason, but a new, highly restrictive abortion law had gone into effect in Texas that barred almost all abortions after six weeks into pregnancy.

Though it can make people sick and uncomfortable, most women today don't die if they're forced to miscarry at home. But an ectopic pregnancy *can* be deadly if it's not treated, and instructions to just go home and wait till it gets worse start to become a game of Russian roulette.

An ectopic pregnancy is when a fertilized egg implants in the fallopian tube, which happens in roughly 2 percent of pregnancies. There may be a detectable heartbeat at first, but since there's no room to grow inside a fallopian tube, the embryo doesn't develop. If the tube ruptures, it can be fatal.

Grand Rapids–based Allison M. didn't know she was pregnant when she began bleeding and had severe pain in her side. "I thought it was just a bad period, so I lay down with a heating pad, and it didn't subside," she told us. Urgent care confirmed she was pregnant but sent her straight to the ER. "They said, this is life-threatening. You need to go right now."

She passed out while they were taking her blood pressure in the ER, and an ultrasound confirmed internal bleeding and the ectopic. "They told me they need to do surgery right away, and I might have to have a full hysterectomy and a blood transfusion," she said. "I went under not knowing if I would wake up and never be able to have kids."

She ultimately lost one fallopian tube. "I was pregnant, and it was gone, all in one day," she said. She eventually went on to have two living children.

When trigger laws went into effect after *Dobbs*, these little-known complications were in the spotlight as lawmakers worked through how or when to allow for exceptions. (Some exceptions are for rape, incest, or to save the life of the mother. On paper, it's simple; in reality, it's quite complicated. How do you prove you've been raped, let alone under extreme time constraints? How do you decide the mother is sick enough to save her life?)

In 2019, then Ohio State Representative John Becker, a Republican, sought to limit insurance coverage for abortion procedures but would offer funding for "a procedure for an ectopic pregnancy that is intended to reimplant the fertilized ovum into the pregnant woman's uterus." That medical proce-dure doesn't exist. Becker told the *Cincinnati Enquirer* that he never actually researched whether it was legitimate medicine, and he had gotten some help from the local Right to Life Action Coalition lobbyist.

After some public outcry over the measure, Becker wrote an op-ed in the newspaper where he said that he spoke with medical doctors from the American College of Obstetricians and Gynecologists who, yes, told him that it was not a viable medical procedure and reiterated it was dangerous and could be deadly for the mother. But he instead decided to rely on journal reports from

1980 and 1917 that offered a slightly different take. (Yes, you read that right, 1917. Penicillin wasn't discovered until 1928.)

The measure failed. But Missouri passed an abortion ban in 2019 that became law in 2022, and medical professionals who perform or induce abortion can be charged with a felony punishable by prison time. (So who's laughing now, we guess.)

In 2016, Tampa Bay, Florida–based Saya H. was thirty-four when she was diagnosed with an ectopic pregnancy. She was devastated and spent the weekend "unimagining my new life and waiting for my miscarriage." First, she had to have an ultrasound "of every corner of my insides to listen for the heartbeat of the thing I couldn't save."

"I remember feeling embarrassed to ask if there was anything I could do to save my baby, even if it was, like, major surgery. They said no, and it's extremely dangerous for you not to take care of this. They never used the word abortion, but it was always in my mind."

It was caught early, so they treated her with a methotrexate injection, which is 90 percent effective in ending the pregnancy but meant she couldn't get pregnant again for three months because it is a chemotherapy drug too. To be clear, the procedure often used to treat ectopic pregnancy is not the D&C or D&E that are most associated with abortion. Yet it's still mired in the political chaos, because the way the punitive laws are written can delay or deny care.

The shot ultimately failed, and Saya had laparoscopic surgery eight days later to remove the embryo from her fallopian tube.

There's also something called a molar pregnancy, which occurs when fluid-filled sacs or tumors develop inside the uterus instead of a placenta. There are both full and partial molars, and during a partial, there may be initial development of a fetus, but it cannot survive. The treatment is—you guessed it—a D&C. These occur in less than 1 percent of pregnancies in the United States and are very rarely discussed. They require monitoring HCG levels for some time as well as oral chemo pills like methotrexate. If a molar pregnancy turns cancerous, it can be fatal.

"I wish I would have known that I could have had one. I truly wish that I had been even remotely educated about it," said Traverse City, Michigan–based Allison B., who had a partial molar pregnancy and a miscarriage between her two living children.

Many people aren't even aware that there are this many types of pregnancy loss. The category that falls in the latest gestational term is stillbirth, which in the United States is generally defined as the loss of a baby after twenty weeks. Practically speaking, stillbirth is generally hard on the body—most people labor and deliver the baby. Childbirth is far more dangerous than abortion or miscarriage, and childbirth with no living child at the end is particularly grueling.

South Florida–based Nathalie C., who lost her daughter Toni at twenty weeks after she went into premature labor because of fibroids and preeclampsia, told us, "We need to educate women and tell them this can happen. I know they don't want to scare anyone, but they don't tell you what will happen if you lose a baby, that you may deliver, that you may have to have a D&C. No one wants to talk about it. Nobody wants to confront such a thought that a little baby can die. There's a lot of fear and judgment about it. But there has to be a way for women to know this is a possibility before it happens and they have absolutely no information."

Stillbirth Happens, People

The way stillbirth is treated in the United States, you'd think it never happened. But at least twenty-one thousand babies were stillborn in 2020, which translates to about 1 in 175 deliveries in the United States. Black women suffer stillbirth at 10.3 per 1,000 live births, Native American women 7.2 per 1,000 births, Hispanic women 5, white women 4.8, and Asian or Pacific Islanders 4.2. The CDC says the rates are likely higher in practice because of a lack of uniformity in how they are reported. And the number of deaths rose during the COVID-19 pandemic.

The annual number of stillbirths in the United States far exceeds the number of deaths among children ages zero to fourteen years from preterm birth, sudden infant death syndrome (SIDS), accidents, drownings, fire, and flu combined, according to the March of Dimes.

But there is no good data collection on stillbirth and its causes. (Picking up on a theme?) Stillbirths aren't counted in the infant mortality tally kept by the CDC. Death certificates are the only real source of national data on this, but the definition of stillbirth varies so widely from state to state that it's not clear all stillbirths are even getting recorded. Not every stillbirth gets a death certificate, and if you go to a clinic, it isn't counted in the state's vital statistics. In many states, stillbirth is listed as the cause of death, but stillbirth isn't a cause of death—it's a descriptor that a baby was born dead. The baby could have died because of issues with the umbilical cord or the placenta or during a difficult delivery. This lack of information makes the data impossible to analyze.

We get it. It's awful to hear about all this. There's wild superstition around pregnancy, and even just thinking your baby might be in trouble sends people into a doom spiral. (After her twins died, Rebecca considered wearing a T-shirt that said "Dead Babies Aren't Contagious" when every parent at kindergarten pickup abruptly stopped speaking to her.) But there is also a not-so-subtle paternalism in some corners of medicine where doctors don't want to make women anxious by telling them something potentially disturbing. If knowledge is power, maybe if we learned and talked more about this, we could prevent some of it from happening?

In 2019, Erica Bailey had an easy pregnancy—for a while.

"In hindsight, my son's movements were slowing down in those last weeks," she said. But she chalked it up to the much-perpetuated idea that "babies run out of room in the third trimester." (The movements should change rather than slow.) "But I literally had never heard anyone talk about stillbirth. It never crossed my mind."

She was thirty-nine weeks when she became concerned that

she hadn't felt movement, and she and her mom went to triage, where a fetal doppler and an ultrasound showed her son Rhoan had died in utero.

"My life split in half in that moment. I felt like such a failure. My job was to protect this baby, and I couldn't even do that," Bailey said.

She became a Count the Kicks ambassador, a group advocating to have expectant parents track fetal movement throughout pregnancy. She counted kicks religiously with her second son, and at thirty-six weeks, she noticed decreased movement. A nonstress test showed his heart rate was decelerating. She was induced that day, and he was born healthy. "The stillbirth rate has been unchanged for decades, and I can't handle that. I hate that it falls on the backs of loss parents to change this, but no one else is going to," Bailey said.

Consider this: SIDS, where a newborn dies seemingly without warning before their first birthday, is similarly mysterious. In the 1990s, the National Institutes of Health kicked off a major awareness push that revolved around something so simple: putting babies to sleep on their backs instead of their stomachs. Over the past thirty years, SIDS deaths have declined by more than 70 percent. Now, there are roughly thirty-four hundred cases annually of sudden unexplained infant deaths, including fourteen hundred SIDS deaths.

Think about how much you hear about SIDS and how little you hear about stillbirth. But there's a simple awareness solution to help reduce stillbirth too, according to the American College of Obstetricians and Gynecologists. After your baby starts to kick, you can keep track of how often you feel that movement. It requires some focus, and the key is to notice major changes, but it's simple and easy to communicate, and there are easy-to-use apps.

Marny Smith, who delivered a stillborn son, Heath, at thirty-six weeks, is a founding member of PUSH for Empowered Pregnancy, an all-volunteer stillborn prevention nonprofit. At the time of her loss, she had never heard of kick counts. Had she known, she would have gone to the hospital immediately when she noticed reduced fetal movement. But—and she's not wrong—she thinks many pregnant people don't want to be seen as "hysterical" (thanks, ancient Greeks) and act panicky and worried. Why though? Who are we trying to impress?

"Doctors don't bring up stillbirth because they don't want to make their patients anxious. Well, would you not tell them they had cancer to avoid making them anxious?" Smith asked us. "It's ludicrous to say you can't educate women about counting kicks to avoid scaring them. What you're saying is you don't want to educate them, don't want to empower women to make decisions about what's going on in their body, the information they're receiving from their baby. I believe that withholding information from pregnant women is putting them and their babies in danger."

The Rainbow Clinic in Mount Sinai Hospital in Manhattan is the first of its kind in the United States designed solely to provide specialized care for the subsequent pregnancies of those who have experienced stillbirth. (It takes its name from the colloquial term "rainbow baby," used to describe a successful pregnancy after a loss.) It opened in 2022, created in partnership with Smith's nonprofit, PUSH. A second clinic opened in Los Angeles in 2023.

Dr. Joanne Stone, a maternal-fetal medicine specialist, heads the clinic, which offers genetic counseling, nutrition counseling, social workers, genetic testing, and frequent ultrasounds and fetal monitoring. Patients can schedule appointments as often as they want, and fetal movement is tracked both by the doctors and the patient more frequently. (Colleen really wishes this existed when she was struggling through two other pregnancies.) They offer preconception consultations for those who want genetic counseling before getting pregnant again, which is available to anyone, even if they are outside Manhattan.

Every staff member is trained with a six-hour video session to make sure that everyone—front desk, sonographers, medical assistants, nurses, and doctors—is treating these patients with language and care they need in what is usually a very high-stress, very emotional pregnancy. NICU staff and pediatricians as well as the nurse managers on labor and delivery and postpartum floors also receive the training, and the room is marked by little rainbow footprints so everyone knows not to say things like "Is this your first baby?"

Each patient gets personalized medical management, and all have Dr. Stone's email address. "They all know, no matter what, you just reach out to me," she said. One patient wasn't feeling fetal movement at thirty weeks, so Dr. Stone kept that patient on the labor floor until she delivered at thirty-seven weeks because even though the monitoring was normal, the patient couldn't feel the baby move. "I do whatever I have to to keep them safe and to feel cared for," Stone said. "They know I don't care if they want to come in every day for monitoring if it makes them feel comfortable."

The clinic receives outside funding to allow this level of care. Unsurprisingly, no one's insurance is covering unlimited sonograms.

"The guidelines are to deliver after thirty-nine weeks, but there's not a single patient in my clinic who is going to make it to thirty-nine weeks," she said. "High anxiety is an indication to deliver earlier, and most go around thirty-seven weeks."

Social workers follow up the day after the delivery, within a week, and after two weeks to see how the parents are doing, and there are frequent postpartum depression screenings.

"Some people are high risk, and you can't take that risk away," Dr. Stone said. "Black women are high risk, and you can't fix structural racism, but you can make sure that they're being heard, that you're addressing all their anxieties and getting frequent monitoring,"

Women who have experienced stillbirth are almost five times as likely to experience another stillbirth or severe maternal complications, and up to a quarter are preventable, according to the Rainbow Clinic. They want to standardize data collection procedures and share data to try to make a dent in the stillbirth rate. The model is based on the Rainbow Clinic in the UK, which published data that showed their patients only had a 1 percent recurrent still-birth rate. "That is incredible," Stone said. "It's going to take time to get our numbers like that, but if we can get that data, we can show this model of care is applicable in other settings."

A Profound Loss

Colleen asked to do testing on the baby's remains after the D&E procedure so that she could get to the bottom of what happened and hopefully prevent it in the future. They could find no reasons.

Autopsies aren't routinely encouraged. They aren't guaranteed in hospitals even if they are requested; Smith says she paid $1,000 out of pocket in New York, a figure that could easily deter even upper-middle-class parents from seeking one out.

Rebecca was discouraged from sending her stillborn son for autopsy, because it would delay burial and likely would not reveal answers. After learning about stillbirth expert Dr. Harvey Kliman from those we interviewed, she sent her 2014 placenta pathology from that pregnancy to him. The results showed that her twenty-week stillborn died as the result of a genetic abnormality. The prenatal genetic screenings had all come back normal, so it never occurred to her that it was a genetic issue. But those tests screen for a limited number of chromosomal abnormalities—the ones usually caused by a wonky egg—and there are nearly limitless possible genetic misfires, though rarer. Nine years and $400 later, she had an answer. She texted Colleen, "I don't know how I feel. Not worse? So…score."

Though she was past the point of blaming herself, it did still help a little to have confirmation that there was absolutely nothing she could have done, and her living sons were unlikely to pass along anything that would affect their eventual children. Those answers had been sitting on slides from the pathology lab for almost a decade, and she would never have known if not for this book.

The American College of Obstetricians and Gynecologists published an obstetrics care consensus report jointly with the Society for Maternal-Fetal Medicine in 2020 that detailed how a lack of uniform protocol for evaluation and classification of stillbirths—and decreasing autopsy rates—are hampering study.

"A significant portion of stillbirths remains unexplained even after a thorough evaluation," they wrote. They suggested that evaluation of a stillbirth should include a fetal autopsy, thorough examinations of the placenta and umbilical cord, and a genetic evaluation. They also recommend referring someone to a grief support group and watching out for signs of depression. Signs of depression. This would be, how do you say? A major understatement. The people we interviewed registered stillbirth as a profound loss.

"He was perfect. Just perfect," Portland, Oregon–based Crystal H. told us about her baby Ezra, who was a full-term, seven-pound fourteen-ounce baby. She has an answer, but it doesn't make her feel any better: There was a knot in the umbilical cord that choked off nutrients. He died the day before she was set to be induced to deliver him, at forty weeks and four days.

"It has shattered our lives," she said. Crystal talks about him all the time. She has to talk about him to survive. This makes a lot of people uncomfortable, because they don't know what to say or how to handle her grief.

There's a difference between the biological experience of a stillbirth and an early miscarriage. "It feels very different," said Joanne Cacciatore, founder of the MISS Foundation, an international nonprofit that serves families whose children have died; she's also a professor at Arizona State University who researches grief and the loss of a child. "For example, I work with a woman— her child died, and then she had three or four subsequent miscarriages early, in the first trimester. They were intensely painful for her, not just because she had miscarriages but because she was losing over and over and over again."

Nneka Hall's daughter Annaya was stillborn at thirty-nine weeks after undiagnosed preeclampsia caused the placenta to fail. She worried something was wrong but was told her worry was because of her history of depression. It was her third pregnancy, she knew something was off, but she felt like everyone was blowing her off. "They literally gaslit me to believe it was all in my head, and then weeks later, she died, and they said, 'These things happen.'"

She got little counsel on what to do; she felt confused and upset and exhausted.

"They brought her to me, and no one told me what I could do. I never even saw her hands or her hair until the pictures because I was afraid to unswaddle her," said Hall, now a doula. "We're afraid of death. Now I know you have to show parents that they're just babies. She just looked like a sleeping baby."

They were waiting for an imam to come give a blessing and discovered the nurses had kept the baby in a storage room, not in the morgue. She said the nurses forgot about the baby girl because she couldn't cry. Because of this, the baby was no longer in a condition for Hall's older children to meet her.

Awful, right? But Hall isn't the only person we interviewed who reported that their baby was temporarily misplaced at the hospital! Part of the problem is that hospital staff don't get bereavement training very often, especially in smaller hospitals. But we also lack a social understanding for this kind of loss; we sweep it under the rug and forget babies in storage rooms and then tell the parents to get over it and try again for another.

So many people mentioned that it was a travesty that they didn't know miscarriage and stillbirth were not uncommon and could happen to them. It's unsurprising. In *What to Expect When You're Expecting* and *Great Expectations*, two popular prenatal books, any negative reproductive outcome is segregated into its own section in the back. Loss is an appendix, not part of the main story.

Some of those we spoke to believe pregnancy loss should be integrated into school health classes, gynecological exams, prenatal education, and childbirth classes. "When all sex ed focuses on is that you shouldn't get pregnant, here's how to prevent it, it sends the message that when you want to be pregnant, it's easy and it all goes well," said Crystal Clancy, a perinatal mental health specialist based in the Twin Cities area through her practice Iris Mental Health and Wellness. "The trick here would be to do it in an age-appropriate way so that teens don't hear, 'oh, well then, it isn't that easy to get pregnant.'"

Clancy also said pregnancy loss and the statistics should be mentioned at every exam—even if it's long before the patient is even thinking about pregnancy and not just for those who identify as female. "Even if they're not in a place to hear it yet, it's still information. It has to be normalized as part of routine healthcare, to have it be as commonplace as being asked how regular our periods are."

Lacey M., who lives in central Washington, was pregnant six times in six years. She has had two living children as well as miscarriages and a TFMR. "I did so much research after my own losses, and I was shocked at how little I knew but also that nobody else knew," Lacey said. "I'm like, 'how could you not know any of this?' But why would they? We don't teach anything. I had an abstinence-only education. So of course most people don't know anything. They're not taught anything about sex or reproduction, let alone loss."

Addressing the possibility beforehand also puts pregnant people in a better position to know what's normal and what isn't. Bleeding, for instance, doesn't necessarily mean a miscarriage; how much bleeding matters. Or patients could be supplied with a pregnancy loss kit of a specimen collector and pads, just in case. Or they could be given a better sense of what's a normal amount of bleeding and cramping with a miscarriage and what warrants a trip to the ER.

"We fail our patients when they don't know what it means

to miscarry, that they could deliver their baby at home," said Sue Villa, the perinatal bereavement coordinator for Edward-Elmhurst Health in Chicago's west suburbs. "We need to be better at preparing our patients for what can happen. What do you do when you pass the tissue? Do you flush the toilet? That can be so traumatic."

This lack of education and accurate information adds to fear and worry, and it sets the stage for PTSD, therapists told us.

A Choice between Awful and Awful Is No Choice at All

Some parents end a wanted pregnancy for a variety of reasons, among them because their babies can't survive outside the womb or would have a truncated life marked by suffering and pain; because they feel unequipped emotionally, physically, or financially to handle a diagnosis; because the birthing parent's health means they cannot continue a pregnancy. If we barely talk about stillbirth, TFMR is even less discussed. We are now capable of learning a raft of details about the baby we carry thanks to more specific and better testing that can be done with a simple blood test. Unfortunately, that greater access to diagnoses does not necessarily mean there are treatments, and it's on the parents to decide what to do with that information.

Kate Carson, an administrator at the Ending a Wanted Pregnancy Facebook group, didn't discover until her thirty-fifth week of pregnancy (forty weeks is full gestation) that her baby had brain abnormalities. "The more pregnant I got, the more I was observing symptoms that didn't seem right. The way she moved was wrong. She moved all the time. I would tell my team, something is wrong, she never stops moving. They would say, that's great! Because they were looking for fetal demise. But they weren't hearing what I was saying. She didn't sleep. She didn't rest. She shook all the time."

She was so anxious that her midwife ordered an ultrasound, and that was when they discovered severe brain abnormalities that gave her daughter a very slim shot of making it to age one, with age three being almost impossible.

Carson says she was given the option of giving her baby only one of two precious gifts: peace or life. She chose peace.

"Sometimes you are just not willing to take a risk on something as important as your child's well-being, and sometimes you have to choose an outcome that you hate to mitigate that risk."

There are only a few doctors who can or will do this, fewer still after the *Dobbs* decision limited the states where abortion is available after twenty-four weeks. Carson went to one of them, Colorado-based Dr. Warren Hern. She had to come up with $25,000 up front as well as money for travel and a hotel.

The first day, the baby was given a euthanizing injection. Then it took two full days to open the cervix, after which Carson delivered. Dr. Hern brought her the baby himself, wrapped in a blanket. She had the baby's cremains sent to her home. Less than twenty-four hours after delivery, she was on a plane back to Boston.

Margot Finn of Ending a Wanted Pregnancy traveled to Dr.

Hern in Colorado too after her daughter was diagnosed with a grave case of lissencephaly—a life expected to last two to six years, marked by respiratory infections, painful seizures, and frequent surgeries.

By the time Finn had enough information about her child's diagnosis, she was past the legal twenty-four-week limit for abortion in Michigan. At twenty-three weeks, six days, all she knew was that her baby had a 70 percent chance of mild to moderate cognitive impairment and only a 30 percent chance of more severe problems. At that time, she wanted more information. Maybe her baby could have a life that wasn't full of pain.

"Waiting for a definitive diagnosis was a privilege I only had because I could pay to travel halfway across the country on short notice and front the $12,500 for an out-of-network abortion," she wrote in an op-ed for Slate. "The only thing I could imagine that would have been worse than my daughter dying is my daughter living," Finn wrote. She continued, "The only thing worse would have been to feel personally responsible for every bit of her suffering thereafter, wishing I could give her peace and being unable to do it."

None of these people wanted any of this to happen. They had to make a terrible choice, and they were doing what they believed was the best and most caring thing for their babies. That's what being a parent is.

Other pregnant people make different choices, equally grueling. A Minneapolis-based loss parent who asked to be called Hooyo, the Somali word for mother, was sixteen weeks pregnant with her first child when she found out her baby didn't have kidneys and would not survive outside the womb.

"As a Muslim, I didn't want to be the one to end life, and I continued to carry him to let what happens happen. I decided to carry the pregnancy through, and whatever weeks we have with him, we'll make meaningful," she told us. "It obviously changed the whole pregnancy. We were never planning to bring home a baby. We were planning a funeral. We didn't buy anything, we didn't set up a room—all those things you think about when you first find out you are pregnant."

She and her husband went on vacation and tried to make memories while she was still pregnant.

At thirty-two weeks, she gave birth, on March 11, 2020—the day before the World Health Organization declared COVID-19 a global pandemic. March 12, the hospitals were shut down, and she would have had to do it all alone.

"One of the biggest things that I hold on to, I can't imagine giving birth alone in those circumstances. My heart goes out to many birthing people who gave birth to a dead baby during COVID," Hooyo told us.

Parents who make this choice can direct that there be no intervention upon birth. Hooyo says her son likely died during delivery; he was gone when she held him. They were able to spend time with him and later perform the Janazah prayer, the Islamic funeral prayer for the deceased.

"It's crazy the way the memory is so intact," she told us. "The details ingrained in my memory. I think because I knew it was the only time we would have with him, I tried to absorb it all intentionally. I can smell the room if I think about it. I remember every minute, exactly what happened."

The experience has also transformed her work; a doctoral candidate, she's now shifted gears to research postpartum care after stillbirth, largely because she, like many others we spoke to, felt there was no clear path or no answers on what to do or how to grieve. She says most of postpartum care is largely in the context of live births, and the death of a baby coupled with the physiological response of a postpartum body needs more attention.

There are roughly 250 different places in the United States that offer perinatal hospice for parents who are not at medical risk and want as much time with the baby as they can. Doctors monitor the birthing parent and the baby and help them prepare for what will happen after the baby is born. But this service isn't routine or free, and it isn't offered everywhere. Only certain pregnant people are eligible, depending on whether it will be safe for them to continue pregnancy and deliver. Some people can't bear the thought of waiting for their babies to die in utero or directly after, and some can't bear the thought that they will. Dr. Steve Calvin, a maternal-fetal specialist in Minnesota, said that patients ask him whether terminating the pregnancy is necessary—whether they have to do it. He said he's had some patients bullied by their providers into terminating, especially genetic counselors.

"I've always tried to be very careful," he told us. "I just say here are the facts of what your baby has, it's really serious, and I'm almost certain this is lethal. You are aware that ending the pregnancy is one of your options, but you could also continue the pregnancy to have the baby with you as long as possible. We are supportive of both those options."

Palliative care means they will monitor the baby and the birthing parent, but just like in end-of-life care, they won't do anything to intervene, except to make the baby comfortable. Generally, the babies die either in the hospital or shortly thereafter. The care is centered around supporting the parents so they can focus on making meaningful memories.

But what if it's not your choice? One such story reported by Frances Stead Sellers in the *Washington Post* detailed the case of one couple whose baby was diagnosed with a fetal anomaly. Deborah Dorbert and her husband, Lee, made a painful decision to end the pregnancy. At the time, Florida law banned abortion after fifteen weeks, but there was an exception that permitted a later termination if physicians agree in writing there is a fatal abnormality. But the doctors didn't sign off in this case. She couldn't afford to travel out of state.

"That's what we wanted," Dorbert told the *Post*. "The doctors already told me, no matter what, at 24 weeks or full term, the outcome for the baby is going to be the same."

Instead, she had to tell her toddler son that the baby she was carrying would never come home. She suffered intense anxiety and depression. On March 3, 2023, she delivered baby Milo, born with Potter syndrome, which meant he had nonfunctioning kidneys and underdeveloped lungs among his many medical problems. Everyone wanted him to live, but he survived only for ninety-nine minutes.

"When he came out you could hear him gasping for air. He was really trying to breathe," Dorbert told the *Post*. "He didn't cry when he was born and he didn't open his eyes at all, but I mean, he struggled."

Morgan Nuzzo, the nurse-midwife who cofounded a third-trimester abortion clinic, wondered to us: "If a baby lives for ninety minutes and is struggling, do we feel good about that? Some people choose that, but my values align with something fast and quick. We have folks come in who say I can't bear to take this baby off life support—I can't make the decision after it's born. I totally get that."

For a growing number of women living in states with strict abortion laws like Dorbert, it's not a question—they have to carry the baby as long as it survives. Palliative care and support might be a welcome answer, but the palliative care field is small; when we spoke, Dr. Calvin had only roughly three instances out of thirty-three hundred births where the palliative care model was an option because of maternal health concerns. In 2019, a committee with the American College of Obstetricians and Gynecologists studied roughly forty hospitals and found where 41 percent of the deaths were neonatal, only 2 percent received palliative care, in part because of a lack of training, physician education, and other barriers. Still, the benefits justify their continued development, the committee reported.

Palliative care is also largely rooted in Christianity and causes discomfort to some on the abortion rights side of things. Proponents of palliative care say it transcends the abortion debate and is an option for women who are looking for as much time as possible. This is, yet again, a complicated, gray area where politics shouldn't really be an issue. If we all thought about pregnancy loss on a spectrum, then it wouldn't be a problem for parents to decide whether they'd prefer to terminate or find palliative care for a baby with a fatal diagnosis.

When all this is happening, the birthing parent often isn't focused on their own health or well-being; they're trying to manage a terrible, complicated, and upsetting end of a pregnancy. But they probably ought to be, because maternal mortality in the United States, or the rate at which a person dies within a year of childbirth, is among the highest in the developed world.

CHAPTER EIGHT

Sick and Dying

How Discrimination Creates Circumstances for Pregnancy Loss

The nationwide rate of infant mortality—when a baby born alive dies—is on the decline (though embarrassingly high compared with other wealthy nations). But maternal mortality rates are alarmingly high, and they're expected to rise even more in the aftermath of the Supreme Court decision to reverse abortion protections. These are deaths tied directly to childbirth and often coincide with pregnancy complications and can be related to miscarriage and fetal death too. The United States has 32.9 maternal deaths per 100,000 live births. (The next closest, by comparison, is the United Kingdom with 10.9 per 100,000 births.) The data for Black women is 69.9 deaths per 100,000 live births, making them nearly three times more likely to die than white women during pregnancy or within a year of the end of the pregnancy. Black women are also far more likely to suffer miscarriage, stillbirth, and other complications.

Anushay Hossain, in her book *The Pain Gap* about how the medical world treats female pain, particularly that of women of color, puts it this way: "Maternal mortality ratios tell us how well a country's healthcare system in general is functioning. In America, our maternal mortality rates are a stark reminder of how little we actually value women's health."

For all birthing people over the past fifty years, we've medicalized pregnancy to the max, where most are giving birth in hospitals (unless you deliver in a birthing center or in a bathtub at home, but those are mostly available to women of privilege). We're scheduling inductions and C-sections and getting epidurals. Not all bad, but it's possible the illusion of control is making some of us forget how deadly childbirth can be.

"It's really underappreciated that pregnancy is dangerous," said Dr. Sarah Prager, the ob- gyn and professor at the University of Washington. That danger is present for all women, but especially for women of color.

A recent study on racism's effects on Black women in the United States found, very plainly, that the impact "on obstetric health inequities is notable, with Black communities experiencing higher rates of preterm birth, low birth weight, infant mortality, and maternal mortality."

The disparities for Black and Native American women are the most stark and baked into the very history of the nation, but healthcare inequity is demonstrable across all people of color.

"Dealing with racism in our daily lives is a major factor in our health and well-being. The experience of racism makes

Black people sick, whether it's mental and emotional health or even physical health," Jamila Taylor, a reproductive rights advocate, told us. She's had many women approach her to say they're afraid to get pregnant because they are worried they won't survive it.

Mistrust of the medical world runs deep with good reason. There are many cases throughout our history where Black people were abused by the medical community. The Tuskegee experiment, forced sterilizations, and the story of Henrietta Lacks are among the most well-known examples, but that's just a small sample. There is also some proof that Black doctors take better care of Black patients than white doctors do; infant mortality for Black newborns was halved when they were cared for by Black rather than white physicians, one study found.

Black, Indigenous, and Hispanic women are far more likely to experience preterm birth and complications in childbirth such as preeclampsia, gestational diabetes, and preterm labor. But their pain is also more prone to be minimized and their concerns less likely to be believed. Scientific data suggests a significant amount of these issues may be preventable, if only everyone was getting proper health care. Serena Williams, one of the most recognizable women on earth, nearly died in childbirth because no one was listening to her complaints about her declining health. After her first baby was born in 2017, doctors and nurses dismissed what she was trying to tell them about her pain and previous experience with blood clots, she wrote in a harrowing first-person account. Finally, a scan that she insisted on showed blood clots in her lungs, and further surgery revealed more clots in her abdomen. (She had a healthy delivery with her second child in 2023.)

Tori Bowie, an Olympic gold medal–winning sprinter, was found dead in her Florida home in 2023. She'd been eight months pregnant. No one had heard from her in a few days, so police did a welfare check and discovered her in bed. An autopsy showed that she had gone into preterm labor and died from complications of childbirth because of respiratory distress and eclampsia, which usually has lots of signs and symptoms as long as medical professionals are looking for them, like elevated blood pressure, protein in the urine, headaches, and shortness of breath. The baby was stillborn. This woman was an elite athlete in peak health. She won three medals for Team USA at the 2016 Olympics. Yet, she died alone in her house.

After Bowie's death, one of her teammates, Tianna Madison, shared on Instagram that she also nearly died while giving birth to her son in 2021. What's perhaps even more disturbing is what else she divulged: "THREE (3) of the FOUR (4) of us who ran on the SECOND fastest 4x100m relay of all time, the 2016 Olympic Champions have nearly died or died in childbirth," she wrote, referring to herself, Bowie, and Allyson Felix, who had a baby in 2018.

If doctors won't listen to one of the most famous and wealthiest living athletes or watch out for Olympic gold medalists, how can the everyday Black woman stand a chance?

Tomeka I. from the greater Charlotte area told us that looking back, she wonders how her story was even possible from a risk management standpoint—her career field. She was pregnant in 2017 and was forty-one when she delivered, which put her at a higher risk of preeclampsia. They gave her a baby aspirin regimen and, when a blood test revealed anemia, iron pills.

Her pregnancy had been pretty easy, no morning sickness, and she walked for thirty minutes every day on her lunch break. That May, she started with weekly appointments, and they thought her son was measuring small. They sent her up to maternal-fetal medicine to get a same-day ultrasound, which was inconclusive because the umbilical cord was blocking their view. The following week, he failed a nonstress test, but after another ultrasound, they said he was fine. She was thirty-five weeks pregnant and thought she had cleared all the hurdles.

She went to a Mother's Day dinner with family and awoke the next morning with a bad stomachache. She vomited and then was able to go back to sleep—she assumed she had food poisoning. The next day when she stood up, she passed out, and an ambulance took her to the hospital. They gave her a fetal doppler and an ultrasound in the ER, which revealed her baby had died, and the doctors told her she had HELLP syndrome, a pregnancy complication associated with preeclampsia. It's an acronym that stands for hemolysis, elevated liver enzymes, and low platelet count. The cause is unknown. (It hasn't been studied.)

"I had no idea what it was. We were so confused," she told us. "They didn't explain it. I think we ended up googling it. They said they needed to induce me. I immediately asked for a C-section. I said, 'I don't think I can deliver him. My son just died. Please let me have surgery,' and they said no but didn't explain why. There was no explanation for what was happening to my body."

Her heart rate was shifting wildly, so they transferred her to another hospital, and a resident picked up her CT scan and realized Tomeka was bleeding internally. They rushed her for the C-section she had asked for earlier without explaining the sudden change of heart.

"I had a liter of blood in my stomach, a softball-size clot on my liver, which ruptured that night," she told us.

Her baby boy, Jace, was born just after midnight. The rest of her family got to hold him while she was unconscious, but she only got five minutes before the nurses took him away. There was no cooling device in her room that allows some parents to spend more time with their babies. Why are there such uneven standards of care for people who suffer loss? Why do some people get the whole suite of care and others nothing at all?

"And because I was intubated, I couldn't talk to him. I couldn't say 'I love you,' or 'I'm sorry,'" she told us. "I was never able to use my voice to talk to him. That was stolen from me, and I can never get that moment back. That's what still chokes me up now."

Tomeka was initially released after a week and then was readmitted the day of Jace's services because she had an infection from the liver embolization. She spent forty-five days in the hospital total, including treatment with aggressive antibiotics and having part of her liver removed. She missed her son's funeral.

Afterward, her friends asked whether doctors had taken urine samples. She had one to verify her pregnancy, then never again.

Urine samples are routine in pregnancy checkups—we had to give a urine sample every time we saw our doctors throughout our pregnancies. Protein in the urine is a sign of preeclampsia. The abdominal pain Tomeka had? Also a sign. So is vomiting. They also weren't checking her blood, which would have likely found something too. She had a handful of blood draws, the last being the first day of her third trimester. As it turns out, none of this is required. Blood and urine samples are just recommendations.

"I was like, what in the hell? I didn't know that should have happened. This was my first pregnancy," she said. "The first thing you think when you lose a pregnancy is 'what did I do?' I have two master's degrees. I went to every appointment. I went to that OB for years. For them not to check my blood and urine, especially after identifying me as high risk, how could that be? This could have been prevented or caught earlier if they had done their job."

She is now the executive director of Jace's Journey, which was founded in 2019 to address racial disparities in maternal health outcomes and advocates for a risk management checklist for providers to reference during every appointment.

Health Problems and Pregnancy Loss

Maternal morbidity—the short- or long-term health problems that result from being pregnant or giving birth—is also pervasive in the United States. More than sixty thousand women nationwide per year suffer from severe maternal morbidity with problems like sepsis, eclampsia, renal failure, stroke, or pulmonary embolism. Hundreds of thousands more have diseases that make their pregnancies more difficult and more dangerous and can lead to the unwanted end of their pregnancies and permanent issues after the baby is born. This too is a far more pronounced problem for people of color in the United States.

A 2016 analysis of five years of data found that Black college-educated mothers who gave birth in local hospitals were more likely to suffer severe complications of pregnancy and childbirth than white women who did not graduate from high school. And then in 2020, researchers examined data on 591,455 deliveries at forty hospitals in New York City from 2010 to 2014. They calculated risks of serious complications, like heart failure, respiratory distress, blood transfusions, or hysterectomy. They found that Black and Latina mothers were more likely to experience delivery complications even when they had the same kind of health insurance and gave birth at the same hospital.

Michelle Drew, a midwife in Delaware, runs the Ubuntu Black Family Wellness Collective, which is aimed at providing holistic reproductive care to Black people. She said many of her clients come to her because they distrust hospitals and doctors, and they are hoping to be believed and just, you know, cared for medically and emotionally. As part of her work, she curated a list of therapists to help women through pregnancy. "It's really important for us that they be able to talk to someone who understands what it means to be a Black woman every day," she told us.

In order to help this crisis of maternal mortality and morbidity, a World Health Organization study in 2021 recommended—get this—more midwives! Turns out the presence of a midwife is associated with fewer cesarean sections, lower preterm birth rates, and lower episiotomy rates, in part because they adopt a more holistic approach to childbirth, treating it more like a life event and less like a medical disability.

"Research consistently demonstrates that when midwives play a central role in the provision of maternal care, patients are more satisfied, clinical outcomes for parents and infants improve, and costs decrease," according to an issue brief by P. Mimi Niles and Laurie Zephyrin for the Commonwealth Fund, a foundation with the mission to promote a high-performing, equitable healthcare system.

That's right, folks. The same midwives run out of town by the ob-gyns at the turn of the last century are now the ones recommended for better childbirth outcomes. (Cue screaming into pillow.)

The *Dobbs* Effect

When the Supreme Court moved to overturn abortion protections in 2022 in the case *Dobbs v. Jackson Women's Health Organization*, there wasn't much thought given to pregnancy loss at all. (You've probably picked up on that theme by now.) The assumption was very much that these were separate things. In some ways, this argument also plays right into what we've been saying: pregnancy is increasingly a choice for many people, and therefore if your pregnancy has ended, that's *also* your choice. Except, of course, the 20 percent of pregnancies that end in miscarriage. Except, of course, when your baby has a fatal anomaly and you don't know how to proceed.

As it turns out, it's sometimes difficult to know whether the end of a pregnancy was a miscarriage or a medication abortion, because the body does similar things. "Heartbeat laws," which have been enacted, as of this writing, in Alabama, Georgia, Kentucky, Louisiana, Missouri, North Dakota, South Dakota, and Texas, ban abortion after the point when a so-called fetal heartbeat can be detected. This occurs as early as six weeks into pregnancy when an ultrasound picks up the grainy pulsing of what will eventually become a heart. These laws assume that if there's still this pulsing, this "heartbeat" as we colloquially call it, the pregnancy is still viable. But doctors told us there can still be activity detected even as the miscarriage is happening. There are no separate miscarriage bells that go off inside the body when the pregnancy ends for unintended reasons. And most ob-gyns do not want to see you until you're at least eight weeks pregnant— two weeks past the limit on abortion in at least one state.

"Even some ob-gyns will repeat misinformation," Dr. Sarah Osmundson, an ob-gyn in Tennessee, told us. "There's no difference between an abortion and a miscarriage medically. Your body doesn't know if there is a heartbeat or no heartbeat."

Given how our culture pushes us to think about pregnancy, it makes sense that many of us are attached almost immediately. Fighting for a medical procedure for your miscarriage seems unnecessarily cruel then, doesn't it? These laws—which we'll discuss in the next section—now vary so widely from state to state that it's difficult to understand how or when you can get medical care. Even medical professionals are confused.

It's only been a short time since the protections fell, and already the effects are serious. NPR journalists spoke to a thirty-three-year-old woman named Christina who lives in the Washington, DC, area. She and her husband were thrilled when they found out she was pregnant. But at her first prenatal appointment, there was no heartbeat, and her hormone levels were low, so her doctor said she was having a miscarriage. They laid her options out: have a D&C, take medicine to make the pregnancy tissue come out faster, or wait it out. She waited, leaving for Ohio for a family wedding. She started bleeding. At her dad and stepmom's house, she crawled into a bathtub so she wouldn't make a mess.

"I was passing blood clots the size of golf balls," she told NPR. She woke her husband, and they went to a nearby emergency room.

At the time, Ohio banned abortion after six weeks. (As of this writing, it's twenty-two weeks, following a lawsuit, and Ohio voters in November 2023 passed a constitutional amendment ensuring abortion access.) The restriction, like many in other states, did not explicitly restrict miscarriage care, but it can have that effect anyway.

Christina went to the ER soaking menstrual pads with blood and was turned away. She went home and eventually lost so much blood that her husband called 911, and she was returned to the same ER, this time in an ambulance. She then finally got medical treatment and had the D&C procedure. She didn't know for sure why she was sent home, but the requirement to prove she was miscarrying rather than aborting "could have cost me my life that day," she told NPR.

It's basic math, doctors told us. "Just practically, fewer abortions is going to mean more pregnancies, and more pregnancies will mean even more miscarriages," Dr. Prager told us.

Miscarriages account for roughly nine hundred thousand emergency department visits in the United States each year. But in some hospitals, doctors aren't trained in procedures to manage the care. Dr. Prager cofounded the Training, Education & Advocacy in Miscarriage Management (TEAMM) project, which trains healthcare teams to perform pregnancy loss care in emergency and clinical settings, because some women haven't established a relationship with an ob-gyn by the time they miscarry. The group has conducted workshops in more than one hundred sites in nineteen states. But as abortion restrictions continue in states nationwide, the number of medical providers taught the procedures is diminishing.

The "gold standard" in medical miscarriage management is the abortion regimen—mifepristone combined with misoprostol. But due to the FDA's extra regulation of mifepristone—and numerous lawsuits—many patients are only offered misoprostol. The FDA currently allows for medication abortion up to nine weeks, while the World Health Organization says it's safe for up to twelve weeks. Inevitably, more pregnant people will rely on the medication later in pregnancy in states where a procedure is not available. This is done in other countries somewhat successfully, but the risk is that all the tissue won't be passed (a bigger risk in later pregnancies), and women will not seek medical attention because they're afraid of being prosecuted. The side effects of these restrictions mean fewer people are able to be treated for miscarriage, and for those who are further along, D&E procedures will become less available as new laws are passed.

Morgan Nuzzo, one of only a few nurse-midwives trained in all-trimester abortions, cofounded a Maryland clinic that opened in October 2022, after *Roe* fell, and is currently the southeasternmost facility in the United States that offers abortions in late pregnancy. Ninety percent of her clients come from out of state. One heartbreaking reality: She sees children every week, some as young as nine, and her clinic also takes care of people who have developmental disabilities and/or are nonverbal. The clinic keeps tissue samples for pathology so detectives can try to locate rapists.

Nuzzo has noticed one outcome of the Supreme Court's decision has been that the restrictions are pushing some people into later abortions, because they have to come up with money, transportation costs, and sometimes childcare. Care is priced at five figures over the twenty-six-week mark because it requires three days of a provider and staff on call twenty-four hours a day. It's already limiting; many people cannot afford it.

She told us that a young couple came to end their wanted pregnancy because of a fetal anomaly and brought a blanket that their midwifery practice had knitted. Nuzzo called their home practice to give them an update. "The whole practice was there, saying, 'How is she? Is she OK?' They were so glad she was with me. This is community care. This is family care. It's really important to offer that care and not operate in silos."

Proponents of abortion restrictions say that miscarriage or stillbirth aren't what they are after and that doctors and nurses should feel OK treating these conditions with whatever medical means they have at their disposal. But it isn't working out that way. It's hard to know exact numbers, but there have been more than one hundred cases in at least a dozen states where people suffering pregnancy complications had delayed care, according to news reports, lawsuits, and scholarly journals. Doctors say that number is much, much higher. And when we say delayed, we mean nearly died from blood loss, or they were told to wait outside a hospital until they got sicker, or they were turned away because the doctors couldn't be sure if they were miscarrying or whether it was a complication from a medical abortion. Some were forced to carry their terminal babies only to deliver and watch them die. Others would have had to travel to receive care and could not afford the costs. Some who live in areas with less restrictive laws also have to wait because of the backlog of appointments from out-of-state residents. These delays will add up to more maternal deaths, not fewer, doctors tell us. But because of the difficulty in collecting proper maternal mortality and morbidity data, we might not know for years just how bad it gets on the ground.

Above all, though, doctors and academics say the people who suffer the worst in this landscape are low income and people of color, especially Black women, because of racism, socioeconomic status, and complicating health factors.

"Post-*Dobbs*, existing mistrust is likely to increase as clinicians become hesitant to provide evidence-based patient care for conditions such as pregnancy loss and ectopic pregnancy due to fear of legal repercussions," according to a column in the medical journal *Lancet* in 2023.

Looks like that's exactly what is happening.

PART III

The Legal Morass

CHAPTER NINE

How Birthing Bodies Are Regulated

The Laws That Increasingly Govern Pregnancy

*R*oe v. Wade was decided in 1973, when the Supreme Court declared a woman had the freedom to choose whether to end her pregnancy under the U.S. Constitution.

A woman named Norma McCorvey (under the legal pseudonym Jane Roe—she didn't go public until years later) became pregnant with her third child. McCorvey had a troubled life, and she gave the first baby to her mother to raise; the second she put up for adoption. This time, in 1969, she wanted an abortion.

But she lived in Texas, where abortion was illegal except to save the mother's life. McCorvey tried to find a doctor but got nowhere and was referred by a friend to two female lawyers who had been looking for just such a client to challenge abortion laws in the state. They filed a lawsuit against Dallas County district attorney Henry Wade, arguing that the Texas law violated McCorvey's right to privacy, a right enshrined by the U.S. Constitution. McCorvey wasn't looking to be the voice of a feminist generation or the head of a class-action lawsuit—she just wanted a way out of her pregnancy. Which she didn't get, to be clear. By the time of the court's decision, she'd already given birth and the child had been adopted.

Abortion Was Law

Every year, roughly seven thousand cases end up at the doors of the Supreme Court, but only a fraction are argued before the nine justices, about 100 to 150 annually. That's because the justices get to *choose* what cases they hear. And they aren't deciding what to take based solely on legal matters or whose case is number one in line or who filed the earliest. It all depends on who the justices are and the political, legal, and social forces of the moment colliding to create the circumstances under which they decide what issues they want to rule on. When the Supreme Court chooses to take up a case, they read all the court documents and hear arguments, and then a justice takes the lead and writes a majority opinion. And that's it. There's no one else to ask, no other manager to see.

Sometimes, the court is weighing in to settle a major argument nationwide, like the 2000 decision that ended the recounts and declared George W. Bush the winner of the presidential election in *Bush v. Gore*. Sometimes they weigh in to right a culturally accepted wrong, like the *Brown v. Board of Education* case, which desegregated schools. Which means, when the court agreed to take on the *Roe* case, it *wanted* to rule. And rule it did. In a seven-to-two majority opinion, it decided women had a right to abortion under the Constitution.

"This right of privacy, whether it be founded in the Fourteenth Amendment's concept of personal liberty and restrictions upon state action, as we feel it is...is broad enough to encompass a woman's decision whether to terminate her pregnancy," wrote Justice Harry Blackmun in the opinion.

The Fourteenth Amendment has five sections, and not all are relevant to this argument, but the first section goes like this: "No state shall make or enforce any law which shall abridge the privileges or immunities of citizens of the United States; nor shall any state deprive any person of life, liberty, or property, without due process of law; nor deny to any person within its jurisdiction the equal protection of the laws."

When Blackmun was weighing how to decide the case, this was where he decided to rest the crux of his opinion—that a person had a right to privacy when it came to their medical decisions. The word "privacy" actually isn't used in the amendment, but it is interpreted that way and has also been used to interpret other landmark cases.

Blackmun found that the states could not regulate abortion in the first trimester, but in the second trimester and beyond, states could impose restrictions that were related to *maternal health*, and then when the fetus reaches "viability" (that very subjective and tricky concept), the state could prohibit abortion as long as there were exceptions to save the life of the mother. Blackmun studied how botched abortions had harmed women and was attempting to regulate the health of the mother. (At the time, the rights of the fetus were not considered on the same footing as the rights of the mother—something that's vastly different today.)

There are some legal scholars—including the late Supreme Court Justice Ruth Bader Ginsburg—who felt that the decision was on shaky ground because it relied on the Fourteenth Amendment. Ginsburg thought the decision would have been harder to challenge if it was grounded instead in the equal protection clause of the Constitution and the right to gender equality. "Also in the balance is a woman's autonomous charge of her full life's course," she wrote.

Speaking to a packed auditorium at the University of Chicago Law School in 2013, she said that a case she had argued would have been a better candidate to codify the right to an abortion, and she wished she'd had the chance. It was right around the same time, 1970, when U.S. Air Force Captain Susan Struck became pregnant while in Vietnam. Quixotically, the policy of the air force was for her to leave the military or have an abortion on the base. She wanted neither—she was going to give the baby up for adoption. But she was still forced out of Vietnam, and she sued. Ginsburg was an ACLU attorney who represented Struck. But the air force changed its policy before she could argue it.

"The idea was 'Government, stay out of this,'" Ginsburg told the auditorium on the fortieth anniversary of the decision. "I wish that would have been the first case. The court would have better understood this is a question of a woman's choice." The idea that the case was decided as a matter of privacy opened it up to challenges left and right, Ginsburg argued, because the right is only inferred, not explicitly spelled out, in the Fourteenth Amendment. She was correct. (Ginsburg famously postponed her retirement from the court, thinking she could do so when the first female president was elected in 2016. Donald Trump defeated Hillary Clinton, Ginsburg died in 2020, and Amy Coney Barrett was confirmed to replace her, a process that took only thirty-eight days, among the fastest confirmations ever. And, well, we know how that shook out.)

It Didn't Last Long

Bit by bit since the right was first enshrined, state laws have steadily encroached on the right to an abortion, as did federal limitations like the Hyde Amendment. These laws did not ban abortion outright, because it would not have been allowed under the Supreme Court's decision. But they whittled away access to make things harder for people who needed the care, particularly for low-income people.

In Missouri in 1986, for example, legislation that restricted abortion contained a preamble that read, "The life of each human being begins at conception," and "Unborn children have protectable interests in life, health and well-being." Missouri restricted public employees and public facilities from performing abortions "unnecessary to save the mother's life," and physicians were mandated to perform "viability testing" before they performed abortion. Lower courts struck down the law, and three years later, the Supreme Court weighed in on a case called *Webster v. Reproductive Health Services*. Former Justice William Rehnquist wrote the majority opinion that allowed some of the provisions to go through, including the viability testing and the public funds restriction. Of the preamble, Rehnquist wrote that "This court has emphasized that *Roe* implies no limitations on a state's authority to make a value judgment favoring childbirth over abortion…and the preamble can be read simply to express that sort of value judgment."

The Missouri preamble stood, and in 2018, Americans United for Life used it in its "model legislation and policy guide" as an example of how to frame the idea of the fetus or baby (or whatever you want to call it) as a person—one with the same rights as a twenty-year-old or ten-year-old or fifty-year-old.

By 1992, another challenge reached the high court. The Pennsylvania legislature changed abortion laws in 1989 to require a twenty-four-hour waiting period and "informed consent," which meant a minor needed the approval of at least one parent to proceed and a wife needed to indicate that she'd told her husband about the decision. Planned Parenthood, which operated affordable healthcare clinics around the country, sued, and *Planned Parenthood of Southeastern Pennsylvania v. Casey* reached the Supreme Court.

By this time, the court had its first woman on the bench, Sandra Day O'Connor. (O'Connor was long retired by the time she died in 2023, and things have improved gender equality-wise on the Supreme Court. As of 2023, there are four women on the high court; three are considered left-leaning and one right-leaning.) O'Connor wrote the opinion along with two other justices, and in doing so, she established a new piece of the puzzle, what's called an "undue burden"—does the regulation create a substantial obstacle before the fetus attains viability? Under this legal idea, they upheld many of the restrictions sought by Pennsylvania. The one the court struck down was the wife's requirement to alert her husband.

This opinion opened the door, and dozens of restrictions were passed in the years before *Roe* was fully overturned. Waiting periods, parental notifications, and abortion bans after twenty weeks all became more prevalent across the country. At the same time, the way abortions were treated changed, and the number of clinics and doctors who performed them shrunk. According to a 2020 study by Stanford University researchers, more than half of medical schools either offered no formal education or only a single lecture on abortion. Barriers to teaching, the authors said, included "restrictive state legislation and hospital policies to relocation of abortion care to outlying clinics away from areas medical students rotate."

This was a slow but very steady creep, and to what degree it affected people depended on race and economic status. Clinics struggled under new restrictive laws that created ever more obstacles to operate. Hospitals were not making up the difference in care, unwilling to get involved in the business that could be politically fraught and sometimes dangerous because of protesters and threats of violence or because of religious affiliation. This, combined with a persistent and effective antiabortion movement that touted ideas like "life begins at conception" and a Supreme Court that was moving steadily to the political right over the decades, leads us to the case that overturned *Roe*: *Dobbs v. Jackson Women's Health Organization*.

Meanwhile, the antiabortion movement had mobilized substantially. Over the past fifty years, trigger laws were passed by (mostly white male) lawmakers in roughly thirteen states that would automatically ban abortion if *Roe v. Wade* were to fall. Other states sought to define the idea, symbolically at the time, that life begins at conception. Miscarriages, stillbirths, and other types of pregnancy loss were hardly considered or even discussed during the creation of this type of legislation.

For those who supported abortion rights, these laws were widely considered unlikely to ever pass, because *Roe* was a "landmark"—a particularly influential case that changed the interpretation of existing law. While there's no rule that says landmarks cannot be overturned, they were considered untouchable. (Wishful thinking, ye feminists of yore.) Still, it's not like the 2022 decision that overturned the *Roe* opinion fell out of the sky.

By the time the *Dobbs* case was filed in the spring of 2018, there was only one licensed abortion facility in the entire state of Mississippi: Jackson Women's Health Organization. The lawsuit was filed by a doctor there who went to the courts to stop a new Mississippi law that banned abortion after fifteen weeks. The heart of this case is that tricky issue of viability, a moving target in pregnancy. The Supreme Court had previously estimated that viability was somewhere around twenty-four weeks. And remember, in the *Roe v. Wade* opinion, Justice Blackmun decided viability was when the state could start regulating abortion. The problem with this entire line of thinking is that viability is highly variable. A baby may be able to survive outside the womb at twenty-one weeks, but there's no guarantee they'll grow up healthy. Maybe they will. It's also possible a baby can't survive at thirty-five weeks or even forty, depending on what has happened with the pregnancy. It's a case-by-case situation that is too varied to make the basis of a blanket policy, doctors tell us.

When the *Dobbs* case reached the Supreme Court, the ideological makeup of the justices was different; now there was a majority of conservatives who had signaled a willingness to restrict abortion access in their legal careers before they ended up at the nation's highest court. Like before, they *chose* to take up the case because they *wanted* to rule. The court ruled in favor of Mississippi and went even further, overruling both *Casey* from the 1990s and *Roe*.

Ginsburg, as it turns out, was right. Justice Samuel Alito's reasoning was, in part, "The Constitution makes no reference to abortion, and no such right is implicitly protected by any constitutional provision, including the one on which the defenders of *Roe* and *Casey* now chiefly rely—the Due Process Clause of the Fourteenth Amendment. That provision has been held to guarantee some rights that are not mentioned in the Constitution, but any such right must be 'deeply rooted in this Nation's history and tradition' and 'implicit in the concept of ordered liberty.'"

What's a Right Anyway?

At the time the Constitution was written, abortion wasn't considered a right. It would not have been considered much at all. (Oh, by the way, at the time the Constitution was written, women couldn't vote, Black people were enslaved, and people routinely died of simple viruses and infections. Not a super inspiring period on which to base modern law.) It was later in the nation's history, as we've explained, that abortion became "a thing" at all.

With the *Dobbs* decision, the justices returned abortion to the states to regulate. Those trigger laws went into effect, and other Republican-led (majority white male) legislatures moved to quickly restrict abortion in many other states. As of this writing, half the country restricts abortion in some way, and some states have made it illegal in almost all cases. There are a couple of escape hatches where the procedure can be performed to save the "life of the mother," but there's also that growing conceit that a fetus has the same rights as the mother. So the "life of the mother" starts to get a little hazy. Whose life is worth more? We don't know yet, legally. The *Dobbs* decision is still playing out, and we don't have settled answers on the ramifications.

Bans on abortion are connected to all other aspects of reproductive health, which reproductive justice activists have been pointing out for decades. Most women who are currently fertile have never lived in a world without legal abortion, and many assumed it was settled law. (Though there were plenty screaming into the void that this was imminent as soon as Trump was elected. Feel free to scan Reddit for how often they were told to calm down. There goes that hysteria again.) Pregnant people embarking on pregnancy today are doing so in a world not encountered for half a century.

Attorney Molly Duane of the Center for Reproductive Rights filed the first lawsuit involving dangerous post-*Roe* reproductive care for pregnant people on behalf of five Texas women (eight later joined on to the case). The lawsuit alleged that the women along with "countless other pregnant people have been denied necessary and potentially lifesaving obstetrical care because medical professionals throughout the state fear liability under Texas's abortion bans."

"It's not good to micromanage the way that physicians provide healthcare in any sphere," Duane told us. "But particularly in the sphere of pregnancy."

That's because pregnancy is not black and white. One of Duane's clients, Amanda Zurawski, said that she had gotten pregnant after grueling rounds of IVF, only to find that she had a condition called cervical insufficiency (see the language chapter one) that caused her water to break prematurely. She was told by several doctors the baby would not survive but that she'd have to wait until the baby's cardiac activity stopped or until the ethics board at the hospital considered her life "at risk" enough for an abortion. She'd lost all the amniotic fluid—necessary for fetal survival—but it just didn't matter.

"I cannot adequately put into words the trauma and despair that comes with waiting to either lose your own life, your child's, or both. For days, I was locked in this bizarre and avoidable hell. Would Willow's heart stop, or would I deteriorate to the brink of death?" she said during a press conference after the lawsuit was filed.

The answer was that she was going to get sick, really sick; she came down with sepsis, an extreme response to infection that can be fatal. She crashed, and doctors induced her at roughly twenty-two weeks. She delivered the stillborn baby and spent several days in intensive care, then a few more in a less critical unit. It's likely she'll have an even harder time getting pregnant now, if she can at all.

"What I needed was an abortion, a standard medical procedure. An abortion would have prevented the *unnecessary* harm and suffering that I endured," she said in testimony before Congress about post-*Dobbs* America. "Not only the psychological trauma that came with three days of waiting, but the physical harm my body suffered, the extent of which is still being determined."

Judge Jessica Mangrum ruled in the summer of 2023 that physicians should use their "good faith judgment." She wrote they should be able to perform an abortion for a patient who has "a physical medical condition or complication of pregnancy that poses a risk of infection, or otherwise makes continuing a pregnancy unsafe for the pregnant person; a physical medical condition that is exacerbated by pregnancy, cannot be effectively treated during pregnancy, or requires recurrent invasive intervention; and/or a fetal condition where the fetus is unlikely to survive the pregnancy and sustain life after birth." But the state attorney general appealed the decision to the state's highest court, so there's that legal limbo again.

The other plaintiffs had similar life-and-death stories, but it doesn't have to be life-and-death to be a discomfiting and frustrating experience. Jessica H. realized she was pregnant, called Planned Parenthood, and was told she couldn't be seen for any kind of prenatal care until she was eight weeks. This was the start of her problems. She was headed out of Texas to New York anyway for a wedding and made an appointment at the Planned Parenthood there. She waited for hours because the clinic was full and was eventually given a blood test that showed the pregnancy was not progressing. When she was offered medication to manage the likely miscarriage, she did not take it, because she had to go to a wedding and was afraid of heavy bleeding during the weekend. She ended up back at home and called her doctor, who agreed to see her but insisted she get another blood test and come back later—the same blood test she'd just gotten in New York. The tests confirmed that the pregnancy hormones were not where they should be, but she couldn't be prescribed medication for the miscarriage for a full two weeks, until her doctor could be sure it was a miscarriage and not an abortion. Two weeks is not a long time in the scheme of things. She didn't nearly die. But because of the abortion laws, she could not access what had been until very recently routine miscarriage care. And all those extra appointments and tests added up, especially for a twenty-five-year-old.

"It was so expensive," she told us. "It was like I was being physically and financially punished for not having a healthy pregnancy."

Louisville, Kentucky–based Emily M. had sailed through the genetic screens and knew she was having a boy, whom she and her husband planned to name Xavier. But her twenty-week scan revealed that he had only one nonfunctional kidney, no lungs, numerous heart defects, and fluid around his stomach and heart.

"We asked what the survival rate was for these types of anomalies, and she told us it was zero percent. That shocked me. In the medical world, I thought there was always a chance, even if one percent. It was flat out zero because no lungs or kidneys is incompatible with life," she said.

They couldn't bear the thought of him suffocating when he was born, so they decided to terminate.

She had spent the time between the diagnosis and procedure hoping he would die naturally in her womb so she wouldn't have to make the decision at all. "I never thought in a million years that I would be sad about my baby still having a heartbeat," she said.

The Baptist hospital referred her to the university hospital, which recommended a D&E as safer than an induction because the physical anomalies would have led to complications during labor. Insurance would not cover the procedure at the hospital, which would have been up to $10,000 out of pocket, so they had to go to the only clinic in Kentucky, where the cost was closer to $2,000.

Kentucky laws at the time put them in an extreme time crunch, because she was twenty weeks and one day, and the cutoff was twenty weeks six days, and Christmas was approaching, when everything would be closed.

The first step was that doctors had to read a document aloud to her. "They said a lot of the information might not be accurate or relevant to our situation, but they were legally required to read it," she said. The item that threw them for a loop was that they had to waive the right to put the child up for adoption. "That one stopped us short. Did we miss something? How would adoption be an option in this scenario? We had to confirm again there was a zero percent chance he would survive, and it still makes me sick that there is a signed document out there somewhere that says that I signed away my rights for adoption and chose abortion with no other information on there," she said.

That started the clock for the state-mandated twenty-four-hour waiting period before the procedure could start. The next day, there was another legal hurdle, serving no medical purpose. "They were required to do an ultrasound, turn it toward my face, and play an audible recording of the heartbeat," she said. "The staff there were really compassionate. You could tell they were just as pissed. I'd already gone through three extremely traumatic ultrasounds in the last forty-eight hours, so they were really kind to me," Emily M. said. They said she could turn her face away, and they could give her earplugs.

"I may have wanted a last look or to listen to the heartbeat one more time to say goodbye, but it was so infuriating that I was being forced to do that, and this law was written by people whose only intention was to shame people for the decision they were about to make. I didn't look, and I did not listen," she said.

They placed the dilators in her cervix, and she returned the next day for the procedure. She went down to the basement, which had six hospital beds. "The hospital gowns didn't fit anybody, and all our asses were out. It was humiliating. We had no privacy whatsoever. The nurses were prepping each one of us, saying our names, our private health information in front of everybody. It was such a weird experience. And they wheeled us into the OR one by one. Every fifteen minutes, they would wheel the next person," Emily M. said. "And everything I did is now illegal in Kentucky. So many people have nowhere to go."

Right now, the United States is a messy patchwork of disparate legislation, and nobody—doctor, lawyer, or patient—quite knows what's legal. Those caught in the middle are at the whim of their particular jurisdiction, court, or healthcare facility while all this plays out in real time.

CHAPTER TEN

Politicians, Restrictions, and Laws, Oh My!

The Mess When We Mix Politics and Medicine

We are wandering into an uncertain future of reproductive health, marked by wildly disparate state legislation that affects accessibility, consistency, and quality of care. Some states have outright banned abortion, and those restrictions are impacting pregnancy loss treatment. Others are enshrining reproductive rights. Women's health advocates are suing. So are those in the antiabortion movement. In many states, there's no clear policy or answers on what will happen when someone ends a wanted pregnancy, and while lawmakers generally say they don't wish to impact miscarriage care, well, that's not the reality in practice. It's unprecedented, and to many of the pregnant people living through them, these new laws feel like a dangerous experiment.

"When we don't talk about women's health, our leaders and governments make policy about women's bodies every day with precious little accurate information," Chavi Eve Karkowsky wrote in *High Risk: Stories of Pregnancy, Birth, and the Unexpected.* "Much of the time, that policy is made by people who have no experience either inhabiting a body with female reproductive capacity or the knowledge of what it requires to care for one. This leads to bad and often dangerous policy."

Some of these restrictive laws have been heavily influenced by evangelical Christianity, and that includes the doctrine which states that a woman should suffer as a punishment for original sin. If you die in childbirth or because of an abortion, it's God's will. Don't blame them, blame Eve, ye olde original bitch.

To put it more bluntly: "There is a strong contingent of extreme mostly politicians but also judges who either don't see or don't want to see the effect these laws are having on women's health care more generally," Jen Klein, the director of the White House Gender Policy Council under President Joe Biden, told us. "Pregnancy loss of very wanted pregnancies is one example at the heart of the problem."

How Restrictions Play Out

In Oklahoma, for example, there were three overlapping laws that regulated abortion and, by extension, women's reproductive health and pregnancy loss. One was a 1910 law that went back into effect after *Roe* fell, making it a crime punishable by up to five years in prison for anyone to perform an abortion or help a woman get an abortion unless it is to preserve her life.

Another, passed in 2022, was a "heartbeat" act that said a doctor can't perform an abortion if a fetal heartbeat is detected. (But remember—what we commonly call a "heartbeat" is actually an electrical impulse, a pre-heartbeat, so to speak, and in miscarriages, that cardiac activity is often detected even as the body is working to expel the tissue.) The 2022 law included a civil-enforcement mechanism, kind of like a similar law in Texas that allows for citizens to file lawsuits against people who perform or obtain abortions. A judge in 2023 struck down everything but the 1910 law. But honestly, who knows what will stand tomorrow?

The impact on the ground has been chaotic. So chaotic, in fact, that zero hospitals in Oklahoma appeared to be able to articulate clear policies, according to Physicians for Human Rights in a joint report with the Center for Reproductive Rights and the Oklahoma Call for Reproductive Justice. A team of research assistants posed as prospective patients and called hospitals in the state to ask questions related to emergency pregnancy care. The questions included whether hospitals could care for them if they had to end the pregnancy to save their own lives. They weren't asking whether they could get an abortion for any reason.

"The results of this research are alarming," according to the report. The research assistants connected with thirty-four out of thirty-seven hospitals statewide that offer obstetric care, and of those thirty-four, twenty-two were unable to provide information on policies or whether there is support offered to doctors when the decision is made to end a pregnancy to save the life of a patient—which is supposed to be the law.

One hospital told a caller "that a pregnant patient's body would be used as an 'incubator' to carry the baby as long as possible," according to the report.

"At one hospital, a staff member put the simulated caller on hold, and after consulting with a hospital physician, told the caller, 'Nowhere in the state of Oklahoma can you get an abortion for any reason,' even though the bans have exceptions."

Dr. Michele Heisler, one of the leaders of the study, told us that the thing that unnerved her the most was not that hospitals were unwilling to provide care; it was that so few could articulate what it would mean practically for someone who needs emergency care when pregnant.

"The unfortunate thing is I think the legislators just want to make it so confusing. I think they're very happy that this is having a chilling effect on hospitals and clinicians," she told us. "I mean, it's so vague and ambiguous, because they really don't want there to be any clarity. They want it to be vague and ambiguous."

Across the country, thirteen states have banned abortion outright, in most cases with no exceptions for rape or incest. Except for Mississippi, which allows for an abortion in the case of rape but not incest. (What?) These states also have "personhood" laws, which treat the fetus as a person—on equal standing with the mother, with the same legal rights. In Oklahoma, for example, an "unborn child" is defined as a human fetus or embryo "in any stage of fertilization until birth."

Other states have banned abortion after six weeks or twelve weeks or fifteen or twenty weeks, and many of those too have laws that suggest the fetus is a person. In Louisiana, Attorney General Jeff Landry argued the ending of a life-threatening pregnancy isn't an "abortion," nor is the removal of an ectopic pregnancy. But when pressed on how those determinations would be made on the ground, he had no answer. So when a doctor is faced in the moment with the choice of saving the mother or the baby, and the fetus is legally considered a person too, whose life takes precedence? Who is more worth saving? And is the doctor going to be charged with a crime for making the wrong decision?

In March 2023 in Texas, a man sued three women under a wrongful death statute, saying they helped his ex-wife end her pregnancy. He was represented by the former Texas solicitor general who wrote the abortion ban. The women countersued and raised some troubling counterclaims (beyond the obvious), including that he admitted in a police report that he went through his wife's phone and then used the text messages as the frame of his lawsuit against the women.

Such concerns over privacy invasion are growing. In Nebraska, for example, prosecutors used Facebook messages between a mom and her daughter that discussed an effort by the mother to help her daughter procure abortion medication. The teenager was past the twenty-week mark where it becomes illegal in the state, and the two were accused of burning and burying the remains. They were charged with crimes including concealing a death and mishandling human remains; the daughter, who was then seventeen, was initially charged as an adult. Facebook, now called Meta, turned over the messages to law enforcement after it was served a warrant. The girl was sentenced to ninety days in jail following a plea agreement. Her mother got two years in prison.

Most of the laws in place today are either trigger bans or passed through legislatures. But when voters are given the choice, they reject harsh abortion rules. In 2022, voters rejected ballot measures in Kansas and Kentucky that would have resulted in stricter restrictions. Voters approved ballot measures to establish the right in California, Michigan, Ohio, and Vermont. And in Montana, they rejected a measure that was called the "Born-Alive Infant Protection Act." The law would have required medical care to be provided to babies born alive after induction, C-section, or those same methods for an abortion.

And voters tend to reject the personhood idea too, when it is presented to them instead of passed by legislators. Personhood measures attempted over the years in Colorado, North Dakota, and Mississippi failed. In Mississippi, a state constitutional amendment that would have declared fertilized eggs to be people was rejected by 58 percent of voters. The effort against it was driven by a woman who needed fertility treatments and saw the law as a threat to that type of treatment as well as miscarriage care.

But in Alabama in early 2024, the state's Supreme Court ruled that frozen embryos were children, following a legal battle over whether couples could pursue a wrongful death lawsuit against a Mobile fertility clinic over an incident in 2020 where frozen embryos were destroyed. IVF remains a political football in the state as of this writing.

Support for legal abortion has risen since the *Dobbs* decision.

A record high 69 percent of Americans think first-trimester abortions should be legal, and a near-record high 34 percent said abortion should be legal in all cases.

Whether or not someone wants to have the abortion is almost beside the point in many of these cases, and the collateral effects for people who didn't want to end their pregnancies—or for healthcare in general—are massive. Many of the abortion clinics also provided low-cost healthcare and birth control to areas where it wasn't readily available, and many of those clinics have closed, leaving not only "abortion deserts" but healthcare deserts.

In one example, the only abortion provider in West Virginia, the Women's Health Center, dropped its lawsuit against the state's ban. Lawsuits, by the way, can be costly even if filed by nonprofit legal groups. The group said in a court filing that it wouldn't be able to provide care any longer because it didn't have physicians available. Meanwhile, one of the doctors is moving to a clinic just over the state border in Maryland where abortion is legal.

"There is a tremendous overlap between states where they aren't only interested in going after abortion rights and policies that would help women and families or contraception. They're related," Klein, the White House adviser, told us.

It should not be a surprise that the states with the most extreme abortion-related bans are also the states where maternal health is the direst. According to the CDC, Arkansas's maternal mortality rate is 43.5 per 100,000 births, followed closely by Mississippi at 43, then Alabama, Tennessee, Louisiana, Kentucky, and Georgia. Those states also have among the strictest abortion restrictions in the nation. (And their infant mortality rates are higher too, compared with the rest of the country.) So it's not like these states are doing a great job caring for pregnant people and their newborns.

A University of Colorado at Boulder study has estimated that it's going to get even worse following the end of federal abortion protections, simply because pregnancy is more fatal than abortion. The study found mortality would increase overall by 24 percent in the years after the *Dobbs* decision—which is 14 percent higher than initially projected.

Any major challenges to these abortion laws are not likely to make it to the Supreme Court or at least would not change the opinion of this court, because the justices have already made their views quite clear. Federal laws take precedence over any state laws, so the only real way to ensure blanket protections for women's reproductive health or to create a set of standards that address maternal mortality, maternal morbidity, stillbirth, ectopic pregnancy, or miscarriages would be through federal law. But the political divide in Congress has widened into the Grand Canyon over the past ten years, and there would need to be some bipartisan support for that type of law. (In related news, the Supreme Court's record disapproval rating stands at 59 percent; Congress has a 78 percent disapproval rating.)

Politics as Usual

Erica Bailey's stillbirth experience changed her politics. She grew up conservative Baptist in West Virginia and now lives in Missouri, which had one of the first trigger bans after *Roe* fell in 2022. "When my baby died, I became a magnet for other's stories of loss. People from all facets of my life were coming out of the woodwork to comfort me with their own tragedies—miscarriages, stillbirths, and infant deaths. I immersed myself in support groups and heard all these stories of loss. I gained so much empathy. I feel horrible that's what it took, but it completely changed me. It broke my heart and lit this rage in me. Anyone who shits on loss parents, I'm going to fight you. I'm going to stand up for anyone who has to go through this hell and have barriers to access the healthcare they need and deserve."

She's not alone. Women in reliably conservative states have rejected efforts to restrict abortion. A 2022 Pew Research Center poll found that 66 percent of all women say abortion should be legal in most or all cases. That same poll found 36 percent of Republican women disapproved of the Supreme Court's ruling.

The decision has inspired some women to run for office, like Allie Phillips in Tennessee, who was pregnant in 2022 and discovered her daughter, Miley Rose, had a fatal abnormality. She traveled to New York because the procedure to end the pregnancy was illegal in Tennessee.

Generally speaking, Democrats want to codify abortion protections and Republicans want to restrict them, though there are some exceptions on either side. But wanting to do something is different from being able to do it or choosing to spend the political capital to do it, especially in Washington.

Roe was overturned with a Democrat in the White House and Democrats in control of Congress. Democrats did try to pass a federal law around women's reproductive health in the weeks after a draft of the *Dobbs* opinion leaked from somewhere inside the majority conservative Supreme Court, but they failed.

Other pieces of legislation focusing on the health and well-being of women and babies have been pending in Congress for years, proposed laws that don't even touch on abortion, stymied still by the nationwide debate.

One such act, the stillbirth prevention legislation called the SHINE for Autumn Act, focuses on three main issues: enhanced stillbirth data collection, research, and education, including an awareness campaign not dissimilar to those that helped reduce SIDS deaths. The legislation was named for Debbie Haine Vijayvergiya's baby Autumn Joy, who was stillborn in 2011. She's campaigned for stillbirth awareness for the last twelve years. And she's had some statewide success; in 2014, her home state of New Jersey passed a law that required the state to establish policies and procedures for the sensitive management of each stillbirth as well as establish protocols for evaluating fetal deaths to ensure accurate and complete data is sent to the state.

Two Democratic representatives, Lauren Underwood from Illinois and Alma Adams of North Carolina, introduced the Black Maternal Health Momnibus Act, twice. There are thirteen bills in the act that, taken together, attempt to address the maternal mortality and morbidity crises in the United States for Black women. The bills do things like extend the federal Special

Supplemental Nutrition Program for Women, Infants, and Children eligibility in postpartum and breastfeeding periods, fund community-based organizations that work to improve maternal health, and improve data collection to better understand maternal health in the United States and inform solutions to address it. Some parts of the legislation have been adopted, but the act hasn't passed.

The Democratic Biden administration was doing what it could to manage the fallout from *Dobbs* using a 1986 law already on the books, called the Emergency Medical Treatment and Labor Act (EMTALA), that is meant to prevent hospitals from refusing to treat patients who need emergency care. The U.S. Department of Health and Human Services sent out guidance nationwide shortly after *Roe* fell specifically to remind healthcare providers in pregnancy-related emergencies to stabilize the condition of the mother—including performing an abortion or inducing labor if necessary.

"An emergency condition may include a condition that is likely or certain to become emergent without stabilizing treatment. Emergency medical conditions involving pregnant patients may include, but are not limited to, ectopic pregnancy, complications of pregnancy loss, or emergent hypertensive disorders, such as preeclampsia with severe features," the guidance stated. And the federal law trumps the state laws on this.

This guidance is meant to give cover to doctors and hospitals where abortion is largely illegal to treat patients who need the care. The Justice Department sued Idaho in 2022 over its abortion law, which allowed for the arrest and prosecution of medical providers just by showing abortion had been performed, regardless of the circumstances around it. The doctors can defend against this only if the procedure was necessary to prevent the *death* of the pregnant woman—not if it merely prevented serious harm. And they were supposed to wait until the woman was near death, even if the patient could face major permanent injury as a result. This would be like if you walked into an emergency room at the start of a heart attack, and doctors couldn't intervene until right before your heart finally stopped beating. The lawsuit included testimonials from perplexed and concerned Idaho doctors. A U.S. District Court judge found that the doctors should comply with federal law, not the state law, but left the other parts of the ban in effect. Then, Idaho state officials appealed, and, as of this writing, it's headed to the Supreme Court where we expect many of these challenges will end up.

Attorney General Merrick Garland made clear the lawsuit was meant to be a signal to other states looking to put physicians in the same predicament. "We will use every tool at our disposal to ensure that pregnant women get the emergency medical treatment to which they are entitled under federal law," he said in a statement following the judge's ruling. "And we will closely scrutinize state abortion laws to ensure that they comply with federal law."

In Texas, state law says abortion is illegal except to deal with a "life-threatening physical condition," and the provider must also offer the "best opportunity for the unborn child to survive" except if it increases the risk to the mother. Antiabortion doctors there sued the federal government over the EMTALA law, suggesting that it was forcing them to provide abortions. A Texas U.S. District Court judge agreed with the antiabortion doctors, allowing federal law to override state law only when there is a conflict between the survival of the mother and the "unborn children."

One year after the fall of *Roe*, more than twenty-five million women ages fifteen to forty-four—or roughly two in five—are living in states where abortion access has been limited since the Supreme Court decision. More than 5.5 million are living in states where there are restrictions pending in the courts. And bans on abortion after twelve weeks into pregnancy are on the books in nearly every state in the southeast. Pregnant people living in these states will inevitably suffer from these laws, because the lines are so very blurry when you get into individual cases. Who knows what it's going to look like a year from now?

It's also becoming harder to tell from the outside whether someone's had a miscarriage or an abortion, because medication abortion at home is more common. This means that in many cases, enforcing regulations is going to rely on investigating pregnancy loss.

One such method is the "floating lung test," which is being used in some places to determine whether a woman suffered a stillbirth or "murdered the baby." It's as medieval as it sounds: medical examiners perform an autopsy and submerge the baby's lungs in water. The idea is if they float, it's a crime, the pseudoscience reasoning being that it indicates there is air in the lungs, so the baby must have been born alive. Except the test is deeply flawed.

Dr. Gregory Davis, a forensic pathologist at the University of Kentucky College of Medicine and a consultant to the office of the medical examiner in Kentucky, told ProPublica that the test was "an outrageous breach of science." There are many different ways that air can enter the lungs of a stillborn, he said. "There's no way you can determine live birth versus stillbirth with this test."

Restrictive laws are having a compounding effect on reproductive healthcare. Doctors and other healthcare professionals in states where abortion is restricted are already relocating or not pursuing residencies or jobs in those states. "Public health experts predict that in a few years, patients in abortion prohibited states, where the ranks of obstetricians are already shrinking, will experience even greater barriers to reproductive health care," wrote Jan Hoffman in the *New York Times*. This problem too may lead to worse care in those states because there will be fewer doctors willing to practice there. And that doesn't just extend to obstetrics—the slight majority of medical school graduates are female and ending their training in their early thirties, prime baby-making time. Those oncologists, pulmonologists, and cardiologists may not want to themselves be patients in abortion-restricted states.

Texas, for example, already has one of the most significant physician shortages in the country, which is expected to increase by more than 50 percent over the next decade. The shortage of registered nurses, around thirty thousand, is expected to double over the same period.

Another possible side effect of these laws? Infant deaths have risen in Texas since the state banned abortion. In 2022, about twenty-two hundred infants died in Texas, 11.5 percent more than in 2021. This is attributed in part to an increase in overall births since the ban. But the spike in infant deaths caused by genetic and birth defects was 21.6 percent, suggesting "that many Texas patients who would have otherwise terminated pregnancies with fatal defects are being forced to carry them to term."

Mississippi isn't much better, with more than half the state considered a maternity care desert—with no hospitals providing obstetric care, no ob-gyns, no midwives. Idaho has a near-total ban, with exceptions for the mother's life, rape, or incest, and those require a police report. They also have an abortion trafficking ban, which prohibits taking minors to other states for abortion care. Not likely a coincidence, Idaho is also the only state in the country to stop tracking maternal mortality rates. Activists say it's because they don't want anyone to know how deadly these laws may be in practice.

So what we're seeing these days are states with abortion restrictions have less access to (and worse overall) medical care, leaving pregnant people who can't afford to move or travel at the mercy of bad outcomes. And some of those outcomes end up criminalized.

CHAPTER ELEVEN

When Pregnancy Loss Is a Crime

The Legal Peril around the Loss of a Baby

On January 4, 2020, just a few months before a global pandemic burst into the world, nineteen-year-old Brittney Poolaw, a member of the Comanche Nation, was roughly seventeen weeks pregnant when she miscarried in the bathroom of an apartment in Lawton, Oklahoma. She called the father of the baby first, and he told her to call 911. When the EMTs arrived, she was sitting on the toilet, quietly, solemnly, bleeding. The baby was in the toilet bowl. He had not been born alive, and the umbilical cord was still attached. Poolaw's condition was worsening, and she was taken to the emergency room at Comanche County Memorial, where she began to hemorrhage. The doctor treating her said she had a partial placental abruption, where the placenta comes undone inside the uterus prematurely. She had an infection and was losing a lot of blood. She was distressed and in pain.

The remains of the baby were also brought to the hospital. In Oklahoma, any miscarriage after twelve weeks must be reported to the state department of health, and Oklahoma issues a death certificate. And at Comanche County Hospital, any pregnancy loss over twelve weeks is also reported to the medical examiner, which investigates suspicious death. Other states, like California, treat fetal deaths at or after twenty weeks as "unattended deaths" that require a coroner to investigate, though there is a movement to change that after complaints that it suggests the mother did something to cause the death of her baby.

In Poolaw's case, an autopsy and further testing were ordered. The doctors and nurses at the hospital were growing suspicious because Poolaw admitted that she'd used drugs. In Oklahoma—as in many other states—people can be charged with child neglect for using illegal drugs while pregnant. But prosecutors were planning a more serious case.

About half of miscarriages before twelve weeks occur because the embryo isn't developing properly, usually because of a chromosomal abnormality. According to the American College of Obstetricians and Gynecologists, "the reasons for most still-births are unknown." Contributing factors include a birth defect or genetic disorder, infections in the pregnant person, complications of labor, umbilical cord issues or placenta problems, and problems with the health of the birthing parent. A large portion of fetal deaths are simply listed as "unexplained." There are some studies linking problems to drug use; a 2014 study on methamphetamine use in particular showed the drug, the use of which has increased dramatically over the past few decades, "was found to be associated with specific patterns of increased maternal and fetal morbidity and death." Compared with nonusers, pregnant women who used meth had increased hypertensive diseases, gestational hypertension, severe preeclampsia, and eclampsia.

Drug Use and Pregnancy Loss

There are few studies that identify a direct link between substance abuse and stillbirth, according to a review of medical studies done in 2018 by researchers at the University of Hawaii. Restricted fetal growth was the most common complication in all types of substance abuse, they found.

Dr. Claire Coles, a professor of psychiatry and behavioral sciences and director of the Maternal Substance Abuse and Child Development program at Emory University in Georgia, has, for more than forty years, studied teratogens, which are substances that cross the placental barrier and interfere with normal fetal development and may cause problems in utero and out. Alcohol is one example; drugs are another, including legal medication. Her program is the data mother ship on what environmental or ingested substances travel from mother to baby. She has a huge body of work, including a recent publication titled "Fifty Years of Research on Prenatal Substances: Lessons Learned for the Opioid Epidemic."

"It's interesting," she told us. "When we started with alcohol in 1980, nobody was interested in hearing about this. People have always been sort of aware there are issues there, but they mostly ignored it. There was this (wrong) idea that the placenta would protect the baby from whatever. It was a solid barrier."

But it turns out it's not much of a barrier after all, and most things get into the bloodstream, including drugs (legal and illegal), alcohol, poisons like mercury and lead, and pollutants. But according to Coles, it isn't that teratogen automatically equals infant death. The reality is far more complex, as are the ideas on how to deal with teratogens and perceived teratogens.

"There are lots of different strings that get involved in this," she told us. "How we regard women and pregnancy and all that. If you're using cocaine, anything wrong with a child must be your fault. Alcohol is more complicated because it's legal and accepted."

Coles studied women who were roughly thirty-four weeks pregnant and above and who were serious crack cocaine users. She followed 110 children for more than twenty years. She compared the kids who were exposed to the drug in utero with those who grew up as their neighbors and found very little difference.

This is not to say that she—or we for that matter— condone drug use during pregnancy. Children born addicted to substances go through withdrawal and can have lifelong complications, physically, mentally, and emotionally. The question is whether there's a scientific basis to charge someone with a crime or whether it's moral panic on the part of the lawmakers. And there's no easy way to answer it.

"I think the fear of these things is used to punish women," Coles said. "Get the law out of it. That is what I believe. On the other hand, I run a clinic in which we see children alcohol- and drug-exposed. The stories we hear would take the paint off the walls. Yes, there are people who shouldn't be having children."

"But it's a very complex and difficult issue," she went on. "One woman was telling me she was drinking three six-packs a day. What she needed was a good treatment program. I understand the frustration of people who pass laws. They've seen the negative consequences of addiction. I just can't advocate for a governmental system in which the response is to punish. It solves no problems."

The lines are much blurrier when it comes to pregnancy and the environmental causes of miscarriage and loss.

In Poolaw's case, the fetal autopsy showed the liver and intestines were outside the fetus's body. It was possibly a condition called gastroschisis where a hole in the abdominal wall near the belly button causes the organs to grow outside, but it wasn't entirely clear. No genetic testing was done. A toxicology screen and blood work ordered for both her and the baby uncovered traces of methamphetamine in her system and in the baby's liver and brain.

The underlying premise in Oklahoma is that when someone miscarries after twelve weeks, it might have been nefarious, like a person doing something to contribute to the end of their pregnancy, and that was even before abortion was formally banned in the state once *Roe* fell. Oklahoma is one of thirty-seven states (plus the federal government) that have laws allowing for homicide charges for causing the loss of a pregnancy. (In 1986, there were zero laws like this.) The laws were initially meant to punish someone if a pregnant woman is hurt or killed and the baby she's carrying is also harmed or perishes as a result. But that isn't how they have been used in practice.

At first, these types of charges were mostly levied against Black women, and that was no coincidence. Guidelines to qualify for welfare were based on stereotypes about "welfare queens" during the Reagan era and persisted until the 1990s, which led to policies that included a cap to discourage those receiving federal aid from having more children. Loretta Ross and Rickie Solinger wrote in *Reproductive Justice* that these politics portrayed "all single mothers as persons of color and all persons of color as dependent on public assistance." (Most women on welfare are not Black, but Black women are more likely to receive funds from Aid to Dependent Children.) This era was all about crack, not methamphetamine or opioids, and the stereotypes of crack babies and/or crack mothers denigrated women of color as being unfit. Between 1986 and 1998, thirty-five states passed laws dealing with prenatal narcotic exposure. Jennifer Johnson, the first woman convicted of a crime after giving birth to a baby who tested positive for drugs, had sought treatment for her addiction while pregnant and been turned away. By 1990, the ACLU estimated that 70 percent of the prosecutions for prenatal abuse were women of color.

Seeking to prosecute a woman for harming her baby is viewed

as moral justice. But that standard isn't equally applied when a pregnant woman is killed. Actually, *homicide* is the number one cause of death in the United States for pregnant women and those who have recently given birth, according to researchers from the Harvard T. H. Chan School of Public Health. Even with the nation's abysmal maternal mortality rate, a pregnant woman is still more likely to be a victim of homicide than to die from obstetric causes, researchers found in 2022. Those killings are a mix of gun deaths and domestic violence. The United States has a higher rate of intimate partner violence than other comparable nations, and that violence is often fatal, they found. Homicides of pregnant women grew during the pandemic too.

Still, the researchers noted that "few perpetrators of intimate partner violence are ever convicted, and many loopholes allowing access to firearms remain." And—shocker—there's no good data out there to identify risk factors. "Recent studies have been limited by large amounts of missing data on the pregnancy status of women who have been killed. Details on relationships and patterns of abuse leading to homicide charges during pregnancy and in the postpartum period are also minimal," they wrote.

Many of these state homicide laws are also used to charge pregnant women with a crime when the authorities believe she's done something to harm the baby, fetus, embryo, or fertilized egg. This means she's probably more likely to be *convicted* of homicide than *protected* from being the victim of one. Nationwide, pregnant women who use certain drugs have been jailed for this, but so have women who have refused C-sections or medical advice, delivered their children without medical supervision at home, been suicidal, or suffered accidental falls. They are charged with crimes like manslaughter, endangerment, criminal recklessness, and neglect. As lawmakers in some states look to remove provisions in abortion law that protected pregnant people from criminalization, they don't have to look very far in how to prosecute.

Looking to Prosecute

In 2013, in the *Journal of Health Politics, Policy and Law*, attorney Lynn Paltrow and sociologist Jeanne Flavin documented 413 cases of arrests and detentions of women between 1973 and 2005 where being pregnant was a critical part of the crime, though Paltrow has said it's likely a "very serious undercount" of what's really happening. The organization Paltrow started, National Advocates for Pregnant Women (now called Pregnancy Justice), advocates for and helps arrange legal representation for pregnant people charged with crimes. The organization has also filed support briefs in federal cases involving reproductive health at the Supreme Court. In a new follow-up to their study, they found 1,396 cases nationwide from 2006 to 2022—the number has more than doubled in half the time, and it's also likely an undercount. Going forward, the nonprofit is going to try to track every arrest in real time, a massive undertaking considering how many women are being charged criminally and how many more stand to be following the end of *Roe* protections.

In Oklahoma alone, forty-five women were charged with pregnancy-related crimes from 2017 through 2021, almost entirely for drug use, according to the Frontier, a nonprofit Oklahoma news site. But only eighteen of them received drug treatment as part of pretrial or an order to complete it, the news site found. So it certainly doesn't appear the cases are being set up as a deterrent to stop other women from using drugs or that there's a substantial effort to help end the addiction.

In 2017, a woman named Adora was charged with murder after she delivered a stillborn baby at Adventist Health Hanford in California. The baby tested positive for methamphetamine, and a doctor told police he thought the drug caused the death. She pleaded guilty to a charge of "voluntary manslaughter of a fetus"—a charge that doesn't actually exist in California law—and was sentenced to eleven years in prison. Her conviction was overturned in 2022.

In 2019 in Pleasant Grove, Alabama, a woman called Marshae was charged with manslaughter. She was five months pregnant at the time and was accused of starting a physical fight with another woman, who then pulled a gun and shot Marshae in the abdomen, killing the baby. Alabama's laws grant a fetus the same legal rights as a full-grown human. The prosecutor dropped the charges after a huge outpouring of criticism over the case.

Also in Alabama, Faith Victoria, twenty, was charged with chemical endangerment of a child, a homicide. She'd delivered a stillborn baby at roughly thirty-eight weeks, nearly full-term, at Madison Hospital. The sheriff's office said she'd continued to use methamphetamine throughout her pregnancy and that an autopsy had been performed, though cause of death was not clear.

"Nobody should fear arrest or prosecution or the loss of any rights because of being pregnant," Paltrow, who has since retired, told us. "But they ought to, because we are entering a new world order."

In 1999, Regina McKnight was the first woman in the United States to be prosecuted and convicted for having a still-born, according to *Policing the Womb: Invisible Women and the Criminalization of Motherhood*, by legal scholar Michele Goodwin, an expert on reproductive justice. The book documents the rise of these types of prosecutions and details the questionable reasons for them. McKnight was twenty-two, poor, Black, and homeless in South Carolina. She suffered depression and anxiety after the death of her mom and began to use cocaine. Her medical records were turned over to police, who said the death must have been caused by drugs, Goodwin reported.

The prosecutor, Greg Hembree, said he wanted to make her an example. "If you kill a child by showing extreme indifference to human life then you're guilty of homicide by child abuse, just like the guy who's guilty of murder," he said at the time.

Goodwin wrote that in McKnight's case, the state had built and rested its prosecution on the fact that she birthed a dead baby. The prosecutor claimed that he did not care whether the drugs she ingested were illegal or not: "'if we determine you are medically responsible for a child's demise, we will file (homicide) charges.'"

McKnight's conviction was eventually overturned in 2008 by the South Carolina Supreme Court, in part because of faulty scientific evidence presented at the trial, but by then, she'd already served a decade in prison.

Dana Sussman of Pregnancy Justice said the organization has found the trend has shifted in the past few years: now more white women are being arrested, mostly for drug use. Disproportionately, women of color are still targeted at a higher rate even as the number of white women arrested has increased.

"It's almost like white women are not embodying the idealized version of white motherhood, and I think it's in part because of the trends in moral panic around drug use and meth and opioid usage," Sussman told us.

In her book, Goodwin takes readers through multiple cases where women were charged with crimes while pregnant and where the law seems to overreach dramatically. In one, a Florida woman in 2010 was confined to bed rest at only twenty-five weeks—something that is ordered when a pregnancy is in jeopardy—and the hospital staff appealed to the court to keep her hospitalized over her objections. The court stated, Goodwin wrote, "that as between a parent and child, the ultimate welfare of the child is the controlling factor."

Two dozen states do not allow life support to be removed from a pregnant woman. In Texas, thirty-three-year-old Marlise Munoz collapsed in 2013 when she was fourteen weeks into her pregnancy from a blood clot that entered her lungs. She was declared brain dead, but hospital officials refused to remove life support because of the law. "For the most part, Americans may take end-of-life decision-making for granted. Most people assume that their medical directives carry substantive weight in the law," Goodwin wrote. The problem is that most of us don't know these kinds of laws even exist.

Even grief is policed. Colorado-based Rachael M. told us she delivered her baby at thirty-three weeks in August 2021. She thought she'd have a preemie, but instead her daughter died after three days because of a lack of oxygen in utero. On her baby Emsley's due date, about seven weeks after she was born, Rachael had a panic attack. Her husband suggested they go see her therapist. "It was kind of an emergency appointment because I was really hysterical and crying and trying to catch my breath," she told us. She had a history with anxiety, which was exacerbated by grief.

But when they arrived, the therapist, who used to be a psychiatrist in the psych ward at a nearby hospital, told them to go there.

"We were shocked," Rachael said. "What do you mean? I'm not going to hurt myself. This is just a very traumatic day. I was in shock for the first six weeks, and now on the due date, it's hitting me all at once."

Rachael and her husband felt they had no choice and didn't want it to escalate further, so they drove to the hospital while the therapist followed them. Rachael's husband is a firefighter who sees a lot of mental health emergencies, and he couldn't believe what was happening. He thought his wife needed rest and maybe anxiety medication.

"Before I knew it, they stripped me, took my phone and my things, and said you're going to downtown Aurora for a few days. My husband was beside himself. He said it felt like I was being kidnapped. They walked me out and put me in a caged van."

They drove her to a facility near Denver. "All I could think was, where am I? This doesn't feel like a safe place. I don't belong here. I am begging them to let me go, and they show me to a little room and say this is where you're going to be. I spent two days on my knees crying, begging to be let go, trying to tell them my story."

Meanwhile, her husband was working with their families and lawyers to get her out. She continued to plead her case, but everyone said she had to speak to the head doctor.

On Monday morning, the doctor came in, and he said, "You're a grieving mother. You have no place being here. I'm going to get you out." He said, "You want a child. Focus on that. Heal your grief. This is not where you belong."

Even still, she couldn't actually be discharged until the following day, a Tuesday—almost the entirety of the five-day hold.

Grief looks weird. Some of the people we spoke to were quiet about what happened, and it came out in other ways, like needing to sleep or feeling depressed or watching a lot of dumb reruns. For others, the grief was a slow burn, a low-level anxiety that never went away. Others had panic attacks. Some cried. Others didn't. It's just impossible to paint a composite photo of grief. But unless they fit into a specific category—sad but not too sad, talking about it but not too much or for too long—eyebrows get raised.

During Brittney Poolaw's trial in Oklahoma, she cried often, her face obscured by a black mask because of pandemic precautions. Poolaw's Comanche Nation makes its own laws, but the miscarriage she suffered was on state grounds. According to trial testimony, Poolaw told the nurse at the hospital that she'd known she was pregnant since October. She didn't know if she wanted to have a baby. But she didn't know how or where to get an abortion, so she did nothing. No prenatal care, no doctor's visits. And she kept using methamphetamine, by her own account, telling the hospital nurse that "she uses it whenever she was mad, she would use it to forget. When she didn't want to think about things, that's when she would use it."

She was arrested and charged with manslaughter, and because she couldn't afford the $20,000 bond, she was in jail for a year and a half awaiting trial. The probable cause of death for the baby was "intrauterine fetal demise," which is a catchall term that means there isn't one clear reason. The medical examiner, Leonardo Roquero, testified that he found the conditions that impacted the death to be "congenital abnormality—that is referred to the evisceration or the defect in the abdomen in which the liver and the intestines were out," he told jurors.

The other findings were the infection of the placenta, partial abruption, and funisitis—an infection of the umbilical cord. Roquero said the toxicology report also revealed methamphetamine in the baby's liver and brain and said that the presence of meth "in a baby or in a stillbirth or the presence of methamphetamine during prenatal period and in the presence of the baby increases the rate of stillbirth of a newborn."

On cross-examination by Poolaw's public defender, Roquero said that the conditions he listed, minus the meth use, would have contributed to the likely cause of death.

"And your report lists all of those conditions, but can you say with certainty that it was the methamphetamine that caused all of those other conditions?"

"No," Roquero said.

During Assistant District Attorney Christine Galbraith's closing argument in the brief trial, she chronicled a life in distress. Poolaw was poor. In a lousy relationship. She'd already had one baby. She went to a Native American hospital to try to get care but didn't have ID and was turned away. She turned to drugs to forget. She sounds like someone who needed help.

"We have a situation here where a defendant put her wants over the needs of baby boy Poolaw. She chose meth over his health," she said to jurors. And later: "The defendant had one job; her job was to keep baby boy Poolaw alive."

The trial lasted one day. Poolaw's attorney only cross-examined a few witnesses. He gave no opening statement nor closing argument. He called no witnesses of his own.

Galbraith, the prosecutor, told the jury that they didn't need to believe meth was the cause of death. They just needed to believe it was at least a contributing factor to convict her. Jurors returned a guilty verdict in less than three hours, and she was sentenced to four years in prison.

Pregnancy Justice worked to get Poolaw a different appeals attorney, who filed an intention to appeal the verdict. Dana

Sussman thinks the verdict could have been overturned and sent back for a new trial, but Poolaw was told there was no guarantee she'd be acquitted in a second trial, and that's true. Because she'd been in jail since her arrest, she was nearly done with her time. She decided to drop her appeal and finish out her sentence.

It was better than taking her chances again with the Oklahoma legal system.

CHAPTER TWELVE

Life and Death Certificates

How a Piece of Paper Came to Define Loss

When Mike Pence was governor of Indiana, shortly before he became the vice president, he signed HB1337 into law. Among other things, it decreed that "a miscarried or aborted fetus must be interred or cremated."

It included specifics on how a hospital or clinic could confirm the burial had happened. The process could be done anonymously, and the parents didn't necessarily have to name the miscarried or aborted fetus. (How generous.) A lawsuit wound its way through appeals before reaching the Supreme Court in 2016, which rejected most of the law but kept the part about the disposal of remains. The court declined to take a fresh look at the case in May 2023 after a second lawsuit was filed, so the law was left on the books.

The idea was to force people who had abortions into thinking about the consequences, and it hewed closely to the notion—popular among some lawmakers in Indiana and other conservative-leaning state legislatures—that people who had abortions and those who provided abortions should pay or at least feel guilty. "Unborn babies are more than medical waste," Indiana attorney general Todd Rokita said in 2022. "They are human beings who deserve the dignity of cremation or burial."

That's great, Indiana. We're happy for you. We assume, since you care so much about the dignity of remains, that you're going to get behind stillbirth awareness campaigns or scientific study to determine what causes late-term miscarriages? Maybe you'll allow for bereavement leave from work for people grieving a pregnancy loss? Help them pay for a memorial? Offer state-funded support groups for the postpartum depression that may follow? Maybe work miscarriage awareness into sex education classes? Oh wait. Indiana doesn't require sex education in classrooms. It does, however, mandate that schools choosing to teach sex ed emphasize abstinence. Maybe we won't hold our breath.

The laws focus on the "humane and dignified disposal of human remains." They were designed in part to punish those who have abortions in a state that restricts them, but they also spill over into pregnancy loss.

"These laws also send the unmistakable message that someone who has had an abortion or miscarriage is responsible for the death of a person," wrote the attorneys in the failed lawsuit challenging the Indiana law. "As a result, they have caused many abortion and miscarriage patients…to experience shame, stigma, anguish, and anger."

The attorneys also argued that the laws "coerce pregnant

people who obtain abortion and miscarriage management care to engage in rituals that are associated with the death of a person." We have a cultural script for what to do when someone dies, but the state doesn't mandate how we handle the funeral. And when we're dealing with a liminal state of pregnancy and loss, everything gets more complicated. Because you're not burying or cremating a fully grown human. In some cases, remains don't resemble a baby at all. It's impossible to know how you are going to feel in that moment when the situation happens to you. And now, in Indiana anyway, you must do what the government demands you do.

In a post about her research on the blog *Nursing Clio, Lost* author Shannon Withycombe wrote, "It is dangerous to think that miscarriage is now somehow imbued with certain natural and inalienable meanings as a death, a tragedy, and something gone wrong."

The Indiana law raises an interesting question: What happens when you miscarry at home? Many people we spoke to said they passed tissue in the toilet. Do people have to dig it out, seal it in a baggie and send it to the hospital for burial? Let's face it, the usual instinct is to flush. It doesn't mean that you're not sad. It just means you don't know what the hell to do. Couldn't it compound the grief and trauma to have to then take those remains to be buried? Are you going to get arrested if you flush the toilet?

In Indiana, the law states that pregnant women can use the healthcare facility's final "method of disposition," but they're responsible for the costs if they choose their own location. The law also requires a certificate of stillbirth for non-live births at twenty weeks gestation or later. If someone delivers or miscarries at a hospital, there are methods to dispose of remains already in place, usually mass graves.

Burial Bingo

Cleveland-based Brittany had a miscarriage at roughly ten weeks. She went in for a D&C procedure and checked the box for burial. She knew it would be in a mass plot, knew the name of the cemetery, and asked numerous times to be notified when the remains would be moved. When she and her husband went to visit, they searched the infant section but never found it. The entire process seemed to drag out her sadness over the miscarriage, and she wondered whether there could have been a more sensitive process.

State laws regarding fetal remains differ. Most hospitals offer to take care of the remains free of charge, which varies by hospital and often by religious affiliation of the hospital. Some incinerate the remains with medical waste like tumors or kidney stones, while others opt for unmarked mass burials at cemeteries, and sometimes parents can find out a general area if they wish to visit. (Though Brittany's experience shows that isn't always the case.).

Catholic and other Christian cemeteries often have miscarriage and infant areas that are free or cheaper than the main areas of the cemetery. Jewish law does not traditionally allow parents of a baby that did not live for more than thirty days to attend the funeral or know where the child is buried, but that has changed among reform rabbis who now allow it for the parents to find closure.

Most of the clinics where the parents we talked to terminated for medical reasons offered a lower cost option for cremains, which were sent to their home a week or two after the procedure.

Those who opt to bury or cremate on their own pay a funeral home. Private burials include outlays for the funeral, burial plot, casket, and marker, and the median cost for a funeral and burial was $7,848 in 2021. Cremation is usually thousands of dollars cheaper. Some funeral homes will waive or reduce the fee for a cremation or funeral for a miscarriage or stillborn, and nonprofits like the Tears Foundation can help offset the costs, but none of this is guaranteed and puts the onus onto a bereaved family. Many just can't afford a burial or private cremation and have to use the free hospital service. Among the dozens of people we spoke to, the most important element in how to handle these decisions was choice—that they had an option to get remains or not, had the option to have a service or not. But the prohibitive costs and proscriptive laws sometimes mean there's no choice at all.

The registrar of vital records in each state issues a "certificate of fetal death" or some type of legal record when a stillbirth happens. The National Center for Health Statistics tracks fetal deaths after twenty weeks, but it was only in 2018 that every state adopted a standardized report on deaths, which would make it easier to count them and derive any data on causes. Miscarriages are not counted in any tally. Abortions are.

It's not like any of this is terribly new. It's just gaining steam in the post-*Roe* and post-*Dobbs* world. In *Motherhood Lost*, author Linda Layne wrote about an Ann Landers column from 1998 in which a New Jersey woman had a full-term stillborn and wrote that the state laws required that she and her husband dispose of their stillborn, but they couldn't claim the baby on their income taxes. She suggested "our government ought to allow grieving parents a way to recognize that their stillborn child existed."

This is the paradox inherent in laws like this—they demand recognition that a fetus is a person deserving of a burial but don't bestow that "personhood" onto stillbirths in a consistent way.

Erica Bailey gave birth to a stillborn in Missouri, where abortion is now essentially banned. "My precious son who lived for 39-weeks, was not seen as a person in the eyes of the law. We did not receive a birth certificate, even though I still gave birth to his 7-pound 6-ounce body," Bailey wrote in *Motherwell*. "We were not able to claim him as a tax dependent, even though we paid for all the same things in preparation for his arrival, in addition to the funeral, burial, headstone, and years of trauma therapy at $150/hour. In the eyes of my very 'pro-life' state, he didn't even exist."

How Do You Honor This?

Joanne Cacciatore, the professor who studies grief and trauma, was instrumental in the passing of a so-called Missing Angels

Act (not her phrase) in Arizona in 2001. In 1994, she gave birth to a baby, Cheyenne, whose heart stopped beating about fifteen minutes before she was born. She got a death certificate in the mail, but she wanted a *birth* certificate. She gave birth after all. But no such record existed. Cacciatore worked with a focus group of other bereaved parents to convince the state legislature to make a change. And it worked. In September 2001, the first birth certificate for a stillborn baby was issued in the United States. It reads: a certificate of birth resulting in stillbirth.

The idea behind this, Cacciatore told us, was to honor the babies, honor the parents who labored and delivered, but also to align with the laws already in place that required stillborn babies to be buried or cremated. It was for parents who are already traumatized and struggling with ways to make sense of what happened, particularly because we're so bad at talking about any of this openly. Cacciatore makes a distinction between stillbirth, though, and miscarriage and abortion. She doesn't think miscarriage is on the same level biologically, because it occurs at an earlier stage in pregnancy. There is no giving birth, no milk coming in.

Now forty-three states (most through the grassroots efforts of grieving families) issue some kind of memorial certificate of stillbirth or a certificate of birth resulting in stillbirth. Many are on request—it's not automatic but is an alternative to the "certificate of fetal death" Cacciatore received when her daughter died.

These certificates are for the purposes of memorial only; they don't hold any legal sway and aren't equivalent to a personhood law. But the abortion debate has consumed this too. Antiabortion advocates seized on these laws as proof of what they've been arguing for the past fifty years—that life begins at conception and that abortion is wrong. Cacciatore has been adamant that her movement isn't about right to life; it's about recognition and grief for people who lost a very wanted baby.

This has spread to first-trimester losses. Former Florida governor Rick Scott made the state the first to offer death certificates to women whose pregnancies end after nine weeks but before twenty weeks. Idaho's Unborn Infants Dignity Act does the same. Other efforts, like one in Wyoming in 2018 that would have required a mandatory "certificate of non-viability," failed to pass.

The biggest critics of these efforts have been, perhaps unsurprisingly, advocates seeking to safeguard abortion rights. Most major groups, like Planned Parenthood and the National Organization for Women, opposed this kind of legislation on the grounds it could create pathways for antiabortion groups to pass more personhood laws and to further restrict abortion. For many loss parents, this too feels cruel. But to some extent, maybe it has. Look at where we are right now.

"Concern about Missing Angel Acts remains because once a category or status is established, it may take on a life of its own," wrote Columbia University professor Carol Sanger, a legal scholar specializing in reproductive rights. "Legal status is a common— indeed an important—mechanism for the distribution of value and goods in a society, and over time more substantive benefits may attach to that status. For example, over time posthumous citizenship became a source of immigration benefits for kin in a kind of 'rights creep,' as the meaning, use, and entitlements of that status expanded."

Now that *Roe* has been overturned, maybe it's time to start rethinking how we view pregnancy loss and abortion, said law professor Jill Wieber Lens. She, like so many others, started to work on stillbirth issues because she suffered one, her baby, Caleb.

"There's still this fear that anytime you start talking about fetal lives, you are going to endanger *Roe* even more, which is impossible," Lens told us. "I think if we could all get a little bit more realistic about how inefficient human reproduction is, I think it would benefit everyone, right? If we were honest, like 70 percent of fertilized eggs don't turn into people, because they don't implant in the first place, we'd all be better off, and we'd be able to allow for the space that people need when, you know, they give birth to a dead baby."

Lens and fellow legal scholar Greer Donley argued in a guest essay in the *New York Times* in 2022 that the line between abortion and pregnancy loss has always been blurry. "But over the past few decades, the anti-abortion movement has forged a cultural bright line between the two experiences, promoting dueling narratives of 'bad' mothers who voluntarily cause fetal death versus 'good' mothers who grieve unpreventable pregnancy loss," they wrote. The abortion rights movement has also created problems "by minimizing focus on the fetus, to ensure that the pregnant person's interest can never be outweighed. That has allowed many in the movement to avoid the difficult question that pregnancy loss raises: What was lost?"

There's something about that piece of paper though. Whether it's a memorial or a death certificate, it helps ground the loss. And its absence can also cause bureaucratic difficulties. Because Colleen went to an abortion clinic, she wasn't given a death certificate. At the time, they told her they'd test the remains, but neither she nor her husband thought through what would happen afterward. Where would the baby end up? And she didn't start asking until years later.

Some fetal remains are buried on Hart Island, a potter's field in New York City off the coast of the Bronx where more than one million bodies are buried. Human remains end up there because people were too poor to afford a private burial or the body went unidentified in the morgue. Historically, though, it's been very difficult for anyone to access the island to pay respects. That's because the property was managed for years by the NYC Department of Correction; prisoners at Rikers Island jail tended to the grave sites. But in 2019, stewardship of the land went to the city's Department of Parks and Recreation. After years of legal wrangling, you now can get on the island by ferry to a gazebo that overlooks some of the grounds, but in order to go to a grave you need a death certificate.

Colleen doesn't have one. She can't remember the exact date of the procedure, only that the baby was dead during the ultrasound appointment five days after their wedding. The only paperwork Colleen had on the procedure was lost during a move from New

York. While doing research for this book, she called the city to ask if she could go and was told she needed the certificate. But when she called the clinic, they told her they don't keep medical records that long, and they wouldn't say for sure where remains from 2012 would have ended up. It was a safe bet, Colleen was told by the clinic, that the remains of her baby had been sent to Hart Island.

Here's the grand catch-22 of it all: she would've had a death certificate if she had gone into labor and delivered the baby in the hospital instead of going for the procedure at the clinic. Delivering a dead baby felt like it would be too much. But it turns out she gave up something else by opting for the procedure: the ability to mark the death as a death—the end of the baby boy they'd been preparing to meet. Shouldn't there be some way to bypass the politics of all this?

Colleen didn't think to ask any of these questions at the time because she was struggling under a lot of grief and shame. She mistakenly thought she would pretend like nothing happened and everything would be fine, but it didn't work like that. She wasn't fine. And now she wonders if the baby is out there somewhere. She's in a liminal state of a different sort.

Loss in the Workplace

This paperwork conundrum causes problems on the job too. It's no secret that there aren't many workplace protections for working mothers. There is no shortage of stories of women showing up within days of giving birth, pumping breast milk in a toilet stall because there's nowhere else to do it, or being unable to take time off (or punished for doing so) to care for a sick child. (Remember how well that whole pandemic went for caregivers?) Pregnancy loss has been mostly ignored at work until recently, and there are (meager) signs of improvement.

Most of those we interviewed described a Kafkaesque drama of bureaucracy to obtain leave, in which some took unpaid because it was all they were eligible for, and those who had decent leave mostly benefited from the help and sympathy of individual coworkers and managers more than any standardized policy.

Isabel, who works for a federal agency in Washington, DC, had a thirty-nine-week stillbirth due to an umbilical cord knot in 2023. She wasn't eligible for paid parental leave, "because I no longer had a baby to bond with," and she had only accrued 3.5 weeks in her time at the job to take for her own recovery from a vaginal delivery. She had used up some leave during her pregnancy. Her bosses created a leave transfer program, so other employees could donate time for her to extend beyond six weeks. In total, she was able to take twelve consecutive weeks.

On top of this, the federal parental bereavement policy is two weeks paid. And Isabel's bosses were advocating for her to qualify because she could bank it for later in the year, when she or her child got sick. She was denied.

"Liberal politics shy away from paid leave for stillbirth and miscarriage because they think it will be an attempt to codify personhood for fetuses," Isabel said. "I don't want to advocate for a policy that leads to restrictive abortion laws. A coworker suggested that all you should need is a medical cert from a doctor saying a person needs this much leave. But low-wage women have so little access to healthcare, even that would be hard for them. What we need are policies that think about the actual people giving birth, what they actually need."

Isabel said she thinks people are worried about the effects of leave for stillbirth on reproductive justice because they do not understand stillbirth, and a law would just have to be crafted the right way.

"Other countries have easily solved this issue by including language in their laws on stillbirth, usually saying that if you give birth after twenty, twenty-four, or twenty-six weeks gestation— the lines are drawn slightly differently everywhere—you are entitled to maternity or parental leave," she said. "This is not about fetal personhood age but about the weeks of gestation at which you have to give birth via vaginal delivery or C-section. This also would be inclusive of terminations. This is ideal."

Her bosses were outraged by the denial, and she did get an exception. "All of my leave was due to relationships and luck," Isabel said. "Not to mention that I was still wearing postpartum diapers at six weeks."

Sacramento-based Jodi M. works for a regional nonprofit. When she had a miscarriage, her female coworkers were very sympathetic, and the bookkeeper tried to code her time off as bereavement days to be helpful. "The chief of operations [a cisgender male] called me and said, 'I'm sorry, but you can't use bereavement time for this.' Why are you calling me about this?

Who gives a shit? And he said, 'Well, it's not a funeral.' And I said, 'Listen, don't ever tell a woman who lost a child that what she's going through isn't a funeral. I don't care how you code it or how you code the time off or whether it's unpaid, whatever. I don't care.' I was shaking and sobbing when I hung up."

Most people we talked to had no idea what they qualified for and either had to do rigorous research to figure out what was available or were lucky enough to have a manager or coworker guide them through the process. Many went back early because they didn't think they met the requirements, though some also went back as a distraction from grief or because they financially just didn't have any other choice.

What are the possible ways to get time off? The Family and Medical Leave Act gives employees the right to take unpaid leave of up to twelve weeks to care for their own serious health conditions, which includes miscarriage. (The fine print: you have to work for an employer with fifty or more employees within a seventy-five-mile radius of one another, have worked there for at least one year, and have clocked at least 1,250 hours within the twelve months preceding taking the benefit. People at smaller companies would not qualify.) So even unpaid leave is only available to 60 percent of the workforce, with nothing to prevent the remaining 40 percent from being fired.

Employees could possibly also cobble together sick leave and short-term disability and take leave or get accommodations under the Americans with Disabilities Act if the miscarriage, stillbirth, or other pregnancy loss had a complication that "substantially limits a major life activity." (Not something that most miscarriages would qualify for.) The Pregnancy Discrimination Act says that an employer cannot treat you worse than other employees because you are pregnant or have a condition related to pregnancy, but what does that mean if you lose the baby? For example, high blood pressure after preeclampsia may qualify for accommodation, but that person is still at work; it's not a reprieve.

Bereavement leave has become more common in the last five years but is still a patchwork of laws and individual private-sector policies.

Illinois passed a fairly comprehensive Family Bereavement Leave Act that went into effect in 2023, which requires companies to provide ten days of unpaid leave for employees who experience a miscarriage, stillbirth, unsuccessful fertility treatment (IUI or IVF), failed surrogacy agreement, failed or nonfinalized adoption, or diagnosis affecting fertility. This is available to the employee or to a close relation of someone experiencing one of these losses.

Utah; Pittsburgh; Boston; Portland, Oregon; and Washington, DC, also offer paid bereavement leave that include miscarriage or stillbirth. California has pregnancy disability laws that allow an employee to take partially paid, protected time off due to a miscarriage. But it's all pretty random and spotty. As of 2022, according to the National Partnership for Women & Families, fourteen states, nineteen cities, and four counties have laws mandating paid sick leave for medical needs, which can apply to employees dealing with mental and physical health issues due to pregnancy loss. ("Can" being the operative word.)

Although much state and federal legislation is at various stages of attempted passage, the fact remains that bereavement leave is not a federal requirement and is mostly reliant on individual company and private-sector policies. A smattering of companies allow for compassionate or bereavement leave, but not many. None that are America's largest employers. (The largest being the federal government.)

The answer to whether someone qualifies seems to be a hard maybe—you can try your luck if your company has a bereavement policy, but no guarantees. A study from NFP, a property broker, benefits consultant, and wealth and retirement plan adviser, finds that nearly one quarter of bereavement leave policies allow an employee to take time off for a miscarriage or a failed in vitro fertilization. Not much.

Part of the problem is the inconsistency of the bureaucracy in each state and the arbitrary nature of where the line gets drawn between miscarriage or stillbirth. "So you get a birth or death certificate when your baby is born at twenty weeks, but if it happened at nineteen and a half weeks, you get neither. Nothing happened legally. That's a crazy solution," Kristen Swanson, the nurse practitioner who has worked in the pregnancy loss space for decades, told us.

The paperwork matters for both emotional and bureaucratic reasons. Some parents want a piece of paper that recognizes that their child existed; practically, you may need a death certificate to qualify for bereavement leave or a birth certificate to qualify for a tax credit.

It's hard to overstate how confusing and inconsistent all this is. Even some well-meaning policies don't cut it. For instance, the New York State Paid Family Leave policy enacted in 2018 does not cover stillbirth bereavement. It includes language that the leave allows "eligible employees to bond with their new child, care for family members with serious conditions and assist loved ones when family members are deployed abroad." The word "bond" has led to those with stillborns to have their paid leave revoked—"linguistic red tape" that excludes them. As of 2023, there were efforts underway to fix what many think was an unintended consequence of a well-intentioned law.

Rachel Unkovic, mother of a stillborn daughter who died after cord compression, volunteers for the PUSH advocacy organization. "People who deliver stillborn babies often don't receive important benefits, such as parental leave and death certificates. It's not because the birthing parent had their body wrecked any less, has less milk coming in, or isn't very busy parenting (in our case, finding a funeral home and planning a funeral)," she told us by email.

A handful of states offer a one-time state stillbirth tax exemption during the year of birth. Minnesota offers a tax credit that is a one-time financial relief to offset unanticipated expenses of funerals, burial, testing, and therapy. The others offer a tax deduction like the dependent child tax credit that can be claimed each year for living dependent children. Some stillbirth parents find this helpful, but it has also been used as a political cudgel.

Amanda Pinkham-Brown is an educational researcher in

a PhD program who had a full-term stillbirth and is gathering narratives from teachers who have experienced pregnancy loss. "A lot of people go back to work soon after their loss, because there isn't much available leave, and a lot end up having to white knuckle it," Brown said. "It's adding to teacher demoralization, especially after the pandemic."

Jackie Mancinelli, a high school English and ESL teacher in New Jersey, founded the nonprofit Start Healing Together to support educators experiencing pregnancy loss and infertility by advocating for rights in the workplace. They help with bargaining contract language and work as intermediaries between teachers and administrators and unions to help secure leave and create individual plans to return to work after a loss or for time off during fertility treatments.

In 2014, Mancinelli was a nontenured teacher at a new school, so she went to work the day after finding out by ultrasound that she had a missed miscarriage. In 2016, she lost her son Richard an hour after an emergency C-section at thirty-three weeks, five days due to a rare fetal-maternal hemorrhage. She went on to have two complicated pregnancies with her living daughters and founded the organization after her youngest was born in 2021, in tribute to Richard.

"When I had my loss, I had to figure out everything on my own and wondered why it wasn't being done on a bigger scale," Mancinelli told us. "There's such a need for this, and it's so shrouded in secrecy and shame." She has created language for union contracts to allow bereavement leave for pregnancy losses.

"The goal is to try to maximize paid leave options," she told us, and the language has been approved for her union, the New Jersey Education Association, and is endorsed by the National Education Association.

Currently, in places that offer a stillbirth certificate, she recommends a parent find out if they collect stillbirth data and count it within the fetal demise statistics for the state and at which week—twenty or twenty-four or beyond. That language can be used to negotiate bereavement leave because it "counts as a child legally," Mancinelli said. "But our contract language lists out every single loss you can have from a chemical pregnancy on up, so it is incredibly inclusive, and you can't say an ectopic is only sick leave. No, it's bereavement leave. We want to try to protect the sick days because that's a huge part of maternity leave for teachers. In New Jersey, we have paid family leave, but if your baby dies, you no longer qualify. You're only caring for yourself, and you need to be caring for someone else to qualify."

What. A. Mess.

Many we spoke to felt the need to suffer quietly or to at least try to hide how they felt because capitalism is pretty indifferent to the trials of any individual human by design. But the poor policies were exacerbated when the suffering became obvious in the workplace.

Ashley L. from central New York had a TFMR at seventeen weeks, five days for trisomy 21 after having to wait two weeks for official confirmation of the diagnosis. She worked at an open-concept office. "I was crying on the phone at my desk," she said.

Her boss brought her to the conference room, and "all I got out was 'something's wrong with the baby.' I hadn't worked there that long, and everyone was like, 'What's the deal with the new girl?'" A follow-up ultrasound confirmed severe abnormalities that were incompatible with life. She took five weeks short-term disability after the termination and had retained products of conception (basically lingering tissues), so over the summer, she had eight separate blood draws and a methotrexate shot to clear it. This was followed by two early miscarriages.

She asked to work from home the day she was expecting confirmation of the miscarriage, but her boss's "sympathy had expired," she told us. Her boss mentioned lost productivity and suggested she "take some long walks." Ashley gave notice soon after, and her boss said, "'I think it would be better for your mental health if today was your last day,' and she helped me to my car."

Though the emotional side is important, it isn't the only issue. A 2021 study showed that pregnancy loss is associated with about a $2,500 loss in annual income. And many ended up switching jobs or industries. (Some to move into advocacy.)

Boise, Idaho–based Angelica Kovach worked as a NICU nurse. After her stillbirth at thirty-three weeks, four days, her coworkers set up a GoFundMe for her. She was able to take twelve weeks paid leave. "My work was so wonderful to me," Kovach said. "It hurts my heart that there are people out there that have to go straight back to work and don't have time to heal from the delivery, let alone process what happened after losing a baby."

She eventually switched out of the NICU and into a new role

teaching a medical assistant course following her stillbirth and a fourteen-week miscarriage because it was too hard to be around the babies. She was very transparent about it in the interview for her new job, telling her new boss, "I lost two babies, and it has gotten too difficult to work on the floor," she said. "It would feel disingenuous to intentionally omit two of my children and what their deaths have done to me, so I was up front."

Similarly, Texas pediatrician Jenna C. took twelve weeks off after her son, Connor, was stillborn at full term. When she returned, she only saw kids five years and up for about six months. "I couldn't go to the nursery yet or to labor and delivery and see a healthy newborn," she said. When she finally did go back, it took time to adjust. "I was thinking, how weird that this baby was born and is alive and fine. Nothing bad happened to anyone. How?"

Westchester-based Taylor was a teacher when she had her eighteen-week loss, and the school arranged for her to have two paid months off. "They quietly kept paying me and told me I could come back when I was ready," she said. "It was such a golden example of how a boss and a business should operate because when I came back, I was ready to come back."

But PTSD made it hard to continue teaching. "Holding space for the kids had been one of my favorite parts of the job. I couldn't do it anymore. I was this leaky container," she said. She took a year off to work on a writing project. "It's really hard to live in your body as a postpartum person without a baby."

There's only so much you can power through.

PART IV

The Making of Meaning

CHAPTER THIRTEEN

The Stories We Tell

Myths and Narratives around Pregnancy and Loss

It's tough for any actual person to thread the needle on the very narrow acceptable cultural story around pregnancy loss. Requirements for this gig: You must grieve, but quietly and privately—a dignified sadness that no one has to witness. This can last maybe a couple of weekends—a month, tops—of eating pints of Ben & Jerry's while weeping and watching Bravo before reemerging into society with a full face of makeup and a readiness to try for a baby again, whipping your diaphragm into the air like Mary Tyler Moore's beret. If it goes on too much longer, you risk veering into crazy lady territory. ("Crazy" meaning a woman over age seventeen having a big feeling for more than six weeks.) You should be a straight, heterosexual, cis woman willing to sacrifice herself at all costs for this and any future pregnancy and do whatever it takes to ensure there is a living child in the future. You should consider this loss a personal failure and spend weeks, months, or years feeling like garbage about it, questioning every move you made that could have contributed to it while you fester silently in your own stew of guilt, shame, and sorrow. (Must be proficient in acting as America's social safety net without pay.)

If followed to the letter? Blame and shame. If you don't fit the description? Add judgment to the mix. Is it any wonder that silence is a defining feature of pregnancy loss?

Quiet Riot

The conventional wisdom is that a pregnant person should keep mum about a pregnancy until about twelve weeks. (The actual length of time varies, but this was the most common recommendation mentioned among the experts and pregnant people we interviewed.) The other so-called safe milestones were after hearing the (not quite a) heartbeat on the fetal doppler, after the first trimester, after the noninvasive prenatal genetic testing came back clear, or after the twenty-week anatomy scan (though you might be showing by then)—all chosen because they are supposed to signal that the pregnancy has passed into some magical Shangri-La where nothing can go wrong from there on out, the threshold after which you are guaranteed to end with a full-term, healthy baby. (If only.)

Kate Watson, who teaches bioethics, medical humanities, and constitutional law at Northwestern University's Feinberg School of Medicine and is the author of *Scarlet A: The Ethics, Law, and Politics of Ordinary Abortion*, called this silence the "cultural confinement period," a version of the Victorian rule where a woman couldn't go out in public once visibly pregnant.

So many are complicit in perpetuating this idea: doctors, therapists, pregnant people, and grandparents. But why? Presumably in part to protect anyone from having to share bad news. And almost certainly to protect everyone else from having to hear it.

"Folded into this notion is the idea that you don't tell people because if you lose the pregnancy, then you don't have to tell people you lost the pregnancy," said psychologist Jessica Zucker.

Those who abide by this delay "inadvertently collude in the silence-making by their decision not to reveal their pregnancy until after the first trimester," anthropologist Linda Layne wrote in *Motherhood Lost*.

Of course, miscarriage, stillbirth, and other pregnancy loss seems uncommon as a result. Nobody is hearing the "untelling" of 20 percent of pregnancy announcements. A 2015 study showed the majority of those surveyed thought miscarriages occurred in 5 percent or less of all pregnancies. (Nope.) Between one-third and one-half of women will experience pregnancy loss, and one in four women will get an abortion. That same study showed there was also widespread misunderstanding of what could cause one—76 percent thought a stress event, 64 percent thought lifting a heavy object, 28 percent thought using an IUD, and 22 percent thought using oral contraceptives. (Half of miscarriages are due to chromosomal issues, a genetic mismatch that nobody can control. But it's comical to think that these survey respondents assumed pregnant people were waiting until their first trimester to move that fridge out of the basement. The ideal time.)

Of those surveyed who had experienced a miscarriage, 37 percent felt they had lost a child, 47 percent felt guilty, 41 percent felt they had done something wrong, 41 percent felt alone, 28 percent felt ashamed. If no one talks about any of these experiences—either in a medical or a personal setting—the gaps in knowledge get filled with googling (oh, the googling), message boards, and online information of varying quality. Zucker refers to it as the "strident trifecta" of miscarriage—silence, stigma, and shame.

People are less likely to share their stories because they think it's rare and therefore think they must have failed, a shame spiral that leads to fewer people sharing and the cycle continuing.

"Rather than being made public and important, the loss can become a private and nameless torment," wrote Kim Kluger-Bell in *Unspeakable Losses: Healing from Miscarriage, Abortion, and Other Pregnancy Loss*. All this turns the pregnant person into a failure instead of someone who needs support.

Reva Judas, who runs the Jewish infant and pregnancy loss support organization NechamaComfort, said, "Guilt is huge. Our clients think 'I shouldn't have gone on vacation. I shouldn't have eaten fish. I should have known that my baby stopped kicking. I should have called my doctor earlier.' They feel like they should have been able to control it, so they must have done something wrong."

"You have one job: keep that thing inside you until it's time to come out," said Chicago-based Jennifer H., who lost one of her twin sons after going into premature labor. "It's all you have to do. The guilt can be crippling."

Minnesota-based Crystal Clancy, the perinatal bereavement counselor, says guilt and shame are almost universal among her clients. "Even if a doctor has done an amazing job saying there's nothing you could have done to cause this, they are thinking, what if I had gotten to the doctor sooner? What if I hadn't eaten that tuna sandwich or not taken that medication or not gotten that manicure? They still have that niggling sense," she told us. "For others, it may be more that they believe they deserved it because of who they are versus what they did."

After her daughter was stillborn at thirty-four weeks in 2014, Parlier, California–based Lorena Tapia founded Project Loreal, which donates memory boxes to numerous hospitals and grief support groups. Tapia had just had her baby shower on a Saturday when she went into labor Sunday morning. "I gave myself a pedicure. I sat on the floor and painted my toenails, not knowing the cord was already wrapped around her neck. If I hadn't done that, would she be here? I dissected everything and backtracked, trying to see what I could have done differently."

Fish, mani-pedis, and approved medicines are unlikely to cause miscarriages or stillbirths, and there's not much one can do to stop premature labor once it's in motion, doctors told us. (Though doctors can sometimes slow it down in some circumstances.) There are a lot of complicated reasons a person spontaneously loses a pregnancy, and almost none are caused by everyday living. The onus pregnant people put on themselves is heartbreaking. This is one of the perverse outcomes of the fallacy of control we talked about in previous chapters—none of us can control a genetic misfire, but if we don't know what causes miscarriages and we don't know how many people have them, then we just marinate in our own guilt and shame. It's empirically not a great system.

Many of those we spoke to had to "untell" the news of their pregnancies. Cassandra H., who lives in the Washington, DC, area, had asked her ob-gyn when she should share the news of her pregnancy and got the twelve-week advice "because the risk of miscarriage is less by then. I shared at fifteen weeks and then felt foolish when I lost it."

Colleen didn't tell too many people outside her family that she was pregnant, though it was obvious, especially because she wore a hastily purchased black-and-white dress to her own wedding after the ivory one she'd initially chosen didn't fit anymore. She was clearly pregnant in the photos. Failure, immortalized! She wasn't sure who she needed to untell; she couldn't even recall what she'd said to some people. One person thought she was getting a divorce and was relieved to discover it was "just a miscarriage." "You can always have another," she was told. Ahem.

Though many who shared before a loss dreaded that initial untelling, many wished they had shared sooner so that they could tell friends and family about their loss to combat their own isolation. Journalist Jessica Levy wrote in the *Washington Post* that this is outdated. "During a successful pregnancy, silence forces us to make excuses for being tired, for missing work to go to doctors' appointments, for running to the bathroom. During an unsuccessful pregnancy, it forces us to suffer alone. In both cases, it causes us to shy away from asking for help when we need it," she wrote.

The majority of those who did share the news of their loss talked about how shocked they were when people came out of the woodwork to share their own losses. This secret society only makes itself known to new initiates, like a uterine Skull and Bones. Most got an outpouring of (usually private) messages saying, "This happened to me too." Rebecca had waited until seventeen weeks to announce on Facebook that she was pregnant with her third boy, assuming she had entered that supposed safety zone. She then publicly shared the news of her stillborn at twenty weeks (the worst kind of "Facebook official") and then handed the phone to her husband to avoid reading any of the responses. After a couple of hours, he said, "I think you should read these. Everyone you know has had something like this happen." She was inundated with private messages of sympathy and shared stories—some from people she had known for years without being aware they were also in this secret bummer club.

People were especially blown away by the stories that were revealed within their own families. Older generations lost their pregnancies in a culture that told them to suck it up, have another, and not talk about their losses.

In the week after Nneka Hall's daughter was stillborn, her grandmother lost patience with her. "I was completely distraught, and she was kind of angry, probably triggered, and said 'You need to stop this. I didn't act like this when I lost my son.' We started pulling it out of her. Before my mother, she had lost a baby to crib death. We didn't know." Hall hadn't heard the story, and neither had her mother or aunt who were born after the baby who died.

Priscilla G., a Filipino Chicago-area pediatrician, lost her son soon after birth when it was discovered that he had hemoglobin Barts, a genetic anemia more common in Southeast Asians. "My mom had lost two babies—one at four months pregnant and one at seven months. Back in the 1970s, they didn't do autopsies. And my mom never talked about it, ever. I had known about them in passing, but she didn't open up about it until I lost my son. We pieced together that those babies probably had the same condition."

Melat, an East African who moved to America when she was five, said family members opened up about losses after her son Axum was stillborn. "I had people reach out who had similar things happen. The people who said, 'I know what this is like,' I felt like I could actually talk to them because they knew the pain. I wasn't alone."

Xaviera Bell's son Xander died soon after birth after she went into premature labor at twenty-one weeks. "My mother wanted me to pray. In the Black community, you fall right back into God's lap," Bell said. "The cancer that invades the Black community is silence. My mother kept saying, 'I don't know how to help you.' I was thinking, you lost five children before me. And she still didn't think she was equipped to help me. But we are not our mother's daughters. What worked for them is not what's working for us now."

Marny Smith, of PUSH, lost her son Heath in 2019. "Once you have a loss, you find out other people in your family had a loss. Other friends had a loss. Everyone you know has had some type of loss—miscarriage, TFMR, stillbirth, whatever it may be. So it's crazy that we don't talk about this as a society. Once my son Heath died, I felt the taboo. I still feel it, but at the same time, my son is dead so what's the worst thing that can happen to me at this point? It already happened. If I say how I feel and that causes someone to feel uncomfortable, well, guess how uncomfortable I'm feeling? I'm the one who has to live with this."

This silence is pervasive across the culture. Any kind of pregnancy loss is rarely depicted on movies or TV.

"How many positive pregnancy tests have I seen in media versus how many miscarriages? Not 25 percent of them," said Margot Finn. "I'm sure some of that has to do with who has written the vast majority of media, and it's not mothers. How long have all of the Oscars focused on sad, Coen brothers films. It's crime, desperation, the American West. Important 'man' stuff. We're missing that whole chunk of people's experience."

Medical shows eventually get around to touching on pregnancy loss at some point, but we're not sure a show that's on for seventeen seasons gets extra credit for featuring a handful of episodes where pregnancies go sideways. The most-cited example of an "abortion movie" is *Dirty Dancing*, which sneaks social commentary about the dangers of illegal abortions and class relations in the 1960s into a movie that made the rounds at many of our childhood sleepovers. (But really the only thing anyone remembers about that movie is "Nobody puts Baby in the corner." And they shouldn't. She's radiant.) Though we compiled a meager list of media that featured pregnancy loss— *Up, Fleabag*, and *The Time Traveler's Wife* came up alongside select episodes of TV shows—very few did so as a central plotline or passed the Bechdel test (a test that determines whether at least two women discuss something other than a man in a fictional work).

The majority of the depictions portray happy pregnancies (which evolve seamlessly from morning puke to live birth), spooky sad ladies who lost a baby and are carrying around a doll with a vacant stare, and torture birth porn like in *Game of Thrones* and *The Handmaid's Tale*, which both brutalize pregnant women with an unflinching gaze to prove that "the birthing bed is a woman's battlefield," as the *House of the Dragon* creators put it. (Cool, thanks for the update. Those of us who have given birth had no idea that it is bloody and brutal until that queen got torn open for eight minutes.) We aren't *Game of Thrones* fans—we don't like dragons, rape, or incest—but we're not so sure that moving from a show that featured horrific sexual assaults on the regular to a spin-off known for its grisly birth scenes is such a feminist improvement. (Also, prioritizing the potential heir over the mother or even attempting a C-section would not have been done in earlier eras in American or European history, as it was in the pilot, but who knows what goes on in dragon realms?)

Silencing miscarriages, anthropologist Layne wrote in *Motherhood Lost*, comes from the American notion of meritocracy (if we work hard enough for long enough, we'll get where we want), overblown expectations of what science can make possible, and a preference for linear narratives and optimism—we like a story that proceeds seamlessly and gets tied up with a bow in the end. And twenty years after her book was published, all that still checks out, but there's an addition—the fact that social media has amplified the extreme performative nature of pregnancy.

Pull Yourself Up By Your Ovaries

The silence of pregnancy loss is countered by the very public (and perfectly filtered and composed) experience of modern pregnancy. Now, being pregnant demands a carefully curated Instagram announcement, maybe with an evergreen sprig framing a pair of baby Hunter boots atop a onesie that reads "Baby Jones, coming 2024." It's a post of the actual sonogram, as though we wouldn't believe our former high school classmate was expecting unless she posted the contents of her uterus as proof. It's a pregnancy photo shoot, one as a couple cradling the belly near a pond, mountain, or forest, depending on the local topography, and one where the mother is wearing a flowing gown in the woods or in a meadow, with her skirts blowing in Mother Nature's gentle breeze, for she is now Gaia, giver of life. It's an elaborate gender reveal announcement that involves popping a balloon or shooting confetti or cutting into a cake to reveal pink or blue. (A trend so out of control that it has started a forest fire and at least four deaths, and even its originator has decided enough is enough.) The kicker is the gorgeous postpartum snug with the newborn parked on the chest of a mother wearing contour makeup. (A human has just exited your body. For the love of God, allow this one moment to accept your pores.)

Part of this is rooted in wanting to publicly celebrate pregnancy rather than hide it away, which is a good instinct. But it's all wrapped up in a sheen of relentless positivity, one unquestionably tied up in consumerism. It's just a modern iteration of an age-old stereotype of motherhood, one where she has to be "perfect"—self-sacrificing, beautiful, and uncomplaining. Donna Reed in lululemon. This is all exhausting enough when a pregnancy works out, but the very same cultural script also seeps into our perceptions of loss, for the perfect mother would never lose a baby in the first place, and if she did, it would be done with dignity and with only a very tiny amount of blood. (Or maybe just that blue liquid they use in period commercials.) Then she would pick herself up and resume her quest toward motherhood perfection.

The point here is that stereotypes—and the dearth of real experiences of pregnancy loss and grief—at best mute our true voices and at worst disallow any room for nuance and choke off public discussion of miscarriage and grief. Ridiculous standards only create a space for assumption, blame, and ignorance. And all contribute to a perceived failure at motherhood.

Another old chestnut influencing our perceptions of loss is the American prosperity narrative—if you work hard enough, focus hard enough, and just keep at it, you'll get what you want. (The bootstraps method of pregnancy.) This pregnancy didn't work out? Just try again! For those undergoing fertility treatments, there's some capitalism at play too—they are literally paying for it, so it's not unreasonable to expect results. And if you had previous losses or hardships, there's a sense that you have paid your dues. Those earlier attempts should be iterative or at least somehow have contributed to "earning" a good result.

"I had convinced myself it was going to be all good," said Debbie Haine Vijayvergiya, the SHINE for Autumn Act advocate, who was pregnant after a series of losses. "I had to believe that I had paid my dues to the fertility gods and that nothing worse could happen to me." That pregnancy ended in stillbirth, her daughter Autumn.

Saya H.'s IVF retrieval resulted in twelve eggs and ended up with two high-quality genetically normal embryos. "All that for two shots at a baby," Saya said. The first transfer failed. "It never crossed my mind that you could go through that and spend that amount of money and not end up with a baby. I felt so embarrassed by how much stock I put into that embryo that wasn't really a baby yet. But eventually I realized I was allowed to grieve. I was allowed to acknowledge that I had gone through what I had both physically and emotionally and didn't have to be embarrassed for hoping, for falling into the fantasy that this science experiment was going to work," she said.

The second transfer was successful, and she has one living son. "I would have loved to have had a second child, but I will never go through IVF again. Your body endures too much."

Try, try, trying again isn't as easy as it sounds when the trying could involve hormone injections that cause mood swings, discomfort, and bloating; cramping and bleeding large chunks of tissue and possibly a fetus out into the toilet; surgery that suctions uterine lining out through a vagina; or giving birth to a dead or soon-to-be-dead baby. Making a family isn't like building a computer in a garage, swapping out different motherboards on the way to kicking off the tech revolution. The pregnant person has to go through something physical every time. (Despite flippant commentary about using abortion as birth control, every pregnancy ends with at least some bloody passing of tissue. It can be as mild as a period or as major as a full-term infant, but there's really no easy out.)

Women are supposed to sacrifice themselves at all costs for motherhood—even if it means putting her own body on the line to get that happy ending and produce that offspring. That cost is up to and including her own life, as we showed in the medical and legal chapters. At the 2023 March for Life, the first since the fall of *Roe*, speakers were touting the sacrifices of women who died in childbirth as martyrs. Feminist writer Jessica Valenti wrote that the antiabortion crowd knows more women will die post-*Dobbs*, so they have to make the maternal losses "palatable."

Jane Armstrong, the perinatal mental health therapist who works with TFMR patients, had to terminate a pregnancy for medical reasons. "We have a conceptualization of motherhood as an absolute sacrifice under any circumstance, and I don't think I appreciated how damaging that was until I was grappling with it through my own loss," she said. "Am I a bad mother for not sacrificing my entire future, every dime I've ever earned and will never earn again because I won't be able to work outside the home, my marriage, and my own physical and mental health, and I might not have been able to have other children we hoped to have—that's the expectation? All this against a backdrop in America where we put mothers on a pedestal and don't do anything for them. We just say, 'Hey, you're great. Here's flowers,' and rely on them for everything."

Kate Carson, one of the administrators for the Facebook group Ending a Wanted Pregnancy and an outspoken abortion advocate, didn't find out until thirty-five weeks that her baby had a severe seizure disorder and numerous brain anomalies. She is at peace with her decision to terminate but says there's something that isn't as well received. "It's really easy to talk about saving my daughter and really hard to talk about saving me. But I for sure saved me too," Carson told us. "And I've saved myself over and over again since then because I realized I was worth saving."

Jessica Van Wyen transferred her last embryo after her TFMR, and that pregnancy ended in miscarriage. She and her husband have decided to stop after seven and a half years of trying and will not have a biological child. "If you're not willing to go into crippling debt, if you're not willing to put yourself through and explore every single opportunity no matter the physical and emotional cost—if you stop before you scorch your life to the ground—you just didn't want it badly enough," she said. "I held a dead baby in my arms. I've been through a miscarriage. I've been through failed transfers. How much more am I going to put myself through? Even if it was all free, I don't know that I could do it."

This is why the concept of the "rainbow baby" can be so polarizing. *Rainbow baby* is a newish term for the child born (alive) after a miscarriage, stillbirth, TFMR, or perinatal loss, in use since about 2008, the idea being that the new baby is symbolic of a rainbow after a storm. It has become its own culture, with rainbow onesies, rainbow baby showers, rainbow baby announcements.

Most who hate the term didn't like to think of the child they lost being a storm, while those who embraced it thought of the grief and trauma as the storm. It's tricky, because some people are worried it reinforces the idea that one baby is swapped out for another.

"People were so relieved when we had a living child, like the cosmic scales were balanced," said Brooklyn-based Gabriella B., who lost her first pregnancy at thirty-one weeks after a placental abruption resulted in an emergency C-section.

"Are there other possible endings to this story that aren't happy, maybe just OK but still meaningful and true?" said Westchester-based Taylor, who had a loss at eighteen weeks and isn't sure future children are possible. "Are there endings to the story that don't involve me putting my uterus on the line again? I have a living child. I would love for him to have living siblings, but I don't know if that's in the cards. I have to fight in medias res before I decide whether it's imperative to produce this rainbow baby."

As we showed in previous chapters, there was a backlash anytime women enjoyed some modicum of freedom in American history. The notion of the self-sacrificing mother was often weaponized in those backlashes, particularly anytime abortion has been invoked since the 1850s, with the same basic argument: abortion is an aberration because it means a rejection of what should be her natural state—motherhood. This led to the creation of the abortion straw woman—a harlot who selfishly refuses to be a mother and is trying to avoid the consequences for supposedly wanton sex. This straw woman doesn't exist (she never has), but the silence imposed by the stigma of pregnancy loss means there's nothing to counter it.

As *The Turnaway Study* showed, "women make thoughtful, well-considered decisions about whether to have an abortion," and those decisions are "overwhelmingly [a story] of people in ordinary circumstances wanting to have some control over their bodies, their childbearing, and their lives."

Guess what? Sixty percent of those in the study were already mothers.

Deciding How We Feel

Politics, the cultural perceptions of motherhood, and silence have all contributed to a culture where those who suffer pregnancy loss are only allowed to feel one way (sad) and do one thing about it (grieve, briefly and quietly). But people are just no longer willing to follow that script, and they're changing the landscape in real time.

As we have talked about earlier, pregnancy isn't just a biological experience; it's influenced by the society and culture at the time. Linda Layne, the anthropologist, interviewed those in pregnancy loss support groups to observe how parents saw their own losses and concluded that pregnancy tests, ultrasounds, medically managing pregnancies at earlier stages, and pro-life campaigns that focused on the fetus contributed directly and indirectly to the "construction of fetal patienthood and personhood, and had a number of unintended consequences for pregnancy loss," including "[moving] up the time and pace with which many American women began to socially construct the personhood of a wished-for child."

Those who are excited about their pregnancies start building that story as soon as they find out. Julia Bueno wrote in *The Brink of Being: Talking about Miscarriage*, "the more we think, plan, daydream, or dream about our longed-for baby, the deeper the grooves in our mind become." It's simple neuroscience that the more we think about something, the more the neural connections strengthen and shape our connection to it.

Pregnant people and their partners are encouraged to create a pregnancy around the idea that bringing a healthy baby home is the only possible ending and then are dropped when that doesn't happen. They're left in a vacuum created by the abortion rights movement, which ignored miscarriage and stillbirth for fear of going down a slippery slope to fetal personhood. The antiabortion movement, meanwhile, capitalized on mourning miscarriages as a way to cement fetal personhood, which is how you get laws like those passed in Indiana. None of this is designed around the feelings of a person who has experienced a pregnancy loss, so naturally it doesn't work for them. All right, then what's the solution?

Well, there could be a move away from encouraging bonding so early. Historian Lara Freidenfelds wrote that in Greece and Israel, doctors do not encourage or expect bonding during early sonograms, because they see it as a strictly medical exam to look for problems in the pregnancy, whereas early sonograms in America use language about "meeting the baby," even when what's in there is little more than a gestational sac. Layne said for the millions of pregnant people who miscarry, "it would be better psychologically not to determine their pregnancies so early, not to start investing in the social construction of fetal personhood until a later date, when the chances of ending up with a take-home baby are significantly greater."

But it may be hard, if not impossible, to put that genie back in the bottle.

A more practical option may be what feminist Kate Parsons called a "relational" model of pregnancy. This was a concept repeatedly described in our interviews, even though most of those we spoke to didn't know this term specifically.

Many people experience multiple kinds of these losses, like a really effed-up bingo card. They know how their stillbirth differed from their miscarriage, their traumatic delivery from their textbook pregnancy. They may have been relieved by an abortion when they were young and unprepared and didn't think about it at all but later grieve for months over a failed IVF embryo transfer. Though some struggled with how to reconcile those feelings with personal politics, it made sense to them that they would feel differently about each pregnancy. Because every pregnancy is different, even when they're all successful, because of life circumstances. For example, you don't get to nap with that second pregnancy if you have a toddler in the house. These people intuitively understood that how you relate to the pregnancy determines your attachment and experience with it. The end. No politics, no further expectations.

This way of thinking supports abortion as a morally valid choice and also allows pregnant people to consider the fetus inside them a baby without contradicting one another.

Law professors Jill Wieber Lens and Greer Donley argue that using this relational model—where every pregnancy means something different to the pregnant person—can recognize those who feel loss without ceding ground on abortion rights—even more important in post-*Roe* America when the two are intertwined. And aligning an abortion rights strategy with pregnancy loss would help counteract the narrative that all pregnancies end with a "healthy, live birth to a smiling mother." If abortion, miscarriage, and stillbirth instead were perceived as normal, even if undesired—certainly more common than most consider them to be statistically—"pregnancy endings could help fight the stigma that affects all adverse pregnancy outcomes and benefit all pregnant people."

"I work in reproductive rights," said Maryland-based Catherine, who lost a daughter at three days old after having to deliver early due to preeclampsia. "I have been attached to our embryos, and we mourned when they didn't stick. Watching our daughter grow up knowing she was an embryo makes them mean something in a new light. But I guess the difference to me is this was our intentional choice. It was our choice to transfer and gestate those embryos and carry them to baby. If it was not our intentional choice, it wouldn't have meaning to me."

Orlando-based Kelsey Garcia-Abdin said, "I would never tell my friend who had an abortion that she killed her baby. But I would never want her to come to me and tell me my embryo is not a baby. And I just don't see the problem there. It's up to the individual to decide what it means to them."

For many we spoke to, the overarching idea was that it was about being pro-bodily autonomy, whether that was gender-affirming care or reproductive justice—being supported as a dignified human being in a given scenario.

Anthropologist Layne says that since "personhood is culturally constructed," it "may be undertaken with some embryos and not others." Feminist bioethicists have called this "calling into personhood"—basically, the fetus does not have inherent personhood; someone else has to draw it out. The relationship is bestowed by the pregnant person, not necessarily by biological stages. If a pregnancy is unwanted or unable to be kept, or if a person with recurrent losses is trying to protect their own feelings, this may be delayed or never happen at all. This explains how much-wanted but failed embryo transfers are devastating, how a miscarriage that ends a pregnancy with a terrible partner can be a relief. In contrast, the antiabortion position is that personhood is presumed at conception, no matter the context.

It also gives a name to something that many pregnant people know to be true—they're perfectly capable of being excited by their own ultrasound without subscribing to or even being interested in antiabortion rhetoric. It's not unheard of for them to be thrilled with one pregnancy and conflicted about another. "This is not inconsistency but rather an awareness of context," Lens and Donley wrote.

Though this may seem foreign to those born in a post-*Roe* world, it's historically truer to how Americans used to think about pregnancy. "No one in earlier times would be surprised that people really loved and wanted some of their babies and did not want others," historian Freidenfelds told us.

Or to put it more bluntly: "It's almost like we should be allowed to think for ourselves," said Sacramento-based Ashley P.

This model allows for a spectrum of reactions without demanding a gallon of tears as a prerequisite but also allows for that gallon if you need it. As writer and historian Daniela Blei wrote, "speaking openly about miscarriage means making room for everyone to talk about miscarriage, no matter what they say."

Some we spoke to talked about their great relief alongside sadness when a miscarriage occurred before they had to make a hard decision about a fetus with anomalies or when they were able to get out of a horrible marriage because of one, or how they were absolutely gutted by their TFMR and also really happy when it was over.

"I am very much against abortion, but the passing of that baby for me personally was the best thing that could have happened in that situation," said Ohio-based Kelly, who had a first-trimester miscarriage. "I would have been tied to my ex-husband for another eighteen years if that baby was born."

Miscarriage posts tend to be embraced and supported when they are about grief and devastation. A pregnant person who is ambivalent or relieved or even happy that it's all over is marginalized and extremely unlikely to share those stories. In 2009, Penelope Trunk, columnist, blogger, and CEO of Brazen Careerist, tweeted relief that she was miscarrying because then she wouldn't have to get an abortion and was pilloried—for oversharing, for being relieved, for talking about abortion. A news anchor on CNN asked her, "Young lady, do you have no shame?" She was forty-two. A mother. A professional. She herself said there shouldn't be a "correct" emotion for miscarriage. If women's pregnancies can end (or be experienced) in a myriad of ways, why too can't their responses also vary? Even saying "suffering" a miscarriage presumes at least physical distress, if not also emotional. She may be crying about the loss or the loss of control over her own body, her future plans, or the death of the embryo or fetus.

"There can be joy and relief in it," said Morgan Nuzzo, who co-runs the all-trimester abortion clinic in Maryland. "I have met so many people who even when they were devastated said, 'I just want to get this over with. I need this nightmare to be done now.' And they are relieved and sad, and a lot of times, they aren't sad about the abortion but because of how much time, effort, and money it took to obtain the abortion."

Doctors and midwives shared with us that patients often express relief about miscarriage behind the closed doors of an exam room. These feelings are not new. This is how women have been feeling for *centuries*. It's society that is shifting.

This relational model allows a pregnant person to decide what each pregnancy means for them. It also puts the person carrying the pregnancy back into the equation. What are they feeling about what's happening to their own body? This doesn't solve many of the problems on a legal or medical scale, but it does at least free a pregnant person from the strictures of a script that only allows for endless sacrifice, isolation, and grief. It's a start.

I Am a Parent

One of the benefits of changing up this tired old story is it also allows pregnant people and couples to decide how they fit into parenthood.

Those who lose a husband are widows; a wife, widowers. Children who lose their parents are orphans. But there isn't a word for the parent, siblings, or any other relationship to the loss of a child, or a baby.

"The first Mother's Day when I didn't have a baby was hard because she wasn't there," said Memphis-based Michelle Goldwin Kaufman, whose daughter Maya lived for one week in 2014 and who had a fifteen-week miscarriage in 2017. "I kept thinking, am I a mother? Am I not a mother?"

"I don't think people realize if your child has not lived outside the womb, they are still your child," said Crystal H. of Portland, Oregon. "Ezra was not just my hopes and dreams. He was real."

Long Beach–based Cynthia, whose son Daniel died five hours after being delivered during premature labor at twenty weeks in 1992, said, "Five minutes ago, I was an expectant mom. Now they're telling you you're not a mom. But you are. I'm still a mom to that baby, and I remember him every day. His siblings talk about him. He is very much a part of our family."

Colleen even avoids asking the question "Is this your first?" because she never knew how to answer it when she became pregnant again. If she said yes, she was further denying the existence of their baby boy, and if she said no, she risked making total strangers uncomfortable. And who really has the time to help strangers out of the discomfort matrix while you're, say, just waiting in line for a bodega egg and cheese?

Those who are not going to have a living child really struggle. They wonder, *Am I technically a parent? Can I own the term mother?* Many we spoke with who were in this situation said they are parenting a baby who died by celebrating birth-days or doing charity events in their baby's name or lobbying for change in some way. They referred to that as "parenting a legacy."

TFMR therapist Jane Armstrong, who terminated for medical reasons during her first pregnancy with her son, Frankie, told us, "A lot of people don't know how to answer the question of how many children they have," she said. "Do I say two if I have one living and one dead? Do I say one, but am I leaving my baby who died out? You're doing this instant calculus in your head." Armstrong said a solution is to answer, "'I have two at home.' For anyone who has experienced a loss, this could ping something in their head, and they will know what that means, and someone else may blow right past it. For the parent, it means they answered the question, left the space in their heart for the baby, and not spilled their guts to a stranger in a grocery store."

Undoing the Silence

When we had our losses, Instagram was pretty new, and Facebook and Reddit groups were hard to find. (Technology moves fast. These platforms are already falling out of favor.) There were message boards, but those were intense and full of abbreviations that made it seem like hieroglyphics for the uninitiated. (DH for dear husband, LC for living child, etc.) Now, a generation of loss parents, mostly forty and younger, are refusing to maintain the silence of older generations. They are sharing their experiences and creating communities along the way.

Overland Park, Kansas–based Ashley B. had a series of five miscarriages, and she is public about it on social media. "I had quite a few people reach out and say, 'I appreciate you being so open about your losses,' and told me about a loss that they had that they had never told anyone publicly about," she said. "It's a weird feeling. It makes me feel there's a positive side, that telling my story has affected somebody else in a way that they feel less lonely. And they understand that absolute physical feeling of loss, the emotion, and the pain, other than someone who has gone through it."

Erica Freeman created *Sisters in Loss*, a podcast and support network for women of color who have experienced miscarriage or loss or have had difficulty conceiving. She has recorded hundreds of episodes over the last five years and interviews people who tell their stories of infertility, miscarriage, stillbirth, or TFMR. Freeman said she wants to give women of color a space to talk freely about what happened but also make other people feel less alone.

"The added stress of being Black in America adds on to how your body processes stress and holds on to stress, and then if you suffer pregnancy loss, that also adds to how your body processes stress and grief," said Freeman, who is also a doula educator and coach who personally had two traumatic birth experiences. "Some people may not say anything. Others who have experienced multiple losses in our community, we really stress and advocate finding a trusted birth team outside of your ob-gyn, having a doula or a supportive partner that could look like a lot of things—a reproductive health individual, a therapist for pelvic floor. We just want to highlight the options."

Jessica Van Wyen, who grew up Mormon, has been speaking about her TFMR publicly on podcasts and other forums. She says she does so deliberately to try to reach religious moderates who may understand. "I'm hoping women who hear my story or have friends and family who do, if they find themselves in these circumstances, they will remember and seek me out so they don't have to be alone," she said. "I didn't know anybody who had terminated for medical reasons. I didn't know what the process would be like. I was terrified and so lonely. With everything that happened with *Dobbs*, it's only going to get harder."

Kiley Krekorian Hanish's son Norbert died of a liver cyst at thirty-five weeks in 2005. At the time, there weren't many internet resources or in-person support groups. "It was so isolating. I tried to move on, but when you don't deal with it, it's festering." When she did find a community, she said, "I heard people talk, and it really resonated. I think those thoughts too! I'm not crazy. I wanted to get people together to break the feelings of isolation. Although I'm not a religious person, this entire journey felt spiritually inspired." She started with retreats and then a Facebook page that grew in the wake of the film *Return to Zero*, inspired by her stillbirth experience. She formed the nonprofit Return to Zero: Hope in 2019, an organization that has grown to include virtual and in-person support through webinars, workshops, support groups, and retreats as well as support, resources, and training for healthcare providers working with bereaved families.

"Women are storytellers, and we want to help each other out, and I just feel like if we all keep talking about it, twenty years from now, it won't be an issue," said Traverse City, Michigan–based Allison B., who had the partial molar pregnancy and also a miscarriage.

Almost everyone we spoke with felt that the move away from silence was a key element of changing the way we think about pregnancy loss.

"We do need stories, we need emotions, we need science, and we need to help people pull their heads out of their asses," said Westchester-based Taylor.

Stories are ephemeral, but keepsakes are tangible. And these grieving parents are also creating a marketplace out of their desire for a remembrance they can touch.

CHAPTER FOURTEEN

Talismans

The Growing Market for Objects That Commemorate Loss

W e're a culture that loves a keepsake. It's a tactile way to keep a memory close. They change meaning over time, taking on a newer, more substantial place in your psyche when, for example, your kid grows up and a macaroni necklace reminds you of their childhood. Or that old concert T-shirt reminds you of your carefree teen years.

For people who lose pregnancies, a keepsake may be all they have; there's no stable of memories on which to dwell, only the idea of what could have been. But things get tricky when we talk about marking a pregnancy loss. We are not supposed to memorialize that baby with a sonogram image framed over the mantle, display photos of the stillborn, keep a blanket bought for a nursery on the couch, or show anyone the onesie you wanted to put on your newborn when you left the hospital.

But we do.

Some people keep little footprints. Some buy clothing for the baby they will never get to dress. Some have the calendar page from the time they found out about the pregnancy. Rebecca bought two separate small chests—one for her stillborn son, a larger one for the twins, each with their names and dates (not really a birthday yet also kind of) carved into a heart on the front. They each contain photos that she has only been able to bear to look at once, the impossibly tiny outfits knitted by volunteers that are tinged with traces of viscera, imprints of their feet, a blessing certificate from the hospital chaplain, and even the discharge paperwork, hastily gathered in the rush to leave the hospital and plopped in a pile. The chests sit neatly in a row on the top shelf of her closet. She never looks at them but will also never get rid of them. When she reorganized her closet after a renovation and brought them down temporarily, her youngest son, then four, couldn't resist taking a peek, reporting, "Those treasure chests had weird stuff in them."

Part of keeping these items out of sight is because they make us sad, that's true. But it's also because we don't want to make people uneasy and people are undeniably made uncomfortable by items meant to memorialize the death of a baby.

Many of the people we interviewed spoke about how there's no place to put this kind of sadness, no way to release it into the world, so hanging on to something and stuffing it in a drawer is about all they felt they could do.

We humans struggle in particular with intangible loss; it's all about what you hoped would be. For those who have to deliver, they may hold the baby for just a brief moment. There's a sonogram, a photo of the pregnant belly, maybe a hospital blanket. In the end, these things become more than just items. They're talismans, meant to give people something—quite literally—to hold on to.

"Your keepsakes represent a tangible connection to your baby that you can see, touch and hold," Deborah L. Davis wrote in her book *Stillbirth, Yet Still Born*. "Keepsakes also connect you to your memories and lend a feeling of being close to your baby or babies."

Some psychologists, nurses, and doctors have realized that a keepsake can aid in healing and have added tangible objects to a bag for people to take home from the hospital. Organizations knit or make tiny clothes for hospitals to keep on hand for babies who are delivered dead or die soon after. Jen D., the U.S. veteran who lives outside Chicago, had a stillborn baby and one who died six weeks after he was born from heart complications. She makes receiving blankets named in honor of her daughter, Olivia, and donates them for memory boxes in hospitals around the country. They're stitched together with ribbon, and when parents say goodbye to the baby, they pull the ribbon—they keep half, and the baby gets the other half. She got the idea because she heard a lot from parents who felt like they were sending babies to their graves alone and cold, and the idea haunted them. And her.

"I wanted to give parents something they could touch," she said. "It seems simple. But I guess it isn't."

Somewhere to Put the Grief

After Jenn C.'s sixteen-month-old daughter Madison died, she had two other children. Five years later, though, she heard about the death of a teenage boy, an acquaintance. Knowing the pain and grief his mother must be feeling triggered her own latent grief over the death of her daughter, who died during her afternoon nap. Even though her daughter was a toddler, so many people had used the same words they use for a miscarriage. They told her, "It's for the best." "Just have another baby." "It was God's will…all the crap that was always said to bereaved parents," Jenn told us. "I was really shamed. For how long I was grieving her and missing her and not just getting on with my life." "You had more children," they said. "You should be happy."

"I had a lot of guilt around my grief, and I didn't know what to do with it," Jenn said. She'd be seized by the desire to buy clothing or toys. "I needed stuff. I needed it. Yeah, no rhyme. No reason. I just knew I needed it."

With the pain of her own daughter's death resurfacing, she also needed an outlet, someplace to put that grief. She had always been drawn to art, she said, and she started experimenting with making sculptures. She was pulled to a specific type of sculpture inspired by an email someone forwarded her titled "Marzipan Babies." She tried her hand at creating her own miniature newborn dolls. But they were not cherubic infants or sleepy toddlers. She was crafting anatomically correct fetuses using polymer clay.

This type of keepsake isn't for everyone. These things can

seem—how shall we put it—downright creepy. She makes them proportionate to that of a fetus at a specific gestational age, and they are accurate—she uses fetal developmental guides from the Mayo Clinic as a guideline. She often wonders how the hell she ended up making these, especially when it wasn't a miscarriage or stillbirth that prompted the trauma, but there she was, sculpting from clay hundreds of fetuses at various stages over and over again.

These fill a void for a certain type of loss parent, especially those who long to see and hold the fragile baby they lost in the early weeks or months of pregnancy. Eventually, she started selling her sculptures on Etsy in a shop she called My Tangible Peace, and she's sold thousands. Midwives call her and order full sets. Each one is made to order, one of a kind. She can make a baby to hold in your hands, or for lesser-developed fetuses, she puts them in resin. She makes sculptures for grieving parents who, like her, just needed something to touch and hold. And she makes sculptures for professionals and educators who desire a more accurate representation of the development process from what is found in medical supply stores.

One thing she won't do, though, is make them look more like "babies." These sculptures look exactly like developing fetuses. Sort of like a pollywog in the earlier stages and, as weeks progress, more like what we think of as a baby. She gets requests sometimes, she said, from right-to-life groups that want the clay creations to make a point for their antiabortion campaigns but don't like how they look.

"But that's what they look like in the womb!" Jenn explains. "I don't make the rules here."

As we said, the fetus has become important iconography to the antiabortion movement. Anyone young enough to be pregnant right now—even someone who isn't especially political or antiabortion—has grown up with the fetus as a symbol of pregnancy, and that has trickled its way to the marketplace. For Christians in particular, the image denotes a life lost.

Jenn has sold to parents, to families and friends of bereaved parents, though she cautions friends that this may not be the most benign way to say condolences. A small resin heart with a tiny dot of a fetus costs about $15, and the prices go up from there; a twelve-week-old fetus encased in resin is $150, a polymer clay twenty-week-old sculpture is $175. She can mix ashes in with the clay if you so desire. On her page, she makes it very clear she's a kindred spirit, and she hears a lot of really sad stories in the process. Her reviews are glowing.

"I literally can barely find the words," one customer wrote. "This has been amazing. Opening the box and finding the sculpture, it was like seeing her again for the first time."

A Growth Industry

This type of item is quite niche. But the general market for pregnancy loss keepsakes is growing—and fast. Of the dozens of sellers we contacted on Etsy, almost all told us that sales for miscarriage or pregnancy loss keepsakes are ballooning. Right now, Etsy, which posted $2.4 billion in revenues in 2022, is the most searched site for pregnancy loss mementos. This is unsurprising due to the nature of the site but also based on who is buying and selling. By the company's own statistics, around 83 percent of its sellers are women as of 2022, and just slightly less—81 percent—of its buyers are women. Much in the same way that social media allowed women who endured pregnancy loss to find one another, Etsy is bringing this community together.

The items for sale in this realm can be broken down into overlapping subsections. There are items of quiet or loud grief, religious or secular. There's jewelry and other wearables, objects to display on a wall or shelf, and consumables—a gift package with a candle and some granola, stuff like that.

If you're not into Jesus, the options are much more limited. One seller offers a watercolor titled "Jesus Christ holding gender neutral baby miscarriage baby loss." Another will send a calligraphy saying that reads, "Miracles are coming." Many of the products are for "angel mamas," because an angel baby is the one who died (a rainbow baby, remember, is the baby you have after you lose a baby).

There are Christmas ornaments with tiny footprints that cost $30. Memorial boxes. Stones with sayings like "Planted on earth, blooming in heaven" for a mere $20.99. Wind chimes. Hanging wall art. Statues of angels, of Jesus holding angels, of stand-alone babies. Key chains emblazoned with ultrasound photos. Sayings like "I may have held you in my womb for a moment, but I will hold you in my heart forever." A website that looks and feels kind of like the Goop of pregnancy loss offers a $115 "care for still-birth box" or "care for miscarriage box" that includes things like heavy-duty pads, tea, and a pamphlet on healing.

Lancaster, Pennsylvania–based Jessica Van Wyen underwent IVF for four and a half years before becoming pregnant, and it seemed like everything was going fine until twenty-three weeks, six days when the sonogram showed significant and devastating brain abnormalities. (The abortion cutoff in Pennsylvania is twenty-four weeks.) She and her husband had to wait an agonizing week before their appointment at Children's Hospital of Philadelphia, where the diagnosis was even worse than her doctor at home had suspected. She and her husband ended the pregnancy at twenty-six weeks.

"This was a much-wanted child. I loved my son so desperately that I wanted to spare him any pain," said Jessica, who named her boy Jacob. She and her husband traveled to a clinic in Washington, DC, for the procedure ending her pregnancy, where she received very compassionate care and their requests to hold the baby and have time with him after he was born were honored. For two hours, she and her husband held him, rocked him, talked to him, and played a lullaby on repeat, a time she described as "sacred."

She was grateful they gave her his hat and blanket and made handprints and footprints as keepsakes. His left handprint bore a telltale sign of her husband's family—an "exact miniature replica" of a little bent pinkie, like three generations of his father's family before him. She sent a small part of Jacob's ashes to a website called Close By Me that specializes in pendants and items made from the ashes of loved ones. She purchased three pieces incorporating his ashes—a ring for her, a necklace for her husband, and a Christmas ornament to hang every year.

Hanging Near Your Heart

Jewelry as a talisman is particularly popular. Louisville-based Emily M. ended her pregnancy in December 2021; at the twenty-week anatomy sonogram, where doctors do a thorough accounting of all the baby parts and organs, her son Xavier had fatal anomalies. In her office, she keeps a "pretty box" that contains "trinkets that people gave me as 'grieving gifts,' if you will," she said. A friend got her a necklace from Etsy with a forget-me-not seed in the middle, and her sister bought her one with her initials, her son's initials, and a sun symbol. "I wear them all the time," she says. "Then there's always something with me."

Kellie Abernethy is among the Etsy sellers making jewelry specifically designed for miscarriage gifts. She started making jewelry after her own miscarriage, when she felt like she needed a remembrance but didn't quite know what. Like a lot of people, she felt embarrassed by needing something to remember the pregnancy particularly because she was just a few weeks along. There was a bouquet on her counter that had some baby's breath, and she thought, huh, maybe she could preserve it. She taught herself a simple technique, preserving a tiny piece of the flower in resin and encircling it. She wore it around her neck and felt better, and she thought maybe other women could use one too. Abernethy opened her shop in March 2020 and has since sold more than eighty-seven hundred necklaces at roughly $35 each.

"Most people are really supportive in the first week or two, and then they sort of forget. But you don't," Abernethy told us. "So it's really something to see people remembering grieving moms."

Another Etsy seller, Erin Cherry, is a music teacher who until 2023 made peg dolls through her shop MyPrettyPeggy. She originally started as a custom toy shop, making little dolls for dollhouses, wooden cars, and the like. A year into it, a previous customer for whom she had painted peg dolls, each in her family's likenesses, "went through a miscarriage and asked me if I could update their family to include this missing little one."

Cherry, whose pregnancy loss dolls came to comprise all her business, often included a note to comfort the parents that also took the onus off the gifter to find just the right words. The note read, in part, "The pain of losing a preborn baby is very real. You were planning for and falling in love with an irreplaceable child... The person giving you this gift knows that you are grieving and loves you." It concluded, "Grief is hard work. Loss has touched and changed you. Know that one day, happiness will begin to sneak back in. In the meantime, please be gentle with yourself."

Cherry suggested that the doll could be carried around in a pocket, set in a special spot, used for play therapy, or buried as a stand-in for an intangible loss.

Like most of what we refer to as "loss Etsy," Cherry had personal experience: seven miscarriages in seven years. "I hated that lonely feeling of going about my life and no one knowing that I was a wreck inside, missing a person I had never met," she told us. "It occurred to me that my smallest doll size was the perfect, discreet, pocket-size doll that a woman could carry to remind herself that it was all real—that longed-for life had started and then stopped—and her grief was valid even if it was unrecognized by those around her." The customer could choose the specific design of the doll, asking for particular clothing, a blanket, or a symbol like a butterfly, or they could choose one with forget-me-nots emblazoned on the front.

Everyone here is making money; none of this is charity. But there is an emotional collateral to this work because of our inability as a society to talk about pregnancy loss openly. When customers order from these sellers, they often give a mountain of personal details. Some are buying for friends; some are the pregnant people themselves. "There have been many times I've stayed up late talking with a stranger who was miscarrying alone in the hospital or who just had a devastating ultrasound," Cherry said. "I've gotten to know many people who are on the rough roller coaster of recurrent miscarriage, and they came back again and again so they could have their whole family represented at home."

That's quite a lot of grief to take in for a simple business transaction. Imagine if every time you got a coffee, your barista heard about your deepest, most painful memories. (Maybe then your name would be spelled right?) It's not really their job to shoulder the burden of all this sadness, but the anonymity seems to offer a certain appeal, particularly because grieving people have so few outlets, and this type of grief is so discomfiting to friends and family. Much like life in Jurassic Park, grief…uh…finds a way.

Psychologist Rayna Markin says in many of her therapy sessions with grieving parents, the pain is compounded because they're grieving in isolation—it makes the pain of the loss that much worse. Sending long, detailed emails to someone you're buying a necklace from is one way to blunt that feeling.

For her part, Abernethy was doing this work through two other pregnancies. Unsurprisingly, reading all these terrible stories of loss and grief did something to her. There's an emotional cost to her work that she didn't expect and feels a bit conflicted by; she appreciates her customers, because their continued support has made it possible for her to stay home with both her babies and work on jewelry in her little studio in the basement after they go to bed at night. But it takes a toll, reading thousands of missives on grief and loss every day, and she also feels a sort of survivor's guilt because she has two healthy babies.

"It was at times hard to have people sharing their stories with me," Abernethy said.

But for Abernethy and many of these sellers, the keepsake was a gesture that the baby mattered. They wanted their customers to feel understood, their loss acknowledged.

"What a relief it is to be seen when your baby was invisible," Cherry said.

Memento Mori

Of this entire sad oeuvre, one of the most polarizing is photos. As a courtesy, hospitals usually take photographs if someone must deliver a baby who dies or is no longer living, but those images can be jarring and upsetting even for the parents, who are often in the same space as the happy ones down the hall holding their living babies.

This is where photographers like Minneapolis-based Jessica Person come in. She spends most of her time capturing the earliest moments of a brand-new family, exhausted and delirious and happy, clutching tiny babies swaddled in blankets, dressed in frilly onesies, or decked out in some fluffy animal ears. Person and her husband (who is also her work partner) have done hundreds of sessions with newborn babies.

But she also takes photos for parents who have just suffered through labor, only to be faced with a painful loss and an odd and awful predicament: just a few moments of time with their baby. For these families, Person volunteers her time. She takes extra care. She treads lighter, stands in the background, and clicks away, capturing images that are raw, painful, and very tender. Her goal is to provide parents with something they can put on a mantle, which sounds simple but is anything but. She is capturing a moment of both deep love and deep pain.

Person volunteers her time with a nonprofit organization called Now I Lay Me Down to Sleep, a national network of photographers who give their time to make beautiful images of the babies and provide black-and-white prints as mementos to the parents. Many of the people who do the work have been through it, not unlike the Etsy sellers, so they already understand some of the issues that might come up. Person herself had a son who died just minutes after he was born; they'd gone through IVF and wanted the baby so badly, only to discover there were severe genetic problems and he wouldn't live.

Most hospitals in metropolitan areas will offer something these days, even if it's not an affiliation with a more formalized group. "I think it's where we are now with care," Person said. "Which I am thankful for, because it hasn't been this way for very long."

These professionals are careful about keeping the images from turning macabre. These are a modern-day version of "memento mori" photos that rose in popularity during a profound shift in familial culture that solidified during the Victorian era. They were photos of dead children, often dressed as though they were still living. As historian Lara Freidenfelds details in *The Myth of the Perfect Pregnancy*, "mothers, distraught at their losses and no longer so willing to see children's deaths as God's will, developed an elaborate culture of mourning. Americans began to see children's deaths, compared with the passing of adults, as especially tragic."

Parents would often commission portraits of their deceased children, laid out for burial or alongside other family members. Photography was in its infancy at the time, and subjects were required to be still for long periods of time, making the deceased something of an ideal subject. According to author Jay Ruby in

Secure the Shadow: Death and Photography in America, there were three general styles. Two were designed to deny death—to imply the deceased wasn't in fact dead—either through mimicking sleep or by posing deceased children with living siblings. The last, though, is more akin to how it's done today: a portrayal of the deceased with family in mourning. In his book, Ruby amassed a collection of images; some force you to peer closely to determine who exactly is dead. Many people of the era perfected this distant stare because they had to sit still for so long.

But these images can seem deeply creepy: sepia photographs of mothers staring at the camera with a frozen, haunted look, their small children propped up beside them or in their arms, some set with eyes open. In one gut-wrenching Victorian image, a family poses for a portrait with two small cribs and two small infants. In another, a little girl is dressed alike with her deceased twin, and they sit there together, one with eyes open, the other closed.

The book, published in 1999, also includes contemporary images of people holding their stillborn babies, but it's long out of print. What Person and photographers who volunteer for the nonprofit are trying to do is normalize this type of memorial.

"One of the most humble privileges that we can take on as photographers I think is to be one of the people who helps create that record that this baby was here," she said. Now I Lay Me Down to Sleep photographers share the images only with the baby's family; they do not use them or post them online to promote their own work. But the families of course can post them if they wish. "Because that's not why we're there, right. We are entering in that family's space to document," she said, later adding, "Everybody needs something different when they go through this kind of tragedy, everybody needs something different to heal, but for many families, photography can be a really important part of that."

Atlanta-based mom Kareen Bronstein was in shock when she went in for an ultrasound at thirty-four weeks and learned there was no fetal heartbeat. Twelve hours later, she was induced and delivered Noam. This was in 2015, and months later, her doctor checked in and asked how she was doing. "I said, I'm angry. I have regrets. I wish I had held him. I wish I had the option. I wish someone had asked me," she told us.

Her doctor said he had asked, though she did not get the message in the haze of trauma in the delivery room. "I wish someone had looked me in the eye, gotten my attention, and said, 'You should really consider doing this even though it seems impossible.'" Something to shake her from her shock to make her understand there would be no second chance. "I don't want to blame. It's just a really big regret for me."

Her doctor contacted the hospital and was able to track down two photos someone had taken of her son—a nurse, someone on staff, she isn't sure who. "Those are my only keepsakes, those two pictures," Bronstein said. She contacted Now I Lay Me Down to Sleep, which also offers a service to clean up raw images not taken by their volunteer photographers. "Now I have a beautiful black-and-white picture of him," she said. "It's still digital. I haven't done anything with it yet. But maybe one day, I will want to frame it. I'm so thankful to have it."

Cash Rules Everything Around Me

American capitalism has yet to meet a market it doesn't like, but it certainly prefers a cheerful veneer. The pregnancy loss market may be growing, but it's still populated largely by sellers who have some kind of personal experience with loss, more motivated by that than by cornering a captive audience for a stroller that can scale Everest. It feels just about on the brink, though, especially as we get ever so slightly better at acknowledging pregnancy loss.

It makes sense that commodification would catch on; the market already drives so much about pregnancy. Americans spend billions on baby products alone, not counting all the extras floating around like nipple cream, doulas, lactation consultants, night nannies, or the advances in technology that aid in conception and childbirth.

It wasn't always this way. Colonial-era women would have some baby garments, a few hats, or a cradle that they would likely make themselves. (Of course, these women also died from childbirth a lot more, and their infants and children died at higher rates, so there wasn't a lot of motivation to buy stuff for a baby they weren't sure they would meet.) Also, mass production didn't exist—people had fewer things in general, and what they did have they kept a lot longer. But these long-standing patterns were changing at the turn of the nineteenth century as Americans got richer and goods became easier to produce. Wealthier families started to spend some of that newly earned money on their babies, who were much more likely to live than they had been previously.

By the turn of the twentieth century, Sears was selling baby goods across the entire catalog and would soon realize that creating a separate baby book had a lot of spending potential. Entire magazines devoted to baby stuff have been published since the 1930s, most notably *American Baby* and *Baby Talk*, and in the heyday of magazines, they were strategically placed in more than ten thousand doctors' offices around the nation. Now, of course, we have the internet and an ever-increasing mountain of crap dedicated to babies that costs more and more money. The global market is huge: the stroller market alone is estimated to be about $8 billion, baby care products another $50 billion or so, and apparel is another $62 billion.

None of this includes the growing costs today of conception or adoption. Debora Spar, a Harvard University professor, chronicled the rise of this market in her 2006 book, *The Baby Business: How Money, Science, and Politics Drive the Commerce of Conception.* The modern market for IVF began in earnest in the late 1980s and has ballooned into a massive industry that often includes surrogacy and is worth billions, she said.

"I think all parts of the baby-making process are part of the market in ways that make people so deeply uncomfortable that we kind of deny it," said Spar.

Pregnant people are often described as a coveted market with "unlimited spending capabilities."

For example, Hearst publications' modern-day marketing advice to advertisers for selling to pregnant women includes "Use nesting instinct: During their pregnancy, women develop a nesting instinct and have an urge to get everything in order for the baby's arrival." And "Use beautiful images: Women like to feel beautiful, even while they are pregnant."

But advertisers do not necessarily have consumers' best interests at heart. According to a World Health Organization/ UNICEF report from February 2022, more than half of parents and pregnant women from nations around the world who were surveyed said they'd been targeted by marketers pushing formula, much of which is in breach of international standards on infant feeding practices. The report uncovered unethical marketing strategies to influence parents' feeding decisions for a market that's worth more than $55 billion.

Though pregnancy is big business, there's little mass market right now in the pregnancy loss realm, which has evolved from consumer pull rather than market push, as many Etsy sellers told us. But there are signs it is coming. Mainstream websites like Parents now advertise "10 Miscarriage Gift Ideas That Show You Care." Amazon features "baby loss" products on its website.

Maybe, just maybe, that's not such a bad thing if it means more societal recognition of this type of loss, said Spar. "If the market can come and add something that you pay a price for but that makes people feel better, I don't think that's a bad trade-off," she said.

Then again, some of this feels off. There's something unsettling about capitalizing on grief. Not necessarily the artisans and fellow grief-stricken parents who have created handmade pieces and given time to their clientele, but the mass market is where it gets sort of unfeeling. And there's a significant potential downside related to the way our personal data is collected, sold, and used.

I Always Feel Like Somebody's Watching Me

BabyCenter is a behemoth website dedicated to pregnancy and having babies. "Track your baby's development," the website suggests. "Get expert guides from the world's #1 pregnancy and parenting resource, delivered via email, our apps and website." According to their data, they have more than nine million users.

You give them the estimated due date or click whether you're trying to get pregnant and provide your email. You're off to the races, and so are they. You've just handed them valuable data they can use to hone marketing and advertising directly on all the baby paraphernalia you may or may not actually need.

"BabyCenter has an incentive to attract newly pregnant visitors and hold their maximum possible attention and interest," historian Freidenfelds details in her book. "Visitors are likely to come to the site already excited to think about and plan for their babies, and BabyCenter has every incentive to amplify this excitement, even when many visitors' pregnancies are destined to miscarry."

Those cute little emails detailing that the baby is the size of a lentil, blueberry, lemon? They can keep coming once the baby is already gone. Rebecca returned from delivering her twenty-week stillborn to an email that her baby was the size of a banana. She shuddered and hit unsubscribe. Another email came. He was (wasn't) a carrot. Unsubscribed again and changed the settings on her profile. By twenty-four weeks, an ear of corn. She desperately reached out to the company and emotionally asked to be removed. "My baby died. Please remove me from these updates." But still, they came. At twenty-six weeks—scallion—she emailed every contact whose email she could find through internet searches, the press room, and the contact page, begging to be removed. This time, it worked, and she was sent an apology. That was 2014.

By 2019, the website gave the option to "delete this child" in their app to stop information from coming, and if you do it, a note arrives that reads "We're deeply sorry for your loss. We'll stop sending you emails and notifications related to this child and won't customize our site or apps for this child any longer."

If you remove the child (interesting that they use the word "child"), it promises to erase all photos, milestones, and announcements associated with the pregnancy on their website and mobile apps. It also offers resources for coping with pregnancy loss and articles about honoring the baby and understanding miscarriage in general.

But even that can be painful—you have to delete the baby you wish you were holding.

The truth is that big corporations are gathering data to bombard this very lucrative market early to ensure brand loyalty. BabyCenter is a massive marketplace; tucked alongside the parenting advice and doctor-approved articles are items for purchase, thanks to algorithms tracking what you click. To sign up for Babylist, a website that hosts baby registries and shopping, you give them information including the existence of a partner, that partner's name and email, due date, gender of the baby, whether it's a multiple, number of other children, type of pregnancy (a surrogate or IVF), your address, your phone number, and other details about your lifestyle. The website in turn uses that data to market directly to you and filter items based on your preferences. It may also give your data to other companies that want to sell you things. And you agree to it; it's all laid out in the privacy policy on its website.

After Rebecca lost the twins, she ordered the memory boxes from Etsy to store their mementos. The seller was lovely and sympathetic. The problem was the ever-tracking, unsympathetic algorithm. After purchasing the boxes (and a ring that included the birthstones of all her children—living alongside the dead), every time she opened Etsy, up popped a statue of a pregnant woman with the belly blasted open, hollowed out and empty. What did this statue even mean? Was it meant to symbolize loss? Was it like some kind of gothic thing? Do people actually think an exploded belly is comforting? (Can we just caution you, dear readers, that if you are thinking of buying something for a friend or loved one who has miscarried or lost a baby, do not, we repeat, do *not* buy them a statue of a woman with an exploded belly. Or really for any other reasons.) For Rebecca, whose uterus really did basically explode, taking an ovary with it, it was extra awful. It followed her on every site—ads popping up unbidden everywhere she went on the internet. The twins died two weeks before Christmas, so she was trying to finish shopping while recovering from hemorrhaging and major surgery, and there it was, at every turn. There was no one to contact, no one to ask to stop. The best Rebecca could do was search for other consumer goods to try to push this unwelcome curse off her feed, defeating capitalism with capitalism.

A 2022 *Los Angeles Times* article with the headline "How Instagram and TikTok Prey on Pregnant Women's Worst Fears" detailed how pregnant women were barraged with videos of stillborn babies and miscarriage on the "for you" section of TikTok. One woman, according to the article, tried to use the "not interested" button, but the videos kept appearing, and by her third trimester, it was half of all the videos she saw on the massively popular social media app. We spent a little time looking for these videos, and they're disturbing. They're also riddled with false information. The "for you" feed and Instagram's reels rely on algorithms to provide a steady stream of videos. The women in the article reported they were identified as pregnant by their online behavior. But instead of content suggesting they buy something, they were targeted with content on all the terrible possibilities.

Pamela Caine, the loss mom who runs the Griffin Cares Foundation in honor of her infant son who died in 1996, has a different perspective after the passage of time. "When Griffin would have gone to the prom, I got mail from tuxedo companies. That's how long and how insidious this sharing of baby information can go. But my feelings on this have changed over the years. I'm twenty-six years out from loss. It used to enrage me; it could take my breath away. But now when I get something addressed to Griffin, I keep those things. It feels like he's out there in some way."

In an effort to humanize the algorithms a little, for at least a few years, there have been "opt out" search engines that allow their users to explain why they don't want to see certain content. It doesn't always work. Gillian Brockwell wrote in a 2018 column for the *Washington Post* that she was the "ideal 'engaged user'" when she was pregnant, Instagram hashtags and all. When her baby was stillborn, though, she couldn't get away from all the ads.

She clicked "I don't want to see this ad" and even answered "Why?" "Do you know what your algorithm decides, Tech Companies?" she wrote. "It decides you've given birth, *assumes a happy result* and deluges you with ads for the best nursing bras (I have cabbage leaves on my breasts because that is the best medical science has to offer to turn off your milk), DVDs about getting your baby to sleep through the night (I would give anything to have heard him cry at all), and the best strollers to grow with your baby (mine will forever be 4 pounds 1 ounce)."

Recently, some companies have started to ask if consumers

want to opt out of Mother's Day emails and promotions. In the spring of 2022, Google finally allowed users to limit ads in certain categories including pregnancy, parenting, dating, and weight loss (which joined alcohol and gambling, the previous categories). A win, right? Not necessarily. The controls don't limit what type of data Google collects from users, only what ads show up. It's not perfect, so things often sneak by, and it doesn't necessarily change the ads found in specific websites, just within the search engines. Those who want to avoid at least some of the onslaught can try dmachoice.thedma.org to prevent baby product companies from sending junk mail, but that won't do anything about the nonstop ads for belly bands on Instagram.

Why are we so willing to hand over our personal data to an industry where our information is sold and resold and our every move is tracked? Why do we tell our sad stories to strangers on the internet in exchange for a necklace? Because we are so desperate to find a community.

A Very Symbolic Tree

Keepsakes fill a void created by a lack of ritual or societal support. It's a stand-in, it seems, for what we don't have. Markin, the psychologist, says that the loss of the baby is devastating, but what's worse is grieving alone. In her 2018 article in the medical journal *Psychotherapy*, she wrote, "In stark comparison with other types of losses, when a pregnancy is lost, there are no communal rituals for grieving, no customary religious or social gatherings, no condolence cards or flowers."

Rebecca bought a garden stone with the boys' names and birth/death dates about a month after the twins died. The grief was still fresh, and they hadn't yet held a funeral because she was still recovering from the hemorrhage. But when it arrived, her husband recoiled. "I hate it," he said. "Please don't put that out." It was January in Chicago anyway, not backyard weather, so it awaited its fate in the basement.

In the spring, Rebecca tried it out by the memorial tree they had planted, so the living sons had something tangible to focus on, an empty belly being too hard to conceptualize at ages five and three. (The tree was endangered by a suspected fungus. Hot tip: If you make a big fuss about a tree memorializing dead babies, be ready to pay an arborist while desperately explaining, "We really, really need this tree to survive. It's a very symbolic tree." The arborist responded, "I do a lot of work on symbolic trees." Don't worry. The tree made it.) But the stone, tucked underneath, looked too much like a tomb, and her husband didn't want to see it every time he mowed the yard. For Rebecca, it was a tribute. For her husband, it was macabre. Finally, it found its permanent home amid creeping Charlie adjacent to the swing set, where her boys liked to say "hey guys" to it as they played and now acknowledge it every once in a while.

What seemed urgent three months after the loss seems slightly less so eight years later. For others, the talisman may always hold that same zing, a bruise to push in lieu of memories to share. Buying memorial objects is creating an ad hoc ritual where there hasn't traditionally been one in our culture.

CHAPTER FIFTEEN

Mourning Rituals

Muddling through a Way to Grieve

M ine actually wasn't that bad. So many people had it worse," Colleen said, insisting that her stillbirth at six months hadn't ranked as high on the grief scale as the losses of the people we had spent months interviewing.

"You have to stop saying that. It was bad. It's all bad," Rebecca said.

At the time, we were standing outside an otherworldly garden full of giant mossy trees, preparing to participate in a Buddhist ceremony commemorating lost pregnancies and children who have died. We had met up in Oregon from our respective cities for a whirlwind thirty-four hours over Mother's Day weekend. One of the women we'd talked to for this book was coming too. The rules of the event, one of the few open to the public in the United States, dictated that everyone who attended must participate—no observers allowed. This was how we came to find ourselves wandering through a small forest and partaking in mild to moderate crafting at the Great Vow Monastery, about an hour outside Portland.

The ceremony is based on those held in Japan for Jizo, a serene, childlike bodhisattva who watches over children and babies who have died—including miscarried, stillborn, and aborted fetuses. The interrupted pregnancies are called *mizuko*—"water babies"—not just because the fetuses exist in the womb in amniotic fluid but because the souls of children who die before their parents cannot cross the river to the afterlife. Jizo hides them in his clothing to protect them from devils and helps them journey out of this limbo state, so the story goes. He's a friendly looking guy, dressed as a simple monk, placidly smiling, and is often depicted holding (usually equally cheerful) babies. The immediate appeal for us was that he isn't morose or dour—happy, not tortured. (A marked difference when you grow up around crucifixes and statues with open chest cavities.)

Jizo became popular in Japan following World War II. Japan had not expected to lose the war, and the nation struggled mightily in the wake of the atomic bombs. There was a major uptick in abortions as families were unable to care for additional children. (Abortion was the only birth control method widely available at the time. The pill remained restricted in Japan until 1999, and their culture doesn't have the same religious hang-ups about abortion as we do in the United States.) Families were looking for something to mark what may have been a wanted pregnancy or at the least was circumstantially ended. The *mizuko kuyo* ceremonies began.

There are Jizo statues all over Japan, usually bedecked with some kind of red cap or cloak—part of the ritual is to sew clothes for Jizo to use while he's caring for the unborn. In Japan, this grief is not hidden away. People leave tokens out in shrines that are often located in parks with swings and slides for siblings to play on.

Our way into the *mizuko kuyo* ceremony was through Jan Chozen Bays, a Buddhist monk who founded the Oregon monastery and who holds a few such ceremonies a year. This woman has seen some things. She used to be a pediatrician with a specialty in detecting child abuse, and she told us how she attended autopsies, cataloged injuries, and testified against abusers routinely. She starts off her book *Jizo Bodhisattva: Modern Healing & Traditional Buddhist Practice* with these anecdotes—it's a brutal way to start a book about a Buddhist saint of sorts who watches over dead children. But Colleen, a former crime reporter who has reported on more than enough murdered children, understood her description of working with "clinical efficiency" while trying hard "not to think of the horror of these children's last hours and days." No wonder Bays was looking for a way to honor lost children.

In addition to commemorating miscarriage, stillbirths, and abortions, Bays expanded the ceremony a few years ago for anyone who has lost a child of any age. Our group was a mix of all. This is one of the only rituals that commemorates pregnancy loss in America, and it doesn't make a moral claim on abortion either way. Attendees can feel conflicted, happy, sad, relieved, or any which way and just want to mark that it happened. For people who have had miscarriages, it can offer a sense of closure, particularly because funerals are rarer for miscarriages than stillbirths.

About twenty of us gathered in a theater-in-the-round type of room, with crafting materials placed on center tables. Bays gave a little lecture on the ceremony, how it began and why she does it. We had been given fair warning that we would need to make or bring offerings to leave with the statues as a tribute. Rebecca brought seashells, because the hospital gave her seashells for each of her babies who died, and she still has absolutely no idea why after years of investigation. (Chicago is famously *not* by the sea. Like solidly in the middle of the land.) Her kids said she should leave something funny, "because you're a funny mom and everything about the babies shouldn't always be a bummer." So Rebecca glued googly eyes to three shells and made a little personalized necklace for a statue. Colleen, who cannot craft and told Rebecca this would be yet another example of how she failed this poor baby, brought a handkerchief to turn into a pocket on a bib she sewed for a Jizo. It turned out very cute, and Rebecca made her a pipe cleaner heart, which she tucked into the pocket. The room was very quiet as everyone worked, though some people cried quietly while creating their tributes.

After the totems were made, the next step was to go out to the dense, primeval garden where dozens of little Jizo statues were nestled inside the grove, bearing little red hats and other items left behind by others. These tokens stay behind forever—they never clear them out. They return to the earth, just like we all do. Ashes to ashes and all that.

As we were preparing to head into the garden, Colleen hesitated. "I don't like the idea of leaving a totem there. I already feel like I left my baby's remains somewhere I can't visit. I don't want to spiritually split him in half like a horcrux." We were sitting with Bays and other monastery residents, on long folding tables outside under a tent, having a (vegan, of course) lunch prepared by the monks. The spot looked out over this endlessly green Oregon valley. Bays, across from us, told Colleen she could take the totem home with her if she liked, the point was that it was up to us what we wanted to do, and how we wanted to feel or proceed. She was a guide, nothing more. It was the first time Colleen had ever even thought about what she wanted. The whole thing had felt so out of control, from getting pregnant accidentally to the loss of the baby to keeping silent and right down to losing the mementos in the move. It was the first time she felt like maybe her grief was useful and even necessary. Could a ceremony like this fill a need for others trying to create meaning? Maybe. But first we should probably talk about America and its disastrous attitudes toward grief.

Good Grief

In 2018, America was transfixed when a female orca named Tahlequah gave birth to a calf that died after a half hour. She carried the calf for seventeen days, for more than one thousand miles. Her relatives in the pod occasionally helped her carry the calf and may have helped feed her. The calf was born breech, and tooth marks on her body suggested the relatives helped pull her out of Tahlequah. Why is it so hard for us to be supportive when a fellow person loses a baby?

To be fair, it's not just about pregnancy loss. America shies away from all grief, a side effect of a culture that elevates relentless optimism and plowing through hard times and sidesteps feelings at all costs.

But our culture is particularly bad at "out of order" losses— when a child dies young, before his or her parents. For most of human history, this was all too common. The Victorians, (remember them?) created an entire culture around death, which started to wane between the 1920s and the 1940s when more children were surviving as medicine advanced. The expectation that your child will make it to adulthood is less than one hundred years old. Culture leaned (not unreasonably) into this happy development by chucking its rituals for those child deaths in the hopes no one would need them.

This is compounded by the fact that people are overall less familiar with death due to medical progress and longevity, and death is happening in hospitals rather than at home, where families had previously tended to their deceased loved ones. French historian Philippe Ariès wrote that for thousands of years prior to the twentieth century, death was a significant community event, and grief was part of the fabric of life. After that, death was made invisible as it was removed from the home and community, medicalized by being placed in healthcare facilities, and administered by the funeral industry.

A side effect of this removal of death and grieving from the mainstream community experience was the modern "need for happiness," Ariès wrote in *Western Attitudes Toward Death from the Middle Ages to the Present*, and "the moral duty and social obligation" to at least appear happy, no matter how you actually feel, became the predominant attitude in Western culture. (America led this shift with its cultural insistence on optimism, but it had legs. America's top exports: oil, cars, and don't be sad-ism.) Talking about death, sadness, or anything that wasn't "happy" became taboo, and those who didn't conform were pressured into silence or dismissed as rude, morbid, crazy, or just a big bummer. Neither Wednesday Addams nor Debbie Downer are known for their popularity.

"There's a silencing of the self around a woman's experience when it comes to her body and reproduction," Rayna Markin, the psychologist who specializes in pregnancy loss, told us. "The loss of a baby in particular is a very traumatic loss. It's not something as a society we tend to acknowledge... The loss of a baby violates our sense of right and wrong and of a fair and just world. Elderly people are supposed to die, and babies are supposed to be born."

We feel entitled to feel good all the time in our culture, said Joanne Cacciatore, the expert on traumatic death and managing that trauma. Her studies have included research on bereaved parents, on mothers of stillborn babies and whether it was more or less beneficial for them to hold the baby after birth, and on grief and trauma in the victims of the Sandy Hook, Connecticut, school shooting in 2012. Cacciatore also runs the Selah Carefarm, a center for people affected by traumatic experiences.

"Anything that doesn't feel good gets rejected. It's marginalized," she told us. "That sort of toxic positivity—you've heard it—just 'choose joy.' This doesn't help grieving people." Cacciatore uses the example that if she smashes your toe with a hammer, "telling you to choose fucking joy isn't helping." Our culture clings to "closure," Cacciatore wrote, "to wrap grief in a bow and send it off on its way, anywhere else but in the here and now." When silence doesn't work as the first line of defense, the next step is cutting grief off at the knees.

There are so many modern ways of short-circuiting grief, but it actually has pretty ancient roots. Megan Devine wrote in her gold-standard book on grief, *It's OK That You're Not OK*, that most of Western culture is built on the idea that if something goes wrong, you did something wrong—"suffering is the price of sin"—and if you're a swell person and something *still* goes wrong, well, never fear, there's a reward in heaven. Eastern traditions, she says, emphasize compassion, but maybe bad things wouldn't happen to a more spiritual person—you must be working off bad karma or storing up good karma for a future self, so rise above it. Find the good.

Either way, shut your yap and count your blessings.

Christianity—the most dominant culture in the pregnancy loss space—has a panoply of short circuits, many of which came up in our interviews. As author Rachel Lewis wrote in her book

Unexpecting: Real Talk on Pregnancy Loss, "Christians often preach an unbiblical, and uncompassionate theology of suffering. Such as, 'everything that happens to you is God's will.' (That teaching is not in the Bible.) 'God will never give you more than you can handle.' (Death is the biological definition of more than you can handle.) 'God needed this baby more than you do.' (Why? Does he collect babies?) 'Your baby's in a better place.' (So, you'd rather your kids go to heaven now than stay on earth?) None of that reflects God's heart for the grieving."

Alishia Anderson, an author and advocate who lost a son to stillbirth, has a father who is a pastor. "The anger that I felt toward God was very strong, but I also stayed connected to God. It was a weird conundrum," Anderson said. "When you grow up in the church, you don't question God. He knows, you'll be fine, everything will work out. I had numerous conversations with my dad about how church can sometimes be a hindrance for parents who are grieving, especially Black church. You can pray and still seek counseling or help without feeling like you are betraying God."

Religion was a comfort to many of those who practice, but others found it complicit in the culture to move on, not dwell, accept that there must be a plan.

Psychotherapist Megan Devine wrote that grief is seen as a "malady"; "we see it as something to overcome, something to fix, rather than something to tend or support." Grief is bad because it hurts (and certainly isn't happy), so we need to move past the pain. This is why people spend so much time trying to "help" by making statements that Devine calls "the second half of the sentence." She wrote, "for each of these familiar comforting statements, add the phrase, 'so stop feeling so bad.' At least you had her for as long as you did (so stop feeling so bad). He died doing something he loved (so stop feeling so bad). You can always have another child (so stop feeling so bad)." We would add, "This was for the best," "Nature took care of it," "At least you know you can get pregnant," "At least it was early on," and "You can try again."

"I got a lot of 'Why are you so sad? So many people have it worse,'" Ashley L. of Central New York, who terminated her pregnancy for medical reasons at seventeen weeks, told us. "It's not a grief Olympics. Can you imagine saying to someone with happy news, 'Well, other people are having a better day than you. They're happier than you, so your happiness doesn't matter.'"

Pregnancy loss has its own variation on this, the "Well, have you thought of…" statements. These are intended to somehow "solve" the problem at hand with a series of suggestions that (potentially could) lead to a baby. Have you thought of doing fertility again? Doing embryo testing? Using an egg donor? Using a surrogate? Adopting? Fostering? These are the reproductive equivalents to putting your nose to the grindstone, pulling up your bootstraps, and powering through at all costs. The problem with these suggestions is that many of them are prohibitively expensive or maybe just not a possibility for many reasons. None are a cure for mourning pregnancy loss, which needs attention on its own, not a solution to wipe the slate clean.

"It's so invalidating when everyone around you is giving you advice like just do IVF, just adopt, things like that," said Amy Watson, a Utah-based baby loss coach through her company Smooth Stones. "It's on top of grief that isn't acknowledged."

Chicago-based Jennifer H. was pregnant with twin sons when her water broke at twenty-seven weeks. She was given steroids to help develop their lungs, but the contractions were too much, and she had a C-section ten hours later. The boys were rushed to the NICU. One twin—her son, William—coded after thirty-three hours. "I watched thirteen people work on a three-pound baby for over an hour."

Her surviving twin was in the NICU for sixty-six days. They dismantled a crib, canceled a baby shower. "People would say, at least you have a healthy child. At least you're OK. Am I? I just watched my son bleed out. I don't know what part of that you think is OK," Jennifer said.

Devine wrote in *It's OK That You're Not OK* that we only know stories of how pain can be redeemed. "We're left with no stories that tell us how to live in it. We have no stories of how to bear witness. We don't talk about pain that can't be fixed. We're not allowed to talk about it."

"Don't act like I am a crazy emotional woman. This was a terrible thing that happened to me," said Nathalie C. of Hollywood Beach, Florida, who lost her baby at twenty weeks due to preterm labor. "I feel like I'm wearing a costume of my own body. I'm just muddling my way through."

"There's no handbook to deal with this," Westchester-based

Nicole O. told us about her TFMR and miscarriage. "I have lost more than anyone that hasn't been through this could ever imagine or be able to identify. It has affected me on every possible level. I look at a picture of myself before, and I look different. People don't understand. You lose so much of yourself."

Roughly 75 percent of women experienced miscarriage and stillbirth as more than a lost pregnancy, according to qualitative research on the experience of attachment and loss in pregnancy. As we have said, this is a newish phenomenon. Mourning miscarriages started in the 1980s, mostly when middle-class white women began experiencing it as grief. So perhaps it's unsurprising that some of the people of color we interviewed said the pregnancy loss space is often dominated by "white lady bullshit."

"Grief is not a Black thing. We don't have time for it," said Xaviera Bell, who lost a son to preterm labor. "We have to go back to work. We have to raise children. We have to be moms. Grief is equivalent to breastfeeding in the Black community. Maybe 30 to 40 percent of Black people do it. We don't have the time. You don't grieve. You manage, and you keep going."

Her son's death catapulted her into the maternal health space. She is now the executive director of the nonprofit Zeal of Xander and the Black Birth Institute in Florida, which work to engage Black bereaved parents and improve Black maternal health and Black infant mortality.

"My crying period is kind of over," she said. "I can't be effective and emotional simultaneously. I'm parenting a legacy and trying to change this space as much as I can."

Grief and mourning are very culturally dependent, shaped by religion, race, and class. Mourning is also often a luxury—for those who can get off work, for those who have time, money, and health insurance to grieve and heal, for those who are allowed to have feelings. For instance, Latina and Black communities are less open to therapy, so many who run support services try to advertise groups without using language that's too feelings-oriented. Grief is personal, but it also has cultural norms that can enhance or complicate the mourning process.

"How do Black women grieve? It's hard for us," said midwife Michelle Drew of the Ubuntu Collective in Delaware. "We have this superwoman stereotype in our culture that says we're supposed to move on. Be strong. Not let it bother us. That's an impossible standard."

Grief Is Like a Fingerprint

Pregnancy loss falls under a few nebulous grief categories, which makes it even harder to process and memorialize. One is *disenfran-chised grief*, a term coined by Kenneth Doka, a renowned expert on grief, death, and dying, defined as "a loss that is not or cannot be openly acknowledged, socially sanctioned, or publicly mourned."

"Miscarriage is often a very silent and invisible loss. People are very used to what's called retrospective grieving, when someone who is older dies and you have all these memories with them," Markin told us. But grief after miscarriage is largely "prospective grieving. It's the loss of your hopes and dreams for the future. For some women, when the miscarriage happens, I think part of it becomes grieving the loss of all the fantasies that were supposed to happen."

For those who find out the baby has died before the actual miscarriage or birth or have decided on TFMR, the grief may be *anticipatory grief*, when you mourn what's to come while still pregnant. It's also called *intangible grief* for the same reason— there's nothing to hold on to, which is where the talismans from the previous chapter come in.

This intangibility makes it hard to mark and define, which can lead to a tendency toward a hierarchy of grief—who is entitled to sadness and for how long. Sherokee Ilse, one of the pioneers in pregnancy loss grief, wrote that typically, people assume the length of the pregnancy is equal to the amount of grief you will feel. "Yet, you cannot measure the amount of attachment and love by the size of the body or the length you have known someone. Love cannot be so easily quantified and measured," she wrote in *Empty Arms*.

Colorado-based Rachael M. was at a yoga class and told another woman she lost a daughter the previous year. "She had all this sympathy on her face and asked, 'How old was she?' I said I was thirty-three weeks pregnant, and she waved her hand and scoffed and said, 'Oh, OK.' Apparently, I didn't hit whatever age she deemed sad. If I say I was in my third trimester of pregnancy, people don't connect it as a great loss. But if I say, 'We lost our daughter a few days after she was born,' they say, 'I'm sorry. That's so hard.' It's fascinating to see the difference."

Grief professionals and organizations are very intentional about not creating a hierarchy of grief. It isn't proportional to gestational age or on any logical timeline.

Kiley Krekorian Hanish, the founder of the pregnancy loss nonprofit Return to Zero: Hope, gave birth to her stillborn son, Norbert, at thirty-five weeks pregnant in 2005. She said every experience of grief and trauma is individual. "You don't know the history of someone else's fertility journey. It is in our human nature to compare—my loss wasn't as bad as this person's, mine was worse than this. Although we are inclined to do this, we should try to be aware when we are doing it and let those thoughts go."

Aviva Cohen is a perinatal mental health psychotherapist who built her Chicago-based practice around infertility, pregnancy loss, perinatal loss, and postpartum depression. "Grief is a chronic condition. It comes and it goes, but it is also like a fingerprint," Cohen told us. "The way that you grieve and the way that I grieve, even if we're grieving as parents, it's not the same. That's the explanation for why a woman could have a loss at six weeks and she takes three months off work. And another who loses a baby at six months or a year and they want to be back at work. I don't think we can ever say how long grief is supposed to last. It's so unique to each person."

Sue Villa, the perinatal bereavement coordinator at Edward-Elmhurst Health in the Chicago suburbs, says she is intentional about creating programs that don't compare losses. "We don't break down our support groups by gestational age," she told us.

"We recognize that every loss is a loss. The minute you find out you're pregnant, that's your baby. We don't want to say that one person's loss is greater than another's. We're all feeling that sense of loss and parenting the babies who aren't here. People come who have had an ectopic, people come after six-week miscarriages, and some who lose a baby at full term. And they understand each other."

Lack of Ritual

There really aren't any specific rituals, traditions, or a collective understanding to shepherd people through pregnancy loss in America. Some of the old standards—a funeral, a burial, a blessing—can apply, but mostly, it's unrecognized in the greater societal sense.

Catholics only baptize the living, so a fetus that never took a breath, even a full-term stillbirth, would not be baptized, though they can have a blessing. Hindus do not have rituals after death for children who do not yet walk, because they ascend into the next world instantly as "divine souls" and need no protection. Islamic belief maintains that the soul is breathed into a baby 120 days after conception. Losses before this period do not require a service, but the baby may be buried if the parents wish.

In Jewish culture, life begins at birth or after thirty days, depending on interpretation. A burial is required after quickening, but the tradition is that the rabbi would bury the baby, the parents would not know where the baby is buried or attend the funeral, and there would be no service or shiva. "Jewishly, I understand it," said Lori Sagarin, director of congregational learning at Temple Beth Israel in Skokie, Illinois, of the traditional law. She has spoken to hundreds of parents about loss after her full-term stillbirth in 1990. "If you had to go into mourning every time an infant died in the ancient world, that's all you would do. But it no longer fits our reality."

Reform Judaism is more flexible and reinterprets the text that there's no obligation to hold services until the baby reaches thirty days old, but it is an option. Sagarin says rabbis approach rituals in a more collaborative way today, and "their role is to help families with rituals that will give them solace and comfort."

Memphis-based Michelle Goldwin Kaufman, whose daughter lived for one week in 2014, held a Jewish burial service and a shiva. "I said, she's real and she matters. I'm going to do these things to honor her."

Reva Judas's firstborn son, Pesach, died of a congenital heart defect after twelve hours in 1986. "There was no support. I was told to go home and get pregnant," she said. In 2010, she founded NechamaComfort, a New Jersey-based Jewish organization that helps people who experience losses from early miscarriage to age one. They offer mostly virtual individual and group support as well as education and training for doctors, clergy, medical personnel, funeral homes, and the community at large. Judas, whose father was a rabbi, works with everyone on their level of observance and helps with Jewish burials, coordinates with the rabbi or temple if the family wants a shiva, and helps with choosing prayers as well as connecting with funeral homes.

We really don't have any secular traditions. The closest America comes to a national mourning ritual is dropping off a casserole that freezes beautifully. Yet the family that suffers a pregnancy loss often doesn't even rank a hot dish. This lack of recognition reinforces the idea that it should be mourned in silence and isolation. Without any rituals, the grief is slower to abate, according to Markin and her colleague Sigal Zilcha-Mano. "Given this, it is no wonder that studies have found that perinatal grief is often chronic, severe, and long-lasting, and that it does not show the typical linear decline over time as found with other types of grief," they wrote. (This doesn't really work. In *The Body Keeps the Score*, Bessel van der Kolk showed that the body must express itself, or trauma takes up permanent residence and comes out sideways in myriad ways—addiction, suicidal ideation, and PTSD among them.)

"I think that part of what makes mourning a pregnancy loss so hard is that it's the only kind of loss we don't have a culturally sanctioned mourning ritual for. In other religions, even if someone isn't religious, there are structured rituals," Markin told us. "It can feel very isolating."

Where silence keeps the loss parents isolated, mourning helps them incorporate it into their own lives. The keepsakes, the rituals—they help the process and allow others to participate for support, validation, and comfort.

Back when birth was still an exclusively female joint

—midwives, mothers, sisters, and grandmothers tending to a woman delivering—there was a cultural language for loss (though, as we've discussed, the definition of loss was much different). As childbirth became more medical, more paternal, and less emotional, another layer of that support was lost. Her discomfort was slowly shushed out of existence while, insidiously, the cultural timeline of what qualified as a "baby" moved earlier. So a pregnant person is more likely to feel grief at a time when there are almost no mourning rituals or even language to mark it. Make your baby real—but only if it lives. In the event it doesn't, the onus is also on the parent to memorialize the baby without a cultural script and even less support. (Emotional labor really knows no bounds.)

After all the rituals involved in initiating people into parenthood (baby showers, pregnancy announcements, etc.), there's no ritual to make the pregnant person whole again after a loss. It all abruptly stops, a highway to nowhere. "There are no rites to incorporate the woman," as feminist anthropologist Linda Layne puts it. This can be especially hard when there are secondary losses, as Hanish of Return to Zero: Hope told us, like those who lost their vision for the future, trust in their bodies, fertility, or relationships such as a spouse, partner, family, or friends. "There's all these other losses that happen as a result of a pregnancy that ends," Hanish told us. "It impacts every part of your life."

"We have such a strong concept around the birth of a baby. We show up for each other, we have showers, we bring food, we have our hand-me-downs. We have such a strong sense of community, and you need that when you lose your baby too," said Seattle-based Malina W., who terminated for medical reasons. "You still need that village, but we just get weird. People get so weird."

If we started putting this all together—mourning, allowing for sadness, allowing for the articulation of a pregnant person's feelings in a real way—we could affect an entire generation's ability to process grief in a healthy way. Their grief, their feelings, would start to matter.

Utah-based Watson, the baby loss and bereavement coach, incorporates life coaching, grief tools, trauma-informed care, and cognitive behavioral therapy tools into her online coaching. "My coaching centers on finding yourself after a loss because it breaks everything down into pieces. I help people put that back together."

"You carry that grief with you every day. You learn how to live your life around it and incorporate it into your life," Villa said.

Elizabeth H. lost a twin at twenty weeks that she had to carry until she birthed the surviving twin at full term. "In terms of the cultural script, it's a weird one. I didn't lose the pregnancy. I got the baby I planned for right about the time I planned. It's been nine years, and I still don't know what to make of the whole thing. I ended the pregnancy with exactly the third child I had planned. But it changed me."

Many we interviewed became advocates. This is admittedly due in part to the volunteer bias of our interviews—advocates were likely to answer our call for stories—but it's also because of the nature of the space. They felt alone, saw a need somewhere, and felt obligated to fill it as a tribute to their baby or to help future loss parents.

"Loss moms are the most energized people I have ever met, because we can't parent our kid the same way we can our living children. This is the only thing we can do. And if this helps us to say our baby's name and to share their story to remind people not only that they mattered and are so deeply loved, it's worth the no sleep, the stolen hours here and there. We want to help others because we know what it's like," said Mancinelli, the advocate for bereavement leave in teachers union contracts.

Stillbirth advocate Vijayvergiya said, "The first time someone hears the word 'stillbirth' should not be when it happens to them. The more we talk about stillbirth, the less it can be ignored."

We heard variations of this over and over again, that this was a cooperative of helpers. But that isn't to say that anyone must turn their experience into their life's work or even meaning. (Remember, we don't subscribe to the happy endings theory of loss.)

"If there's meaning to be had, it's because we choose to create it," said Van Wyen, a Lancaster-based TFMR mom who is now a facilitator through Return to Zero: Hope. "But there's an unrealistic expectation that everyone become an advocate or head a support group or dedicate their lives to it in some way, and that's not fair. They're allowed to just find joy in their own life and keep surviving, and that's meaningful. I do not approve of the message that God or the universe has done this to you so greater good can come out of it. Humans are resilient. That's one of the most beautiful things about us. We have a right to choose what's right for us."

We ourselves have heard this—that losing five pregnancies between us is somehow all worth it because we wrote this book. Let us put it straight—we would happily not have gone through any of it. But we live in reality, we move forward, and writing is the only marketable skill either of us have, so here we are. One doesn't justify the other.

Postpartum Care

The care received in the postpartum process sets the stage for how a pregnant person will process grief—whether it compounds the trauma or starts the healing process.

"It's not just a loss, it's a trauma. At the time of the loss, you as the grieving parent are in a traumatized state. You don't necessarily have the wherewithal to think about your options and your decisions," said Markin. "That's why it's so important to have support around you—when you're in a state of trauma and shock and disbelief, you can't always think of these things. Ten years from now, am I going to want a grave site? It's hard to think like that in the moment, but we don't always provide much support for people in this state or necessarily know what to say or how to support them."

Those we interviewed mentioned the need to repeat options, guide the family through possibilities and ideas of how to make memories with their baby, and leave them with information so they have something to look at when the shock wears off.

Trauma-informed care would allow people to know they can ask for handprints or footprints or hold the baby, for example.

Alishia Anderson, the author who lost her son DJ to stillbirth, wishes there were better protocols to help postpartum grieving people. "Most of us have never done this. Who would know when you're still trying to process that you have a dead baby in your arms that you should take a picture?" she wrote.

Those who don't say goodbye may regret it later—especially because there are no redos. Amie Lands wrote in *Navigating the Unknown*, "research has shown that families who have met, bathed, dressed and spent time with their baby are better able to cope in the healing process; it helps our brains to comprehend what has happened and these activities allow you to parent your child in the only way that you can."

Watson also volunteers through Share Parents of Utah at local hospitals. She had losses at fourteen and thirty-nine and a half weeks as well as six living children and has been working in the baby loss space for about a decade.

"I've walked in and found babies in buckets with paper towels on them and walked in and found a clean baby that the family is holding, and that's at the same hospital," Watson told us. "The difference is whether they came through the ER or labor and delivery. Even if L and D has beautiful bereavement care and cute blankets and memory boxes, the ER is its own planet."

This came up frequently in our interviews with those working in hospitals: that there's no standard of care from hospital to hospital and often not within departments of the same hospital.

Through Watson's volunteer work, she helps the families dress the baby, makes hand and feet molds, takes footprints, can call a photographer, and also connects them with support groups.

"We have blankets and two identical hats—the family gets one to keep that's the same as the one the baby wears. Those things are really important. It changes a body into a baby, especially if they are in different conditions. Some babies look a little rough, but the plaster molds are so cool because you can see the fingernails and the palms of their hands, and it's so sweet," Watson said. "It's such a tender time. You have to be really gentle and only do what they're comfortable with."

Return to Zero: Hope offers free training that smaller hospitals can do virtually, particularly those that are outside a large hospital network that may offer such training in house.

"No one should go home from a hospital thinking they're the only ones who ever lost a baby," Watson said.

Cohen, a therapist who has a pregnancy loss and infertility-based practice in Chicago called the Blossom Method, also runs support groups, one of which Rebecca attended for a year. "There should be somebody like me on staff in every OB practice around the country. It should be mandatory. Between the anxiety people feel and the concerns they have, even if nothing ever goes wrong."

Cohen says there needs to be literature for each situation (ectopic, miscarriage, stillbirth, TFMR), so people leave with something that explains what to expect. "So they know what's going to happen, mentally and physically. So they know their milk may come in, and if it does, this is what you need to do," she said.

Colleen didn't understand that milk would come in, though she believes she was told. (See above on repeating instructions.) Either way, she was not prepared for it, on Thanksgiving night, while she sat at work alone in the newsroom, her shirt drenched with milk for the baby she'd never feed. Though no one suggested she'd need counseling or therapy either, she did go to a therapist who after a few months forgot she had a stillbirth, and when she reminded him asked her why she was "fixated" on it. She stopped going.

Villa, the perinatal bereavement coordinator for Edward-Elmhurst Health, runs a pregnancy grief program that has existed since 1987. She follows up with anyone who comes through the entire hospital system with a pregnancy loss—doctor's offices, emergency rooms, ambulatory care for early losses, and anyone who is admitted to the hospital. (She gets a weekly census report based on medical coding as well as direct referrals from physicians.) She sends them information about support groups, a closed Facebook page for families to connect with one another, and events where families can hear the baby's name read out loud in memoriam. For those on the labor and delivery floor or the NICU with babies who aren't going to live, she offers ideas on how they can make memories in the short time they have.

"I don't think enough people assign the word 'traumatic,'" Villa said. "Going through pregnancy loss is going through an emotional and physical trauma. And it's such a lonely place."

Kristen Swanson, the Seattle-based nurse practitioner who has done decades of work counseling women on grief and miscarriage—she was among the first to publish research on the very specific grief around pregnancy loss—said just a simple recognition that something happened and they were allowed to be sad went a long way. Just by not immediately telling someone "You can have another" or "You'll get over it," you're already helping. Swanson said that some women would go into a sort of trance explaining what had happened, going over the details of what they felt, smelled, saw. All she really had to do was listen.

"I realized it's a profound moment, but who do you get to share it with?" she asked. "I'm more like a witness, I guess would have been the best word. But a witness who has witnessed so many of these, I understand what people go through."

Texas-based Melat held her stillborn son, and her family members came to visit. "I wanted my family to grieve this properly, but I really didn't want to have a funeral. The nurses took the baby into another room and had him wrapped in a knit blanket with the lighting dimmed so you couldn't see all the details. He looked like a healthy baby, and they walked everyone who wanted to see him into the room in groups of one or two," Melat said. "That helped start the healing process." The nurses also went out and brought her a teddy bear that was a hot pad. "I was so glad I had that, because I didn't realize how empty my arms would feel."

Jill A. from central Massachusetts induced at twenty-three weeks at her home hospital after her daughter was shown to have a life-limiting diagnosis. She did a pregnancy photo shoot beforehand and then was able to stay with the baby for two days with the assistance of a cooling bassinet. "I told the nurse, you need to take her from the room because I can't leave her in an empty room," she said.

The postpartum grieving process has gotten more attention at major hospitals, and some are starting to design not just programs but physical spaces around best practices. Megan Gargano wanted to honor her daughter, Luna, who was stillborn in 2019. She and her husband felt supported by the hospital staff and nurses, who had bereavement training. But the room, of course, was intended for a live birth. "We wanted to design a room where the care was in tandem with the space," Gargano said, who fundraised and worked with the bereavement, nursing, and ob-gyn staff to help create the space.

The result is the Butterfly Suite at the Cleveland Clinic Akron General, which is in another part of the postpartum wing, with a separate entrance and a larger floor plan than most rooms. (After laboring and recovering in a postpartum room until the birthing parent is stable, the family can move to the suite.) "It's a home-like space for families to make memories. One of the things that's really hard, we don't get to go home and read to our kids or hold them in their beautiful nurseries. It's a homey environment where they can take all the time they need," Gargano said. There's a rocking chair, books, and a Bluetooth speaker to read a story or play a song. The room has little cards to explain the areas of the space, where families can choose clothing (including angel wraps for early losses), bathe the baby, and a reminder that a nurse can schedule family photos. "A visual reminder is important. There's so much that just was not registering with me when we lost Luna," Gargano told us. The room is large enough for family to visit, and there's a cooling bassinet that looks less clinical but prolongs the time a family can stay with the baby.

There are blankets, bassinets, and small beds from the UK-based Cuddle Cot and Florida-based Caring Cradle that keep the body cool. These give parents the time they need so that they can decide when they are ready to go. Many large hospital systems in major cities have at least one, and about half of those in the United States are in hospitals because of private fundraising, not hospital investment.

Gargano fundraised $30,000 for the space but thinks hospitals should include a room like this in their budget line. She is trying to expand to other hospitals in northeast Ohio and consults with people across the country who want to create them in their local hospitals. "I say, here's everything I know. Go do it," Gargano said.

A similar suite in West Penn Hospital in Pittsburgh was created after Becky Keenan delivered a stillborn son at thirty-five weeks and overheard a round of applause when a baby was born in the room next door. It's a soundproofed labor and delivery space for a family who is delivering a stillborn or one who will not live long, connected to a waiting room so extended family can be together.

Making Your Own Ritual

Grief is involuntary, but mourning is voluntary, wrote Deborah L. Davis in *Empty Cradle, Broken Heart.*

Some of those we interviewed were people of faith or at least relied on their cultural backgrounds to fill in the gaps of what to do when a baby dies. What we found interesting was that even religious people were blending faith with secular mourning rituals.

The "continuing bonds" concept of grief holds that the relationship just changes after a death rather than ends. "Old grief theory wants people to 'move on' or 'get over' the loss of their loved one. However, it can be helpful to think about 'moving forward' and integrating the loss. There is the possibility of having a relationship with your child who is not with you in the physical form," Hanish told us. That continuing relationship has taken many forms among those we've talked to. A candle lighting, a special day where you do the same thing every year, visiting a cemetery or park. "Then you can still parent your child but in a different way."

Families were creative and individualized in how they memorialized their baby or honored their own grief. Some created a garden. Some said goodbye to the urn or memorial shelf every night or did an annual memorial walk. Some went to psychics, though not all found that comforting. Tattoos were by far the most common ritual among those we spoke to—about 60 percent had them or were considering them, usually in tandem with their partners. "I feel like a tattoo was a way to memorialize the loss by reclaiming my body," said Boston-based Margaret P. who had a thirty-four-week stillbirth. "I was completely out of control in losing the pregnancy, but I can choose how I present my body in public. And it's something that I can look at and remember."

Another popular tribute was acts of service. Rachael M. donated 250 ounces of breastmilk after her daughter died at three days old through an organization that distributes it to NICU families. TFMR parent Jill A. from central Massachusetts leaves "a generous tip" at restaurants and tells a quick story about Hadley, their daughter who had rare brain abnormalities. They will leave a note like, "This should have been our daughter's second birthday. We wanted to do something nice in our daughter's memory. Take this tip and do something nice for someone else." (Cacciatore's MISS Foundation sells cards to do the same.)

Pediatrician Priscilla G., whose son died of genetic anemia, donated his heart valves and his corneas. They received a medal from the Gift of Hope. "Our baby was a hero but never took a breath," she said. Jenna C., also a physician, donates school items in memory of her stillborn son. Her mom is a retired kindergarten teacher, and they print out a school supply list and donate a big bag to a school with fewer resources.

The most inspirational thing that came up over and over with loss parents was the freedom to change their mind or mark an anniversary differently based on how they felt.

"You don't have to do the same thing you did last year," said Leah Mele-Bazaz, who had a twenty-six-week stillbirth and is the author of the memoir *Laila: Held for a Moment.* "You also don't have to do anything. The fifth year, the anniversary hit me so much harder compared to previous years. Each year feels different."

Jacqui L. of Chicago lost her first son to stillbirth. "I didn't hold him. I'm OK with it because it was how I felt," she said. "It took seven years to name him, eight years to visit his grave, and nine years to feel ready to collect the box at the hospital."

Katie N. and her partner originally hadn't named their baby who they lost to TFMR—they called them Little Bebop. They decided to go to a local river, scattered wildflower seeds, and named the baby Nova. "We made it a naming day," she told us.

Though the postpartum moments have a strict timeline just based on biological realities, everything that comes after doesn't. You can change your mind. There's no right way to honor your baby, and you have the rest of your life to do it. If you want to cry on the anniversary, go ahead. Commemorate it the next day, the next week, or skip it altogether. "Give yourself permission to have some grace for yourself," Katie N. said.

Rebecca had a redo funeral for her TFMR twins when the first went badly. She and her husband had delayed the funeral by eight weeks to allow time to attend her husband's beloved grandpa's funeral and to physically recover from the emergency hysterectomy. (It was not a great couple of months.) The deacon who had been so gentle at her stillborn son's funeral had passed away. The next obvious choice was a local priest who had been dismissive of the stillbirth, telling her not to be sad because now the baby was in heaven. (Another short circuit. It pissed her off.) The funeral home said no problem, they worked with a new priest who would do it. Well, the imported priest bailed the day before the service when someone he knew better died. (This must be the clergy equivalent of getting invited to a cooler party.) There wasn't much time to improvise, but the funeral home said they had it covered. The graveside service ended up being headed by one of the members of the family who ran the funeral home. He read "Amazing Grace" like a poem, cried sloppily, and then said "Well, that's all I got." It would almost have been funny save for, you know, the tiny casket. The whole thing lasted less than five minutes.

The service had just been Rebecca, her husband, and their parents, and they all left more annoyed than comforted. It gnawed at her that it had been such a garbage tribute. The funeral for her stillborn had been beautiful and healing. This one had just added to the wound. Then all at once, she realized—we don't have to accept this. We can just have a do-over. She called the chaplain who had been so kind at the hospital, an Episcopalian priest, and asked if he would do a service when the gravestone went in at the cemetery. In the spring, he performed a ceremony of his own thoughtful design, with secular-leaning readings and a recognition of the cumulative traumas that had come before. It honored the babies and acknowledged that they as parents also needed to heal. They both immediately felt better.

This has led to what Rebecca calls the "fuck it, more funerals" philosophy. Let us give you permission: Don't like the funeral? Have a redo. Is the memorial you did last year no longer serving you? Do a different one. Are you feeling too overwhelmed to do anything this year? It's fine! Nobody is grading you. Do what feels right.

Moving Forward

Back in Oregon, it was time for the *mizuko kuyo* ceremony. We walked alongside the other participants into the beautiful, wooded area with dozens of Jizo statues scattered throughout. Some were big, some were tiny, and all were adorned or surrounded by various tributes—knit hats that were starting to decay, brightly painted rocks, necklaces, bibs, and laminated memorials to specific children. We stood in a semicircle in a clearing in front of a giant tree—actually two trees that grew together, fittingly. Bays and two other female Buddhists (a welcome change from our upbringing) read the names of the babies and children that had been volunteered and led us in Buddhist chanting.

Then one by one (or, in the case of couples, two by two), we lit incense and walked into the garden to choose the Jizo upon which we wanted to bestow our tokens. Colleen and Rebecca split up for this part, each choosing one that appealed to us, and met up to walk back out together. It was very sweet and emotional but not at all depressing. We both ended up leaving our totems behind in the garden. And now, Bays told us afterward, the garden was ours, and we could return anytime we wanted to visit it.

We met when we were ten years old. We walked home together every day after school through eighth grade, pausing to swing at the park until we split off to our respective houses. We spent our free time biking back and forth to each other, leaving our ten-speeds slouched around town as we watched MTV, checked out the Baby-Sitters Club books at the library, or walked Rebecca's dog back and forth in front of the house of our crush of the moment in the hopes that he would come out and immediately fall in love. We watched *Say Anything* dozens of times and ate more raw cookie dough than was medically advisable. And now, more than thirty years later, we were driving back from memorializing our dead babies. It would have been poetic symmetry had we rallied to watch a Cameron Crowe movie, but room service didn't have any raw cookie dough, and we were both pretty emotionally spent. We settled for a dinner at the hotel restaurant and diligent note-taking

Both of us are viciously opposed to the notion of "the journey," that any pain is worthwhile and can be redeemed in life lessons or spun into art or meaning, like cashing in a casino chip. But it's undeniable that we both found meaning in writing and researching this book—in interviewing people also trying to make sense of what had happened to them, plus scholars, doctors, educators, therapists, and activists, at a time when an already screwed system is becoming more dangerous by way of laws that misunderstand and/or are completely indifferent to the lives of pregnant people.

The meaning, for us, isn't just about those babies we lost anymore. The pregnancies that ended in trauma, that blasted out our insides. It's about the hope that no one else ends up almost dead from a miscarriage before medicine will intervene, or feels lost and isolated in a confusing knot of grief, or knows nothing of pregnancy loss until it happens to them.

The liberation in making your own ritual, your own meaning? It evolves with you.

AFTERWORD

We're only just beginning to see how the profound changes to reproductive healthcare are impacting American lives. And honestly, it's going to get a lot worse before it gets better. (Wombless Rebecca is headed straight to the colonies if Gilead comes. Colleen may have a shot at Aunt, but brown isn't really her color.) Roughly half the country now has restrictive laws in place. Doctors are moving out of these states, and maternity wards are closing, making even routine obstetric care harder to find. The two-tiered system of reproductive access that has persisted since the passage of the Hyde Amendment in 1976 may become even more draconian and unequal. It's going to take years before things change. In that time, a lot of people will probably become sick and die.

Right now, we're in a moment where only the most horrific,

bloodiest, and most life-threatening pregnancy loss stories break out over the din. But none of this is about auditioning for humanity. Women, people of color, and other marginalized groups are constantly put in a position to lay bare their trauma for a scrap of consideration, begging to matter one personal story at a time. It's exhausting.

The movement to restrict abortion is also tied to other civil rights issues; those seeking to restrict transgender rights draw from the successes of the antiabortion playbook. Tennessee's ban on gender-affirming care, for example, used arguments made in the Supreme Court's abortion ruling. So as one right withers, it's possible many others are next.

There is no proverbial bow to tie around any of this.

But the fall of *Roe* has, for better or worse, brought to light the connectedness of all forms of pregnancy loss and the concept that it can be downright hazardous to ascribe blanket morality to difficult and highly specific medical choices. Those who have experienced ectopic pregnancies, miscarriages, stillbirths, and TFMRs are finding kinship and common ground with one another rather than retreating to their separate corners. The loss space is a fellowship, and these parents feel fiercely protective of one another.

The gray areas between the perfect pregnancy and abortion are discussed more now than most anytime in the last century, thanks to everyday people sharing their stories on social media, the work of advocates, and even celebrities who are more open about their experiences. Anyone speaking up makes it easier for others to do the same and disrupts the shame, stigma, and silence that previously marked this space.

Science also is finally starting to focus more on pregnancy-related complications, and there is, however small, more public discussion of inequitable medical care. But the maternal mortality and morbidity crisis among people of color should be mentioned alongside every issue in this space. This crisis is an everyone problem.

The lawyers, doctors, advocates, and experts we've interviewed think it's going to be at least a decade before ground begins to settle on reproductive care. We're writing this book just as these profound changes are all starting to be implemented, and we have no crystal ball to tell you what's going to happen. But the breakdown of today might just present us with an opportunity. What if, during this period, we can learn from our mistakes and rebuild in a way that allows for all the permutations of pregnancy and loss and the entire spectrum of emotion?

It would have to be a reworked system, one that looks out for the health, humanity, and well-being of all pregnant people.

ACKNOWLEDGMENTS

This book was three years in the making. Well, sort of. Three years from the idea, a decade since our losses, more than thirty years of friendship. Any way you count it, a long gestation.

We are so grateful to everyone who helped us along the way, from the parents who shared their loss stories with us to the experts, doctors, midwives, lawyers, historians, therapists, and advocates who shared their expertise and helped us paint a picture of the current landscape. Any errors in the book are our own.

We would like to thank:

Our agents, Jan Baumer and Sonali Chanchani, who gave us so much confidence when they were interested in our proposal, then helped finesse it and find the right outlet. We were so grateful to have you as partners and loved the symmetry of a two-woman writing team and a two-woman agent team. We are lucky to have found you.

Our editor, Erin McClary at Sourcebooks, who helped shape this book into its final form. We are so thankful that you recognized the value of this work, advocated for it, and took a gamble on a difficult subject matter, to say the least. We are also grateful to the entire team at Sourcebooks who worked on design and promotion. Thank you for supporting our work.

Our readers, Abby Anders, Anne Dashine, Molly Ferris, Elizabeth Kennedy, Joanna Lewis, Ashley Little, Kara Norman, Jenna Shapiro, Alexa Stanard, and Nicole Woitowich, who helped wrestle early drafts into submission. Thank you for your perspectives and support and for reassuring us that we really were onto something.

We would especially like to thank historians Shannon Withycombe and Lara Freidenfelds, who walked us through the history of pregnancy loss; Kiley Hanish of Return to Zero: Hope, who put out a call for sources and offered resources and expertise; Kate Carson and Margot Finn, admins of Ending a Wanted Pregnancy, as well as Jane Armstrong and Sabrina Fletcher, who shared their TFMR experiences and knowledge; linguists Elise Kramer and Jessica Rett, who helped us understand framing, registers, and sociolinguistics; Kate Watson for helping us through linguistic challenges; Jessica Zucker, Marny Smith of PUSH, and Elana Frank of the Jewish Fertility Foundation, who linked us up with sources and provided valuable insight into the pregnancy loss space; Jill Wieber Lens, who channels her rage over ridiculous policies around stillbirth into action; and doctors Sarah Prager, Katharine White, and Lisa Harris, and midwife Morgan Nuzzo, not just for their counsel but for their fieldwork. We also want to thank Jan Chozen Bays for inviting us to the *mizuko kuyo* ceremony. It was so meaningful, and we are truly grateful. We are thankful to everyone who talked to us for this book, and our research was made richer by your perspectives.

We'd like to give a very sincere thanks to the one-hundred-plus people who told us their personal stories of pregnancy loss. Each moved us. Some made us cry, others sent us into a full-tilt rage, and all affected us deeply. Every time we talked to one of you, we felt even more determination that this book was necessary. Thank you for trusting us and for caring about others enough to talk about your own experiences. We are so grateful to you.

REBECCA

I want to thank my husband, Andy, who has been an early reader of almost everything I've written since we were nineteen years old. He read dozens of drafts of various portions of the book, many with me sitting nearby saying, "What part are you on now?" "Why are you laughing?" "Why aren't you laughing?" "Why are you making that face?" "Why aren't you saying anything?" Yet somehow, the marriage survived. He was incredibly supportive and really believed in the book, even when I would turn into a limp noodle and bemoan my life choices. I also want to thank my boys—Alex, Joe, and Danny—for being empathetic and curious creatures and for bringing such consideration to both me and the subject matter. These kids have grown up knowing they have three brothers who died, and it has framed their compassion and nuance on this topic to a degree that most adults haven't achieved. They're pretty exceptional, and I'm so lucky they are mine. I also want to thank my parents, Mary and Ron Little, who watched the boys many times so that I could work, who read early drafts, and who, my whole life, when I said I wanted to jump, not only asked how high but signed me up for leaping lessons and helped me practice. So much love to my siblings, Ashley and Sean; my in-laws, Mickey and Jill; my longtime friends Abby Anders, Anne Dashine, Molly Ferris, Sonja Gill, Joanna Lewis, Hilary McElligott, Maribel Nash, and Alexa Stanard, and all my beloved cousins, aunts, and uncles who were supportive all the way through from kernel of idea to finished book and did the work of reminding me to be a person along the way. Thank you also to Kristin Harvey and Lia, who provided childcare and other assistance that allowed me to focus on my work. Thank you for everything.

Lastly, I have to thank my coauthor, Colleen. It wouldn't be accurate to say that I always knew we would one day write a book about our tragic losses together—that would have been pretty dark and prescient for fourth grade—but our tendency to run along parallel tracks was clear from a young age. Invest in your early friendships, because you never know: one day, you may be swinging at Leavitt Park, hoping that the Virgin Mary doesn't appear and compel you to become a nun, and the next, you'll be hammer texting links to fetus jewelry because you just can't believe what you're seeing. This has been one of the best personal and professional experiences of my life. Thank you for being a friend.

COLLEEN

I would first like to thank my husband, Andrew (not to be confused with Rebecca's husband), who was all in when I came up with this idea, read the book, and offered immensely useful feedback. He even thought of the title for the book. You counseled me through reporting and drafts, relived dark days, and forced me to stick to my writing schedule even when I wanted to sit on the couch and watch *30 Rock* reruns. I love you, and I deeply appreciate your support and care. To our kids, Wyatt and Ruby, thank you for being kind and wonderful and curious about this and everything else. I hope I make you proud, and I love you both very much. To my mother, Maureen, and sister, Claudia, this book is also for you. I honor your losses, and I love you both. I appreciate the support of my giant family, especially my brother, Nico, my uncles, many, many cousins, and the aunts—Mary, Kack, TR, Paula, and also Stacie—and thank them for sharing their stories. Thanks to Jenna and to Deroy Peraza for unfailing support. Thanks also to my longtime friends Kristin Acuff, Amy Dickerson, Emily Larsen, and Hannah Oakes for saying (for years) that I could do this. I'd also like to acknowledge my AP editor Nancy Benac, herself a great writer, who helped me by allowing me to guard my off-work hours so I could research and write. Lastly, thank you so much to Kara Norman, who encourages me to write even when that writing is bad poetry that no one should ever see, and to Elizabeth Kennedy for the hours and hours of discussion about this and everything else in life, and also for Sunday dinners.

And to my coauthor, Rebecca: thank you for agreeing to plumb the very depths of your personal despair for this book. I know we both agree that everything is copy, but extending that to cursed wombs is next level. Working on this book has been exceptionally rewarding. I'm grateful for all your partnership, and not just because we're both type A people who are usually stuck doing all the work in a group project but because we come from the same place, literally and metaphorically, and we both recognize the value of humor as a necessary salve. Not every friend will laugh at your resin baby jokes and get your *Wayne's World* deep cut references. Writing this has been just as good as being the chosen ones to fetch Mrs. Delaney's tea from the teacher's lounge.

APPENDIX: DID YOU SERIOUSLY JUST SAY THAT TO ME?

A near-universal aspect of any loss experience is when those around the grieving person say the wrong thing. We asked everyone we interviewed for the phrases (and actions) they hated and those that really helped.

DON'T SAY:

"Everything happens for a reason."

No, it doesn't. Come on. Do you even believe this, or are you just saying it because you've heard it before? Be prepared to supply the reason why you think they lost the pregnancy or baby. Be equally prepared to be punched in the tenders.

"At least (it happened early/your health is OK/you can have another, etc.)."

No sentence that is intended for comfort should start with "at least." For example, "At least your friend got to take a fun hike before they fell off that cliff." Feeling better yet? Some common examples: "At least you know you can get pregnant," "At least this probably means something was wrong with the baby," "At least you can travel now," "At least you got a few minutes/few days with her." Be wary of the word "just" for the same reasons.

"Count your blessings."

Gratitude practice has its place, but not right now, you hippie. Let the grieving person come to this on their own. Forced gratitude goes against the mission.

"Nature took care of it/there must have been something wrong."

Maybe. Maybe not. Who cares? Someone is sad. You're focusing on the wrong thing.

"Be thankful it happened before you got to know the baby."

Asking someone to be grateful that their hoped-for baby died before they got to know them as opposed to being ripped from them at a later date is really bizarre. Child death is not an inevitable experience for a parent, so you don't need to construct a timeline where it's a comfort.

"I know just how you feel because my (dog/cat/hamster/lizard) died."

Almost half of the people we interviewed had someone say

something like, "My dog died last year, so I know just how you feel," or "My cat is really sick, so I'm going through this too," or "My animals are like my children, so I've been there." Listen, we like pets, but this is not comparable. It just isn't. You did not have to push your dead schnauzer out of your body when he was put to sleep. You do not generally have a series of puppies who die in succession. Comparative grief is always tricky. Stick to "I'm sorry," and grieve your pet's death on its own terms.

"You can always try again/have another baby."

You don't know if that's true. And whether it is or not is none of your business. Also babies aren't mufflers; you don't swap one out for another.

"Your baby is in a better place/you have an angel in heaven/God needed another angel."

This is an example of the short circuit—don't be sad, God wanted this. Well, then he seems like a jerk. Be careful of imposing religion on someone else or of using religion to try to stop up every outlet for grief. Offer prayers if they will be gratefully received, but be aware of your audience.

"Time heals all wounds."

Maybe. Guess we'll see. But right now, it's fresh, so knock it off.

"Let me know if you need anything."

This one seems benign but actually puts the onus back on the grieving person to make an assignment. Grief emotional labor, if you will. It tends to make the person who said it feel virtuous for offering without actually resulting in any help for the griever. Instead try something like, "I'd love to bring you dinner on Tuesday," or "Can I take the kids on Saturday? I'll bring them back after we spend a couple hours at the pool."

"You'll get through this."

This isn't terrible in the scheme of things, but grief isn't something to defeat. Trauma isn't something to wrestle like an alligator. Frequent asks to get coffee, go on walks, go out to dinner, run errands together—repeatedly—help someone walk through grief rather than recommending they conquer it and hold its head aloft like a Scottish king.

Nothing.

We understand this instinct. Many people are afraid they'll say the wrong thing, so they say nothing at all. Or you're worried that if you bring it up, it will make the person sad. Most loss parents, especially in the immediate postpartum period, are thinking about it all the time. You bringing it up won't change that. Use the tips below to say the right thing. Silence isn't helpful.

ALSO AVOID:

Fortune teller statements

"You'll be fine. You'll have a baby. I know it." You don't know anything! Stop it.

Comparisons

There's an old *Far Side* cartoon where a guy with a peg leg says to a guy with a peg head, "Well, I guess that ain't a bad story, but let me tell you about the time I lost this." There can be comfort in sharing a similar story if you have one—you also miscarried, terminated, or had a stillbirth—but be careful not to compete. We're all walking around traumatized. Nobody gets a prize.

Cheerleading

These comments are along the lines of "You can always try again," "This will make you stronger," etc. This just makes it feel like the grieving person should get over it and no one really understands.

Doing anything irreversible

Do not take down the nursery or donate the maternity clothes in an effort to help ease their pain. You can store them out of sight, but don't do anything that can't be undone. Put them aside, and let the grieving parents decide when or how they want to deal with them.

Being a grief vampire

Do not try to get all the dirty details so you can be the one "in the know." Don't pepper them with insensitive or personal questions.

Giving unsolicited advice or trying to find a reason this all happened

No one cares.

Making the grieving person comfort you

There's a concept called "ring theory" developed by psychologist Susan Silk and her friend Barry Goldman. It's pretty simple—the person in crisis is the center in the ring. The next closest people are in the first ring. Keep drawing rings, and keep adding the next closest people. They call this the "kvetching order." The center person can kvetch to anyone. The next closest ring? They can kvetch to the next ring out. But everyone in the rings has to help inward. You comfort in, you dump out. It's brilliant, correct, and effective.

HERE'S WHAT TO DO AND SAY INSTEAD.

- "I thought about your baby today."
- Use the baby's name, if it was given one.
- Sit with them and listen to their story (or sit in silence if that's where they're at) without trying to fix it.
- See if the family wants you to be the one to share the news so they don't have to with friends, family, the hairdresser—anyone who saw them pregnant who may ask about the baby next time.
- Offer to take the other kids out of the house with a specific date and time. "Can Tommy come to the library with us today? I'll pick him up at 11:30 a.m. and have him back by 2 p.m., and I'll feed him lunch."
- Offer to walk the dog.

- Get groceries/drop off dinner/start a meal train/order restaurant meals. Don't expect to stay and chat early on. Just feed them and go away.
- Check in by phone/text/carrier pigeon. Just don't expect a response.
- Listen to the story if they want to tell it. Don't push if they don't. Something like, "I'd love to hear about your baby when you're ready."
- Send actual mail.
- Ask if you can run errands for or with them.
- Send flowers.
- "I'm sad for you" or "I'm here for you."
- Invite them to go out, and don't be deterred if the answer is no at first.
- Make note of the day of the loss and check in with the parents at one month, six weeks, three months, six months, nine months, and one year.
- "I don't know what to say, but I love you very much."
- Invite them to baby showers. Let them decide whether they are ready to go to this or anything else. Taking away more agency isn't helpful.
- "I'm thinking of you today."

RECOMMENDED MEDIA

BOOKS

- *War Against the Weak: Eugenics and America's Campaign to Create a Master Race* by Edwin Black
- *Contraception and Abortion in 19th Century America* by Janet Farrell Brodie
- *The Brink of Being: Talking about Miscarriage* by Julia Bueno
- *Bearing the Unbearable: Love, Loss, and the Heartbreaking Path of Grief* by Joanne Cacciatore
- *Birth: The Surprising History of How We Are Born* by Tina Cassidy
- *Woman of Valor: Margaret Sanger and the Birth Control Movement in America* by Ellen Chesler
- *Unwell Women: Misdiagnosis and Myth in a Man-Made World* by Elinor Cleghorn

- *The Way We Never Were: American Families and the Nostalgia Trap* by Stephanie Coontz
- *Empty Cradle, Broken Heart: Surviving the Death of Your Baby* by Deborah L. Davis
- *It's OK That You're Not OK: Meeting Grief and Loss in a Culture That Doesn't Understand* by Megan Devine
- *Ourselves Unborn: A History of the Fetus in Modern America* by Sara Dubow
- *Disembodying Women: Perspectives on Pregnancy and the Unborn* by Barbara Duden
- *For Her Own Good: Two Centuries of the Experts' Advice to Women* by Barbara Ehrenreich and Deirdre English
- *Witches, Midwives, and Nurses: A History of Women Healers* by Barbara Ehrenreich and Deirdre English
- *Get Me Out: A History of Childbirth from the Garden of Eden to the Sperm Bank* by Randi Hutter Epstein
- *Backlash: The Undeclared War Against American Women* by Susan Faludi
- *The End of American Childhood: A History of Parenting from Life on the Frontier to the Managed Child* by Paula S. Fass
- *The Turnaway Study: Ten Years, a Thousand Women, and the Consequences of Having—or Being Denied—an Abortion* by Diana Greene Foster
- *The Myth of the Perfect Pregnancy: A History of Miscarriage in America* by Lara Freidenfelds
- *Like a Mother: A Feminist Journey Through the Science and Culture of Pregnancy* by Angela Garbes

- *What God Is Honored Here? Writings on Miscarriage and Infant Loss by and for Native Women and Women of Color* by Shannon Gibney and Kao Kalia Yang
- *Babies Made Us Modern: How Infants Brought America into the Twentieth Century* by Janet Golden
- *Policing the Womb: Invisible Women and the Criminalization of Motherhood* by Michele Goodwin
- *The Pain Gap: How Sexism and Racism in Healthcare Kill Women* by Anushay Hossain
- *Empty Arms: Coping After Miscarriage, Stillbirth, and Infant Death* by Sherokee Ilse
- *High Risk: Stories of Pregnancy, Birth, and the Unexpected* by Chavi Eve Karkowsky
- *Revolutionary Conceptions: Women, Fertility, and Family Limitation in America 1760–1820* by Susan E. Klepp
- *Unspeakable Losses: Healing from Miscarriage, Abortion, and Other Pregnancy Loss* by Kim Kluger-Bell
- *The Body Keeps the Score: Brain, Mind, and Body in the Healing of Trauma* by Bessel van der Kolk
- *The All New Don't Think of an Elephant!: Know Your Values and Frame the Debate* by George Lakoff
- *Moral Politics: How Liberals and Conservatives Think* by George Lakoff
- *Motherhood Lost: A Feminist Account of Pregnancy Loss in America* by Linda L. Layne
- *Brought to Bed: Childbearing in America 1750–1950* by Judith Walzer Leavitt

- *Interrogating Pregnancy Loss: Feminist Writings on Abortion, Miscarriage, and Stillbirth* by Emily R. M. Lind and Angie Deveau
- *Delivered by Midwives: African American Midwifery in the Twentieth-Century South* by Jenny M. Luke
- *Abortion and the Politics of Motherhood* by Kristin Luker
- *The Woman in the Body: A Cultural Analysis of Reproduction* by Emily Martin
- *New Handbook for a Post-Roe America: The Complete Guide to Abortion Legality, Access, and Practical Support* by Robin Marty
- *America and the Pill: A History of Politics, Peril, and Liberation* by Elaine Tyler May
- *Homeward Bound: American Families in the Cold War Era* by Elaine Tyler May
- *From Midwives to Medicine: The Birth of American Gynecology* by Deborah Kuhn McGregor
- *Icons of Life: A Cultural History of Human Embryos* by Lynn M. Morgan
- *Medical Bondage: Race, Gender, and the Origins of American Gynecology* by Deirdre Cooper Owens
- *Invisible Women: Data Bias in a World Designed for Men* by Caroline Criado Perez
- *Abortion and Woman's Choice: The State, Sexuality, and Reproductive Freedom* by Rosalind Pollack Petchesky
- *Pro: Reclaiming Abortion Rights* by Katha Pollitt

- *Testing Women, Testing the Fetus: The Social Impact of Amniocentesis in America* by Rayna Rapp
- *When Abortion Was a Crime: Women, Medicine, and Law in the United States, 1867–1973* by Leslie J. Reagan
- *Killing the Black Body: Race, Reproduction, and the Meaning of Liberty* by Dorothy E. Roberts
- *Reproductive Justice: An Introduction* by Loretta J. Ross and Rickie Solinger
- *Abortion after Roe* by Johanna Schoen
- *Birthing a Slave: Motherhood and Medicine in the Antebellum South* by Marie Jenkins Schwartz
- *Modern Motherhood: An American History* by Jodi Vandenberg-Daves
- *The Midwife Said Fear Not: A History of Midwifery in the United States* by Helen Varney and Joyce Beebe Thompson
- *Medical Apartheid: The Dark History of Medical Experimentation on Black Americans from Colonial Times to the Present* by Harriet A. Washington
- *Lying In: A History of Childbirth in America* by Richard W. and Dorothy C. Wertz
- *Your Guide to Miscarriage and Pregnancy Loss: Hope and Healing When You're No Longer Expecting* by Kate White
- *Stillbirth and the Law* by Jill Wieber Lens, forthcoming
- *Lost: Miscarriage in 19th Century America* by Shannon Withycombe
- *Abortion and the Law in America: Roe v. Wade to the Present* by Mary Ziegler

- *After Roe: The Lost History of the Abortion Debate* by Mary Ziegler
- *I Had a Miscarriage: A Memoir, A Movement* by Jessica Zucker

ARTICLES

- Dias, Elizabeth. "When Does Life Begin?" *New York Times*, December 21, 2022. https://www.nytimes.com/interactive /2022/12/31/us/human-life-begin.html.
- Donley, Greer, and Jill Wieber Lens. "Abortion, Pregnancy Loss, & Subjective Fetal Personhood." *Vanderbilt Law Review* 75 (June 1, 2022): 1649–727. https://papers.ssrn.com/sol3 /papers.cfm?abstract_id=4125492.
- Eldeib, Duaa, Nadia Sussman, Liz Moughon, and Adriana Gallardo. "Stillbirths: When Babies Die Before Taking Their First Breath." ProPublica, 2022. https://www.propublica.org /series/stillbirths.
- Markin, Rayna, and Sigal Zilcha-Mano. "Cultural Processes in Psychotherapy for Perinatal Loss: Breaking the Cultural Taboo Against Perinatal Grief." *Psychotherapy* 55, no. 1 (March 2018): 20–26. https://doi.org/10.1037/pst0000122.
- Parsons, Kate. "Feminist Reflections on Miscarriage, In Light of Abortion." *International Journal of Feminist Approaches to Bioethics* 3, no. 1 (Spring 2010): 1–22. https://doi.org/10 .3138/ijfab.3.1.1.

- Petchesky, Rosalind Pollack. "Fetal Images: The Power of Visual Culture in the Politics of Reproduction." *Feminist Studies* 13, no. 2 (Summer 1987): 263–92. https://doi.org /10.2307/3177802.
- Reagan, Leslie J. "From Hazard to Blessing to Tragedy: Representations of Miscarriage in Twentieth-Century America." *Feminist Studies* 29, no. 2 (Summer 2003): 356–78. http://www.jstor.org/stable/3178514.

PODCASTS

- Evans, Robert, and Dr. Kaveh Hoda. "Part One: The Father of Gynecology." *Behind the Bastards.* July 12, 2022. https://www .iheart.com/podcast/105-behind-the-bastards-29236323 /episode/part-one-the-father-of-gynecology-99304866/.
- Freeman, Erica. *Sisters in Loss.* https://sistersinloss.com/.
- Masarik, Elizabeth Garner, and Sarah Handley-Cousins. "Abortion and Birth Control before Roe v. Wade: 19th & 20th c. Family Limitation." *Dig: A History Podcast*, January 7, 2018. https://digpodcast.org/2018/01/07/before-roe-v -wade/.
- Masarik, Elizabeth Garner, and Sarah Handley-Cousins. "Miscarriage in 19th Century America." *Dig: A History Podcast*, February 10, 2019. https://digpodcast.org/2019 /02/10/miscarriage-nineteenth-century-america/.
- Masarik, Elizabeth Garner, and Marissa Rhodes. "Early American Family Limitation." *Dig: A History Podcast*,

April 25, 2021. https://digpodcast.org/2021/04/25/early
-american-family-limitation-2/.

- Matthews, Susan. "Slow Burn: Roe v. Wade." Slate, June 1,
  2022. https://slate.com/podcasts/slow-burn/s7/roe-v-wade.

NOTES

Introduction

Ten to 20 percent: Jonah Bardos et al., "A National Survey on Public Perceptions of Miscarriage," *Obstetrics & Gynecology* 125, no. 6 (June 2015): 1313–20, https://doi.org/10.1097/aog.0000000000000859.

Stillbirths are a smaller subset: "What Is Stillbirth?," Centers for Disease Control and Prevention, last reviewed September 29, 2022, https://www.cdc .gov/ncbddd/stillbirth/facts.html.

According to the Centers: "What Is Stillbirth?"

The odds of being struck: "Lightning Strike Victim Data," Centers for Disease Control and Prevention, last reviewed September 16, 2022, https://www.cdc .gov/disasters/lightning/victimdata.html.

Restricting access and abortion stigma: Jessica Zucker, "'Sometimes It Was Easier to Say I Delivered a Stillborn': Termination for Medical Reasons Post-*Roe*," *Vogue*, June 9, 2023, https://www.vogue.com/article/termination-for -medical-reasons-post-roe.

The United States has 32.9 deaths: Donna L. Hoyert, "Maternal Mortality Rates in the United States, 2021," NCHS Health E-Stats, 2023, https://dx .doi.org/10.15620/cdc:124678; Roosa Tikkanen et al., "Maternal Mortality and Maternity Care in the United States Compared to 10 Other Developed Countries," Commonwealth Fund, Issue Briefs, November 18, 2020, https:// www.commonwealthfund.org/publications/issue-briefs/2020/nov/maternal -mortality-maternity-care-us-compared-10-countries.

Maternal deaths across: Laura G. Fleszar et al., "Trends in State-Level Maternal Mortality by Racial and Ethnic Group in the United States," *JAMA* 330, no. 1 (2023): 52–61, https://doi.org/10.1001/jama.2023.9043.

Black mothers are more: "Working Together to Reduce Black Maternal Mortality," Centers for Disease Control and Prevention, April 3, 2023, https://www.cdc.gov/healthequity/features/maternal-mortality/index.html.

Chapter One

In the first movie: *Look Who's Talking,* directed by Amy Heckerling (Tristar Pictures, 1989), 4:22 to 4:45, https://www.amazon.com/Look-Whos-Talking-John-Travolta/dp/B000J3FY18.

In the second movie: *Look Who's Talking Too,* directed by Amy Heckerling (Tristar Pictures, 1990), 4:24 to 6:29, https://www.amazon.com/Look-Whos-Talking-John-Travolta/dp/B003E2LTZQ.

As the egg moves down: Yasmine AlSayyad, "What We Still Don't Know about Periods," *New Yorker,* April 12, 2023, https://www.newyorker.com/books/under-review/what-we-still-dont-know-about-periods; John L. Fitzpatrick et al., "Chemical Signals from Eggs Facilitate Cryptic Female Choice in Humans," *Proceedings of the Royal Society* 287, no. 1928 (June 10, 2020): 5, https://doi.org/10.1098/rspb.2020.0805.

Then the two cells': Elizabeth Dias, "When Does Life Begin?," *New York Times,* December 31, 2022, https://www.nytimes.com/interactive/2022/12/31/us/human-life-begin.html.

How about that: Dias, "When Does Life Begin?"

Once the sperm and the egg: "Fertilization," in Bruce Alberts et al., *Molecular Biology of the Cell,* 4th ed. (New York: Garland Science, 2002), https://www.ncbi.nlm.nih.gov/books/NBK26843.

The dividing zygote turns: Dias, "When Does Life Begin?"; Yusuf S. Khan and Kristin M. Ackerman, "Embryology, Week 1," StatPearls, April 17, 2023, https://www.ncbi.nlm.nih.gov/books/NBK554562/.

From week three to about eight: "Fetal Development," Cleveland Clinic, last reviewed March 3, 2023, https://my.clevelandclinic.org/health/articles/7247-fetal-development-stages-of-growth.

Incidentally, most abortions and miscarriages: Greer Donley and Jill Wieber Lens, "Abortion, Pregnancy Loss & Subjective Fetal Personhood," *Vanderbilt Law Review* 75 (June 1, 2022): 1665, https://papers.ssrn.com/sol3/papers.cfm?abstract_id=4125492.

Humans are notoriously inefficient reproducers: Dias, "When Does Life Begin?"; Annual Capri Workshop Group, "Early Pregnancy Loss: The Default

Outcome for Fertilized Human Oocytes," *Journal of Assisted Reproduction and Genetics* 37, no. 5 (May 2020): 1057–63, https://doi.org/10.1007/s10815 -020-01749-y.

Sociolinguist George Lakoff talks: George Lakoff, *Moral Politics: How Liberals and Conservatives Think* (Chicago: University of Chicago Press, 2016), 264–65.

The modern Supreme Court: Paula Abrams, "The Scarlet Letter: The Supreme Court and the Language of Abortion Stigma," *Michigan Journal of Gender and Law* 19, no. 2 (2013): 293–94, https://repository.law.umich.edu/cgi /viewcontent.cgi?article=1025&context=mjgl.

(Gretchen, stop trying: *Mean Girls*, directed by Mark Waters (Paramount Pictures, 2004), 39:59 to 40:05, https://www.amazon.com/Mean-Girls -Lindsay-Lohan/dp/B000HZGBJC.

So in a culture where we have: Kim Kluger-Bell, *Unspeakable Losses: Healing from Miscarriage, Abortion and Other Pregnancy Loss* (New York: Harper, 2000), 123.

Many people feel invalidated: Kate Parsons, "Feminist Reflections on Miscarriage, in Light of Abortion," *International Journal of Feminist Approaches to Bioethics* 3, no. 1 (Spring 2010): 2, https://doi.org/10.3138/ijfab.3.1.1.

"We recommend that providers": Kiley Krekorian Hanish, phone interview with the authors, May 19, 2022; Kiley Krekorian Hanish, email message to the authors, August 8, 2023.

"Terms like 'products of conception'": Kelsey Garcia-Abdin, phone interview with the authors, April 12, 2023; Kelsey Garcia-Abdin, email message to the authors, August 7, 2023.

"I don't know what category": Michelle Goldwin Kaufman, phone interview with the authors, March 15, 2023.

"We definitely talk about": Katie N., phone interview with the authors, April 23, 2023.

Many view this as a failure: Linda Layne, *Motherhood Lost: A Feminist Account of Pregnancy Loss in America* (New York: Routledge, 2013), chapter 10, Kindle.

"At that stage of pregnancy": Jess C., phone interview with the authors, April 14, 2023.

"I talk about it sort of": Margaret P., phone interview with the authors, April 18, 2023.

New York–based Nicole O.: Nicole O., phone interview with the authors, January 27, 2023.

"If I tell somebody": Sarah Prager, phone interview with the authors, July 20, 2022.

A D&E (dilation and evacuation): Donley and Lens, "Abortion, Pregnancy Loss."

"But in my career": Prager, phone interview.

Later pregnancy losses and abortion: Greer Donley and Jill Wieber Lens, "Why Do We Talk about Miscarriage Differently from Abortion?," *New York Times*, August 2, 2022, https://www.nytimes.com/2022/08/02/opinion/abortion-miscarriage-roe-dobbs.html.

"Let's just call it": Kimberly Nordyke and Ryan Gajewski, "Chrissy Teigen Reveals She Had an Abortion to 'Save My Life for a Baby That Had Absolutely No Chance,'" *Hollywood Reporter*, September 15, 2022, https://www.hollywoodreporter.com/news/general-news/chrissy-teigen-miscarriage-abortion-john-legend-baby-jack-1235221899/.

The Catholic, antiabortion LifeNews.com: Tierin-Rose Mandelburg, "Chrissy Teigen's Miscarriage Can't Be an Abortion, Because Abortions Purposefully Kill Babies," LifeNews.com, September 19, 2022, https://www.lifenews.com/2022/09/19/chrissy-teigens-miscarriage-cant-be-an-abortion-because-abortions-purposefully-kill-babies/.

These organizations and antiabortion medical groups: Micaiah Bilger, "Doctors Confirm Removing Baby's Body after Miscarriage Is Not an Abortion," LifeNews.com, December 12, 2022, https://www.lifenews.com/2022/12/12/doctors-confirm-removing-dead-babys-body-after-a-miscarriage-is-not-an-abortion/.

As law professors Jill Wieber Lens: Donley and Lens, "Abortion, Pregnancy Loss."

On his podcast: Candice Ortiz, "Ted Cruz Argues Chrissy Teigen's Abortion Was Actually a Miscarriage Since It Saved Her Life," Mediaite.com, September 26, 2022, https://www.mediaite.com/podcasts/ted-cruz-argues-chrissy-teigens-abortion-was-actually-a-miscarriage-since-it-saved-her-life/.

Writer and historian Daniela Blei: Daniela Blei, "The History of Talking about Miscarriage," The Cut, April 23, 2018, https://www.thecut.com/2018/04/the-history-of-talking-about-miscarriage.html.

Texas's ban specifies that: Kate Zernike, "What Does 'Abortion' Mean? Even the Word Itself Is Up for Debate," *New York Times*, October 18, 2022, https://www.nytimes.com/2022/10/18/us/abortion-roe-debate.html.

The American Medical Association: Zernike, "What Does 'Abortion' Mean?"

As journalist Christina Cauterucci wrote: Christina Cauterucci, "The Kind of Life That Texas Really Values," Slate, July 22, 2023, https://slate.com/news-and-politics/2023/07/texas-abortion-ban-infant-deaths-samantha-casiano.html.

When abortion is deemed a: Carmel Shachar, "The Only Moral Abortion

Is…," Bill of Health, July 21, 2022, https://blog.petrieflom.law.harvard.edu/2022/07/21/moral-abortion-ectopic-pregnancy/.

Morgan Nuzzo, a certified nurse midwife: Morgan Nuzzo, phone interview with the authors, May 22, 2023; Joyce Arthur, "The Only Moral Abortion Is My Abortion," *Joyce Arthur's page* (blog), September 2000, https://joycearthur.com/abortion/the-only-moral-abortion-is-my-abortion/.

"I resist modifiers": Prager, phone interview.

"There is definitely a nuance": Katie N., phone interview.

Abortions after twenty weeks: Donley and Lens, "Abortion, Pregnancy Loss."

"There are two types": Nuzzo, phone interview.

Alison Dreith, director of strategic partnerships: Alison Dreith, phone interview with the authors, March 9, 2023.

"We need to talk about abortion": Dreith, phone interview.

"Sometimes I don't even like": Sabrina Fletcher, phone interview with the authors, August 30, 2022.

"I don't think most people": Jane Armstrong, phone interview with the authors, May 30, 2022.

Fletcher, who became a bereavement doula: Fletcher, phone interview.

"Did I really choose it?": Heather Pew, phone interview with the authors, January 12, 2023.

"Some in our group say": Margot Finn, phone interview with the authors, March 1, 2023.

"I had to sit there": Rebecca S., phone interview with the authors, January 25, 2023.

"I'm really not ashamed": Yvette, interview with the authors, April 18, 2023.

"One of my canned phrases": Nuzzo, phone interview.

"The word abortion was hard": Malina W., phone interview with the authors, March 15, 2023.

"Being so visibly pregnant": Laura T., phone interview with the authors, January 17, 2023.

Cleveland-based Brittany: Brittany, phone interview with the authors, February 15, 2023.

"He was using words like": Kristen Swanson, phone interview by the authors, May 5, 2022.

Geriatric pregnancy used to: Rachel E. Gross, "Please Don't Call My Cervix Incompetent," *Atlantic*, January 25, 2023, https://www.theatlantic.com/health/archive/2023/01/geriatric-pregnancy-old-outdated-medical-terms/672834/.

Geriatric pregnancy gave way to: Gross, "Please Don't Call."

This is how it is medically coded: Gross, "Please Don't Call."

It used to be taught that: Emily Martin, *The Woman in the Body: A Cultural Analysis of Reproduction* (Boston: Beacon Press, 2001), 45.

"The language we use": Lacey M., phone interview with the authors, February 3, 2023.

A 2018 study found that: Anna P. Goddu et al., "Do Words Matter? Stigmatizing Language and the Transmission of Bias in the Medical Record," *Journal of General Internal Medicine* 33, no. 5 (May 2018): 685–91, https://pubmed.ncbi.nlm.nih.gov/29374357/.

Some suggestions include replacing: Tassia Agatowski, "The #Renaming-Revolution Glossary Is Here," Peanut, May 11, 2023, https://www.peanut-app.io/blog/renaming-revolution-glossary.

"I didn't know I had been": Ashley B., phone interview with the authors, April 12, 2023.

"People need to hear the word": Nneka Hall, phone interview with the authors, March 4, 2023.

"It's heteronormative assumption": Ashley P., Zoom interview with the authors, April 21, 2023.

"There is a complete lack": Tina Mody, Zoom interview with the authors, April 11, 2023.

The American College of Obstetricians and Gynecologists: "Inclusive Language," American College of Obstetricians and Gynecologists, February 2022, https://www.acog.org/clinical-information/policy-and-position-statements/statements-of-policy/2022/inclusive-language.

Family Equality, a nonprofit: "Trans Family Building," Family Equality, accessed April 27, 2023, https://www.familyequality.org/family-building/trans-family-building/.

The American Civil Liberties Union: Gross, "Please Don't Call."

Transgender studies scholar Paisley Currah: Paisley Currah, "Feminism, Gender Pluralism, and Gender Neutrality: Maybe It's Time to Bring Back the Binary," *Paisley Currah* (blog), April 26, 2016, https://www.paisleycurrah.com/2016/04/26/feminism-gender-pluralism-and-gender-neutrality-maybe-its-time-to-bring-back-the-binary/.

"Growing up and living": Catherine, phone interview with the authors, April 17, 2023.

There is very little research: Damien W. Riggs et al., "Men, Trans/Masculine, and Non-Binary People's Experiences of Pregnancy Loss: An International Qualitative Study," *BMC Pregnancy and Childbirth* 20 (2020): 482, https://doi.org/10.1186/s12884-020-03166-6.

"While some talked about": Carla Pfeffer, phone interview with the authors, April 18, 2023.

Chapter Two

Abortion was referenced in: Katie Hunt, "Abortion Is Ancient History: Long Before *Roe*, Women Terminated Pregnancies," CNN, June 23, 2023, https://www.cnn.com/2023/06/23/health/abortion-is-ancient-history-and-that-matters-today-scn/index.html.

Colonial women were playing a numbers: Susan E. Klepp, *Revolutionary Conceptions: Women, Fertility, and Family Limitation in America 1720–1820* (Chapel Hill: University of North Carolina Press, 2009), 4; Mary Beth Norton, *Liberty's Daughters: The Revolutionary Experience of American Women, 1750–1800* (Ithaca, NY: Cornell University Press, 1996), 71.

Nearly one in five children: Klepp, *Revolutionary Conceptions*, 70.

It was also one of the only: Judith Walzer Leavitt, *Brought to Bed: Childbearing in America 1750–1950* (New York: Oxford University Press, 1986), chapter 2, Kindle.

Her friends, neighbors, mother: Norton, *Liberty's Daughters,* 78; Leavitt, *Brought to Bed*, chapter 2, Kindle.

The follow-up to the lying-in: Richard W. Wertz and Dorothy C. Wertz, *Lying In: A History of Childbirth in America* (New Haven, CT: Yale University Press, 1989), 5.

In *Celebrating the Family*: Elizabeth H. Pleck, *Celebrating the Family: Ethnicity, Consumer Culture, and Family Rituals* (Cambridge, MA: Harvard University Press, 2020), 164.

Approximately one in thirty women: Lara Freidenfelds, *The Myth of the Perfect Pregnancy: A History of Miscarriage in America* (New York: Oxford University Press, 2020), 15; Klepp, *Revolutionary Conceptions*, 61.

Cotton Mather warned: Leavitt, *Brought to Bed*, chapter 1, Kindle.

Pregnant poet Anne Bradstreet: Jeannine Hensley, ed., *The Works of Anne Bradstreet* (Cambridge, MA: Belknap Press of Harvard University Press, 1967), 224.

Though some historians do: Norton, *Liberty's Daughters,* 75.

Babies would often fail to thrive: Klepp, *Revolutionary Conceptions*, 61.

In her letters, Abigail Adams: Janet Farrell Brodie, *Contraception and Abortion in 19th Century America* (Ithaca, NY: Cornell University Press, 1994), 41; Norton, *Liberty's Daughters*, 73–75.

Alexander Hamilton grew impatient: Klepp, *Revolutionary Conceptions*, 206–7.

A woman could be prosecuted: Brodie, *Contraception and Abortion*, 39.

And those guys would whip: James A. Cox, "Bilboes, Brands, and Branks," *Colonial Williamsburg Journal*, Spring 2003, https://research.colonialwilliamsburg.org/Foundation/journal/spring03/branks.cfm.

Lara Freidenfelds, a historian: Freidenfelds, *Myth of the Perfect Pregnancy*, 43.

But if she had some: Freidenfelds, *Myth of the Perfect Pregnancy*, 21.

Pregnancies lost further along: Freidenfelds, *Myth of the Perfect Pregnancy*, 25.

Historian Barbara Duden noted: Barbara Duden, "The Fetus on the Farther Shore: Toward a History of the Unborn," in *Fetal Subjects, Feminist Positions*, ed. Lynn M. Morgan and Meredith W. Michaels (Philadelphia: University of Pennsylvania Press), 13–25.

But very much like today: Freidenfelds, *Myth of the Perfect Pregnancy*, 21.

A 1766 obituary: Julia Cherry Spruill, *Women's Life and Work in the Southern Colonies* (New York: W. W. Norton, 1998), 52.

The attitudes around all: Freidenfelds, *Myth of the Perfect Pregnancy*, 38.

British herbalist Nicholas Culpeper's: Brodie, *Contraception and Abortion*, 42.

Fun fact: the Nirvana song: Angie Martoccio, "Nirvana's 'In Utero': 20 Things You Didn't Know," *Rolling Stone*, September 21, 2018, https://www.rollingstone.com/feature/nirvana-in-utero-trivia-kurt-cobain-722109/.

Tansy was also thought to: Brodie, *Contraception and Abortion*, 43.

"But it wasn't like": Lara Freidenfelds, phone interview with the authors, January 12, 2023.

"Abortion was so 'deeply rooted'": Molly Farrell, "Ben Franklin Put an Abortion Recipe in His Math Textbook," Slate, May 5, 2023, https://slate.com/news-and-politics/2022/05/ben-franklin-american-instructor-textbook-abortion-recipe.html.

The first enslaved people: Nikole Hannah-Jones and Mary Elliott, eds., "The 1619 Project," *New York Times Magazine*, August 18, 2019, https://www.nytimes.com/interactive/2019/08/14/magazine/1619-america-slavery.html.

In 1808, Congress ended: "The Act Prohibiting the Importation of Slaves, 1808," National Archives, last reviewed January 7, 2022, https://www.archives.gov/education/lessons/slave-trade.html.

This, coupled with the expansion: Stephanie R. M. Bray and Monica R. McLemore, "Demolishing the Myth of the Default Human That Is Killing Black Mothers," *Frontiers in Public Health* 9 (2021): 675788, https://doi.org/10.3389/fpubh.2021.675788.

Children born to enslaved women: Dorothy E. Roberts, *Killing the Black Body: Race, Reproduction, and the Meaning of Liberty* (New York: Vintage, 2014), chapter 1, Kindle.

Thomas Jefferson, founding father: Thomas Jefferson to John Wayles Eppes, June 30, 1820, Jefferson Quotes and Family Letters, https://tjrs.monticello.org/letter/380.

It's worth remembering: Ibram X. Kendi, *Stamped from the Beginning: The Definitive History of Racist Ideas in America* (New York: Bold Type Books, 2016), 118, 157.

Prenatal care would have come: Jenny M. Luke, *Delivered by Midwives: African American Midwifery in the Twentieth-Century South* (Jackson: University Press of Mississippi, 2018), 27.

Some slaveholders might reduce: Darlene Clark Hine and Kathleen Thompson, *A Shining Thread of Hope: The History of Black Women in America* (New York: Broadway Books, 2009), chapter 3, Kindle.

Pregnancy was unlikely to: Hine and Thompson, *Shining Thread of Hope*, "Motherhood," Kindle.

Most academics working on: Roberts, *Killing the Black Body*, chapter 1, Kindle.

The infant mortality rate: Roberts, *Killing the Black Body*, chapter 1, Kindle.

Frederick Douglass said: Frederick Douglass, *Narrative of the Life of Frederick Douglass, an American Slave* (Peterborough, ON: Broadview Press, 2018), 94.

Slaveholders would break up: Marie Jenkins Schwartz, *Birthing a Slave: Motherhood and Medicine in the Antebellum South* (Cambridge, MA: Harvard University Press, 2009), 19; Roberts, *Killing the Black Body*, chapter 1, Kindle.

Because of this: Roberts, *Killing the Black Body*, chapter 1, Kindle.

As Marie Jenkins Schwartz: Schwartz, *Birthing a Slave*, 96.

These Victorian mothers were: Freidenfelds, *Myth of the Perfect Pregnancy*, 60.

And though it started: Freidenfelds, *Myth of the Perfect Pregnancy*, 60.

But a side effect of these: Sara Dubow, *Ourselves Unborn: A History of the Fetus in Modern America* (New York: Oxford University Press, 2011), 20.

Regulars were usually: Kristin Luker, *Abortion and the Politics of Motherhood* (Berkeley: University of California Press, 1984), 29.

Barbara Ehrenreich and Deirdre English: Barbara Ehrenreich and Deirdre English, *For Her Own Good: Two Centuries of the Experts' Advice to Women* (New York: Second Anchor Books, 2005), 46.

Healing was female when: Ehrenreich and English, *For Her Own Good*, 46.

Getting a foot in the door: Leslie J. Reagan, *When Abortion Was a Crime: Women, Medicine, and Law in the United States, 1867–1973* (Oakland: University of California Press, 2022), 68.

But the regulars weren't very good: Leavitt, *Brought to Bed*, chapter 2, Kindle.

Regardless, the doctor would: Schwartz, *Birthing a Slave*, 37.

When slaveholders called: Schwartz, *Birthing a Slave*, 34, 50; Harriet A. Washington, *Medical Apartheid: The Dark History of Medical Experimentation on Black Americans from Colonial Times to the Present* (New York: Harlem Moon, 2006), chapter 1, Kindle.

By 1845, enslaved women: Schwartz, *Birthing a Slave*, 237.

He had them on a: Deirdre Cooper Owens, *Medical Bondage: Race, Gender, and the Origins of American Gynecology* (Athens: University of Georgia Press, 2018), 38.

They were given opium: Washington, *Medical Apartheid*, chapter 2, Kindle.

These surgeries would have: Washington, *Medical Apartheid*, chapter 2, Kindle.

Sims notes that during: J. Marion Sims, *The Story of My Life* (New York: D. Appleton, 1884), 238.

Anushay Hossain wrote in: Anushay Hossain, *The Pain Gap: How Sexism and Racism in Healthcare Kill Women* (New York: Tiller Press, 2021), 151.

Sims's white physician apprentices: Washington, *Medical Apartheid*, chapter 2, Kindle.

It is not known if Sims: Deborah Kuhn McGregor, *From Midwives to Medicine: The Birth of American Gynecology* (New Brunswick, NJ: Rutgers University Press, 1998), 53.

The procedure Sims is so: Washington, *Medical Apartheid*, chapter 2, Kindle.

The J. Marion Sims statue: William Neuman, "City Orders Sims Statue Removed from Central Park," *New York Times*, April 16, 2018, https://www.nytimes.com/2018/04/16/nyregion/nyc-sims-statue-central-park-monument.htm.

The doctors were much more likely: Owens, *Medical Bondage*, 20.

This access to bodies: Washington, *Medical Apartheid*, chapter 2, Kindle.

Julius was shot out: Ellen Gutoskey, "Why Is It Called a Cesarean Section?" *Mental Floss*, June 13, 2022, https://www.mentalfloss.com/posts/why-is-it-called-a-cesarean-section; "Cesarean Section: A Brief History," U.S. National Library of Medicine, last updated July 26, 2013, https://www.nlm.nih.gov/exhibition/cesarean/part1.html; Donna Sarkar, "Are Cesarean Sections Named after Julius Caesar?" *Discover*, February 24, 2021, https://www.discovermagazine.com/health/are-cesarean-sections-named-after-julius-caesar.

This lack of access: Shannon Withycombe, *Lost: Miscarriage in 19th Century America* (New Brunswick, NJ: Rutgers University Press, 2019), 5.

"The fetus served as": Withycombe, *Lost*, 140.

A baby had previously been: Withycombe, *Lost*, 154.

"They could say, midwives": Shannon Withycombe, phone interview with the authors, January 13, 2023.

Interestingly, at a time: Withycombe, *Lost*, 21.

Literacy rates skyrocketed: Elizabeth Garner Masarik and Sarah Handley-Cousins, "Miscarriage in 19th Century America," February 10, 2019, in *Dig: A History Podcast*, 48:53, podcast, https://digpodcast.org/2019/02/10/miscarriage-nineteenth-century-america/.

There was a veritable smorgasbord: Brodie, *Contraception and Abortion*, 232.

None of these methods would: Brodie, *Contraception and Abortion*, 73.

"It doesn't have to be super reliable": Freidenfelds, phone interview.

And it was widely used: Ellen Chesler, *Woman of Valor: Margaret Sanger and the Birth Control Movement in America* (New York: Simon and Schuster, 2007), chapter 3, Kindle.

In the U.S. in 2020: Rachel K. Jones et al., "Long-Term Decline in US Abortions Reverses, Showing Rising Need for Abortion as Supreme Court Is Poised to Overturn Roe v. Wade," Guttmacher Institute, last updated December 1, 2022, https://www.guttmacher.org/article/2022/06/long-term-decline-us -abortions-reverses-showing-rising-need-abortion-supreme-court.

By the mid-nineteenth century: James C. Mohr, *Abortion in America: The Origins and Evolution of National Policy* (Oxford: Oxford University Press, 1979), chapter 3, Kindle.

Middle- and upper-class women: Reagan, *When Abortion Was a Crime*, 68.

Women in major cities would: Reagan, *When Abortion Was a Crime*, 70.

Immigrant and working-class: Reagan, *When Abortion Was a Crime*, 74; Brodie, *Contraception and Abortion*, 228.

Storer blamed newfangled ideas: Elizabeth Garner Masarik and Marissa Rhodes, "Early American Family Limitation," April 25, 2021, in *Dig: A History Podcast*, 49:09, podcast, https://digpodcast.org/2021/04/25/early-american -family-limitation-2/.

It's also likely that restricting: Brodie, *Contraception and Abortion*, 274.

An opinion of the American Medical Association's: Jodi Vandenberg-Daves, *Modern Motherhood: An American History* (New Brunswick, NJ: Rutgers University Press, 2014), chapter 3, Kindle.

"Perhaps it is inevitable": Susan Faludi, *Backlash: The Undeclared War Against American Women* (New York: Broadway Books, 2020), chapter 14, Kindle.

Storer asked white Protestant women: Reagan, *When Abortion Was a Crime*, 11.

Abortion "has always been a contest": Sarah Churchwell, "Body Politics: The Secret History of the US Anti-Abortion Movement," *Guardian*, July 23, 2022, https://www.theguardian.com/books/2022/jul/23/body-politics.

When abortion had been readily accessible: Masarik and Rhodes, "Early American Family Limitation."

These early laws were really more: Lara Freidenfelds, "When the Constitution Was Drafted, Abortion Was a Choice Left to Women," *Washington Post*, May 23, 2022, https://www.washingtonpost.com/outlook/2022/05/23/when -constitution-was-drafted-abortion-was-choice-left-women/.

"Almost all states got": Withycombe, phone interview.

Many of these doctors were also: Freidenfelds, phone interview.

"They insist there is no": Freidenfelds, phone interview.

As body historian Barbara Duden wrote: Barbara Duden, *Disembodying Women: Perspectives on Pregnancy and the Unborn* (Cambridge, MA: Harvard University Press, 1993), 94.

Doctors, irritated that women: Masarik and Rhodes, "Early American Family Limitation."

As historian James C. Mohr wrote: Mohr, *Abortion in America*, chapter 9, Kindle.

By the late nineteenth century: Masarik and Rhodes, "Early American Family Limitation."

Philosopher Iris Marion Young wrote: Iris Marion Young, *On Female Body Experience: "Throwing Like a Girl" and Other Essays* (New York: Oxford University Press, 2005), Section 2, Kindle.

Similarly, by the 1880s: Withycombe, *Lost*, 60.

The man who went after this: Brodie, *Contraception and Abortion*, 259.

His dislikes included pornography: Brodie, *Contraception and Abortion*, 270.

The Comstock Act passed in 1873: Reagan, *When Abortion Was a Crime*, 13; Withycombe, *Lost*, 19.

Various lawsuits threaten access: Laurie Sobel and Alina Salganicoff, "Q & A: Implications of Two Conflicting Federal Court Rulings on the Availability of Medication Abortion and the FDA's Authority to Regulate Drugs," KFF, April 8, 2023, https://www.kff.org/policy-watch/q-a-implications-of-two-conflicting-federal-court-rulings-on-the-availability-of-medication-abortion-and-the-fdas-authority-to-regulate-drugs/.

Some states went beyond: Brodie, *Contraception and Abortion*, 256; Karen Abbott, "Madame Restell: The Abortionist of Fifth Avenue," *Smithsonian*, November 27, 2012, https://www.smithsonianmag.com/history/madame-restell-the-abortionist-of-fifth-avenue-145109198/.

Chapter Three

By the early twentieth century: Freidenfelds, *Myth of the Perfect Pregnancy*, 87.

Infant mortality in particular: Vandenberg-Daves, *Modern Motherhood*, chapter 4, Kindle.

Depressingly, it remains a problem: Joshua Cohen, "U.S. Maternal and Infant Mortality: More Signs of Public Health Neglect," *Forbes*, August 1, 2021,

https://www.forbes.com/sites/joshuacohen/2021/08/01/us-maternal-and
-infant-mortality-more-signs-of-public-health-neglect/?sh=488d8ab13a50.

Most parents still did not: Vandenberg-Daves, *Modern Motherhood*, chapter 4, Kindle.

The Children's Bureau answered letters: Vandenberg-Daves, *Modern Motherhood*, chapter 6, Kindle.

A Mrs. E.S.: Vandenberg-Daves, *Modern Motherhood*, chapter 6, Kindle.

At the same time, the early decades: Freidenfelds, *Myth of the Perfect Pregnancy*, 62.

The move from fatalistically: Paula S. Fass, *The End of American Childhood: A History of Parenting from Life on the Frontier to the Managed Child* (Princeton, NJ: Princeton University Press, 2016), 99.

It was the only federal program: Chesler, *Woman of Valor*, chapter 3, Kindle.

They were deeply ingrained: Ehrenreich and English, *For Her Own Good*, 103.

But they lacked formal training: Helen Varney and Joyce Beebe Thompson, *The Midwife Said Fear Not: A History of Midwifery in the United States* (New York: Springer, 2016), 15.

They were "less likely": Angela Garbes, *Like a Mother: A Feminist Journey through the Science and Culture of Pregnancy* (New York: Harper Wave, 2018), 23.

This movement to delegitimize: Hossain, *Pain Gap*, 145–46.

Moreover, doctors were also: Ehrenreich and English, *For Her Own Good*, 107.

Midwives were banned from hospitals: Leavitt, *Brought to Bed*, chapter 7, Kindle.

Whether Sadie really existed: Chesler, *Woman of Valor*, chapter 3, Kindle.

The average number of children: Stephanie Coontz, *The Way We Never Were: American Families and the Nostalgia Trap* (New York: Basic Books, 2016), 206.

Former president Theodore Roosevelt: Chesler, *Woman of Valor*, chapter 8, Kindle.

He was very interested: Churchwell, "Body Politics."

But Sanger also thought: Reagan, *When Abortion Was a Crime*, 36.

She opened her first birth control: Chesler, *Woman of Valor*, chapter 8, Kindle.

Sanger, like most in the contemporary: Reagan, *When Abortion Was a Crime*, 36.

In 1928, she published: Blei, "History of Talking About Miscarriage."

One mother of four wrote: Leslie J. Reagan, "From Hazard to Blessing to Tragedy: Representations of Miscarriage in Twentieth Century America,"

Feminist Studies 29, no. 2 (Summer 2003): 359, https://www.jstor.org/stable /3178514.

In fact, Nazis credited: Adam Cohen, *Imbeciles: The Supreme Court, American Eugenics, and the Sterilization of Carrie Buck* (New York: Penguin, 2017), conclusion, Kindle.

It was common knowledge: Roberts, *Killing the Black Body*, chapter 2, Kindle.

Planned Parenthood now includes: "Our History," Planned Parenthood, accessed September 2, 2023, https://www.plannedparenthood.org/about-us /who-we-are/our-history.

The Great Depression saw a: Gary Cross, *The Cute and the Cool: Wondrous Innocence and Modern American Children's Culture* (New York: Oxford University Press, 2004), 27–28.

With men in and out: Reagan, *When Abortion Was a Crime*, 132–33.

Women in all these circumstances: Elizabeth Garner Masarik and Sarah Handley-Cousins, "Abortion and Birth Control before Roe v. Wade: 19th & 20th c. Family Limitation," January 7, 2018, in *Dig: A History Podcast*, 57:23, podcast, https://digpodcast.org/2018/01/07/before-roe-v-wade/.

But doctors during this time: Reagan, *When Abortion Was a Crime*, 132.

So it's no surprise that during: Reagan, *When Abortion Was a Crime*, 146.

Contraceptive manufacturers, with condom makers: Mary Ziegler, *Reproduction and the Constitution in the United States* (New York: Routledge, 2022), chapter 1, Kindle.

It was "widely advertised": Chesler, *Woman of Valor*, chapter 13, Kindle.

The economic reality of: Freidenfelds, *Myth of the Perfect Pregnancy*, 45.

After World War II: Luker, *Abortion and the Politics*, 74.

She wasn't blamed for it: Reagan, "From Hazard to Blessing," 361.

According to Jenny M. Luke: Luke, *Delivered by Midwives*, 27.

The birth rates rose for all: Elaine Tyler May, *Homeward Bound: American Families in the Cold War Era* (New York: Basic Books, 2017), 131.

Women married young: May, *Homeward Bound*, 131.

Childcare absorbed more than twice: Coontz, *Way We Never Were*, 28.

She couldn't have credit cards: Coontz, *Way We Never Were*, 35.

J. Edgar Hoover even blamed: Vandenberg-Daves, *Modern Motherhood*, chapter 8, Kindle.

Women were neurotic or schizophrenic: Coontz, *Way We Never Were*, 35.

An early miscarriage or two: Freidenfelds, *Myth of the Perfect Pregnancy*, 47.

It landed more in the category: Freidenfelds, *Myth of the Perfect Pregnancy*, 47.

Freud, that old pal to women: Julia Bueno, *The Brink of Being: Talking about Miscarriage* (New York: Penguin Books, 2019), 94.

Furthermore, as Julia Bueno details: Bueno, *Brink of Being*, 94.

Sedating women in these tragic: Bueno, *Brink of Being*, 94.

And here's more Freudian fun: Freidenfelds, *Myth of the Perfect Pregnancy*, 47.

In fact, our contemporary interpretation: Withycombe, phone interview.

In 1957, ninety-seven out of every one thousand: Coontz, *Way We Never Were*, 44.

And the proportion of white brides: Coontz, *Way We Never Were*, 43.

Ann Fessler compiled oral histories: Ann Fessler, *The Girls Who Went Away* (New York: Penguin Books, 2007), 2.

Maternity homes were segregated: Fessler, *Girls Who Went Away*, 2.

Women escaped the stigma of unwed motherhood: Fessler, *Girls Who Went Away*, 148.

Abortions remained illegal: Reagan, *When Abortion Was a Crime*, 15.

The means by which to obtain: Luker, *Abortion and the Politics*, 57.

Psychiatric conditions became an indication: Reagan, *When Abortion Was a Crime*, 201.

Those words, according to a 1967 article: Sally L. Satel, "The 'Open Secret' on Getting a Safe Abortion Before Roe v. Wade," *New York Times*, June 4, 2022, https://www.nytimes.com/2022/06/04/opinion/sunday/psychiatrists-abortion-roe.html.

Dr. Alan F. Guttmacher: Satel, "'Open Secret.'"

In the 1950s, roughly 250,000: Coontz, *Way We Never Were*, 260.

In 1953, Alfred Kinsey: May, *Homeward Bound*, 145; Dubow, *Ourselves Unborn*, 64.

In New York City between: Masarik and Handley-Cousins, "Abortion and Birth Control."

Many employers had mandatory leave: Courtni E. Molnar, "'Has the Millennium Yet Dawned?': A History of Attitudes toward Pregnant Workers in America," *Michigan Journal of Gender and Law* 12, no. 1 (2005): 170, https://repository.law.umich.edu/cgi/viewcontent.cgi?article=1093&context=mjgl.

These laws were an outgrowth: Molnar, "'Has the Millennium Yet Dawned?,'" 171.

By the 1950s, historian: Reagan, *When Abortion Was a Crime*, 194.

Chapter Four

Pregnant people are living: "The Rise of Pregnancy Criminalization: A

Pregnancy Justice Report," Pregnancy Justice, September 2023, https://www
.pregnancyjusticeus.org/rise-of-pregnancy-criminalization-report/.

A bounty law in Texas: Texas Heartbeat Act, effective September 1, 2021,
https://capitol.texas.gov/tlodocs/87R/billtext/pdf/SB00008F.pdf; Aziz Huq,
"What Texas's Abortion Law Has in Common with the Fugitive Slave Act,"
Washington Post, November 1, 2021, https://www.washingtonpost.com
/outlook/2021/11/01/texas-abortion-law-history-rights-suppressed/.

A survey in 2022: Whitney Arey et al., "A Preview of the Dangerous Future of
Abortion Bans—Texas Senate Bill 8," *New England Journal of Medicine*, August
4, 2022, https://www.nejm.org/doi/full/10.1056/NEJMp2207423.

In the words of feminist author: Katha Pollitt, *Pro: Reclaiming Abortion
Rights* (New York: Picador, 2015), 3.

Prevention and "control" contributed: Jessica Zucker, *I Had a Miscarriage: A
Memoir, A Movement* (New York: Feminist Press at the City University of New
York, 2021), 43.

Historian Elaine Tyler May wrote: Elaine Tyler May, *America and the Pill: A
History of Politics, Peril, and Liberation* (New York: Basic Books, 2011), 1.

When the pill was approved: Freidenfelds, phone interview.

Women came out of the shadows: Luker, *Abortion and the Politics*, 40.

Americans were largely spared: Leila McNeill, "The Woman Who Stood
Between America and a Generation of 'Thalidomide Babies,'" *Smithsonian*,
May 8, 2017, https://www.smithsonianmag.com/science-nature/woman-who
-stood-between-america-and-epidemic-birth-defects-180963165/.

Chessen's hospital board turned: Dubow, *Ourselves Unborn*, 65.

When she returned home: Luker, *Abortion and the Politics*, 64.

Her case garnered: Megan Brenan, "Gallup Vault: Public Supported Therapeutic
Abortion in 1962," Gallup, June 12, 2018, https://news.gallup.com/vault
/235496/gallup-vault-public-supported-therapeutic-abortion-1962.aspx.

This has been consistent:: Hannah Hartig, "About Six-in-Ten Americans Say
Abortion Should Be Legal in All or Most Cases," Pew Research Center, June 13,
2022, https://www.pewresearch.org/short-reads/2022/06/13/about-six-in
-ten-americans-say-abortion-should-be-legal-in-all-or-most-cases-2/.

The American College of Obstetricians: Dubow, *Ourselves Unborn*, 65.

By 1967, a survey by: Mohr, *Abortion in America*, afterword, Kindle.

Part of the reason this: Abrams, "Scarlet Letter."

Today, restrictive abortion laws: Abrams, "Scarlet Letter."

This change was kicked off: Ziegler, *Reproduction and the Constitution*,
chapter 2, Kindle.

Nixon feared losing conservative: Ziegler, *Reproduction and the Constitution*,
chapter 2, Kindle.

Nixon had discovered: Ziegler, *Reproduction and the Constitution*, chapter 2, Kindle.

The health clinic at: Reagan, *When Abortion Was a Crime*, 196.

Though it is next to: Ziegler, *Reproduction and the Constitution*, introduction, Kindle.

Viability has been a constant: Dias, "When Does Life Begin?"

Public health experts estimated: Johanna Schoen, *Abortion after Roe* (Chapel Hill: University of North Carolina Press, 2015), 24.

Legal abortions before sixteen weeks: Schoen, *Abortion after Roe*, 24.

But the rights granted: Robin Marty, *New Handbook for a Post-Roe America: The Complete Guide to Abortion Legality, Access, and Practical Support* (New York: Seven Stories Press, 2021), 1.

The Hyde Amendment has been: "The Hyde Amendment: An Overview," Congressional Research Service, updated July 20, 2022, https://crsreports.congress.gov/product/pdf/IF/IF12167.

Because those seeking abortions: Ziegler, *Reproduction and the Constitution*, chapter 3, Kindle.

Antiabortion groups: Mary Ziegler, *Abortion and the Law in America: Roe v. Wade to the Present* (Cambridge: Cambridge University Press, 2020), chapter 2, Kindle.

Women's health activists of color: Loretta J. Ross and Rickie Solinger, *Reproductive Justice: An Introduction* (Oakland: University of California Press, 2017), 54–55.

It enshrined subsequent restrictions: Dubow, *Ourselves Unborn*, 110.

As of 2023: "The Hyde Amendment: A Discriminatory Ban on Insurance Coverage of Abortion," Guttmacher Institute, May 2021, https://www.guttmacher.org/fact-sheet/hyde-amendment.

In 2019, that amounted: Diana Greene Foster, *The Turnaway Study: Ten Years, a Thousand Women, and the Consequences of Having—or Being Denied—an Abortion* (New York: Scribner, 2020), 69.

For the three-quarters who do: Foster, *Turnaway Study*, 69.

Keep in mind that: Lane Gillespie, "Bankrate's 2023 Emergency Savings Report," Bankrate, June 22, 2023, https://www.bankrate.com/banking/savings/emergency-savings-report/.

It was also a new: Robert Wuthnow, "Restructuring of American Religion: Further Evidence," *Sociological Inquiry* 66, no. 3 (July 1996): 303–29, https://doi.org/10.1111/j.1475–682X.1996.tb00223.x.

After Nixon's reelection: Reagan, *When Abortion Was a Crime*, xviii.

The divorce rate more: Fass, *End of American Childhood*, 208.

In a 1972 essay: Phyllis Schlafly, "What's Wrong with 'Equal Rights' for

Women?," *Phyllis Schlafly Report*, 1972, https://awpc.cattcenter.iastate.edu /2016/02/02/whats-wrong-with-equal-rights-for-women-1972/.

Around the same time: Churchwell, "Body Politics."

Before then, the movement: Mary Ziegler, *After Roe: The Lost History of the Abortion Debate* (Cambridge, MA: Harvard University Press, 2015), 13.

Being antiabortion was how: Ziegler, *After Roe*, 16.

Formerly Democratic southern whites: Ziegler, *Reproduction and the Constitution*, chapter 3, Kindle.

Their success made the: Ziegler, *Reproduction and the Constitution*, chapter 3, Kindle.

The movement's original goal: Ziegler, *Abortion and the Law*, chapter 1, Kindle.

Laura Palmer by way: Sarah A. Leavitt, "'A Private Little Revolution': The Home Pregnancy Test in American Culture," *Bulletin of the History of Medicine* 80, no. 2 (Summer 2006): 333, https://doi.org/10.1353/bhm.2006.0064.

Love Canal, New York, resident: "Love Canal Fact Pack," Center for Health, Environment & Justice, August 2015, https://chej.org/wp-content/uploads /Love-Canal-Factpack-PUB-0012.pdf.

The EPA eventually banned: Blei, "History of Talking About Miscarriage."

Popular and health media: Reagan, "From Hazard to Blessing," 364.

Now, two-thirds of abortions: "Induced Abortion in the United States," Guttmacher Institute, September 2019, https://www.guttmacher.org/fact -sheet/induced-abortion-united-states.

Historian Freidenfelds lays out: Freidenfelds, *Myth of the Perfect Pregnancy*, 144.

Decidedly religious with a: Reagan, "From Hazard to Blessing," 367–68.

Support groups (mostly among: Reagan, "From Hazard to Blessing," 365.

Historian Leslie J. Reagan cites: Reagan, "From Hazard to Blessing," 368.

Chapter Five

The twenty-four embryo and fetal: Catherine Cole, "Sex and Death on Display: Women, Reproduction, and Fetuses at Chicago's Museum of Science and Industry," *Drama Review* 37, no. 1 (Spring 1993): 55, https://doi.org/10 .2307/1146270.

These are the very same ones: Cole, "Sex and Death on Display."

The museum has displayed: Cole, "Sex and Death on Display."

As cognitive linguist George Lakoff: George Lakoff, *The All New Don't Think of an Elephant!: Know Your Values and Frame the Debate* (White River Junction, VT: Chelsea Green Publishing, 2004), chapter 6, Kindle.

German artist-scientist Friedrich Ziegler: Rose Holz, "The 1939 Dickinson-Belskie Birth Series Sculptures: The Rise of Modern Visions of Pregnancy, the Roots of Modern Pro-Life Imagery, and Dr. Dickinson's Religious Case for Abortion," *Papers in Women's and Gender Studies* 9 (2017): 24, https://digitalcommons.unl.edu/cgi/viewcontent.cgi?article=1010&context=womenstudiespapers.

He won the fair's: Dubow, *Ourselves Unborn*, 25.

At the 1933 Century of Progress: Dubow, *Ourselves Unborn*, 38.

The sculptures depicted something: Holz, "1939 Dickinson-Belskie Birth Series," 5.

Most previous knowledge: Holz, "1939 Dickinson-Belskie Birth Series," 20.

But X-rays of pregnant: Holz, "1939 Dickinson-Belskie Birth Series," 21.

"The story of in utero development": Holz, "1939 Dickinson-Belskie Birth Series," 5.

Canadian Dionne quintuplets: Holz, "1939 Dickinson-Belskie Birth Series," 22.

The cover photo was captioned: Freidenfelds, *Myth of the Perfect Pregnancy*, 103.

Every other one was dead: Freidenfelds, *Myth of the Perfect Pregnancy*; Lynn M. Morgan, *Icons of Life: A Cultural History of Human Embryos* (Berkeley: University of California Press, 2009), 206.

The Nilsson photos: Bueno, *Brink of Being*, 11.

Life **magazine's print run:** Freidenfelds, *Myth of the Perfect Pregnancy*, 103.

"The 'beginning of life' sequence": Duden, *Disembodying Women*, 14.

She wanted to feature photos: Morgan, *Icons of Life*, 199, 202.

The fact that these films: Morgan, *Icons of Life*, 203.

Nilsson's and Flanagan's works: Morgan, *Icons of Life*, 193.

"From their beginning": Rosalind Petchesky, "Fetal Images: The Power of Visual Culture in the Politics of Reproduction," *Feminist Studies* 13, no. 2 (Summer 1987): 268, http://www.jstor.org/stable/3177802.

But there was another important change: Freidenfelds, *Myth of the Perfect Pregnancy*, 103.

Many scholars and feminists peg: Rayna Rapp, *Testing Women, Testing the Fetus: The Social Impact of Amniocentesis in America* (New York: Routledge, 2000), chapter 2, Kindle.

Sonograms "altered the relationship": Withycombe, *Lost*, 38.

The term *bonding* **had:** Janelle S. Taylor, *The Public Life of the Fetal Sonogram: Technology, Consumption, and the Politics of Reproduction* (New Brunswick, NJ: Rutgers University Press, 2008), chapter 4, Kindle.

Yes, they can be exciting: Taylor, *Public Life*, introduction, Kindle.

At six weeks: Selena Simmons-Duffin and Carrie Feibel, "The Texas Abortion

Ban Hinges on 'Fetal Heartbeat.' Doctors Call That Misleading," NPR, May 3, 2022, https://www.npr.org/sections/health-shots/2021/09/02/1033727679 /fetal-heartbeat-isnt-a-medical-term-but-its-still-used-in-laws-on-abortion.

Heartbeats can be detected: Kelly McBride, "In the Intense Debate Over Abortion, Precise Language Doesn't Mean Taking Sides," Poynter, May 31, 2019, https://www.poynter.org/ethics-trust/2019/in-the-intense-debate-over -abortion-precise-language-doesnt-mean-taking-sides/.

Fetal heartbeat is not a clinical term: Simmons-Duffin and Feibel, "Texas Abortion Ban"; Paige Winfield Cunningham, "The Fight Over 'Heartbeat' Further Inflames Tensions in Abortion Battle," *Washington Post*, September 26, 2022, https://www.washingtonpost.com/politics/2022/09/26/fight-over -heartbeat-further-inflames-tensions-abortion-battle/.

The Catholic position changed: Dubow, *Ourselves Unborn*, 6.

Political scientist Petchesky called: Petchesky, "Fetal Images," 267.

Former abortion provider: Schoen, *Abortion after Roe*, 145.

A fetus "the size of": Pollitt, *Pro*, 84.

According to the American College of Obstetricians and Gynecologists: "Facts Are Important: Gestational Development and Capacity for Pain," American College of Obstetricians and Gynecologists, accessed June 10, 2023, https://www .acog.org/advocacy/facts-are-important/gestational-development-capacity-for -pain.

When just 0.9 percent: "Abortion Surveillance—Findings and Reports," Centers for Disease Control and Prevention, last reviewed November 17, 2022, https://www.cdc.gov/reproductivehealth/data_stats/abortion.htm.

President Reagan screened it: Ziegler, *Abortion and the Law*, chapter 3, Kindle; John Rogers, "Producer of 'Silent Scream' Anti-Abortion Film Dies," Associated Press, February 14, 2019, https://apnews.com/article /e704898e599449b79c0657e56403134b.

It was "cultural representation": Petchesky, "Fetal Images," 267.

As Ziegler wrote in: Ziegler, *Reproduction and the Constitution*, chapter 3, Kindle.

The directions were explicit: Clay Risen, "Joseph M. Scheidler, 'Godfather' of the Anti-Abortion Movement, Dies at 93," *New York Times*, January 20, 2021, https://www.nytimes.com/2021/01/20/us/joseph-m-scheidler-dead.html.

"They will start using": Faludi, *Backlash*, chapter 14, Kindle.

The Ku Klux Klan: Faludi, *Backlash*, chapter 9, Kindle.

"Changing the 'fetus' mentions": Hannah Armitage, "Political Language, Uses and Abuses: How the Term 'Partial Birth' Changed the Abortion Debate in the United States," *Australasian Journal of American Studies* 29, no. 1 (July 2010): 25, http://www.jstor.org/stable/41054184.

All this is to say: Duden, *Disembodying Women*, 4.

"Fetal imagery became part": Freidenfelds, phone interview.

"We sentimentalize images": Freidenfelds, phone interview.

This is ideological work: Reagan, *When Abortion Was a Crime*, xix.

Life and choice are not: Freidenfelds, *Myth of the Perfect Pregnancy*, 144.

Instead of being antiabortion: Faludi, *Backlash*, chapter 9, Kindle.

After this semantic switcheroo: Faludi, *Backlash*, chapter 9, Kindle.

As Faludi wrote, "this Orwellian": Faludi, *Backlash*, chapter 9, Kindle.

Lakoff's titular famous example: Lakoff, *All New Don't Think*, introduction, Kindle.

"It's effective politically to": Armstrong, phone interview.

Anat Shenker-Osorio, a progressive: Mary Harris, "Why Abortion Activists Need to Stop Using the Word *Choice*," Slate, May 16, 2022, https://slate .com/news-and-politics/2022/05/abortion-activism-pro-choice-messaging -language-ireland-argentina.html.

"We hear endlessly about": Pollitt, *Pro*, 41.

By the late 1980s: Schoen, *Abortion after Roe*, 247.

This contributed to the view: Schoen, *Abortion after Roe*, 21.

In 1973, 81 percent: Johanna Schoen, "Living through Some Giant Change: The Establishment of Abortion Services," *American Journal of Public Health* 103, no. 3 (March 2013): 416–25, https://doi.org/10.2105/ajph.2012.301173.

After all, the prevention of: Jennifer L. Holland, *Tiny You: A Western History of the Anti-Abortion Movement* (Oakland: University of California Press, 2020), 13.

At least eleven people: Melissa Block, "An All-Trimester Abortion Clinic Prepares to Open in Maryland, One of Few Nationally," NPR, September 1, 2022, https://www.npr.org/2022/09/01/1120124723/an-all-trimester -abortion-clinic-prepares-to-open-in-maryland-one-of-few-nationa.

As Schoen wrote: Schoen, *Abortion after Roe*, 248.

In 2022 after the *Dobbs* decision: Oriana González, "Report: 'Sharp Increase' in Crimes against Abortion Clinics Post-*Roe*," Axios, May 11, 2023, https:// www.axios.com/2023/05/11/crimes-violence-abortion-clinics-roe-v-wade.

They masquerade as healthcare: "Crisis Pregnancy Centers," American College of Obstetricians and Gynecologists, accessed July 23, 2023, https:// www.acog.org/advocacy/abortion-is-essential/trending-issues/issue-brief -crisis-pregnancy-centers.

"Legitimate medical providers" would: Susan Rinkunas, "Woman Sues Anti-Abortion 'Pregnancy Center' after Her Ectopic Pregnancy Ruptured," Jezebel, June 26, 2023, https://jezebel.com/woman-sues-anti-abortion-pregnancy -center-after-her-ect-1850576215.

"I called the morning of": Yvette, interview.

Antiabortion activists were off: "Targeted Regulation of Abortion Providers," Guttmacher Institute, last updated August 31, 2023, https://www.guttmacher .org/state-policy/explore/targeted-regulation-abortion-providers.

In 1990, the ACLU estimated: Lynn M. Paltrow, "Criminal Prosecutions against Pregnant Women: National Update and Overview," Reproductive Freedom Project, American Civil Liberties Union, April 1992, https://www .pregnancyjusticeus.org/wp-content/uploads/1992/01/1992-State-by-State -Case-Summary.pdf.

Approximately one in four pregnant: Marty, *New Handbook*, 2.

The ACA also provided: "Regulating Insurance Coverage of Abortion," Guttmacher Institute, last updated August 31, 2023, https://www.guttmacher .org/state-policy/explore/regulating-insurance-coverage-abortion.

And a 2014 Supreme Court: Burwell v. Hobby Lobby Stores, Inc., 573 U.S. 682 (2014).

"It seemed best for our family": Julie Cohen, phone interview with the authors, April 21, 2023.

"After legalization, the opposite": Freidenfelds, *Myth of the Perfect Pregnancy*, 144.

The effect of this narrative: Freidenfelds, *Myth of the Perfect Pregnancy*, 142.

Plenty of Americans cannot access: "Unintended Pregnancy," Centers for Disease Control and Prevention, last reviewed March 27, 2023, https://www .cdc.gov/reproductivehealth/contraception/unintendedpregnancy/index .htm; "1 in 6 People Globally Affected by Infertility: WHO," World Health Organization, April 4, 2023, https://www.who.int/news/item/04-04-2023-1 -in-6-people-globally-affected-by-infertility.

Yet pregnancy is assumed: Withycombe, *Lost*, 165.

"The narratives our society": Armstrong, phone interview.

"There's comfort in the narrative": Withycombe, phone interview.

Chapter Six

Bethany from Texas was sick: Bethany, phone interview with the authors, June 23, 2023.

To the nurses, she said: Bethany, phone interview.

In 1849, Elizabeth Blackwell: McGregor, *From Midwives to Medicine*, 75.

After more women started: Elinor Cleghorn, *Unwell Women: Misdiagnosis and Myth in a Man-Made World* (New York: Dutton, 2021), 116.

As of 2019, women make up: Stuart Heiser, "The Majority of U.S. Medical

Students Are Women, New Data Show," Association of American Medical Colleges, December 9, 2019, https://www.aamc.org/news-insights/press -releases/majority-us-medical-students-are-women-new-data-show\.

Women and people of color: BNIH Revitalization Act of 1993 Public Law 103–43, https://grants.nih.gov/policy/inclusion/women-and-minorities /guidelines.htm.

"When we were first advocating": Ruth Faden, phone interview with the authors, April 7, 2023.

And as a result, according to a: Irving Zucker and Brian J. Prendergast, "Sex Differences in Pharmacokinetics Predict Adverse Drug Reactions in Women," *Biology of Sex Differences* 11, no. 32 (June 2020): 1–14, https://doi.org/10 .1186/s13293-020-00308-5.

"Unwanted side effects": Zucker and Prendergast, "Sex Differences in Pharmacokinetics."

And in 2013: Nicole Woitowich, "Clinical Trials Are Better at Including Women. But Data Analysis Is Still a Real Problem," *Chicago Tribune*, July 7, 2023, https://www.chicagotribune.com/opinion/commentary/ct-opinion -clinical-trials-research-women-drugs-nih-revitalization-act-20230707 -hcunrc3m5jhjldnstn25vbagoq-story.html.

As Dr. Katherine Wisner: Erin Spain, "Medication and Mental Health during Pregnancy with Katherine Wisner, MD," August 1, 2018, in *Breakthroughs*, podcast, 27:34, https://www.feinberg.northwestern.edu/research/podcast /medication-and-mental-health-during-pregnancy.html; Katherine L. Wisner, Hyunyoung Jeong, and Christina Chambers, "Use of Antipsychotics during Pregnancy: Pregnant Women Get Sick—Sick Women Get Pregnant," *JAMA Psychiatry* 73, no. 9 (September 2016): 901–3, https://doi.org/10.1001 /jamapsychiatry.2016.1538.

Even the list of drugs: "Drug Pregnancy Categories," WikEM, last updated April 2021, https://wikem.org/wiki/Drug_pregnancy_categories.

The National Institutes of Health mandate: "Report of the Advisory Committee on Research on Women's Health: Fiscal Years 2019–2020," National Institutes of Health, 2021, https://orwh.od.nih.gov/sites/orwh/files/docs /ORWH_BiennialReport2019_20_508.pdf.

The statistics are not as good: Tanvee Varma et al., "Reporting of Study Participant Demographic Characteristics and Demographic Representation in Premarketing and Postmarketing Studies of Novel Cancer Therapeutics," *JAMA Network* 4, no. 4 (April 2021): e217063, https://jamanetwork.com/journals /jamanetworkopen/fullarticle/2778908.

In 2022, Harvard Medical School: Alexandra Z. Sosinsky et al., "Enrollment of Female Participants in United States Drug and Device Phase 1–3 Clinical

Trials between 2016 and 2019," *Contemporary Clinical Trials* 115 (April 2022): 106718, https://doi.org/10.1016/j.cct.2022.106718.

Though there are overall improvements: Manisha Vadali, "More Data Needed," Brigham and Women's Communications, June 29, 2022, https://hms.harvard.edu/news/more-data-needed.

Perez wrote, "According to the FDA": Caroline Criado Perez, *Invisible Women: Data Bias in a World Designed for Men* (New York: Abrams, 2021), 23–24.

A 2016 updated National Institutes of Health policy: Nicole Woitowich, Annaliese Beery, and Teresa Woodruff, "Meta-Research: A 10-Year Follow-Up Study of Sex Inclusion in the Biological Sciences," *eLife* 9 (2020): e56344, https://elifesciences.org/articles/56344.

"When this happens, we have no way": Woitowich, "Clinical Trials Are Better."

In her book *The Pain Gap*: Hossain, *Pain Gap*, 55.

According to research from: Saraswathi Vedam et al., "The Giving Voice to Mothers Study: Inequity and Mistreatment during Pregnancy and Childbirth in the United States," *Reproductive Health* 16 (2019): 77, https://doi.org/10.1186/s12978-019-0729-2.

Rayna Markin, a psychologist: Rayna Markin, phone interview with the authors, May 26, 2022.

"I'm about to give birth": Jen D., phone interview with the authors, May 19, 2022.

"Nobody checked up on me": Katie N., phone interview.

"Within the context of": Kelly Treder et al., "Racism and the Reproductive Health Experiences of U.S.-Born Black Women," *Obstetrics and Gynecology* 139, no. 3 (March 2022): 407–16, https://doi.org/10.1097/aog.0000000000004675.

Central Massachusetts–based Emy C.: Emy C., Zoom interview with the authors, March 27, 2023.

Xaviera Bell, who was: Xaviera Bell, phone interview with the authors, March 22, 2023.

Now she knows that: "NIH Study Finds Racial, Ethnic Differences in Fetal Growth," National Institutes of Health, September 29, 2015, https://www.nih.gov/news-events/news-releases/nih-study-finds-racial-ethnic-differences-fetal-growth.

The March of Dimes 2023 report card: "2023 March of Dimes Report Card for North Carolina," March of Dimes, accessed December 3, 2023, https://www.marchofdimes.org/peristats/reports/north-carolina/report-card.

"I always thought if I": Bell, phone interview.

Some have loudly sounded: "ACOG Statement on the Decision in Dobbs V. Jackson," American College of Obstetricians and Gynecologists, June 24, 2022, https://www.acog.org/news/news-releases/2022/06/acog-statement-on-the-decision-in-dobbs-v-jackson.

But the drugs caused: James H. Kim and Anthony R. Scialli, "Thalidomide: The Tragedy of Birth Defects and the Effective Treatment of Disease," *Toxicological Sciences* 122, no. 1 (July 2011): 1–6, https://doi.org/10.1093/toxsci/kfr088.

In 1977, the FDA: "History of Women's Participation in Clinical Research," National Institutes of Health, accessed March 2023, https://orwh.od.nih.gov/toolkit/recruitment/history.

"So regardless if you were pregnant": Nicole Woitowich, phone interview with the authors, May 9, 2022.

Numerous studies showed that unvaccinated: David A. Schwartz, Sarah B. Mulkey, and Drucilla J. Roberts, "SARS-CoV-2 Placentitis, Stillbirth, and Maternal COVID-19 Vaccination: Clinical-Pathologic Correlations," *American Journal of Obstetrics and Gynecology* 228, no. 3 (March 2023): 261–69, https://doi.org/10.1016/j.ajog.2022.10.001.

Women who are vaccinated during: Natasha B. Halasa et al., "Effectiveness of Maternal Vaccination with mRNA COVID-19 Vaccine during Pregnancy against COVID-19–Associated Hospitalization in Infants Aged <6 Months—17 States, July 2021–January 2022," Centers for Disease Control and Prevention, February 18, 2022, https://www.cdc.gov/mmwr/volumes/71/wr/mm7107e3.htm.

There's a lot of "ethically unproblematic": Anne Drapkin Lyerly and Ruth Faden, "Mothers Matter: Ethics and Research during Pregnancy," *Virtual Mentor* 15, no. 9 (September 2013): 775–78, https://doi.org/10.1001/virtualmentor.2013.15.9.pfor1–1309.

"Pregnant people are not just women": Faden, phone interview.

In considering the ethics: Drapkin and Faden, "Mothers Matter."

In 2015, the American College of Obstetricians and Gynecologists: "Committee on Ethics Opinion, No. 646," American College of Obstetrics and Gynecologists, November 2015, https://www.acog.org/clinical/clinical-guidance/committee-opinion/articles/2015/11/ethical-considerations-for-including-women-as-research-participants.

Hundreds of research projects: Roni Caryn Rabin, "A Blood Test Predicts Pre-Eclampsia in Pregnant Women," *New York Times*, July 3, 2023, https://www.nytimes.com/2023/07/03/health/pregnancy-preeclampsia-test.html.

"We are beginning to understand": Woitowich, phone interview.

"This rejection of science": Ullrich K. H. Ecker et al., "The Psychological Drivers of Misinformation Belief and Its Resistance to Correction," *Nature*

Reviews Psychology 1 (2022): 13–29, https://doi.org/10.1038/s44159-021 -00006-y.

"We, doctors, scientists, clinicians": Dr. Jamila Perritt, phone interview with the authors, May 24, 2023.

Chapter Seven

No matter how educated: Katharine White, phone interview with the authors, May 20, 2022.

People of color are at: Sudeshna Mukherjee et al., "Risk of Miscarriage among Black Women and White Women in a U.S. Prospective Cohort Study," *American Journal of Epidemiology* 177, no. 11 (June 2013): 1271–78. https://doi.org/10 .1093/aje/kws393.

"It was not a happy time": Margaret M., phone interview with the authors, March 1, 2023.

"Because of the trauma": Pamela Caine, phone interview with the authors, April 4, 2023.

"It was the picture of the tiny": Krysta H., phone interview with the authors, March 2, 2023.

"The issue, I think": Lisa Harris, phone interview with the authors, July 11, 2022.

For that same reason: Megan K. Donovan, "D&E Abortion Bans: The Implications of Banning the Most Common Second-Trimester Procedure," Guttmacher Institute, February 21, 2017, https://www.guttmacher.org/gpr/2017 /02/de-abortion-bans-implications-banning-most-common-second-trimester -procedure.

The Accreditation Council for Graduate Medical Education: Jan Hoffman, "OB-GYN Residency Programs Face Tough Choice on Abortion Training," *New York Times*, October 27, 2022, https://www.nytimes.com/2022/10/27 /health/abortion-training-residency-programs.html.

In Texas for example: Pam Belluck, "They Had Miscarriages, and New Abortion Laws Obstructed Treatment," *New York Times*, July 17, 2022, https:// www.nytimes.com/2022/07/17/health/abortion-miscarriage-treatment.html.

"I thought it was just a bad period": Allison M., interview with the authors, January 12, 2023.

Becker told the *Cincinnati Enquirer*: Jessie Balmert, "No One Was Talking about Implanting Ectopic Pregnancies—Except This Lawmaker and Lobbyist," Cincinnati Enquirer, May 20, 2023, https://www.cincinnati .com/story/news/politics/2019/12/10/emails-lobbyist-helped-draft-bill -suggesting-docs-could-reimplant-ectoptic-pregnancies/2632532001/.

She was devastated: Saya H., phone interview with the authors, January 12, 2023.

Yet it's still mired in the political: Nuria Diaz Muñoz and Maria Ramirez Uribe, "How Treatment of Ectopic Pregnancy Fits into Post-*Roe* Medical Care," Poynter, July 5, 2022, https://www.poynter.org/fact-checking/2022/how -treatment-of-ectopic-pregnancy-fits-into-post-roe-medical-care/.

These occur in less than: "Molar Pregnancy," March of Dimes, last reviewed October 2017, https://www.marchofdimes.org/find-support/topics/miscarriage -loss-grief/molar-pregnancy.

"I wish I would have known": Allison B., phone interview with the authors, February 8, 2023.

South Florida–based Nathalie C.: Nathalie C., phone interview with the authors, April 25, 2023.

But at least twenty-one thousand babies: "What Is Stillbirth?"; Adriana Gallardo and Duaa Eldeib, "What You Need to Know about Stillbirths," ProPublica, May 3, 2023, https://www.propublica.org/article/what-to-know -about-stillbirths.

Black women suffer stillbirth: "What Is Stillbirth?"

The annual number of stillbirths: "Stillbirth," March of Dimes, last updated October 2020, https://www.marchofdimes.org/find-support/topics /miscarriage-loss-grief/stillbirth.

"In hindsight, my son's": Erica Bailey, phone interview with the authors, February 15, 2023.

Over the past thirty years: Kawai O. Tanabe and Fern R. Hauck, "A United States Perspective," in *SIDS: Sudden Infant and Early Childhood Death: The Past, the Present and the Future*, ed. J. R. Duncan and R. W. Byard (Adelaide: University of Adelaide Press, 2018), chapter 19, https://www.ncbi.nlm.nih.gov /books/NBK513376/; "Sudden Unexpected Infant Death and Sudden Infant Death Syndrome," Centers for Disease Control and Prevention, last reviewed March 8, 2023, https://www.cdc.gov/sids/data.htm.

"Doctors don't bring up stillbirth": Marny Smith, phone interview with the authors, March 2, 2023.

Dr. Joanne Stone, a maternal fetal medicine: Dr. Joanne Stone, Zoom interview by the authors, May 10, 2023.

Women who have experienced stillbirth: "Mount Sinai Collaborates with PUSH for Empowered Pregnancy to Launch Nation's First Rainbow Clinic Dedicated to Reducing Stillbirths," Mount Sinai Health System, March 22, 2022, https://www.mountsinai.org/about/newsroom/2022/mount-sinai-collaborates -with-push-for-empowered-pregnancy-to-launch-nations-first-rainbow-clinic -dedicated-to-reducing-stillbirths; Gallardo and Eldeib, "What You Need to Know."

But those tests screen for: Pathology results from Dr. Harvey Kliman to Rebecca Little, May 25, 2023.

The American College of Obstetricians and Gynecologists: "Obstetric Care Consensus: Management of Stillbirth," American College of Obstetricians and Gynecologists, March 2020, https://www.acog.org/-/media /project/acog/acogorg/clinical/files/obstetric-care-consensus/articles/2020 /03/management-of-stillbirth.pdf; Duaa Eldeib, "Federal Study Calls U.S. Stillbirth Rate 'Unacceptably High' and Recommends Action," ProPublica, March 23, 2023, https://www.propublica.org/article/stillbirths-rate-nih-cdc -prevention-research.

"He was perfect": Crystal H., phone interview with the authors, April 9, 2023; Crystal H., in-person interview with the authors, May 13, 2023.

"It feels very different": Joanne Cacciatore, phone interview with the authors, August 9, 2022.

"They literally gaslit me": Hall, phone interview.

"When all sex ed focuses": Crystal Clancy, Zoom interview with the authors, March 3, 2023.

"I did so much research": Lacey M., phone interview.

"We fail our patients when they don't": Sue Villa, phone interview with the authors, March 21, 2023.

"The more pregnant I got": Kate Carson, phone interview with the authors, March 5, 2023.

Margot Finn of Ending a Wanted Pregnancy: Finn, phone interview.

"Waiting for a definitive diagnosis": Margot Finn, "I Had a Late-Term Abortion. President Trump and Pro-Lifers Have No Right to Call Me a Murderer," Slate, February 7, 2019, https://slate.com/technology/2019/02 /late-term-abortion-support-group-lessons-trust-myself-women.html.

"The only thing I could imagine": Finn, "I Had a Late-Term Abortion."

"As a Muslim": Hooyo phone interview with the authors, April 11, 2023.

"I've always tried to be": Steve Calvin, phone interview with the authors, May 1, 2022.

She couldn't afford to: Frances Stead Sellers, "Her Baby Has a Deadly Diagnosis. Her Florida Doctors Refused an Abortion," *Washington Post*, May 19, 2023, https://www.washingtonpost.com/health/2023/02/18/florida -abortion-ban-unviable-pregnancy-potter-syndrome/.

"That's what we wanted": Sellers, "Her Baby."

But he survived only: Frances Stead Sellers, Thomas Simonetti, and Maggie Penman, "The Short Life of Baby Milo," *Washington Post*, May 20, 2023, https://www.washingtonpost.com/health/interactive/2023/florida-abortion -law-deborah-dorbert/.

"When he came out": Sellers, Simonetti, and Penman, "Short Life of Baby Milo."

"If a baby lives": Nuzzo, phone interview.

Palliative care and support: Calvin, phone interview.

In 2019, a committee: "Perinatal Palliative Care: ACOG Committee Opinion," *Obstetrics & Gynecology* 134, no. 3 (September 2019): 84–89, https://journals .lww.com/greenjournal/fulltext/2019/09000/Perinatal_Palliative_Care_ _ACOG_COMMITTEE_OPINION,.48.aspx.

Chapter Eight

The nationwide rate: "World Population Prospects 2022," World Health Organization, accessed January 2023, https://population.un.org/wpp/.

The next closest: Gareth Iacobucci, "Ireland and UK See Sharp Rise in Maternal Deaths," *BMJ* 379 (November 11, 2022): o2732, https://doi.org/10.1136/bmj .o2732.

The data for Black women: Hoyert, "Maternal Mortality Rates."

Anushay Hossain, in her book: Hossain, *Pain Gap*, 118.

"It's really underappreciated": Prager, phone interview.

A recent study on racism's effects: Treder et al., "Racism and the Reproductive Health Experiences."

"Dealing with racism in our daily": Jamila Taylor, phone interview with the authors, July 25, 2022.

Mistrust of the medical world: Simar Singh Bajaj and Fatima Cody Stanford, "Beyond Tuskegee—Vaccine Distrust and Everyday Racism," *New England Journal of Medicine* 384 (February 2021): e12, https://www.nejm.org/doi/full /10.1056/NEJMpv2035827.

There is also some proof: Brad N. Greenwood et al., "Physician-Patient Racial Concordance and Disparities in Birthing Mortality for Newborns 2020," *Proceedings of the National Academy of Sciences* 117, no. 35 (September 2020): 21194–200, https://doi.org/10.1073/pnas.1913405117.

Serena Williams, one of the: Serena Williams, "What My Life-Threatening Experience Taught Me about Giving Birth," CNN, February 20, 2018, https:// www.cnn.com/2018/02/20/opinions/protect-mother-pregnancy-williams -opinion/index.html.

She won three medals: Pat Graham, "US Sprinter, Olympic Medalist Tori Bowie Dies at 32," Associated Press, May 3, 2023, https://apnews.com/article /tori-bowie-olympics-sprinter-us-f92b339b3dd576866011516285aa674c.

What's perhaps even more disturbing: Tianna Madison (@ Tianna.t.madison), "THREE (3) of the FOUR (4) us who ran on the SECOND fastest 4x100m relay of all time, the 2016 Olympic Champions have nearly died or died in childbirth," Instagram, June 13, 2023, https://www.instagram.com/p/CtccVtiS0A0/?igshid=MTc4MmM1YmI2Ng==.

They gave her a baby aspirin: Tomeka I., phone interview with the authors, April 20, 2023.

More than sixty thousand women: "Severe Maternal Morbidity in the United States," Centers for Disease Control and Prevention, last updated July 3, 2023, https://www.cdc.gov/reproductivehealth/maternalinfanthealth/severematernalmorbidity.html, 7/10/2023.

A 2016 analysis of five years: Hossain, *Pain Gap*, 123.

They found that Black and Latina: Elizabeth Howell et al., "Race and Ethnicity, Medical Insurance, and Within-Hospital Severe Maternal Morbidity Disparities," *Obstetrics & Gynecology* 135, no. 2 (February 2020): 285–93, https://doi.org/10.1097/aog.0000000000003667.

"It's really important for us": Michelle Drew, Ubuntu Collective, phone interview by the authors, June 14, 2022.

In order to help this crisis: "New Report Sounds the Alarm on Global Shortage of 900,000 Midwives," World Health Organization, May 5, 2021, https://www.who.int/news/item/05-05-2021-new-report-sounds-the-alarm-on-global-shortage-of-900–000-midwives.

"Research consistently demonstrates": P. Mimi Niles and Laurie Zephyrin, "How Expanding the Role of Midwives in U.S. Health Care Could Help Address the Maternal Health Crisis," Commonwealth Fund, May 5, 2023, https://www.commonwealthfund.org/publications/issue-briefs/2023/may/expanding-role-midwives-address-maternal-health-crisis.

"Even some ob-gyns will repeat": Sarah Osmundson, phone interview with the authors, March 29, 2023.

"I was passing blood clots": Selena Simmons-Duffin, "Her Miscarriage Left Her Bleeding Profusely. An Ohio ER Sent Her Home to Wait," NPR, November 15, 2022, https://www.npr.org/sections/health-shots/2022/11/15/1135882310/miscarriage-hemorrhage-abortion-law-ohio.

"Just practically, fewer abortions": Prager, phone interview.

Miscarriages account for roughly nine hundred thousand: Lyndsey S. Benson et al., "Early Pregnancy Loss in the Emergency Department, 2006–2016," *Journal of the American College of Emergency Physicians Open* 2, no. 6 (December 2021): e12549, https://doi.org/10.1002%2Femp2.12549.

But due to the FDA's extra: Donley and Lens, "Abortion, Pregnancy Loss."

The FDA currently allows: Sarah Zhang, "The Abortion Pill Can Be Used Later Than the FDA Says," *Atlantic*, June 29, 2022, https://www.theatlantic.com/health/archive/2022/06/how-late-can-you-take-abortion-pill/661437.

This is done in other countries: Zhang, "Abortion Pill."

Morgan Nuzzo, one of only: Nuzzo, phone interview.

It's hard to know exact numbers: Kavitha Surana, "Doctors Warned Her Pregnancy Could Kill Her. Then Tennessee Outlawed Abortion," ProPublica, March 14, 2023, https://www.propublica.org/article/tennessee-abortion-ban -doctors-ectopic-pregnancy; "New Report Details How Post-*Roe* Abortion Bans Are Harming Patients and Providers," Advancing New Standards in Reproductive Health, May 12, 2023, https://www.ansirh.org/sites/default /files/2023–05/Care%20Post-Roe%20Press%20Release%2020230515v2.pdf.

"Post-*Dobbs*, existing mistrust": Sarah Averbach et al., "Failure to Progress: Structural Racism in Women's Healthcare," *Lancet* 57 (March 2023): 101861, https://www.thelancet.com/journals/eclinm/article/PIIS2589 –5370(23)00038-X/fulltext.

Chapter Nine

This time, in 1969: Meilan Solly, "Who Was Norma McCorvey, the Woman Behind Roe v. Wade?," *Smithsonian*, June 24, 2022, https://www .smithsonianmag.com/smart-news/who-was-norma-mccorvey-the-woman -behind-roe-v-wade-180980311/.

Every year, roughly seven thousand cases: "The Supreme Court at Work," Supreme Court of the United States, accessed May 2023, https://www .supremecourt.gov/about/courtatwork.aspx.

"This right of privacy": Roe v. Wade, 410 U.S. 113 (1973), https://supreme .justia.com/cases/federal/us/410/113/.

The Fourteenth Amendment: Constitution of the United States, "Milestone Documents, 14th Amendment to the U.S. Constitution: Civil Rights (1868)," National Archives, https://www.archives.gov/milestone-documents/14th -amendment.

"Also in the balance": Foster, *Turnaway Study*, 164.

But the air force: Alisha Haridasani Gupta, "Why Ruth Bader Ginsburg Wasn't All That Fond of Roe v. Wade," *New York Times*, last updated May 19, 2021, https:// www.nytimes.com/2020/09/21/us/ruth-bader-ginsburg-roe-v-wade.html.

"The idea was 'Government'": Meredith Heagney, "Justice Ruth Bader Ginsburg Offers Critique of Roe v. Wade During Law School Visit University of Chicago Law School," University of Chicago Law School, May 15, 2013, https:// www.law.uchicago.edu/news/justice-ruth-bader-ginsburg-offers-critique-roe-v -wade-during-law-school-visit.

Donald Trump defeated Hillary Clinton: Barbara Sprunt, "How Amy Coney

Barrett's Confirmation Would Compare to Past Supreme Court Picks," NPR, October 1, 2020, https://www.npr.org/sections/supreme-court-nomination /2020/10/01/916644231/how-a-barrett-confirmation-would-compare-to -past-supreme-court-timelines.

Missouri restricted public employees: Webster v. Reproductive Health Services, 492 U.S. 490 (1989), https://supreme.justia.com/cases/federal/us /492/490/.

Of the preamble, Rehnquist wrote: *Webster*, 492 U.S. at 491.

The Missouri preamble stood: "'Missouri Preamble': A Framework for Defining and Protecting Personhood," Americans United for Life, 2017, https://aul.org/wp-content/uploads/2019/07/Missouri-Preamble.docx.

O'Connor wrote the opinion: Planned Parenthood of Southeastern Pa. v. Casey, 505 U.S. 833 (1992), https://supreme.justia.com/cases/federal/us/505 /833/.

The one the court struck down: *Planned Parenthood.*

Barriers to teaching: Roshan M. Burns and Kate A. Shaw, "Standardizing Abortion Education: What Medical Schools Can Learn from Residency Programs," *Current Opinion in Obstetrics and Gynecology* 32, no. 6 (December 2020): 387–92, https://doi.org/10.1097/gco.0000000000000663.

The lawsuit was filed: Dobbs v. Jackson Women's Health Organization, 597 U.S. ____ (2022), https://supreme.justia.com/cases/federal/us/597/19–1392/.

Justice Samuel Alito's reasoning: *Dobbs.*

Bans on abortion are connected: Marian Jones, "Dorothy Roberts on Reproductive Justice: 'Abortion Isn't the Only Focus,'" *Guardian*, August 28, 2022, https://www.theguardian.com/us-news/2022/aug/28/reproductive-freedom -abortion-rights-dorothy-roberts-interview, 4/16/23; Ross and Solinger, *Reproductive Justice: An Introduction*, 9.

The lawsuit alleged that the women: Zurawski et al v. State of Texas et al., criminal complaint, filed March 6, 2023, courtesy of Center for Reproductive Rights, https://reproductiverights.org/wp-content/uploads/2023/03/Zurawski -v-State-of-Texas-Complaint.pdf.

"It's not good to micromanage": Molly Duane, phone interview with the authors, May 5, 2023.

"I cannot adequately put into words": Remarks at press conference by plaintiffs in Zurawski et al. v. State of Texas et al., March 8, 2023, courtesy of Center for Reproductive Rights, https://reproductiverights.org/zurawski-texas -plaintiffs-remarks-press-conference/.

"What I needed was an abortion": Amanda Zurawski, testimony before U.S. Senate Judiciary Committee, April 26, 2023, https://www.judiciary.senate.gov /imo/media/doc/2023-04-26%20-%20Testimony%20-%20Zurawski.pdf.

She wrote they should: Zurawski et al. v. State of Texas et al., temporary injunction order, August 4, 2023, courtesy of Center for Reproductive Rights, https://reproductiverights.org/wp-content/uploads/2023/08/Zurawski-v -Texas_TI.pdf.

Jessica H. realized she was pregnant: Jessica H., phone interview with the authors, May 8, 2023.

Louisville, Kentucky–based Emily M.: Emily M., phone interview with the authors, January 27, 2023.

Chapter Ten

"When we don't talk about": Chavi Eve Karkowsky, *High Risk: Stories of Pregnancy, Birth, and the Unexpected* (New York: Liveright, 2020), xvi.

"There is a strong contingent": Jen Klein, in-person interview with the authors, September 22, 2022.

Another, passed in 2022: Oklahoma State Legislature, Text of HB 1503, passed May 3, 2022, http://www.oklegislature.gov/BillInfo.aspx?Bill=sb1503 &Session=2200.

"The results of this research are alarming": Christian De Vos et al., "No One Could Say: Accessing Emergency Obstetrics Information as a Prospective Prenatal Patient in Post-*Roe* Oklahoma," Physicians for Human Rights, Oklahoma Call for Reproductive Justice, and Center for Reproductive Rights, April 2023, https://reproductiverights.org/wp-content/uploads/2023/04 /OklahomaAbortionBanReport_Full_SinglePages-NEW-4-27-23.pdf.

"The unfortunate thing is": Michele Heisler, phone interview with the authors, April 26, 2023.

In Oklahoma, for example: Oklahoma State Legislature, Text of HB 4327, passed May 26, 2022, http://www.oklegislature.gov/BillInfo.aspx?Bill=hb4327 &Session=2200.

But when pressed on how: Julie O'Donoghue, "Louisiana Health Department Declines to Answer Doctors' Questions on Abortion Law," Louisiana Illuminator, November 1, 2022, https://lailluminator.com/2022/11/01/louisiana-health -department-declines-to-answer-doctors-questions-on-abortion-law/.

The women countersued: Emily Bazelon, "Husband Sued over His Ex-Wife's Abortion; Now Her Friends Are Suing Him," *New York Times*, August 18, 2022, https://www.nytimes.com/2023/05/04/us/texas-man-suing-ex-wife -abortion.html.

They were charged with crimes: Shaila Dewan and Sheera Frenkel, "A Mother, a Daughter and an Unusual Abortion Prosecution in Nebraska," *New York*

Times, August 18, 2022, https://www.nytimes.com/2022/08/18/us/abortion
-prosecution-nebraska.html.

Facebook, now called Meta: Margery A. Beck, "18-Year-Old Nebraska Woman Sentenced to 90 Days in Jail for Burning Fetus after Abortion," Associated Press, July 20, 2023, https://apnews.com/article/abortion-charges-nebraska
-f330455d60aa3c01534bcb74216f8404#.

In 2022, voters rejected: Melissa Chan, "Kentucky Voters Reject Anti-Abortion Ballot Measure," NBC News, November 9, 2022, https://www
.nbcnews.com/politics/2022-election/kentucky-voters-reject-anti-abortion
-ballot-measure-rcna56313.

Voters approved ballot measures: Lindsay Whitehurst, "Kentucky, Michigan Voters Approve Protecting Abortion Rights," Associated Press, November 11, 2022, https://apnews.com/article/2022-midterm-elections-abortion
-8779f3ee57d4d20d54861a5ed6ba72ff.

And in Montana: Mary Beth Hanson, "Montana Voters Reject 'Born Alive' Abortion Referendum," Associated Press, November 11, 2022, https://apnews.com/article/abortion-health-business-montana
-a99111675c40301d1940addca098d599.

The law would have required: Hanson, "Montana Voters."

Personhood measures attempted: Rachana Pradhan and Jennifer Haberkorn, "Personhood Movement Loses Twice," Politico, November 5, 2014, https://
www.politico.com/story/2014/11/personhood-movement-north-dakota
-colorado-112552.

In Mississippi, a state constitutional: Denise Grady, "Medical Nuances Drove 'No' Vote in Mississippi," *New York Times*, November 15, 2011, https://www
.nytimes.com/2011/11/15/health/policy/no-vote-in-mississippi-hinged-on
-issues-beyond-abortion.html.

But in Alabama: Dan Rosenzweig-Ziff, "Alabama Supreme Court rules frozen embryos are children, imperiling IVF," *Washington Post*, February 20, 2024, https://www.washingtonpost.com/politics/2024/02/19/alabama
-supreme-court-embryos-children-ivf/.

A record high 69 percent: Lydia Saad, "Broader Support for Abortion Rights Continues Post-*Dobbs*," Gallup, June 14, 2023, https://news.gallup.com/poll
/506759/broader-support-abortion-rights-continues-post-dobbs.aspx.

The group said in a court filing: John Raby, "Lawsuit Seeking to Revoke West Virginia Abortion Ban Dropped," Associated Press, April 17, 2023, https://apnews.com/article/abortion-lawsuit-west-virginia-f50486
28336f55256cab02015eb9904c.

Meanwhile, one of the doctors: Women's Health Center of West Virginia, https://www.womenshealthwv.org/, accessed December 3, 2023.

"There is a tremendous overlap": Jen Klein, in-person interview.

According to the CDC: "Maternal Deaths and Mortality Rates: Each State, the District of Columbia, United States, 2018–2021," Centers for Disease Control and Prevention, accessed May 2023, https://www.cdc.gov/nchs/maternal-mortality/mmr-2018–2021-state-data.pdf.

And their infant mortality: "Infant Mortality Rates by State," Centers for Disease Control and Prevention, last reviewed September 12, 2023, https://www.cdc.gov/nchs/pressroom/sosmap/infant_mortality_rates/infant_mortality.htm.

The study found mortality: Amanda Jean Stevenson, Leslie Root, and Jane Menken, "The Maternal Mortality Consequences of Losing Abortion Access," *SocArXiv*, June 29, 2022, https://osf.io/preprints/socarxiv/7g29k.

In related news: Devan Coyle, "Supreme Court Approval Rating Declines amid Controversy over Ethics and Transparency: Marquette Poll," CNN, May 24, 2023, https://www.cnn.com/2023/05/24/politics/supreme-court-approval-rating-poll-ethics-marquette/index.html; "Congress and the Public," Gallup, July 2023, https://news.gallup.com/poll/1600/congress-public.aspx.

"When my baby died": Bailey, phone interview.

A 2022 Pew Research Center poll: "Majority of Public Disapproves of Supreme Court's Decision to Overturn Roe v. Wade," Pew Research Center, July 6, 2022, https://www.pewresearch.org/politics/2022/07/06/majority-of-public-disapproves-of-supreme-courts-decision-to-overturn-roe-v-wade/.

The decision has inspired: Charlotte Alter, "She Sued Tennessee for Denying Her an Abortion. Now She's Running for Office," *Time*, October 12, 2023, https://time.com/6320148/allie-phillips-abortion-lawsuit-tennessee/.

Democrats did try: Draft Supreme Court opinion, via Politico, accessed May 2023, https://www.politico.com/f/?id=00000180–874f-dd36-a38c-c74f98520000.

She's campaigned for stillbirth awareness: Debbie Haine Vijayvergiya, phone interview by the authors, May 22, 2023.

Two Democratic representatives: Black Maternal Health Momnibus Act of 2021, H.R. 959, 117th Cong. (2021), https://www.congress.gov/bill/117th-congress/house-bill/959.

TheDemocratic administration: "Emergency Medical Treatment & Labor Act (EMTALA)," Centers for Medicare and Medicaid Services, last modified September 6, 2023, https://www.cms.gov/regulations-and-guidance/legislation/emtala.

"An emergency condition": "Reinforcement of EMTALA Obligations Specific to Patients Who Are Pregnant or Are Experiencing Pregnancy Loss," U.S. Department Health & Human Services, July 2022, https://www.hhs

.gov/guidance/sites/default/files/hhs-guidance-documents/QSO-22–22-Hospitals_0.pdf.

And they were supposed to: "Justice Department Sues Idaho to Protect Reproductive Rights," U.S. Department of Justice, August 2, 2022, https://www.justice.gov/opa/pr/justice-department-sues-idaho-protect-reproductive-rights.

A U.S. District Court judge found: Rebecca Boone, "Idaho Can't Enforce Abortion Ban in Medical Emergencies," Associated Press, August 24, 2022, https://apnews.com/article/abortion-health-texas-xavier-becerra-4ccc7296f015270b0dc66c64e975689c.

"We will use every tool": "Justice Department Sues Idaho."

A Texas U.S. District Court: "Paxton Secures Victory against Biden Administration," Texas Attorney General, August 24, 2022, https://www.texasattorneygeneral.gov/news/releases/paxton-secures-victory-against-biden-administration-blocks-hhs-forcing-healthcare-providers-perform.

More than 5.5 million are living: Geoff Mulvihill, Kimberlee Kruesi, and Claire Savage, "A Year after Fall of *Roe*, 25 Million Women Live in States with Abortion Bans or Tighter Restrictions," Associated Press, June 22, 2023, https://apnews.com/article/abortion-dobbs-anniversary-state-laws-51c2a83899f133556e715342abfcface.

One such method: Duaa Eldeib, "A Lab Test That Experts Liken to a Witch Trial Is Helping Send Women to Prison for Murder," ProPublica, October 7, 2023, https://www.propublica.org/article/is-lung-float-test-reliable-stillbirth-medical-examiners-murder.

"Public health experts predict": Hoffman, "OB-GYN Residency Programs."

This problem too may lead: Sophia Novack, "You Know What? I'm Not Doing This Anymore," Slate, March 21, 2023, https://slate.com/news-and-politics/2023/03/texas-abortion-law-doctors-nurses-care-supreme-court.html.

The shortage of registered nurses: Novack, "You Know What?"

But the spike in infant deaths: Cauterucci, "Kind of Life."

Mississippi isn't much better: Kate Royals, "'Death at Your Toes': A Look Inside a Mississippi Maternity Care Desert," *Mississippi Today*, November 3, 2022, https://mississippitoday.org/2022/11/03/mississippi-maternity-care-desert/.

Activists say it's because: Kathleen McLaughlin, "No Ob-Gyns Left in Town," *Guardian*, August 22, 2023, https://www.theguardian.com/us-news/2023/aug/22/abortion-idaho-women-rights-healthcare.

Chapter Eleven

She was distressed and in pain: Transcript of Brittney Poolaw's criminal trial, December 13, 2021, courtesy of National Advocates for Pregnant Women (now Pregnancy Justice).

In Oklahoma, any miscarriage after twelve weeks: Dana Branham and Carmen Forman, "What We Know, and What We Don't, about Oklahoma's 6-Week Abortion Ban," *Oklahoman*, May 6, 2022, https://www.oklahoman .com/story/news/2022/05/06/oklahoma-abortion-ban-roe-v-wade-ruling -supreme-court-what-we-know/9645486002/.

And at Comanche County Hospital: Transcript of Brittney Poolaw's criminal trial.

Other states, like California: Nigel Duara, "Bill Would End Coroner Investigations of Stillbirths," Cal Matters, September 29, 2022, https://calmatters .org/justice/2022/04/coroner-investigation-stillbirths-anti-abortion/.

About half of miscarriages: Philip John Hardy and Katherine Hardy, "Chromosomal Instability in First Trimester Miscarriage: A Common Cause of Pregnancy Loss?," *Translational Pediatrics* 7, no. 3 (July 2018): 211–18, https://doi.org/10.21037%2Ftp.2018.03.02.

According to the American College of Obstetricians and Gynecologists: "Stillbirth," American College of Obstetricians and Gynecologists, last reviewed June 2022, https://www.acog.org/womens-health/faqs/stillbirth.

A large portion of fetal deaths: M. A. Sims and K. A. Collins, "Fetal Death: A 10-Year Retrospective Study," *American Journal of Forensic Medicine and Pathology* 22, no. 3 (September 2001): 261–65, https://doi.org/10.1097 /00000433-200109000-00012.

There are some studies: Margaret C. Gorman et al., "Outcomes in Pregnancies Complicated by Methamphetamine Use," *American Journal of Obstetrics and Gynecology* 211, no. 4 (October 2014): 429.e1–7, https://doi.org/10.1016/j .ajog.2014.06.005.

Restricted fetal growth was the: Corrie B. Miller and Tricia Wright, "Investigating Mechanisms of Stillbirth in the Setting of Prenatal Substance Use," *Academic Forensic Pathology* 8, no. 4 (December 2018): 865–73, https:// doi.org/10.1177%2F1925362118821471.

She has a huge body of work: Lynn T. Singer et al., "Fifty Years of Research on Prenatal Substances: Lessons Learned for the Opioid Epidemic," Adversity and Resilience Science 1 (October 2020): 223–234, https://doi.org/10.1007 %2Fs42844-020-00021-7.

"It's interesting," she told us: Dr. Claire Coles, phone interview by the authors, May 18, 2022.

Children born addicted to substances: "Neonatal Abstinence Syndrome," Stanford Medicine Children's Health, accessed December 3, 2023, https://www .stanfordchildrens.org/en/topic/default?id=neonatal-abstinence-syndrome -90-P02387.

"I think the fear of these things": Coles, phone interview.

A toxicology screen and blood: Transcript of Brittney Poolaw's criminal trial.

In 1986, there were zero: Michele Goodwin, *Policing the Womb: Invisible Women and the Criminalization of Motherhood* (Irvine: University of California, 2020), 15.

Loretta Ross and Rickie Solinger: Loretta J. Ross and Rickie Solinger, *Reproductive Justice: An Introduction* (Oakland: University of California Press, 2017), 46.

Most women on welfare are not: Washington, *Medical Apartheid*, chapter 8, Kindle.

Jennifer Johnson, the first woman: Coontz, *Way We Never Were*, 146.

By 1990, the ACLU: Paltrow, "Criminal Prosecutions against Pregnant Women."

Those killings are a mix: Rebecca B. Lawn and Karestan C. Koenen, "Homicide Is a Leading Cause of Death for Pregnant Women in US," *BMJ* 379 (October 2022): 2499, https://doi.org/10.1136/bmj.o2499.

Homicides of pregnant women: "Pregnancy-Associated Homicides on the Rise in the United States, Suggests NICHD-Funded Study," National Institutes of Health, September 16, 2022, https://www.nichd.nih.gov/newsroom/news /091622-pregnancy-associated-homicide.

"Recent studies have been limited": Lawn and Koenen, "Homicide."

In 2013, in the *Journal*: Lynn Paltrow and Jeanne Flavin, "Arrests of and Forced Interventions on Pregnant Women in the United States, 1973–2005: Implications for Women's Legal Status and Public Health," *Journal of Health Politics, Policy and Law* 38 (April 2013): 299–343, https://papers.ssrn.com /sol3/papers.cfm?abstract_id=2530100.

In a new follow-up: Dana Sussman, phone interview with the authors, June 6, 2023.

But only eighteen of them: Kassie McClung and Brianna Bailey, "She Was Charged with Manslaughter after a Miscarriage. Cases Like Hers Are Becoming More Common in Oklahoma," Frontier, January 7, 2022, https:// www.readfrontier.org/stories/she-was-charged-with-manslaughter-after-a -miscarriage-cases-like-hers-are-becoming-more-common-in-oklahoma/.

Her conviction was overturned: Gregory Yee, "California Judge Overturns 11-Year Prison Term for Woman Whose Baby Was Stillborn," *Los Angeles Times*, March 18, 2022, https://www.latimes.com/california/story/2022-03 -18/california-judge-overturns-conviction-woman-whose-baby-was-stillborn.

The prosecutor dropped the charges: "Alabama Prosecutors Drop Charges against Woman Whose Fetus Died in Shooting," *Time*, July 3, 2019, https://time.com/5620130/alabama-charges-dropped-marshae-jones/#.

"Nobody should fear arrest": Lynn Paltrow, phone interview with the authors, April 8, 2022.

The book documents the rise of: Goodwin, *Policing the Womb*, 16.

"If you kill a child": Bob Herbert, "In America; Stillborn Justice," *New York Times*, May 24, 2011, https://www.nytimes.com/2001/05/24/opinion/in-america-stillborn-justice.html.

The prosecutor claimed that he: Goodwin, *Policing the Womb*, 16.

McKnight's conviction was eventually: Goodwin, *Policing the Womb*, 43.

"It's almost like white women": Sussman, phone interview.

The court stated, Goodwin wrote: Goodwin, *Policing the Womb*, 82.

"For the most part, Americans may": Goodwin, *Policing the Womb*, 92.

"It was kind of an emergency": Rachael M., phone interview with the authors, March 8, 2023.

And she kept using methamphetamine: Transcript of Brittney Poolaw's criminal trial.

The medical examiner, Leonardo Roquero: Transcript of Brittney Poolaw's criminal trial.

Roquero said the toxicology: Transcript of Brittney Poolaw's criminal trial.

"No," Roquero said: Transcript of Brittney Poolaw's criminal trial.

"We have a situation here where": Transcript of Brittney Poolaw's criminal trial.

Jurors returned a guilty verdict: Asha Gilbert, "After Miscarriage, Woman Is Convicted of Manslaughter. The 'Fetus Was Not Viable,' Advocates Say," *USA Today*, October 21, 2021, https://www.usatoday.com/story/news/nation/2021/10/21/oklahoma-woman-convicted-of-manslaughter-miscarriage/6104281001/.

Dana Sussman thinks the verdict: Sussman, phone interview.

Chapter Twelve

Among other things: House Bill 1337, Indiana State Legislature, 2016, https://iga.in.gov/legislative/2016/bills/house/1337/details.

The process could be done: House Bill 1337, Indiana State Legislature.

The court declined to take: Tom Davies, "US Supreme Court Won't Take Up Indiana's Abortion Burial Law," Associated Press, May 1, 2023, https://apnews.com/article/indiana-abortion-laws-fetal-remains-burial-157a280867b60059d2c2f7ed90e70183.

"Unborn babies are more than": Whitney Downard, "Fetal Remains Law Upheld on Appeal," *Indiana Capital Chronicle*, November 29, 2022, https://indianacapitalchronicle.com/briefs/fetal-remains-law-upheld-on-appeal/.

It does, however, mandate that: Aleksandra Appleton, "Sex Ed in Indiana Isn't Required. Here's What It Looks Like in Schools That Teach It," Chalkbeat Indiana, February 13, 2023, https://in.chalkbeat.org/2023/2/13/23594928/indiana-sex-ed-health-requirements-bill-consent-birth-control-pregnancy-reproduction.

"These laws also send the": Jane Doe no. 1 et al. v. Attorney General of Indiana et al., filed December 21, 2020, https://lawyeringproject.org/wp-content/uploads/2020/12/S.D.-Ind.-20-cv-03247-dckt-000001_000-filed-2020-12-21.pdf.

The attorneys also argued: Jane Doe no. 1 et al. v. Attorney General of Indiana et al.

In a post about her research: Shannon Withycombe, "Meanings and Materials of Miscarriage: How Babies in Jars Shaped Modern Pregnancy," Nursing Clio, October 31, 2018, https://nursingclio.org/2018/10/31/meanings-and-materials-of-miscarriage/.

In Indiana, the law states: "ISDH Guidance for Implementation of Fetal Disposition Requirements from House Enrolled Act (HEA) 1337," Indiana State Department of Health, updated October 28, 2019, https://www.in.gov/health/files/HEA-1337-Guidance.pdf.

Cleveland-based Brittany had: Brittany, phone interview.

The median cost for a funeral: "Average Funeral Cost," Bankrate, July 3, 2023, https://www.bankrate.com/insurance/life-insurance/average-funeral-cost/.

Some funeral homes will: Tears Foundation, accessed October 25, 2023, https://thetearsfoundation.org/.

Abortions are: National Vital Statistics System, Centers for Disease Control and Prevention, last reviewed November 29, 2023, https://www.cdc.gov/nchs/nvss/index.htm.

She suggested "our government": Layne, *Motherhood Lost*, chapter 4, Kindle.

"My precious son who lived": Erica Bailey, "I Used to Be Pro-Life. Then My Baby Died," *Motherwell*, October 12, 2022, https://motherwellmag.com/2022/10/12/i-used-to-be-pro-life-then-my-baby-died/.

Joanne Cacciatore, the grief and trauma: Cacciatore, phone interview; "MISSing Angels Bill—Frequently Asked Questions," MISS Foundation, accessed June 26, 2023, https://www.missfoundation.org/advocacy/missing-angels-bill-frequently-asked-questions/.

She doesn't think miscarriage is: Cacciatore, phone interview.

Now forty-three states: "MISS State and Federal Legislation Initiatives,"

MISS Foundation, accessed June 26, 2023, https://www.missfoundation.org/advocacy/miss-state-and-federal-legislative-initiatives/.

Cacciatore has been adamant: Cacciatore, phone interview.

Idaho's Unborn Infants Dignity Act: Idaho Unborn Infants Dignity Act, accessed December 3, 2023, https://legislature.idaho.gov/wp-content/uploads/statutesrules/idstat/Title39/T39CH93.pdf.

Other efforts, like one in Wyoming: Joel Funk, "Wyoming Lawmakers Advance Miscarriage Certificate Bill," *Wyoming News*, February 22, 2018, https://www.wyomingnews.com/news/local_news/wyoming-lawmakers-advance-miscarriage-certificate-bill/article_b8000aba-17a4–11e8–9dcc-0b478161cd58.html, 6/2023.

"Concern about Missing Angel Acts": Carol Sanger, "Legislating with Affect: Emotion and Legislative Law Making," *American Society for Political and Legal Philosophy* 53 (2013): 38–76, https://www.jstor.org/stable/24220329.

"There's still this fear": Jill Wieber Lens, phone interview by the authors, May 30, 2023.

"But over the past few decades": Donley and Lens, "Why Do We Talk."

Her bosses created a leave: Isabel, phone interview with the authors, April 24, 2023; Isabel, email message to the authors, August 28, 2023.

"The chief of operations": Jodi M., Zoom interview by the authors, April 21, 2023.

The fine print: you have to: "Fact Sheet: Pregnancy Loss and Workplace Rights," A Better Balance, last updated November 8, 2023, https://www.abetterbalance.org/resources/miscarriage-workplace-rights/.

So even unpaid leave: Criado Perez, *Invisible Women*, 81.

The Pregnancy Discrimination Act says: "Fact Sheet: Pregnancy Loss."

This is available to the employee: Carol Warner, "Emerging Trend: Bereavement Leave Covers Reproductive Losses," HRMorning, June 22, 2022, https://www.hrmorning.com/news/bereavement-leave-pregnancy/; Danielle N. Malaty et al., "What Illinois Employers Need to Know about the Family Bereavement Leave Act," Goldberg Segalla, February 9, 2023, https://www.goldbergsegalla.com/news-and-knowledge/knowledge/what-illinois-employers-need-to-know-about-the-family-bereavement-leave-act/.

Utah, Pittsburgh, Boston, Portland, Oregon: Warner, "Emerging Trend."

California has pregnancy disability laws: "How to Manage Pregnancy-Related Leave in California," Society for Human Resource Management, October 14, 2022, https://www.shrm.org/resourcesandtools/tools-and-samples/how-to-guides/pages/californiamanagingpregnancyleave.aspx.

As of 2022, according to the: Amanda Wilke, "Miscarriage and Other

Pregnancy Loss Leave," International Foundation of Employee Benefit Plans, June 1, 2022, https://blog.ifebp.org/miscarriage-and-other-pregnancy-loss-leave/.

The largest is the federal government: "Federal Employers," U.S. Department of Labor, accessed June 25, 2023, https://www.dol.gov/agencies/odep/program-areas/employers/federal-employment.

A study from NFP: Kelsey Butler, "One in Four US Companies Offers Bereavement Leave for Pregnancy Loss," Bloomberg, February 1, 2023, www.bloomberg.com/news/articles/2023-02-01/one-in-four-us-companies-offers-bereavement-leave-for-pregnancy-loss#xj4y7vzkg.

"So you get a birth or death": Swanson, phone interview.

It includes language that the leave: Alexis Young, "Fight to Extend Paid Family Leave to Parents Grieving Still Born Babies Continues," New York Now from WMHT, February 1, 2023, https://nynow.wmht.org/blogs/politics/fight-to-extend-paid-family-leave-to-parents-grieving-still-born-babies-continues/.

The word "bond" has: Young, "Fight to Extend."

"People who deliver stillborn": Rachel Unkovic, email message to the authors, March 7, 2023.

The others offer a tax deduction: "Certificate of Stillbirth/Certificate of Birth Resulting in Stillbirth," Star Legacy Foundation, accessed June 26, 2023, https://starlegacyfoundation.org/legislation/.

"A lot of people go back": Amanda Pinkham-Brown, phone interview with the authors, April 12, 2023.

"When I had my loss": Jackie Mancinelli, phone interview with the authors, March 1, 2023.

"I was crying on the phone": Ashley L., phone interview with the authors, February 2, 2023.

A 2021 study showed: Priti Kalsi and Maggie Y. Liu, "Pregnancy Loss and Female Labor Market Outcomes," Economics: Faculty Publications, Smith College (2021): 17, https://scholarworks.smith.edu/eco_facpubs/57.

"My work was so wonderful": Angelica K., phone interview with the authors, April 14, 2023.

"I couldn't go to the nursery yet": Jenna C., phone interview with the authors, February 28, 2023.

"They quietly kept paying me": Taylor, phone interview with the authors, March 23, 2023.

Chapter Thirteen

Kate Watson, who teaches bioethics: Kate Watson, phone interview with the authors, May 24, 2022.

"Folded into this notion": Jessica Zucker, interview with the authors, June 29, 2022.

Those who abide by this delay: Layne, *Motherhood Lost*, chapter 4, Kindle.

A 2015 study showed the: Bardos et al., "National Survey."

Between one-third and one-half: Donley and Lens, "Abortion, Pregnancy Loss."

That same study showed: Bardos et al., "National Survey."

Zucker refers to it as: Zucker, *I Had a Miscarriage*, 42.

"Rather than being made": Kluger-Bell, *Unspeakable Losses*, 125.

Reva Judas, who runs the: Reva Judas, phone interview with the authors, March 8, 2023.

"You have one job": Jennifer H., phone interview with the authors, May 5, 2023.

"Even if a doctor": Clancy, Zoom interview.

"I gave myself a pedicure": Lorena Tapia, phone interview with the authors, March 1, 2023.

Cassandra H., who lives in the: Cassandra H., phone interview with the authors, March 15, 2023.

"During a successful pregnancy": Jessica Levy, "We Tend to Keep Quiet about Miscarriages. Here's Why That Should Change," *Washington Post*, March 28, 2017, https://www.washingtonpost.com/news/parenting/wp/2017/03/28/we-have-a-tradition-of-keeping-quiet-about-miscarriages-heres-why-that-should-change/.

"I was completely distraught": Hall, phone interview.

"My mom had lost two babies": Priscilla G., phone interview with the authors, January 17, 2023.

"I had people reach out": Melat, phone interview with the authors, May 3, 2023.

"My mother wanted me to pray": Bell, phone interview.

"Once you have a loss": Marny Smith, phone interview.

"How many positive pregnancy tests": Finn, phone interview.

Though we compiled a meager: Rund Abdelfatah and Ramtin Arablouei, "What Is the Bechdel Test? A Shorthand for Measuring Representation in Movies," NPR, April 5, 2023, https://www.npr.org/2023/04/05/1168116147/what-is-the-bechdel-test-a-shorthand-for-measuring-representation-in-movies.

The majority of the depictions: Jordan Williams, "Why That Rhaenyra Birth Scene Had to Happen," Screen Rant, October 24, 2022, https://screenrant.com /rhaenyra-stillborn-baby-graphic-scene-important-house-dragon.

Silencing miscarriages, anthropologist Layne: Layne, *Motherhood Lost*, chapter 2, chapter 8, Kindle.

A trend so out of control: Gabrielle Canon, "California Couple Whose Gender-Reveal Party Sparked a Wildfire Charged with 30 Crimes," *Guardian*, July 21, 2021, https://www.theguardian.com/us-news/2021/jul/21/couple -gender-reveal-party-wildfire-charged; Jack Dutton, "Gender Reveal Parties Have Already Seen Four Deaths So Far This Year," *Newsweek*, April 1, 2021, https://www.newsweek.com/gender-reveal-parties-four-dead-1580477; Jenna Karvunidis as told to Molly Langmuir, "I Started the 'Gender Reveal Party' Trend. And I Regret It," *Guardian*, June 29, 2020, https://www.theguardian .com/lifeandstyle/2020/jun/29/jenna-karvunidis-i-started-gender-reveal -party-trend-regret.

And all contribute to a: Donley and Lens, "Why Do We Talk."

"I had convinced myself": Haine Vijayvergiya, phone interview.

"All that for two shots": Saya H., phone interview.

Feminist writer Jessica Valenti: Jessica Valenti (@JessicaValenti), "I made a TikTok about this very thing a few days ago: Conservatives have been valorizing women who die during pregnancy or childbirth for the last few years—because they knew women were gonna start dying post-Roe & they want to make it as palatable as possible," Twitter, January 20, 2023, 9:32 p.m., https://twitter.com /JessicaValenti/status/1616624841045442562?lang=en.

"We have a conceptualization of motherhood": Armstrong, phone interview.

"It's really easy to talk": Carson, phone interview.

"If you're not willing to go": Jessica Van Wyen, phone interview with the authors, January 11, 2023.

Rainbow baby **is a newish term:** Kelly Burch, "What Is a Rainbow Baby? How the Term for Children Born after a Pregnancy Loss Went Mainstream," Business Insider, June 28, 2022, https://www.insider.com/what-is-a-rainbow-baby-how -the-term-went-mainstream-2020–10.

"People were so relieved": Gabriella B., phone interview by the authors, April 24, 2023.

"Are there other possible endings": Taylor, phone interview.

As *The Turnaway Study* showed: Foster, *Turnaway Study*, 22, 24.

Sixty percent of those: Foster, *Turnaway Study*, 38.

Linda Layne, the anthropologist: Layne, *Motherhood Lost*, chapter 2, Kindle.

Those who are excited about: Bueno, *Brink of Being*, 3.

They're left in a vacuum: Donley and Lens, "Abortion, Pregnancy Loss."

Historian Lara Freidenfelds wrote: Lara Freidenfelds, "8 Myths about Pregnancy and Miscarriage," *Washington Post*, January 2, 2020, https://www.washingtonpost.com/lifestyle/2020/01/02/myths-about-pregnancy-miscarriage/.

Layne said for the millions: Layne, *Motherhood Lost*, chapter 5, Kindle.

A more practical option: Parsons, "Feminist Reflections on Miscarriage."

Law professors Jill Wieber Lens: Donley and Lens, "Abortion, Pregnancy Loss."

And aligning an abortion rights: Donley and Lens, "Abortion, Pregnancy Loss."

If abortion, miscarriage, and stillbirth: Donley and Lens, "Abortion, Pregnancy Loss."

"I work in reproductive rights": Catherine, phone interview.

Orlando-based Kelsey Garcia-Abdin: Garcia-Abdin, phone interview; Garcia-Abdin, email.

Anthropologist Layne says that since: Layne, *Motherhood Lost*, chapter 10, Kindle.

Feminist bioethicists have called this: Donley and Lens, "Abortion, Pregnancy Loss."

In contrast, the antiabortion: Donley and Lens, "Abortion, Pregnancy Loss."

"This is not inconsistency": Donley and Lens, "Abortion, Pregnancy Loss."

"No one in earlier times": Freidenfelds, phone interview.

Or to put it more bluntly: Ashley P., Zoom interview.

As writer and historian Daniela Blei: Blei, "History of Talking About Miscarriage."

"I am very much against abortion": Kelly, phone interview by the authors, January 17, 2023.

A news anchor on CNN: Penelope Trunk, "Penelope Trunk: Why I Tweeted about My Miscarriage," *Guardian*, November 6, 2009, https://www.theguardian.com/lifeandstyle/2009/nov/06/penelope-trunk-tweet-miscarriage.

She may be crying about: Parsons, "Feminist Reflections on Miscarriage."

"There can be joy and relief": Nuzzo, phone interview.

This relational model: Parsons, "Feminist Reflections on Miscarriage."

Children who lose their parents: Sukie Miller, *Finding Hope When a Child Dies: What Other Cultures Can Teach Us* (New York: Fireside, 2002), 19.

"The first Mother's Day": Kaufman, phone interview.

"I don't think people": Crystal H., phone interview; Crystal H., in-person interview.

Long Beach–based Cynthia: Cynthia, phone interview with the authors, April 10, 2023.

TFMR therapist Jane Armstrong: Armstrong, phone interview.

"I had quite a few people": Ashley B., phone interview.

"The added stress of being Black": Erica Freeman, phone interview with the authors, July 20, 2022.

"I'm hoping women who": Van Wyen, phone interview.

"It was so isolating.": Hanish, phone interview; Hanish, email.

"Women are storytellers": Allison B., phone interview.

"We do need stories": Taylor, phone interview.

Chapter Fourteen

"Your keepsakes represent": Deborah L. Davis, *Stillbirth, Yet Still Born* (Golden, CO: Fulcrum Publishing, 2014), 65.

"I wanted to give parents": Jen D., phone interview.

"It was God's will": Jenn C., phone interview with the authors, January 25, 2023.

"I literally can barely": My Tangible Peace, accessed December 3, 2023, https://www.etsy.com/shop/mytangiblepeace?ref=shop_sugg_market.

Right now, Etsy, which posted: "Financials for Etsy Inc.," *Barron's*, accessed December 3, 2023, https://www.barrons.com/market-data/stocks/etsy/financials?mod=article_chiclet.

By the company's own statistics: "Etsy Celebrates Its Community of Female Entrepreneurs," Etsy, March 2, 2020, https://www.etsy.com/news/etsy-celebrates-its-community-of-female-entrepreneurs/; "Distribution of Etsy Shoppers and Buyers in the United States as of 4th Quarter 2017, by Gender," Statista, July 11, 2023, https://www.statista.com/statistics/431950/etsy-us-shopper-gender/.

"This was a much-wanted child": Van Wyen, phone interview.

"I wear them all the time": Emily M., phone interview.

Abernethy opened her shop: Kellie Abernethy, phone interview with the authors, April 21, 2022.

A year into it: Erin Cherry, email message to the authors, May 30, 2022.

Psychologist Rayna Markin says: Markin, phone interview.

"It was at times hard": Abernethy, phone interview.

"What a relief it is": Cherry, email.

"I think it's where": Jessica Person, phone interview with the authors, March 18, 2022.

As historian Lara Freidenfelds: Freidenfelds, *Myth of the Perfect Pregnancy*, 59–60.

"Many people of the era": Jay Ruby, *Secure the Shadow: Death and Photography in America* (Cambridge, MA: MIT Press, 1995), 55.

In another, a little girl: Ruby, *Secure the Shadow*, 57.

"One of the most humble privileges": Person, phone interview.

"I said, I'm angry": Kareen Bronstein, phone interview with the authors, January 23, 2023.

Americans spend billions: "Baby Products Market Size, Share & Trends Analysis Report by Product (Baby Cosmetics & Toiletries, Baby Food, Baby Safety & Convenience), by Region, and Segment Forecasts, 2022–2030," Grand View Research, February 2023, https://www.grandviewresearch.com/industry -analysis/baby-products-market.

By the turn of the twentieth century: Freidenfelds, *Myth of the Perfect Pregnancy*, 122.

The global market is huge: "Baby Prams and Strollers Market Outlook (2023– 2033)," Fact.MR, May 2023, https://www.factmr.com/report/531/baby-prams -and-strollers-market; "Baby Care Products Global Market Report 2023," ReportLinker, February 2023, https://www.reportlinker.com/p06323881/Baby -Care-Products-Global-Market-Report.html?utm_source=GNW; "Baby Apparel Market Size, Share & COVID-19 Impact Analysis, by Type (Top Wear, Bottom Wear, and Others), by Material (Cotton, Wool, and Others), by End-User (Girls and Boys), and Regional Forecast, 2023–2030," Fortune Business Insights, June 2023, https://www.fortunebusinessinsights.com/baby-apparel-market-102106.

"I think all parts": Debora Spar, phone interview with the authors, February 3, 2023.

For example, Hearst publications': Kristen May, "How to Market to Pregnant Women," Chron, https://smallbusiness.chron.com/market-pregnant-women -34417.html.

The report uncovered unethical: "More Than Half of Parents and Pregnant Women Exposed to Aggressive Formula Milk Marketing—WHO, UNICEF," World Health Organization, February 22, 2022, https://www.who.int/news /item/22-02-2022-more-than-half-of-parents-and-pregnant-women-exposed -to-aggressive-formula-milk-marketing-who-unicef.

But there are signs it is coming: Christin Perry, "10 Miscarriage Gift Ideas That Show You Care," *Parents*, October 1, 2022, https://www.parents.com/pregnancy /complications/miscarriage/miscarriage-gifts-that-show-you-care/.

Amazon features "baby loss": "Baby Loss," Amazon, accessed May 26, 2022, https://www.amazon.com/baby-loss/s?k=baby+loss&page=4.

"If the market can": Spar, phone interview.

"Get expert guides": "Baby Development," BabyCenter, accessed July 23, 2023, https://www.babycenter.ca/your-babys-development.

According to their data: "About BabyCenter, L.L.C.," BabyCenter, accessed July 23, 2023, https://www.babycenter.com/about-babycenter/company -information/about.

"BabyCenter has an incentive": Freidenfelds, *Myth of the Perfect Pregnancy*, 117.

By 2019, the website gave: "Pregnancy Week by Week," BabyCenter, accessed July 23, 2023, https://www.babycenter.com/pregnancy/week-by-week.

The website in turn uses: Babylist, accessed July 23, 2023, https://www .babylist.com/registry/new/signup.

A 2022 *Los Angeles Times*: Brian Contreras, "How Instagram and TikTok Prey on Pregnant Women's Worst Fears," *Los Angeles Times*, May 25, 2022, https:// www.latimes.com/business/technology/story/2022-05-25/for-pregnant -women-the-internet-can-be-a-nightmare.

Pamela Caine, the loss mom: Caine, phone interview.

When her baby was stillborn: Gillian Brockell, "Dear Tech Companies, I Don't Want to See Pregnancy Ads after My Child Was Stillborn," *Washington Post*, December 12, 2018, https://www.washingtonpost.com/lifestyle/2018 /12/12/dear-tech-companies-i-dont-want-see-pregnancy-ads-after-my-child -was-stillborn/.

Recently, some companies have started: Eleanor Hawkins and Kelly Tyko, "Brands Allow Customers to Opt Out of Mother's Day Marketing," Axios, April 30, 2023, https://www.axios.com/2023/04/30/mothers-day-2023-marketing -holiday-email-opt-out.

The controls don't limit: Tatum Hunter, "Google Is Letting You Limit Ads about Pregnancy and Weight Loss," *Washington Post*, April 28, 2022, https:// www.washingtonpost.com/technology/2022/04/28/google-block-ads -pregnancy-weight-loss/.

Those who want to avoid: DMA Choice, accessed July 20, 2023, https://www .dmachoice.org/.

In her 2018 article: Rayna Markin and Sigal Zilcha-Mano, "Cultural Processes in Psychotherapy for Perinatal Loss: Breaking the Cultural Taboo Against Perinatal Grief," *Psychotherapy* 55, no. 1 (March 2018): 20–26, https://doi.org /10.1037/pst0000122.

Chapter Fifteen

Jizo became popular: Jan Chozen Bays, *Jizo Bodhisattva: Modern Healing & Traditional Buddhist Practice* (Boston: Tuttle, 2002), 38.

There was a major uptick: Elisabeth Bumiller, "Japan's Abortion Agony,"

Washington Post, October 25, 1990, https://www.washingtonpost.com /archive/lifestyle/1990/10/25/japans-abortion-agony/64704f8d-aeac-4357 -9731-5bf856abb4a4/.

The pill remained restricted: Sonni Efron, "Japan OKs Birth Control after Decades of Delay," *Los Angeles Times*, June 3, 1999, https://www.latimes.com /archives/la-xpm-1999-jun-03-mn-43662-story.html.

People leave tokens out: Jenny Schroedel, *Naming the Child: Hope-Filled Reflections on Miscarriage, Stillbirths, and Infant Death* (Brewster, MA: Paraclete Press, 2016), 14–15.

She used to be a pediatrician: Jan Chozen Bays, phone interview with the authors, March 2, 2023.

But Colleen, a former crime reporter: Bays, *Jizo Bodhisattva*, xxvi.

In 2018, America was transfixed: Ed Yong, "What a Grieving Orca Tells Us," *Atlantic*, August 14, 2018, https://www.theatlantic.com/science/archive /2018/08/orca-family-grief/567470/; "Orca Who Carried Her Dead Calf for More Than 1,000 Miles Is Pregnant," CBS News, June 28, 2020, https://www .cbsnews.com/news/orca-who-carried-dead-calf-1000-miles-is-pregnant/.

After that, death was made: Phillipe Ariès, *Western Attitudes toward Death from the Middle Ages to the Present*, trans. Patricia M. Ranum (Baltimore: Johns Hopkins University Press, 1974), 60, 67–68.

A side effect of this removal: Ariès, *Western Attitudes toward Death*, 64.

"There's a silencing of the self": Markin, phone interview.

"Anything that doesn't feel": Cacciatore, phone interview.

Our culture clings to "closure": Joanne Cacciatore, *Bearing the Unbearable: Love, Loss, and the Heartbreaking Path of Grief* (Somerville, MA: Wisdom Publications, 2017), 56.

Megan Devine wrote: Megan Devine, *It's OK That You're Not OK: Meeting Grief and Loss in a Culture That Doesn't Understand* (Boulder, CO: Sounds True, 2017), 48.

"Find the good": Devine, *It's OK*, 49.

As author Rachel Lewis: Rachel Lewis, *Unexpecting: Real Talk on Pregnancy Loss* (Minneapolis: Bethany House, 2021), 166.

"The anger that I felt": Alishia Anderson, phone interview by the authors, April 13, 2023.

Psychotherapist Megan Devine: Devine, *It's OK*, xvii, 15.

Grief is bad because: Devine, *It's OK*, 21.

"I got a lot of 'Why'": Ashley L., phone interview.

"It's so invalidating": Amy Watson, phone interview with the authors, March 1, 2023.

"I watched thirteen people": Jennifer H., phone interview.

"We're left with no stories": Devine, *It's OK*, 36.

"Don't act like I am a crazy": Nathalie C., phone interview.

"There's no handbook": Nicole O., phone interview.

Roughly 75 percent of women: Donley and Lens, "Abortion, Pregnancy Loss."

Mourning miscarriages started: Reagan, "From Hazard to Blessing," 365.

"Grief is not a Black thing": Bell, phone interview.

"How do Black women grieve?": Drew, phone interview.

One is *disenfranchised grief*: Laurie Meyers, "Grieving Everyday Losses," *Counseling Today*, April 24, 2019, https://ct.counseling.org/2019/04/grieving-everyday-losses/.

"Miscarriage is often a very": Markin, phone interview.

"Yet, you cannot measure": Sherokee Ilse, *Empty Arms: Coping after Miscarriage, Stillbirth, and Infant Death* (Oro Valley, AZ: Wintergreen Press, 2019), 31.

"She had all this sympathy": Rachael M., phone interview.

"You don't know the history": Hanish, phone interview; Hanish, email.

"Grief is a chronic condition": Aviva Cohen, phone interview by the authors, March 8, 2023.

"We don't break down": Villa, phone interview.

Catholics only baptize the living: Ingrid Kohn and Perry-Lynn Moffitt, *A Silent Sorrow: Pregnancy Loss: Guidance and Support for You and Your Family* (New York: Routledge, 2000), 133.

Hindus do not have rituals: Miller, *Finding Hope*, 113.

Losses before this period: Kohn and Moffitt, *Silent Sorrow*, 136.

A burial is required after quickening: Kohn and Moffitt, *Silent Sorrow*, 133–36; Judas, phone interview.

"Jewishly, I understand it": Lori Sagarin, phone interview with the authors, March 9, 2023.

"I said, she's real": Kaufman, phone interview.

"There was no support": Judas, phone interview.

The closest America comes: *Steel Magnolias*, directed by Herbert Ross (Tristar Pictures, 1989), 1:16:40, https://www.netflix.com/title/60001533.

"Given this, it is no wonder": Markin and Zilcha-Mano, "Cultural Processes in Psychotherapy."

In *The Body Keeps the Score*: Bessel van der Kolk, *The Body Keeps the Score: Brain, Mind, and Body in the Healing of Trauma* (New York: Penguin, 2014), 14–15, 70, 143.

"I think that part of what": Markin, phone interview.

The keepsakes, the rituals: Markin and Zilcha-Mano, "Cultural Processes in Psychotherapy."

After all the rituals involved: Markin and Zilcha-Mano, "Cultural Processes in Psychotherapy."

"There are no rites": Layne, *Motherhood Lost*, chapter 4, Kindle.

"There's all these other losses": Hanish, phone interview; Hanish, email.

"We have such a strong": Malina W., phone interview.

"My coaching centers": Amy Watson, phone interview.

"You carry that grief": Villa, phone interview.

"In terms of the cultural script": Elizabeth H., phone interview with the authors, January 13, 2023.

"Loss moms are the most energized": Mancinelli, phone interview.

Vijayvergiya said, "The first": Haine Vijayvergiya, phone interview.

"If there's meaning to be had": Van Wyen, phone interview.

"It's not just a loss": Markin, phone interview.

"Most of us have never": Anderson, phone interview.

Amie Lands wrote in: Amie Lands, *Navigating the Unknown: An Immediate Guide When Experiencing the Loss of Your Baby* (Blythewood, SC: Kat Biggie Press, 2017), 46.

"I've walked in and found": Amy Watson, phone interview.

"There should be somebody": Aviva Cohen, phone interview.

"I don't think enough people": Villa, phone interview.

Swanson said that some women: Swanson, phone interview.

"I wanted my family": Melat, phone interview.

"I told the nurse": Jill A., phone interview with the authors, February 16, 2023.

"We wanted to design a room": Megan Gargano, phone interview with the authors, March 10, 2023.

It's a soundproofed labor and delivery: Anya Sostek, "After Stillbirth of Their Son, Family Creates Butterfly Suite for Grieving Families in West Penn," *Pittsburgh Post Gazette*, December 10, 2022, https://www.post-gazette.com /news/health/2022/12/10/stillbirth-butterfly-suite-west-penn-ahn-perinatal -loss/stories/202212070046, 6/30/23.

Grief is involuntary: Deborah L. Davis, *Empty Cradle, Broken Heart: Surviving the Death of Your Baby* (Golden, CO: Fulcrum Publishing, 2016), 20.

"Old grief theory wants people": Hanish, phone interview; Hanish, email.

"I feel like a tattoo": Margaret P., phone interview.

Rachael M. donated 250 ounces: Rachael M., phone interview.

TFMR parent Jill A.: Jill A., phone interview by the authors, February 16, 2023.

Cacciatore's MISS Foundation: "Send a Kindness Card," MISS Foundation, accessed June 27, 2023, https://www.missfoundation.org/kindness-project/.

"Our baby was a hero": Priscilla G., phone interview.

Her mom is a retired kindergarten: Jenna C., phone interview.

"You don't have to do the same": Leah Mele-Bazaz, phone interview with the authors, March 21, 2023.

"I didn't hold him": Jacqui L., phone interview with the authors, March 22, 2023.

"We made it a naming": Katie N., phone interview.

Afterword

Roughly half the country: Julianne McShane, "Pregnant with No OB-GYNs Around: In Idaho, Maternity Care Became a Casualty of Its Abortion Ban," NBC News, September 30, 2023, https://www.nbcnews.com/health/womens-health/pregnant-women-struggle-find-care-idaho-abortion-ban-rcna117872.

Tennessee's ban on gender-affirming: Mary Ziegler, "Fresh Fallout from the Supreme Court's *Dobbs* Ruling Just Hit Trans People," Slate, July 19, 2023, https://slate.com/news-and-politics/2023/07/supreme-court-dobbs-ruling-trans-backlash.html.

Appendix: Did You Seriously Just Say That to Me?

You comfort in: Elana Pramack Sandler, "Ring Theory Helps Us Bring Comfort In," *Psychology Today*, May 30, 2017, https://www.psychologytoday.com/us/blog/promoting-hope-preventing-suicide/201705/ring-theory-helps-us-bring-comfort-in.

INDEX

ABOUT THE AUTHORS

 Rebecca Little is an accomplished freelance journalist and a former contributing editor for *Chicago Magazine*. She spent years as a beat reporter covering local news and obituaries and has also written about education, feminism, parenting, style, politics and pop culture for clients such as the *Chicago Tribune*, WBEZ, *Crains Chicago Business*, Zagat, Google and the *Irish Times*. She has a master of science in journalism from the Medill School of Journalism at Northwestern University and completed the Second City improv training program. She lives in the Chicago suburbs with her husband and sons.

© Roberto Schmidt

Colleen Long is a staff reporter at the Associated Press and has covered some of the nation's most important news including the White House, the 2020 presidential election, immigration in the Trump era, race and policing, and New York City crime and courts. She has written extensively on the intersection of women and the criminal justice system, including an award-winning story on prison nurseries. Colleen's reporting has appeared in major news publications around the world, and she was part of a team that was a finalist for a Pulitzer Prize in 2019 for immigration coverage. She lives in Washington, DC with her husband and two children.